Bessie Head – Thunder Behind Her Ears

'I write best if I can hear the thunder
behind my ears. Not even *Rain Clouds*
was real thunder yet. Some of my letters to
friends are faint rumblings of it.'

D0874840

Studies in African Literature
New Series

NGUGI WA THIONG'O
Decolonising the Mind
Moving the Centre

DAVID COOK & MICHAEL OKENIMKPE
Ngugi wa Thiong'o*
An Exploration of his Writings

ELDRED DUROSIMI JONES
The Writings of Wole Soyinka

SIMON GIKANDI
Reading the African Novel
Reading Chinua Achebe

EMMANUEL NGARA
Ideology & Form in African Poetry
New Writing from Southern Africa*

ADEOLA JAMES (Editor)
In Their Own Voices
African women writers talk

JANE WILKINSON (Editor)
Talking with African Writers
Interviews with African poets, playwrights & novelists

MILDRED MORTIMER
Journeys through the French African Novel

KENNETH HARROW (Editor)
Faces of Islam in African Literature
Thresholds of Change in African Literature

DAVID KERR
African Popular Theatre

*forthcoming

EAEP Nairobi
HEINEMANN Portsmouth (N.H.)
JAMES CURREY London
DAVID PHILIP Cape Town

Bessie Head
Thunder Behind Her Ears

HER LIFE AND WRITING

Gillian Stead Eilersen

HEINEMANN
Portsmouth NH

JAMES CURREY
London

DAVID PHILIP
Cape Town & Johannesburg

First published 1995 in southern Africa by David Philip Publishers (Pty) Ltd,
208 Werdmuller Centre, Claremont, 7700, South Africa;

in the UK by James Currey Ltd, 54b Thornhill Square, Islington, London N1 1BE;

and 1996 in the USA by Heinemann: A division of Reed Publishing (USA) Inc.,
361 Hanover Street, Portsmouth, New Hampshire 03801-3912

© Gillian Stead Eilersen 1995

ISBN 0-86486-279-2 (David Philip, paper)
ISBN 0-85255-535-0 (James Currey, paper)
ISBN 0-435-08984-6 (Heinemann, paper)

British Library Cataloguing in Publication Data
Available from the British Library

Library of Congress Cataloging-in-Publishing Data
On file at the Library of Congress

Printed by Clyson Printers (Pty) Ltd, 11th Avenue, Maitland, South Africa

Contents

✼

To Britta, Jørn, Kirsten and Niels

Acknowledgements

This is the first full-length work to appear on Bessie Head. That it has taken the form of a biography has been determined to a large degree by Bessie Head herself. Believing that she was working on her autobiography at the time of her death in April 1986, I thought at first that it would be sensible to continue on something half-completed. However, it soon became clear that Head had not begun to write this autobiography when she died; and her preliminary work had presumably consisted of nothing more than sorting through the material she already had. It was this material, mainly a well-organised and extremely extensive correspondence, which nonetheless determined the genre of the present work. Bessie Head's lively, detailed letters to publishers, agents, critics and other literary friends often provide such penetrating comment on her published writing as well as giving rich insight into her ideas and mental speculation that they afford an obvious basis for an introductory study of this important writer. It was with excitement, and a sense of privilege and responsibility, that I delved into this very newly catalogued material for the first time at the Khama III Memorial Museum in Serowe, Botswana, in 1988.

I have many people to thank for help, encouragement, patience and sometimes hospitality during the years that it has taken to write this biography. Many have been most generous in helping me to gain better insight into my subject by sharing their memories of Bessie Head with me. As well as the many interesting contacts I have made in Botswana, South Africa and England, I was also able to interview Harold Head in Canada and enjoy there the warm encouragement of one of Bessie's most loyal friends, Tom Holzinger. These contacts, the many exchanges of correspondence, in some cases lasting several years, and the many telephone interviews have been a long, enriching experience for me. It is inadequate, I know, simply to list all their names in alphabetical order but I hope they will understand and accept my sincere gratitude:

David Ben-Tovim, Kenneth Birch, Dennis Brutus, Tom Carvlin, Patrick Cullinan, Margaret Daymond, Sybil and Alan Dicks, Adriaan Donker, Britta Eilersen, Kirsten Eilersen, Mary and Ronald Emery, Elizabeth Fairbairn, Terence Finley, Elizabeth Firmstone, Ragnhild and Henrik Fischer-Nielsen, Rosemary Forbes, Ruth and Per Forchhammer, Vernon Gibberd, Giles Gordon, Charlotte

Granly, Jane Grant, Sven Hamrell, Nancy Hansen, Mary and Harold Head, Howard Head, Diana Heiberg-Iürgensen, Jean Highland, Caroline Head Hlaba, Tom Holzinger, Mma-Jennings, Gareth Johnson, Patricia Johnson, Gothe Kgamane, Cassim Kikia, Dennis Kiley, Hilda King, Paddy Kitchen, Marit Kromberg, Kerstin Kvist, Bernard Letsididi, Scobie Lekhutile, Ann Langwadt, Ken Mackenzie, Beauty Magula, Marianne and Carl-Gunner Marstrand, Lianne McGregor, Amin Mohammed, Kaiser Ndyetabula, Mmatsela and Hugh Pearce, Folliott Phipson, Veronica Samuel, Lars Ole Sauerberg, Bosele Sianana, Frants Staugård, Robin Stead, Gertrude Stock, Katrin Sell, Stephen Sello, Keld Vorup Sørensen, Winifred Thomsett, Patrick van Rensburg, Randolph Vigne, Hans Christian Vorting, Jørn Wennerstrøm, and Pauline Wills.

I should also like to thank the following libraries and institutions for their help:

Killie Campbell Africana Library, Durban, South Africa
Johannesburg Public Library, Johannesburg, South Africa
Khama Memorial Museum, Serowe, Botswana
Staff of the English Department, Odense University, Denmark
St Monica's Home, Brighton Beach, South Africa
Scandinavian Institute for African Studies Library, Uppsala, Sweden
South African Archives, Pretoria, South Africa
South African Library, Cape Town, South Africa
William Cullen Library, University of the Witwatersrand Library, Johannesburg, South Africa.

Unless otherwise indicated, the photographs are my own.

I received a travel grant from the Scandinavian Institute for African Studies, Uppsala, Sweden, and generous support, comprising both research and travel grants, from Danish International Development Aid (Danida), Copenhagen, Denmark, for which I am grateful.

Finally I should like to thank my mother, Joyce Stead, and my husband, Peter Eilersen, for their invaluable support.

Gillian Stead Eilersen
Kolding, Denmark

South Africa
Against Heavy Odds
1937–1964

Bessie Head as a child in Pietermaritzburg (courtesy Khama Memorial Museum)

1

Childhood
1937–1949

Bessie Amelia Head seemed singularly alone in the world. As her success as a writer brought her increasing renown, she began to admit quite openly that she had no known relatives, not even the 'sense of having inherited a temperament, a certain emotional instability or the shape of a fingernail from a grandmother or great-grandmother'.[1] While this often distressed her, it could also give her a feeling of freedom. 'I just don't fit in and belong anywhere and I tend to pride myself on not fitting in or belonging,'[2] she once said. The picture she gave of her childhood and youth was dramatic, tragic – and fragmentary. Though she did not live long enough to learn the full story of her origins, she did take pride in one thing: that she had been named after her mother.

Bessie Amelia Birch was the second of a family of seven children whose parents, Walter Thomas Birch and Alice Mary, born Bezant, had emigrated to South Africa from England in 1892, the year after their marriage. They settled in Harrismith in the Orange Free State, where the eldest daughter, Florence, was born in the same year and Bessie (called 'Toby' by her family) two years later, on 13 March 1894. Two more sisters and three brothers followed. The family moved to Johannesburg, where Walter Birch built up a thriving business as a painting and decorating contractor. The youngest son, Kenneth, was only three years old when Walter Birch died suddenly on his farm near Witbank in the Transvaal. Alice Birch was left a widow at the age of forty-five.

Two years earlier, on 23 March 1915, and just ten days after she came of age, Toby had married Ira Garfield Emery. He was Australian by birth, the youngest of a family of seventeen children. Ira Emery emigrated to South Africa at the age of sixteen, encouraged by several of his brothers who had served there with an Australian contingent during the Anglo-Boer War and later settled in the country. He got a job on the South African Railways. He was six months older than Toby, lean, wiry and very charming. He was also an up-and-coming sportsman, who had won the Johannesburg Harriers Athletics Club gold medal for the best all-round athlete for three consecutive years.

Toby was also attractive. Her eyes, large, brown and expressive, were set in a square face with a generous mouth. Her brown hair was short and thick, with bangs in the fashion of the day. She was strongly built and slightly plump, giving a general impression of wholesome well-being. She was a good-natured, lively young woman, and very musical.

After a short courtship, the couple were married in a registry office and presented the Birch family with a *fait accompli*. This caused dissension and distress.

Ira Emery was not wealthy and the small house they moved into in Jules Street in the Johannesburg suburb of Malvern in no way measured up to what Toby had been used to. She often found herself alone. Ira spent much of his free time at his athletics club. His interest in sport went far beyond his own achievements and his own club. In 1914 he was involved in the establishment of the South African Olympic Games Committee. It became affiliated to the International Olympic Committee, and Ira Emery became its first general secretary, a post that he was to hold for 49 years.

On 1 December 1915 Toby gave birth to a son, Stanley Garfield. South Africa was by this time sending troops to Europe to fight in the Great War that had erupted the previous year, and shortly after Stanley's birth, Ira Emery left for France to serve with the South African Engineers. He returned two years later, and immediately began to revive amateur athletics as a sport, concentrating especially on building up the reputation of the Johannesburg Harriers. Stanley, generally called Sam, was then at a delightful age. His father lost no time in taking him to his sports meetings. Sam was soon a favourite amongst the club members and later became its official mascot.

There was a further addition to the family on 14 February 1919. A second son, Ronald Irwin, was born. When he was ten months old, tragedy struck. Sam, recently turned four, had been allowed to play with some friends across the road. As he returned home, he was hit by a taxi carrying five prominent businessmen to the horse races at Springs, near Johannesburg. He was killed instantly. The car was travelling so fast that it only drew to a stop a hundred metres down the road. The driver later reported at a police station that he had 'slightly injured' a child.

Toby was in the house when the accident happened. She heard the screech of brakes, heard a child scream piercingly, and rushed into the street to see her son lying in a pool of blood. She gathered the little body to her. 'Neck broken, legs broken, head smashed,'[3] reported the *Star*.

Toby was in a state of total shock. Crying slightly, patting the body, she could not utter a word. Minds crack, they say, or shatter. Stanley's violent death before her very eyes proved more than hers could bear. Everything that was later to befall her had its origin in those few minutes on 17 December 1919.

Ira Emery was as distraught as his wife at the loss of his son. In his grief, he turned on Toby and blamed her for the accident. With Sam gone, Toby and Ira Emery attempted to fill out the bleakness of their days. One thing was clear. They could not go on living in the same house, in the same death trap of a road. They moved to Persimmon Street, Malvern, and there built a house on a small plot of land paid for by Toby's mother. Toby loved gardening and set to work to transform the bare ground. She soon succeeded. Despite the new surroundings and the pleasure of the garden, the marriage never recovered. Toby gradually became more and more subdued.

The baby, Ron, thrived and was her only comfort. Ira Emery worked and trained; went to athletic meetings and to committee meetings; and mourned the loss of his son without being able to share his sorrow or comfort his wife. Instead he continued to blame her for Sam's death. His reproach lurked under the surface of every argument. In 1921 he went off to Australia for six months, managing the South African athletics team that toured the country, and running in it as well. In 1925 he ran his last race, which he won, and then turned to sports administration.

Two of Toby's sisters had settled in the coastal city of Durban in Natal, and she used to take Ronald on regular holidays to visit them. The Durban beaches stretch for miles and are covered with wide expanses of fine white sand; the sea is pleasantly tempered; there are exhilarating breakers or protected rock pools; and sunshine for days on end. Their time was spent on or near the beach; there were outings or picnics with the family, and mother and son enjoyed these holidays to the full.

Otherwise Ron, six by now and attending the local primary school, would retain only two kinds of memories from this time of his life. The first was the quarrels between his parents. To him they seemed never-ending: the angry voices, the heated accusations, the tears. The second was his recollections of his mother at the piano. The worse things got, the more she seemed to seek refuge in her music. She became a different person then; her face glowed, her body moved as freely and as harmoniously as the songs she sang. As she rose from the piano, the sad lost look that he had begun to associate with her returned. Toby began to put on weight, and lost her earlier briskness; she now moved around the house heavily and morosely, locked into a world that only her mother tried to penetrate. Alice Birch kept constant contact with her daughter, urging her to pull herself together. As for her five sisters and brothers, they were preoccupied with their lives, and showed little concern for her problems.[4] Her husband had given her up. Toby faced her predicament alone.

In 1927 it was decided to move Ron out of the home and he was sent to live with his aunt Tillie, Ira Emery's sister. In November 1928 Ira Emery also left, moving into a room in the South African Railways headquarters. The following February, Toby filed a suit claiming restitution of conjugal rights or divorce, with custody of the child and maintenance. The divorce was granted on 22 April 1929.[5]

Toby was given custody of Ronald, in accordance with a deed of settlement that had been drawn up between the parties on 11 March. Ira Emery was allowed to see his son every fourth weekend; and Ronald was to spend a third of his school holidays with his father. Both parents were to have an equal say in his education. Toby was to be paid a monthly maintenance allowance and the house in Persimmon Street was to be transferred into her name. In 1932 Ira remarried.

Toby's mental state deteriorated noticeably after Ira moved away. She still loved him and still referred to him as 'my husband'. Though she had divorced him, she made it abundantly clear that this was something she had done after much pressure from him.

She was now very lonely. Immediately after the divorce, Ira had decided that Ronald should be sent to boarding school. He started at the King Edward VII

School in Johannesburg and stayed there until 1935. Not only did the school provide the boy with a good education; it gave his life an element of stability as well. Toby could look forward to the weekends when he came home. She was devoted to him, and he to her.

She was distraught when she heard that Ira was to marry again. Though she was not supposed to know anything about it, she found out the particulars of the wedding, and went to the service. The presence of her forlorn figure caused some consternation in the wedding party and proved no good omen for Ira's marriage.

Toby could no longer administer her affairs. She did not pay the mortgage on the house, a situation sometimes aggravated by the fact that Ira Emery was not always regular in paying her alimony. Despite their earlier differences, Alice Birch now stepped in and began to help Toby run her life.

In 1933 things reached a crisis. It became clear that Toby was seriously in need of help. In a letter dated 8 March to the Master of the Supreme Court, Alice Birch offered herself as *curator bonis* of her daughter's estate, explaining that she had 'had such a lot to do with this very sad case and the financial parts' that she felt quite capable of carrying out the duties as curator.[6]

Alice Birch was a remarkable woman. Intelligent, determined and energetic, she was also very shrewd, and could debunk anything she thought was ridiculous and pompous with acute, humorous insight. Combined with a good dose of humanity, these qualities produced what her son, Kenneth Birch, has characterised as 'that old-fashioned breed of the non-permissive matriarch'.[7] They also made her an excellent businesswoman, and she immediately began to get her daughter's affairs under control. In April 1933, sewerage, costing £29, was installed in Toby's house which was painted and renovated for £25. Arrears due at the city treasurer's department were paid with an explanatory note that this amount was hard to collect because the maintenance due to Toby from her husband came in irregularly.

Despite this help, Toby's mental state became even more unstable and on 26 August 1933 she had to be admitted to the Pretoria mental hospital.[8] She was registered as a paying patient. Her house was rented out and from then on Alice Birch's bookkeeping abilities were very evident. She had to keep a thorough check on all her daughter's affairs and account for all her expenses to the Master of the Supreme Court. Though she once received a reprimand for sending insufficient details, all Toby's financial affairs from 1933 onwards were painstakingly documented and accounted for by her mother.

During this period Toby was described as 'simple and childish' with 'no insight into her surroundings'. She was 'inclined to ramble in conversation' and suffered from 'loss of memory'. Though she divorced her husband herself, she did not 'recognise the fact' that she was divorced.[9] Elsewhere she was described as having a tendency to extravagance. In early 1934 she addressed letters to both the Governor-General, Lord Clarendon, and the registrar of the Johannesburg law courts in an attempt to enlist help to leave the mental hospital and take a journey overseas with her son. The letters are rambling and disjointed. In one she refers to her 'parents', though her father had died in 1917, and says that 'my husband wants me to be in a position'. Clearly, the divorce was still plaguing her. She asked the registrar to 'kindly instruct my people Mrs A.M. Birch … in terms of the Order of Court dated 29th October 1929 to come and fetch me, as the terms of the Order of Court must be complied with'.[10]

Alice Birch also tried very hard to get her daughter granted six months' leave of absence. The doctors were not very encouraging. She was told that Toby was 'incoherent and foolish' and that there was 'little hope of any improvement in the near future'.[11] Nonetheless, her persuasive powers must have had an effect. A fortnight after being told this, Alice Birch took Toby to the family home in Doris Street, Kensington. She had been granted a six-month leave of absence from the hospital. Alice Birch reported shortly afterwards that she saw a big difference in her daughter's behaviour. 'Her mind is much more steady and reasonable,' she wrote, adding, 'I hope that I have at last accomplished something'.[12] At the end of this period Toby was discharged and in September 1935 Alice Birch reported that she was very much better. Just three months later, however, at the end of that same year, she was readmitted.

After a period of six months she was once more discharged. By this time, her son Ronald had left school and started work with an investment company, later changing to become an apprentice electrician. He lived for short periods with his father, then with a cousin and thereafter with his grandmother.

In October 1936 Toby approached a Johannesburg solicitor and told him that she wished to make her will. Although the solicitor later reported that she appeared 'perfectly normal and quite lucid',[13] she was not legally entitled to sign such a document and it was to be declared invalid. She left all she possessed to her son Ronald. She added that she wished to be buried in the family plot at Brixton in Johannesburg and was under no circumstances to be cremated.[14] She was forty-two years old.

Shortly afterwards she went to Durban to stay with her sisters. She spent some months there, enjoying the shopping and seaside life; she also developed a passion for going to the cinema. In late April 1937 her sister suddenly realised that Toby was pregnant. Though no one was to know this for some time, the father of the child was black. Since 1927 extramarital sexual intercourse between a white and a black person in South Africa had been a punishable offence.

Toby had always been plump and had put on weight with the years, so no one had noticed any change in her figure until she was over six months pregnant. There is no record of how it happened or where. Perhaps it was in Johannesburg before she left for the coast; or shortly after her arrival in Durban. But it is interesting to note in this connection the date of the drawing up of her will: October 1936. It is possible that some dramatic turn of events in her life – a love affair or a rape – could have occasioned it.

It seems that Alice Birch once again took charge. On 16 May 1937, Toby was admitted to Fort Napier Mental Institution, in Pietermaritzburg, the capital of the province of Natal and eighty kilometres inland from Durban. Although its name was originally derived from those of two of the most famous Boer leaders, Pieter Retief and Gerrit Maritz, and it had once been the centre of the Voortrekker republic of Natalia, Pietermaritzburg was later to become a loyal outpost of the

British Empire.

When Toby gave birth to a daughter less than two months after her admission to the mental hospital, the baby was described as 'white' on the birth certificate. Bessie Amelia Emery insisted that the child be given her full name. 'The only honour South African officials ever did me – naming me after this unknown, lovely and unpredictable woman,'[15] this child was to write many years later. But included in the genetic miscellany Toby passed on were also her large expressive eyes, her artistic bent and her love of gardening.

Only at this stage did Alice Birch begin to realise that her illegitimate granddaughter was of mixed blood. The baby had immediately been given out for adoption but the white family returned her because she looked 'strange'. Did the delicate little fingernails have a brownish tinge? Were the wisps of hair too curly? White South Africans have a piercing and well-trained eye in such matters. 'The child is coloured, in fact quite black and native in appearance,'[16] the family solicitor was later to state. Baby Bessie was finally given to a couple named Nellie and George Heathcote, living in the poorest part of the city. As people of mixed race, they were classified as coloured. They took the child in and received a monthly payment of £3 for doing so.

Alice Birch seems to have been very concerned for the baby's welfare. She exchanged letters with the adoption organisation and was personally responsible for sending the monthly cheques. In one report from the social worker, she was told that Bessie was 'a lovesome thing and developing beautifully',[17] which might have been encouraging words to a grandmother but were no help to a little girl who had been plunged by an accident of birth into a world where she would never know the identity of her mother, grandmother, brother, uncles or aunts. These uncles and aunts were by this time thoroughly alarmed by the unexpected implications of this family scandal and wished to have nothing whatever to do with it.

That was not Alice Birch's way. She continued to visit her daughter whenever she came to Durban and maintained a conscientious stewardship of Toby's property, paying her monthly bill of £6 at the hospital and the baby's £3 monthly upkeep with exemplary regularity.

Toby retreated more and more into an unreal world. In one of the low brick barracks which were spread about the spacious Fort Napier grounds, she spent her days. As the name suggests, the hospital had once been part of the city's fortification system. Originally established by the British in 1843, soon after the Boer settlers had submitted to British authority in the region, it was intended to dissuade the Voortrekkers from any attempt at re-establishing their power there. In fact it was the presence of the garrison that had largely been responsible for turning the backward village into a British colonial capital city. British regiments which had served or would later be serving in outposts of the Empire were stationed for a time in Pietermaritzburg. Turf club meetings, elegant balls and amateur dramatics flourished and in the last two decades of the century many of the most beautiful young ladies of the town linked themselves to the British gentry by marrying cavalry officers. The fort played an important role as a military base during the Anglo-Boer War, but after the Union of South Africa was formed in

1910, when Pietermaritzburg lost its status as colonial capital, its significance declined. In 1914, on the outbreak of the First World War, the garrison was finally withdrawn. In 1920, the oldest buildings – the barracks and the redbrick lookout tower itself – were converted into a mental hospital.

Toby wrote her son many letters, always looking forward to the day when they could live happily together again but never telling him anything about his half-sister. In 1939 the Second World War broke out. Ronald, like his father, joined the army. In 1940, before going on active service, he visited his mother. They strolled about the grounds. She was delighted to have him with her, showed off her soldier-son to the other inmates and seemed to be in an excellent state of mind. Then he left for North Africa. A medical note a few days later states: 'Mrs Emery is very well. She seems very happy here and is none the worse for her son's visit.'[18]

In 1943 her health suddenly declined. Alice Birch spent long periods of time with her daughters in Durban and visited Toby frequently. On 13 September 1943 she died. The Notice of Death gives as cause both 'lung abscess' and 'mental disorder' specified as 'dementia praecox',[19] a now obsolete term for schizophrenia and characterised by a premature and marked decline from a former level of intellectual capacity, manifesting itself in apathy, depression or personality disintegration.

Toby was cremated at the Stellawood crematorium in Durban, despite the fact that in her will she had directly stated that 'my body shall not under any circumstances be cremated'. The explanation is that Alice Birch knew nothing of the will. 'I have been entirely unaware of this will being in existence, please advise,'[20] she wrote to the Master of the Supreme Court in early October.

Ronald Emery was in Cairo at the time but had been granted home leave from 18 September. So when he arrived back in South Africa from Egypt on 21 September, his father met him with the news of his mother's death. Shortly afterwards he heard about the illegitimate child, now six years old, and 'coloured'.

During the next year, the estate was wound up. Alice Birch put in a claim for about half of it, maintaining that she had 'paid out monies' from her own pocket from time to time 'to keep the Estate going which prior to my Curatorship through lack of funds, I was unable to recuperate myself at any time'.[21] The Child Welfare Society in Pietermaritzburg also filed a claim for £300 'for the maintenance of a minor female child of deceased'.[22]

The winding-up process was delayed because Ronald was once more 'up North', serving as a lieutenant in the Signals unit of the South African army. At first it seemed as if he was going to contest his grandmother's claim. But he later wrote to her that this was not his intention at all: he had merely hoped to personally 'pay you back every penny which you so unselfishly spent on my mother'[23] instead of letting it be done through an outsider. To his solicitor he wrote: 'If she believes that she is entitled to that claim, which she obviously does, then I am quite satisfied that she gets it ... I honestly believe that by not contesting this claim, a silly family argument will be brought to an end. This, in my opinion, is the important issue.'[24] He was by this time discussing 'the child' quite openly with his grandmother and stating that he was going to make over £300 for her maintenance. 'When that has been done,' he wrote, 'I am having nothing more to do with her.'[25] The final outcome was that after Alice Birch had been paid out her £550 and the child Bessie her £300, there was about £200 left for Ronald. He took the situation philosophically. 'I would rather be penniless ... than feel I had beaten a relation to a financial point,' he wrote in the same letter to his solicitor.

Disillusioned with South African society, Ronald Emery was to travel and live abroad, mainly in Canada, for long stretches of time after the war.

Alice Birch seems to have abandoned the young Bessie after the death of her own daughter. She had tried to do what she could for the child, but family opposition had made her bitter. She lived to the age of ninety-two and was blessed with a clear mind right to the end, but she never again allowed the scandalous family event to be discussed in her presence. Her illegitimate granddaughter was to get no share of her material goods; but by the rich irony of fate, which was to fascinate this granddaughter throughout her life, she was endowed instead with her grandmother's energy, determination and intelligence; with her sense of the ridiculous; and with her stocky little figure.

In the early 1940s the coloured community of Pietermaritzburg lived mostly at the lower end of the city, 'at the bottom of Church Street' (the main street), as people would say. Together with the Indians, already building up a thriving trade for themselves as merchants, the coloureds occupied the middle rung of the racially defined hierarchy which was already in existence in South Africa, to be given an official framework in 1948.

Some of the forebears of these people had been the British soldiers who had garrisoned Fort Napier; others, the Voortrekker pioneers who had moved into Natal under Piet Retief's leadership. In colonial Natal, liaisons between white men and black women were tolerated. But in twentieth-century South Africa, such liberal attitudes were long out of date, and the offspring found themselves consigned to the poorer areas of town. Perhaps one of Nellie Heathcote's grandparents or great-grandparents had been the offspring of an Irish soldier. Young Irishmen, seeking relief from the poverty of their homeland, were numerous in the British Army. This was especially true of the 45th Regiment, the 1st Sherwood Foresters, which had been the pioneer garrison in the city from 1843 to 1853 and established an active Roman Catholic community.[26] Nellie Heathcote was a very devout Catholic.

In Natal, until the turn of the century, coloureds were accorded the same legal status as whites; they retained the franchise even when it was taken from Indians in 1893; they served in white regiments during the Boer War; coloured children went to white schools. By 1905, however, race consciousness was growing stronger and more exclusive, and the system of separate schools for different racial groups had been established. Most coloureds in Natal spoke English; in the other three provinces they spoke Afrikaans.

By the late thirties many coloureds had semi-skilled jobs, or positions requiring a certain amount of responsibility, but were paid miserably for it. Some coloured men in Natal and the Cape still had the franchise, and were registered on the common voters' roll, but this basic right would be removed in the fifties.

The Heathcote home at 73 East Street was poor but respectable. Bessie's fos-ter-father, George, was a cobbler. He was also a member of the Child Welfare Committee. When the newborn Bessie was turned down by the first prospective adoptive couple, he had taken her home to his wife. They already had one adopt-ed daughter, whose father was a white magistrate, and they took in lodgers as well.

Bessie grew into a thin, attractive child, with long thick dark hair, huge expres-sive eyes and a shy smile. Her adopted sister Rhona was fifteen years older than she was. For a while Nellie Heathcote also looked after two boys, but their moth-er claimed them again and took them to England.[27]

These were the war years in Pietermaritzburg. South African soldiers home on leave or wounded English soldiers at one of the many army hospitals in the area thronged the streets. Every so often a troop train would pass through Pietermaritzburg station and people would flock there to see the soldiers off. Sometimes Nellie Heathcote and her two girls would be in the crowd. The little coloured group would keep together at the far end of the platform as the long troop train, with excited young men in uniform hanging out of each window, pulled slowly out of the station. The coaches with white boys would pass first; then would follow the coaches with the coloured soldiers. As they stood at the windows of the departing train, catching grateful sight, at last, of someone they knew, they would be shyer and more uncertain about their role as heroes. All signing up for active service was voluntary, but the black troops could not join combat units, only the auxiliary services. In battle, a life was a life; in politics, how-ever, other rules applied.

The presence of British soldiers in town was also felt in East Street. Lacking their South African counterparts' racial awareness, they would wander down to the poorer end of town in search of illegal home-brewed liquor and attractive black prostitutes. Bessie, aged four or five, would certainly have observed drunk-en scenes in the street, or even next door. It was hardly likely that Nellie Heathcote sold home-brewed beer herself, as suggested by some of Bessie's later writings. She was far too upright for that.[28]

When she was six, several changes occurred in Bessie's life. Her biological mother died in Fort Napier. This event was registered in East Street because Alice Birch decided to give Bessie her mother's toys. Nellie Heathcote had never told Bessie anything about her background. She grew up believing herself to be Nellie Heathcote's daughter. The arrival of the authoritative white woman in their home interested Bessie but did not cause her any uneasiness. Later she remembered her; remembered being grasped and pressed against the pleasantly perfumed person sitting in a chair; remembered what to her seemed a Scots accent. (Alice Birch was from Devon.) Many years later Nellie Heathcote told her how her grandmother had visited her on several occasions. Perhaps the visit in 1943 was the final one before pressure from the family or her own realisation of the hope-lessness of the situation made Alice Birch cut Bessie out of her life and erased her from the collective family memory.

At about the same time Bessie's foster-father died. This made life even more difficult for Nellie Heathcote. After George Heathcote's death, she managed on his small army pension supplemented by the money that came in from letting out rooms.

The event of significance was that Rhona ran away from home. Bessie has a rather bizarre account of the events leading up to this. Rhona had met and fallen in love with a handsome football star. Nellie Heathcote did not know him at all, but when he came to visit Rhona she could see that he had a very dark skin. 'She just hated him on sight ... All the people in South Africa have distorted ideas about colour like that.'[29] According to Bessie, she ended the relationship by throwing urine in the young man's face. Rhona ran away with the football player but soon afterwards met someone named George Billings and married him. She and her foster-mother were later reconciled, and Rhona's daughter, Veronica, was later sent to live with Nellie Heathcote, who brought her up, while Rhona remained in Durban. Veronica Samuel (née Billings), nicknamed Wally after the Duchess of Windsor, Wallis Simpson,[30] became one of Bessie's staunchest admirers.

The question of books and reading was one which caused friction between Bessie and her foster-mother. Bessie started school at the Greyling Street Coloured School and made good progress. She longed to own a book. When Nellie Heathcote received the three pounds paid to her for Bessie's board, they would sometimes go shopping. Bessie would beg for a book from a bookshop they passed. But she had to plead for three months before Nellie Heathcote gave in. She was allowed to choose one about a bear called Fuzzy-Wuzzy. It was the only book she ever owned as a child. Some fifteen years later, Bessie was to reveal, in the first long piece of fiction she ever wrote, some of her intense hunger for words as a child. In her novella, *The Cardinals*, the young protagonist finds a picture book, *The Adventures of Fuzzy Wuzzy Bear*, on a refuse dump. She urges an old man who has befriended her to read it to her. As he does so, pointing to the pictures, 'the words "sea" and "holiday"' leap out at her. She does 'a little skip dance around the old man'. She puzzles over the simple captions but can read them within a week: 'The adventures of the bear became real too and she spent many hours sharing his experiences with him. When he ate an ice-cream, it was as though the melting cream dripped over her fingers. When he swam in the sea, she felt the waves rising to swamp her.'[31]

To Bessie's great distress, she was never allowed to sit in a corner and read. If she did so, Nellie Heathcote would snatch the book away and clip her ear. But if she sat and stared into space, all was well. It was the reading that upset her foster mother. That illiterate people do not allow. They seem to need the constant warmth of communication and idle chatter but not any solitary activity like reading. Books are not of their world.'[32] Nellie Heathcote was often rough with her, according to Bessie. 'She seemed to think I should be violently beaten for the slightest thing,' she wrote to Veronica Samuel many years later.[33]

Bessie was no doubt right in feeling in retrospect that there had been 'something grievously wrong' with her relationship with her foster-mother. Perhaps Nellie Heathcote was puzzled by the strange silent behaviour of her child and wished she would be more like everyone else. Bessie was unfair in calling Nellie Heathcote 'illiterate', however. She may not have been very educated, but she read the newspaper and her Bible daily. According to Veronica Samuel, her eyesight was poor, which meant that she did not like writing letters. But perhaps it was a general feeling of insecurity about the written word that made her get other people to write all the letters she later addressed to the headmistress at Bessie's boarding school, an insecurity Bessie observed and registered.

Nonetheless, Bessie loved her foster-mother. She called it 'an almost fanatic attachment'[34] and said that in spite of the personality clashes 'I adored her, but only through sheer terror of being utterly alone. That was the last, defenceless love I had for any human being.'[35] To Veronica Samuel she wrote: 'I know I loved her and looked after her as I was able but she did bad things to me.'[36]

Veronica Samuel, seven years younger than Bessie, has entirely different memories of her grandmother. Nellie Heathcote seldom showed bad temper. Veronica Samuel was never beaten or even slapped. Nellie Heathcote's religious convictions were such that she would withdraw into her room and pray if she encountered anger or aggression.[37]

Bessie was a quiet and caring child. From an early age she was made to work very hard. She described herself as 'scrubbing an eternally dirty house . . . selling bones and bottles for a shilling for meat, and scouring the fields around the house for wild spinach'.[38] An incident she related to Veronica Samuel illustrates some of the same qualities. She was recalling the time when Veronica, aged four, returned to live in the home in 1948.

You were a horrible little girl to me then because you spoiled things. I was a little girl who looked after everything. I watered the flower garden after school. Indeed I was always working. So when you came we had a flower garden of many coloured daisies. I found you busy pulling the tops off the flowers and throwing them on the floor.

When Bessie tried to stop further damage, Veronica Samuel looked back 'with wicked green eyes' and destroyed two more flowers. She 'deaded' one of her grandma's chickens and ran in to tell her. 'For all these bad things you were never beaten but I was a child who was beaten all the time.'[39]

The daily struggle to make ends meet and bring up the children in her care took all Nellie Heathcote's energy. She was not a politically minded person. A lifetime of training had taught her to ignore the discriminations she suffered as a coloured woman; the continual pinpricks to her dignity. As a Christian, she regarded them as part of the cross she had to bear. That is why the general election of 1948, the same year that Veronica Samuel came to East Street, did not interest her very much, especially as she had no vote. Like most people, she expected Prime Minister Smuts, leader of the United Party, to remain in power. Indeed, she hoped he would. His reputation at home had been enhanced by the role South Africa had played in the Second World War and abroad by his close involvement with the establishment of the United Nations. However, this was not to be. To the dismay of most Natalians, D F Malan's National Party won the election by a narrow majority. To mobilise every vote he could in what was regarded as a confrontation between the Afrikaners and the English, who had monopolised the most important areas of power since the defeat of the Afrikaners in the Boer War in 1902, Malan had rallied his supporters under the catch-phrase *swart gevaar*, the black peril. His solution to this problem was 'apartheid', or separation of the races.

After the National Party victory, Malan introduced laws to bolster the existing racial segregation and give it an official structure. Laws regulating personal contact between the races appeared quickly: the Mixed Marriages Act of 1949 extended the prohibition of marriage between whites and Africans to include coloureds and Indians; and the Immorality Act of 1950 likewise extended the prohibition on sexual intercourse between people of different groups. These won easy popularity for the government among its poorer voters, who feared the encroachment of the other races. That they also caused untold heartbreak was not considered important.

The grand scheme for a genuine separation of the races was at this stage more an election slogan than an ideologically viable plan. Even the government's own experts did not provide clear indications of how apartheid, in the sense of totally removing blacks from white industrial and farming areas, could ever be implemented.

Nevertheless, in 1950 the government introduced the first two laws which were to form the cornerstones of 'grand apartheid': the Population Registration Act and the Group Areas Act. The first in particular caused immediate consternation. It required all citizens to be registered as belonging to one of the official racial groups. Borderline cases were decided by boards set up for the purpose. People who thought they were white found themselves classified as coloured. Coloureds were redesignated as Africans, or what the government called 'Bantu'. Rarely did the scale tip in the other direction. The Group Areas Act enabled the government forcibly to break up the existing residential patterns in urban areas where people of different races often lived side by side, and remove the undesirable groups to other areas, so that each race might live in its own 'group area'. In practice, this meant that the best parts of a city were declared 'white', and the other groups were evicted.

All this legislation was enforced with great harshness. The Population Registration Act was particularly hateful to the coloureds, who until then had often allied themselves with the whites. Many now actively supported the growing anti-apartheid resistance movement. But Nellie Heathcote was not one of these. She suffered the increasing indignities with patience and taught her daughter to do likewise, while the segregation of buses, public conveniences, beaches, post offices, public libraries and municipal parks was institutionalised. The hated notices 'Slegs Blankes/Europeans Only' appeared everywhere.

In 1949 another frightening event touched the Heathcote family closely. Riots between Africans and Indians broke out in Durban, after an Indian trader struck a young black boy. It was enough to release a storm of pent-up violence, which spilled over into other parts of Natal, especially Pietermaritzburg. Poor urban Africans were dependent on the Indian shopkeepers to provide the food they needed in the small quantities they could afford and often with a complicated system of credit and interest built in. Suddenly now, the frustration of seeing these shrewd Indian businessmen growing rich on their poverty in addition to all the other frustrations of their lives, proved too much for them. For three days the

Indian areas of Durban and Pietermaritzburg were overrun by rioters breaking into shops, looting and sometimes setting fire to them. Altogether 42 people were killed and over a thousand injured. East Street and the lower part of Church Street were packed with a surging crowd of Africans. Nellie Heathcote's neighbour, an Indian shopkeeper called Khan, barricaded himself and his family into his house: they survived, though his shop was pillaged. Nellie Heathcote and her household did the same, hardly sleeping for three nights, and very conscious of the poor protection that their old house offered. Gradually, however, things returned to normal.

Meanwhile the initial tensions between Bessie and Veronica Samuel subsided. They spent a lot of time together during the next two years. Veronica Samuel the tomboy admired her quiet and serious Aunt Bessie greatly. Bessie too was conscious of this hero-worship and referred rather proudly to her niece's admiration of her in a letter written from boarding school some years later. After losing touch with each other for 25 years, Veronica Samuel, combining common sense and intuition, 'found' her Aunt Bessie again in 1982.

One of Veronica Samuel's recollections from these early years is of how Nellie Heathcote, Bessie and she prepared for Easter. Every morning throughout the period of Lent they went to early morning mass at St Anthony's Catholic Church in Retief Street. It was here Bessie had been baptised and here both she and Veronica Samuel had taken their first communion when they turned eight. The priest, Father Gabriel, was an Indian. Mass started at six o'clock so an old man with his rickshaw would call for them at half past five and transport them to the church. The air was crisp, even chilly, for winter was setting in, and they had to wrap scarves round their heads and pull their hands into the sleeves of their knitted cardigans as they sat shivering in the rickshaw. These light two-wheeled vehicles were still part of the Pietermaritzburg, indeed the Natal, scene then. Though later to become an elaborately decorated tourist attraction drawn by hefty men in traditional dress, rickshaws at this stage generally served as a poor man's taxi, drawn by thin men in tattered clothes. It was as such that Nellie Heathcote and the girls used them: Nellie Heathcote had a weak heart.[40]

When she was thirteen Bessie was moved from the Heathcote home. It was a Mr Benjamin, probably a member of the local welfare organisation's Coloured Case Committee, as Bessie's foster-father had once been, who took the initial steps. In a letter dated 31 January 1950 he wrote about 'the use' Bessie was to Nellie Heathcote, 'as she made her work hard and her home had got so bad that I had to report and get her removed as soon as possible'.[41] It was Mr Benjamin who decided to approach St Monica's Home through his committee.

Left and above: *Ira G Emery and Bessie (Toby) Birch c. 1914 and 1920*
Below: *The Birch family (c. 1926): Alice Birch is central; Toby Emery and Kenneth Birch centre back row; Ronald Emery centre front row (photos courtesy Ronald Emery)*

Right: *Toby with Ronald in the pram (courtesy Ronald Emery). If one compares this with the photo on page 18, the resemblance between mother and daughter is striking.*

IN MEMORIAM

THE DAUGHTERS OF

WALTER AND ALICE BIRCH

WHO PASSED AWAY

FLORENCE ALICE IN 1963

BESSIE AMELIA IN 1943

Bessie with Howard in Botswana, c. 1968 (courtesy Khama Memorial Museum)

Above left: *Nellie Heathcote's house at 73 East Street, Pietermaritzburg*

Above right: *Bessie with Nellie, her foster-mother (courtesy Khama Memorial Museum)*

Below: *The drive and main building of St Monica's Home (courtesy St Monica's)*

2

St Monica's Home, 1950–1956
Durban, 1956–1958

St Monica's Home was an Anglican mission school for coloured girls. The role of the church in black (and coloured) education in South Africa was a complicated one. Before 1953, in fact, it was the mission schools which provided most of the education available to black people. Such famous institutions as Lovedale and St Matthew's in the Cape, Adams College and Mariannhill in Natal, and Grace Dieu and St Peter's in the Transvaal had an excellent educational record. A whole generation of black leaders emerged from mission school backgrounds. That these schools were also responsible for undermining the cultural patterns of the black people and often unintentionally reinforced the negative values of white South Africa, by making the virtue of humility equal subordination, forgiveness equal passive acceptance and duty equal inferiority, only illuminates the complex nature of race relations in the country.

St Monica's, first called St Cyprian's Mission, started in 1895 as a school for children 'who on account of their colour and poorness of clothing' did not go to the government schools and were 'not welcomed there'.[1] Though it was an outward manifestation of the way in which the South African 'colour question' was taking shape, it was established in a spirit of great dedication and devotion by a Miss Snell, with a minimum of public or diocesan support. The school had to rely on the teachers having 'private means'[2]. This was also the main obstacle for Miss Snell and her successors.

Gradually the school was enlarged to take in boarders until this became its main purpose. Having for a while attempted to provide schooling and training for young coloured girls of 'good' (white) background, it reverted in about 1911 to catering for orphan children or social outcasts. Black mothers, the victims of white male abuse, would often bring children there. 'Most of the children have Zulu, Indian or Cape Coloured mothers and English or Scottish fathers who have deserted them,' wrote the headmistress in 1917.[3] Things improved financially when the school became government-aided. But the real break came in February 1920 when it moved to a large and beautiful property at Hillary, then a little village outside Durban consisting of a railway halt, a small post office, a grocery shop and an Indian store. This brought immense improvements. Though the buildings were dilapidated and not altogether suited for their new purpose, the twenty-acre property was a veritable paradise of unusual trees, a sweeping drive lined with huge palms, ornamental shrubs and a stream flowing through the centre of it. It was at this stage that the name of the home was changed to St Monica's Diocesan Home for Coloured Girls. Two years later Miss Louie Farmer, who was to make such a great contribution to the school, arrived. She it was who responded to Mr Benjamin's enquiries and accepted Bessie Emery as a pupil.

Bessie left behind a distressed foster-mother. Mr Benjamin remarked rather cynically that Nellie Heathcote did not want Bessie to leave because of the monthly board she received for her and because of all the work Bessie did for her. There are many indications, however, that Nellie Heathcote loved Bessie just as much as Bessie loved Nellie Heathcote, whom she had grown up believing to be her natural mother.

Bessie was wrenched away not only from her mother but also from the religion she had grown up with. St Monica's was an Anglican Home. It seems that Mr Benjamin chose to approach St Monica's rather than 'the R.C. Home'. He said that he knew 'that home also – and knew Mrs Heathcote was R.C. and she would have had the child christened in the Church'.[4] He seems to have chosen St Monica's because of the quality of the education. Though a venture into the unknown for Bessie, it also held the promise of a future with, according to Mr Benjamin, more chance to read and study.

Bessie was taken to the Home on 23 January 1950.[5] By that time she had completed Standard 4 at the Greyling Street Coloured School. She was short for her age, a quiet little girl, dressed plainly but very neatly, her black curly hair closely cropped. As she walked up the drive lined with huge royal palm trees and azalea bushes along the grass verge, she must have been aware of a new chapter beginning in her life.

First there was the physical environment to adapt to. During the 1930s and 1940s the Home had gradually acquired the buildings that it needed. The original old white house, called St Monica's and serving as dormitories and classrooms, had been greatly improved after a series of repair projects. Situated at the end of the long drive, it was the focal point of life at the school, which now also had an infant school with accommodation, called St Christopher's, a chapel opened in 1937 and a new block consisting of dining-room and kitchen facilities on the ground floor and a playroom, with a stage, upstairs, equipped with toy cupboards and bookshelves and called the House of Truth,[6] everything paid for from private donations. Stretching out on all sides were other buildings such as the cottage occupied by Louie Farmer, called The Dell, extra classrooms, garages, a laundry, chicken runs and a netball court, all in a setting of tall shady trees and flowering shrubs. The children also had an outdoor dining-room – the long narrow tables and benches placed under the shade of huge mango trees. The buildings were simple and utilitarian but after thirteen years in the poor area of a city, with all its aesthetic limitations, the sheer luxuriance of her new surroundings must have awakened a response in Bessie which she was to express in later years in her desire to surround herself with plants and natural vegetation even under drought conditions.

However, with this enrichment came restrictions. The whole day was partitioned into strictly organised time modules. It began with a cold shower, summer and winter. 'Very healthy it was,' said a former assistant Lady Warden.[7] 'Terrible,' said a former pupil.[8] Before breakfast, the girls had to clean the dormitories and ablution block, the older girls taking on the heavier work. Then came breakfast, consisting of porridge, some fruit and a cup of tea. Further cleaning followed; then morning prayers, prior to starting lessons. As the demands for better educational facilities increased, so did the need for extra staff. This resulted in a redistribution of authority. A Headmistress was appointed to run the school. In Bessie's time this was an English missionary sent out to South Africa by the Society for the Propagation of the Gospel, Miss Bunty Theobald, who was a talented and popular teacher. Louie Farmer, now Lady Warden, and concerned with the extramural activities of the girls, also did some teaching.' One or two members of staff came in every day, but otherwise they lived on the premises. The standard of teaching was high and many of the girls passed the same examinations as white children of the same age. Promising pupils were sent to Durban to complete their education.

Louie Farmer was also an educationist of some vision though of a more rigid nature. Her aim was to give as many of the girls as possible an all-round education to equip them for other and more challenging occupations than the traditional one of domestic help. For those who had started formal education too late or found it too burdensome, however, she had a curriculum that included practical and creative subjects: dressmaking, cookery, nature study, drawing and gardening. Much emphasis was placed on choir work and singing, at which the girls excelled.

The main meal of the day was eaten at midday. This consisted of boiled samp – maize kernels 'stamped and broken but not ground as fine as mealie rice or mealie meal' – and dried beans, the staple food of many black South Africans. On Fridays they had fish; on Sundays, meat. 'Very tasty and nourishing,' said a former assistant Lady Warden. 'Terrible,' said a former pupil.

The afternoons were often taken up with the practical subjects. Gardening was as much a duty as a training. The school had a vegetable garden which provided for its own needs. The flower garden had to be weeded and watered. The girls could also be given other afternoon chores. Very often the only time they had to themselves was the half-hour before supper. This meal consisted of slices of bread and tea or milk. Then came homework, evening prayers and bed. 'There was more work than play at St Monica's,' said one former pupil. 'Religion and work, that was our life . . . And plenty of places that were out of bounds!'

Religious instruction came in two forms. There were the daily and weekly church services; then there was what Louie Farmer called Character Training, both of a corporate and of an individual nature. In making the girls recognise the 'value of the principles of the Christian life and character',[9] her guiding principle was 'Spare the rod and spoil the child', and she worked tirelessly to correct the moral weaknesses of her flock.

There had undoubtedly been rules in Nellie Heathcote's family, but they could not be compared with what Bessie now had to adjust to. Every misdemeanour was punishable: stealing money or items of property, stealing food, breaking things, speaking during silence hours, arriving late, disobedience, telling lies. As well as this, large parts of the huge grounds were declared out of bounds.

Many offences were punished by beatings. The wrongdoer was made to lie on the table in the upper classroom while Louie Farmer caned her. 'Sailing the seven seas' the girls called it, and no one escaped this nautical adventure. Louie Farmer collected up the crimes and meted out the punishments each morning before prayers. 'It was her idea of "Thoughts for Daily Living", said a former pupil.

Another typical form of punishment was being sent to Coventry, where unacceptable behaviour was punished by refusing to let anyone speak to the culprit. This could be extended to a period in solitary confinement for a graver offence. Sometimes Louie Farmer was more ingenious. At some stage during Bessie's time at the Home, one of the girls stole some bread from the kitchen and hid it under the floor of the chapel. After fruitless attempts to get the sinner to confess, Louie Farmer woke the girls each morning at two o'clock and made them search for the bread until breakfast time.

There was much for a young girl to learn at St Monica's; many adaptations to be made. Bessie seemed to manage reasonably well. In the first place, she was bright and did not have to suffer the humiliations of not being able to remember her lessons, though the ordeal of standing up and repeating multiplication tables always frightened her. She was also used to hard work and was by nature orderly.

The agonies that she suffered she kept to herself. She missed her foster-mother and Veronica very much. During her first year at the school, she saw nothing of her family. Visitors were allowed once a month but for Nellie Heathcote such a visit was beyond her means. In March 1951, over a year after her admittance to St Monica's, Bessie was apparently so distressed by the letters she received from her foster-mother that it was suggested by a social worker that Bessie should be told not to write to her any more. However, a more constructive solution was found: Nellie Heathcote went to the Home. She wrote to Louie Farmer after the visit, thanking her for allowing her 'to see and write to Bessie'.[10] She asked to be allowed to send some wool to Bessie, so that she could knit a jersey for herself, and mentioned a dressing-table runner Bessie had been embroidering. This visit probably helped Bessie over her worst bout of homesickness.

Aged thirteen, Bessie broke into print for the first time. An organisation calling itself the Goodwill Council published short essays and poems from schoolchildren of all races in a small magazine in connection with Goodwill Week 1951. Bessie Emery from 'St. Monica's Govt.-Aided Coloured school, Hillary, Natal' contributed a short piece, about 30 lines long, entitled 'The Stepping Stones of Truth'. It was the story of Peter, who was always telling lies. It distressed his parents: 'they punished him but that was of no help.' After having done something particularly 'wicked' – stealing some money from his father – he was transformed by a dream. He dreamt that he tried to cross a broad river on some stepping stones, but he was unable to do so, because they hurt him badly when he stepped on to them. A beautiful lady dressed in 'purest white' explained to him that these were the Stepping Stones of Truth and only he could help himself before it was too late. Peter awoke and rushed in to confess his theft to his father. The story concludes: 'We must help others by Love, just as his guardian angel helped Peter. Punishment only seems to make us worse.'[11] The final sentence could also be taken as a direct comment on Bessie's own school system.

Punishment aside, Bessie showed many signs of settling down at St Monica's, and in a letter from September 1951 Louie Farmer expressed satisfaction with her progress. She reported here that Bessie was 'now in Std VI' and working extremely hard as she still wished to be a teacher. She was 'quite a good pupil' and had made 'great strides in every way since she came to St Monica's'.[12] Louie Farmer also said that Bessie wished to stay on at the school and attend Umbilo High School (with some of the other girls) the following year. This would enable her to take the Teacher's Training Course after Standard 8. St Monica's was going to apply for a bursary for her. Bessie might have settled into a calmer existence had events not taken another, far more dramatic turn.

Bessie had been accepted at the Home as a paying pupil. The £3 per month that Nellie Heathcote had previously received now went to the Home. Her mother's legacy was not large, however, so the welfare organisation and Louie Farmer decided to try and have Bessie declared 'a child in need of care'. According to the Children's Act of 1937, this would mean that her board and tuition would be paid by a government maintenance grant, and the remains of her inheritance, about £40 at that stage, could be kept for an emergency later on.

The first letter relating to this plan is dated 17 August 1951, about 19 months after Bessie first started at St Monica's. In October the question of whether Bessie should be allowed to go to Pietermaritzburg for the holidays was discussed, but neither the social worker nor Louie Farmer considered this a good idea.[13] Apparently, no one thought of telling Bessie. She expected to be going 'home' for the holidays.

Meanwhile, the hearing to determine Bessie's future status was scheduled for 19 December 1951,[14] about the same time as the school holidays were due to begin. In 1975 Bessie described the event thus:

[T]here was no 'coming home'. The English missionary, in charge of the Durban orphanage abruptly announced: 'You can't go back there. That's not your mother.' I went and flung myself under a bush in the school grounds and started to howl my head off. A teacher soon came past and asked what was wrong. 'I'm going to die because they won't let me go home to my mother,' I wailed.

She hauled me off to the missionary principal's office and that lady in turn bundled me into a car and straight to the juvenile section of the Durban magistrate's court. There a young man read something out in a quick gabble, most of which I didn't hear except that he insisted that my real mother was a white woman, not the Coloured foster-mother I'd grown up with. This seemed to relieve the missionary. The law had confirmed it. On return to the orphanage she produced a huge file. Most of what she said was that my mother had been insane and my father was 'a native.' That was the big horror but then there were so many of us at that orphanage who were horrors. [15]

Thus Bessie learnt in part of her true origins. In her version, this gruesome treatment of a child, even by the standards of South African society, is puzzling in its total illogicality; yet it is too strange not to be true. With hindsight it is possible to see that the events did indeed happen as described. Yet Bessie had mis-construed things. She believed she had been taken to court because she threw a tantrum, whereas, of course, the court hearing had been planned long before. Technically speaking, she was taken there for her own good although Louie Farmer had apparently failed to prepare her for the devastating information that she would be given. A shocking example of adult insensitivity, this event shaped and coloured the rest of Bessie Emery's life. Its emotional impact can only be imagined, never assessed.

The findings were that she was a child in need of care, and she was placed in the custody of St Monica's Home. As from January 1952 a monthly grant of £2 5s was paid for her maintenance.[16] For an introspective young girl cut adrift from the only moorings she had known, this development no doubt seemed irrelevant.

Perhaps Louie Farmer unbent a little and tried to comfort the child, as the pro-tagonist Elizabeth is comforted by 'the gaunt missionary . . . in her version of tenderness' in Bessie Head's novel *A Question of Power*.[17] No doubt Louie Farmer attempted to tell Bessie that her real mother was a good woman who cared for her. No doubt the pathetic letter that Toby Emery had written from Fort Napier was produced and read aloud to the young girl. In it her mother stipulat-ed 'that above all things, it was her earnest desire' that her daughter receive an education and that 'some of her money should be set aside' for this purpose.[18]

But the information seemed unreal to Bessie. She belonged emotionally to Nellie Heathcote. She still had to sort out a 'fanatic attachment' to her. Her first reaction was to turn away in disgust from Louie Farmer and the religion she rep-resented. When she had come to St Monica's, she was made to change her reli-gion from one day to the next. Her Roman Catholic faith had not been good enough for Louie Farmer, whose brand of Christianity now apparently permitted such inhumanity:

The lady seemed completely unaware of the appalling cruelty of her words. But for years and years after that I harboured a terrible and blind hatred for missionaries and the Christianity which they represented, and once I left the mission I never set foot in a Christian church again.[19]

Bessie Head wrote this in 1982. Yet it seems that she retained a remnant of affec-tion for the faith of her earliest years. 'When I die,' she told her son many years later, 'contact the Roman Catholic priest.' He did.

She no doubt became more difficult, given to the moodiness and 'sulks' dis-approved of by the teachers. She was no doubt punished more than previously, perhaps also unreasonably so, though her contemporaries did not notice this. 'Bessie was a quiet girl, a good girl,' they maintained. Even the quiet and good did not escape solitary confinement or a sailing trip on the seven seas.

'Bessie was a bookworm, that's what she was.' One of the first results of the experience was to make Bessie choose, blindly now, later consciously, 'to live with books'. And this is one thing St Monica's provided for her. She 'ran through the whole library' and was afterwards fed on Plato and anything she asked for out of private libraries because she 'had become "Teacher's Pet" and remained persistently top of the class'.[20]

She was never much interested in sport and did not go to the ballet classes some of the girls had begun to attend, so she spent the little leisure time that was available to her reading. If she felt she was being victimised, this was a way of keeping herself as invisible as possible.

Though the events in the magistrate's court cast a shadow over her life, the new year brought interesting changes for her. She became one of a small elite group who left St Monica's each morning and took the bus to Umbilo Road High School where they began their secondary education. There was the excitement of getting a new school uniform; of starting new subjects; of having teachers who did not know all her weaknesses; of making new friends.

About this time, Bessie acquired spectacles. Her bookish habits had apparently affected her sight, though later in life she managed without them again. She was still a squarely built little girl, much shorter than most of the others. She had a serious face, dominated by large and sensitive eyes, a face that could suddenly light up in a smile coming directly from the heart. She retained her simple style of dress, though she had a weakness for white bobby socks, always immaculate and fitting her sturdy legs snugly.

In July 1952, after she had been two and a half years at St Monica's, she was granted her first holiday. Conditions in Nellie Heathcote's home were rather cramped, for at this time Rhona Billings and her four children were staying there, and a nephew was occupying the outside room. As well as this, a Mr and Mrs Davis boarded there. However, the authorities allowed her to spend a fortnight with her foster-mother. Probably Bessie arrived in a rickshaw, taking it from the station down to East Street; this is how one of her friends from the Home remembers arriving there once when she visited the Heathcote home with Bessie. It was during this holiday that Bessie had to ask Nellie Heathcote the question that lay heaviest on her heart. 'Are you my real mother?' she asked. 'No,' said Nellie Heathcote, and started to cry.[21] Bessie heard about her grandmother coming to visit her and realised that she remembered the event dimly. As Bessie later told the story, her white mother came from a racehorse-owning family and Bessie's father was believed to be the stable hand. Nellie Heathcote, or Bessie herself, must have embroidered the story with these details. The Birch family had no racehorses.

These were the months of the Defiance Campaign, launched on 27 June 1952. After the tragic riots in Durban in 1947, the Indian and African communities had tried to face and shelve their differences, seeing the greater need to cooperate against a regime of which both groups were victims. One-day strikes in protest against the new laws had been organised and on 6 April 1952, when celebrations of the tercentenary of the arrival of Jan van Riebeeck at the Cape were being arranged, mass protest meetings were held in many parts of the country. The African National Congress and the South African Indian Congress thereafter launched a more ambitious plan: a civil disobedience campaign based on the Gandhian principle of non-violent non-cooperation. After limited success, with the main resistance coming from the Eastern Cape, the campaign flagged and began to die down by October. Some demonstrators who had been charged with occupying premises reserved for whites won an appeal in the Supreme Court on the grounds that the separate facilities provided had not been equal. However, the government replied to the Supreme Court ruling with an Act of 1953 which stated that separate amenities need not be equal. The screw had been given another turn.

The next year, in July 1953, Bessie again went to Pietermaritzburg for a fortnight. Nellie Heathcote was becoming proud of Bessie's achievements. She had just turned sixteen and was preparing to write her Junior Certificate examination, a public examination taken by all pupils of that age in Natal. Nellie Heathcote did an unusual thing. She promised to pay Bessie's examination fees. She did so shortly after Bessie returned to school, going up to the welfare office and paying in £1 10s, which was then forwarded to St Monica's.[22] It was her way of making up for the times she had let Bessie down: over books; over waiting too long to tell her about her real origins.

In November of the same year Nellie Heathcote wrote again to the school. She wanted Bessie to come home for the Christmas holidays. Over a month later and only three days before the school term closed, Louie Farmer answered. Permission was refused because Bessie had been going through a difficult time. This disappointment, coming on top of the strain connected with writing her examinations, was too much for Bessie. She absconded from St Monica's.

On the morning of the last day of term, Bessie and the three other girls attending Umbilo Road High School left the Home at about half past six to catch the bus to school as usual. Bessie mentioned to one of them that she wanted to visit someone at Addington Hospital. 'That's foolish and very risky,' her friend replied. 'Yes,' said Bessie, 'I don't think I dare.' With this remark, the other girls took it that she had abandoned the idea. She then talked about having to get her suitcase at school. Her friends thought this was strange because they had all taken their schoolbags back to St Monica's the day before. On arriving at school, the little group dispersed. Not until the final assembly, when the headmaster, who was giving out the prizes, called Bessie's name in vain, did the girls realise that she was not there. One of them collected her prize, telling Mr Ingle that Bessie was absent. Then they looked for her and, after a couple of hours, returned to St Monica's, thinking that she had gone ahead of them.

Her disappearance caused panic at the Home. In all the thirty years Louie Farmer had been there, she had had only nine girls run away.[23] Bessie's three companions were made to sit alone and write out their versions of what had happened. One concluded her description thus: 'But please Mam I really didn't no that Bessie was going to Maritzburg.'[24] Louie Farmer contacted the headmaster of the school but he was not able to help. Then she got in touch with the welfare organisation in Pietermaritzburg. The next morning a telephone call put her mind at rest.[25] Bessie was with Mrs Heathcote.

This was a new turning-point in Bessie's life: 'I had committed a serious offence by running away from the mission school and had to state my reasons before a juvenile magistrate ... The speech the magistrate made – you go back there, it's all for your own good – was quite all right to me.' In the same article, she explained why she was willing to go back to St Monica's. Something about the intense and dramatic nature of this visit to Maritzburg must have opened her eyes to the 'rigid, set life of the poor'. She noticed the uniformity, the passivity. 'They did not dream of enquiring into the riddle of life or attempting to get above it, as I had partly started to do.' To get out of this environment meant snapping the affection she felt for Nellie Heathcote. Aged sixteen, Bessie did this. She called it 'a blind choice for survival', the choice of 'a life with books'.[26] It was the choice of an individualist that was later woven into the myth of her own identity.

When the results of the Junior Certificate examination were published, Bessie found she had passed. Now a new decision had to be made. She had always talked about becoming a teacher, and she could now take a two-year course which would qualify her for elementary school teaching. It was an inferior form of training to that which white youngsters were offered. But it was a training, and it was decided that she take it.

Bessie's academic success was yet another indication of the steady progress the school had been making. But two events in 1950 were to cast a long shadow over the spacious lawns of St Monica's Home. In that year Hendrik Verwoerd became Minister of Native Affairs; it was he who soon introduced the Bantu Education Act to centralise African education under government control. This Act made it so difficult for the mission schools to continue that many were forced to close down.

1950 was also the year of the Group Areas Act. From the end of 1952, there were rumours circulating to the effect that Durban and its neighbouring municipalities were to be 're-zoned'. Early in 1953, a delegation of smartly dressed officials appeared at St Monica's, asking to be shown around as they needed to gain an impression of the size and state of the school for the new zoning plans. Normally Louie Farmer was proud to show off the premises, having in her mind's eye the way things had been when she came and the circumstances connected with each improvement that had since been made. If she also did so that day, it was only in quick, intense flashes. She was shaken to her roots by the realisation that this product of so many years of hard work was clearly threatened. She could barely answer the polite enquiries civilly.

When the officials drove off, she rushed inside to where some of the older girls were sewing, and in an almost unprecedented outburst, confided to them her fears for the future of the Home on its present property.[27] They were more than justified. In the years since St Monica's had moved there, Hillary had become one of Durban's attractive suburbs. That an institution for orphan coloured girls run by English missionaries should be allowed to nestle undisturbed in the midst of such a beautiful suburb was unthinkable in the new schemes to entrench the white man.

Bessie now had two years left at St Monica's. Louie Farmer had six months. In June 1954 she retired. Everyone who knew her remembers her strict moral standards. 'Good and evil were sharply defined to "Louie", never confused by the greyness with which so many blur their consciences ... One never heard from her lips that common phrase of the second-rate, "That'll do",'[28] said a fellow missionary. 'She was a strict disciplinarian,' said a former pupil, 'but she trained the girls to be individuals, depend on themselves, learn to be honest. She made honesty the most important quality one should acquire.' 'When I look back,' said another pupil, 'I feel that that's where my character was built.' 'Louie Farmer was cruel,' said another. 'Good but harsh. We liked her all the same. When I got married I thought of the Home in a new light. At least we were safe there.'

Yet none of the girls were encouraged to think about their unhappy backgrounds in planning for their futures. They seldom confided personal or family details to each other, never discussed why they were in the Home. 'Somehow,' said one, 'we were made to feel ashamed of why we were there.' 'Why did they want to wipe out our lives?' asked another. 'If we could just leave the home without probing into our own background they would have been very happy.' Then she added, with her special degree of insight: 'It was the missionary spirit of the times. They supported the white side of life and the black side of life was forgotten.' Gertrude Stock, who said this, had trained as a teacher and returned to work at St Monica's under Louie Farmer in the 1930s. In 1963 she became the first (and only) coloured principal of the school.[29]

Louie Farmer's pedagogical methods, inhibitions and taboos belonged in the English boarding school tradition known to generations of children – irrespective of colour – who have been through it. Nonetheless, she cared deeply about her girls and their future, worked tirelessly to place them in safe and rewarding occupations when they left the Home, and kept close contact with many of them in their new lives. Most of the girls admired and respected her, especially as they grew older. But not Bessie. On several occasions whilst there, she told other girls that she thought Louie Farmer was cruel, her punishments too harsh. And this is how she later described her.

Miss Margaret Cadmore replaced Louie Farmer as Lady Warden in June 1954. She was a friend of Miss Theobald's, who suggested her to the Bishop. She brought with her Miss Winifred Thomsett. They had trained as missionaries together at the Josephine Butler Training College for Moral Workers in Liverpool.[30] They spent a month at St Monica's with Louie Farmer before she sailed for England and a short retirement which ended in an untimely death as the result of a fall.

'When Miss Cadmore came, we got sheets and knives and forks.' 'When Miss Cadmore came, we could listen to the radio and dance on Sundays.' 'When Miss Cadmore came, it meant a right-about turn for us.'

Margaret Cadmore had a ruddy complexion, a turned-up nose and a ready smile. She was short and tubby with a very direct manner and a colourful vocabulary of swear words. Her favourite expression was 'What the damn blasted hell is going on here', said Bessie.[31] She had been a nurse during the Second World War, and when her fiancé was killed in action, she became a missionary. It was during the war, she told the girls, that she had learnt to swear. An old schoolfriend knew better: 'She had always used those words and got them and many others from her father. He was an even more vivid, wayward and free person! Truly a wild Welshman! Margaret and he did not get on well together, being too much alike to live in peace.'[32]

No one remained unaffected by her arrival. She made a tremendous impression on Bessie. Her off-beat sense of humour, her unconventionality, her earthiness and common sense, were qualities she had never encountered before.

As one of the oldest and most promising girls at the Home, Bessie was given Margaret Cadmore's full attention. In fact it was not very long before the five girls who were now taking their Natal Teachers' Senior Certificate and who went out every day to Bechet High School, as Umbilo Road High School had been renamed, were moved into her own quarters, The Dell. They needed more time and privacy to study than it was possible to get amidst seventy children. They needed her personal concern.

It was probably at this stage that Bessie, having read everything in the school library, began on Margaret Cadmore's books. Bessie later described her teacher's efforts to get her to understand the poet W B Yeats: 'He [Yeats] used to totally defeat me. One day I told her I could not understand him and she flew off the beam and grabbed the book from my hands: "You're reading him the wrong way. Now hear the lake water lapping."' She also encouraged Bessie to sketch. 'She would stand behind me and shrill: "Life isn't like that, harsh outlines. It's soft, round curves. Caress it with your eyes." I translated this advice to my writing.'[33]

Margaret Cadmore also tried to give the girls some sex education before it was too late. 'She was absolutely frank with the girls about this side of life and was extremely fond of telling us about a man she had loved during the war, and lost. It was like saying: It's quite all right. Everyone has passions. Now this is the sensible thing to do about it.'[34] In Bessie's case, she may have succeeded only in encouraging her romantic and unrealistic idea of men.

Winifred Thomsett, with her little dog Penny, was also an asset to the school. As assistant Lady Warden, she was in charge of the daily running of the Home, from getting up at five in the morning to give out the supplies for the day to taking on the role of handyman. Her calm friendliness, her ability to refrain from moralising and her amazing aptitude for repairing things and finding ways of solving everyday problems made her popular. The girls called her Man Friday. Bessie spent much time with her dog.

There was now more time for fun at the Home. Bessie and her friends were fond of dressing up and putting on sketches. With broom handles serving as banjos and hats pulled on at all angles they would present their Daft Half Hour of songs, sketches and nonsense. Sometimes of an evening they would dance to the radio, the staff joining in.

The next eighteen months were a happy time for Bessie. In Margaret Cadmore she found a friend as well as a mentor. Several letters which Bessie wrote to her have survived, illustrating how the young girl began to blossom at this time. In one written shortly after Margaret Cadmore's arrival at the school, Bessie wrote to tell her how she had run away. 'I hardly knew how to tell it to you last night,' she began.

My reason for doing so now clearly shows me that I had selfishly considered myself and thought I hated staying here, because I had got myself into frequent trouble and was miserable ... I have completely changed my attitude towards life. I have come to realise that we are only important to God in our consideration and service to others. I find this very hard to live up to but it certainly makes me happy.[35]

Her rejection of Christianity was being kept in abeyance for a while.

In December 1954 Bessie was allowed to go home for the holidays. She wrote a charming letter to tell Margaret Cadmore that she had arrived. She could not telephone, she said, because she was 'awfully scared of phoning. Once I phoned my mother and stood holding the phone for about three minutes without saying a word!' She described her journey in the bus and how an old black priest caught sight of 'one of the erring members of his congregation' and 'started to deliver a sermon' over Bessie's head. 'He gesticulated wildly, his eyes bulged, a vein stuck out on the side of his neck and his voice thundered in my ears till my eardrums rattled.' She talked about the 'heroine worship' shown her by her niece Veronica Samuel, and how she struck 'ballet poses' for her and was rewarded 'by the glow of admiration in her eyes'. She described her nephew Dennis teasing her for being fat and the promise he had extracted from her to marry him 'chiefly because of my pathetic attempts at baking'. Margaret Cadmore had given her two pairs of stockings, 'so sheer and lovely I am afraid to wear them. Can you imagine how grown up I am going to feel?'[36] It is the letter of someone who enjoys writing and who knows the recipient will enjoy what she has to say.

The Heathcote family were now beginning to feel the effects of the Group Areas Act. Pietermaritzburg was being re-zoned, and Nellie Heathcote was told that they had to move from East Street, which was to be an Indian business area. This was a worrying time for Nellie Heathcote, as it was for all her neighbours. She finally found a house in an area called the Coloured Village, which was just being established by the municipality.

Towards the end of 1955, Veronica Samuel wrote to Bessie describing their move and adding that 'Gramma hopes you are a good girl not getting cross'.[37] They invited her for the Christmas holidays but that year she was not allowed to go.

Bessie was now approaching her final year of training. Her half-yearly results in 1954 had been good. She had been placed second in the class, and was said to have worked diligently, especially in Educational Methods and in English. Her weak subjects were Arithmetic and Afrikaans. By December 1955 Bessie had lost some of her drive. Her English results were as good as ever, and her teacher appreciated her effort: 'Has worked very well indeed and handles the language capably.' In subjects such as History, Geography and Biology, however, she was said to have lost interest or achieved a disappointing result. She was 'very weak and very lazy' at Arithmetic. But what is worse, she failed her Physical Training examination, receiving the comment: 'Weak. Did not work harder as she was asked to, so she failed.'[38] This was a blow. It meant that she did not pass that year. Her Natal Teachers' Senior Certificate was dated 1 January 1957, and was only issued in June 1957, eighteen months after she should have completed her course. She had had to take a supplementary Physical Education examination at the M L Sultan Technical College at the end of 1956.

On 21 January 1956 it was time for Bessie to leave St Monica's. She was officially discharged from the provisions of the Children's Act on 17 February 1956, and from the beginning of that school year, in January, she was appointed to the teaching staff of Clairwood Coloured School.

In 1959 both Margaret Cadmore and Miss Theobald resigned from St Monica's. In 1969 the Home was moved to Wentworth, into buildings that had previously been police barracks in a wind-blown and undeveloped area. The sloping grounds below the main house at Hillary were levelled; shrubs, bushes and fruit trees were razed to the ground; the old buildings were removed; and modern red-brick classrooms were erected instead. St Monica's Diocesan Home for Coloured Girls was converted into Werda Hoërskool. It became a high school for white children who received instruction in the medium of Afrikaans.

After having lived a strictly regulated life for so many years, Bessie, aged eighteen, was now on her own. Margaret Cadmore had seen to it that she had good lodgings, with a teacher from Clairwood Coloured School, and she ended up living just across the road from the school.

Very soon she realised how protected her own life had been. While she was wrestling with questions about God or W B Yeats, her own people were suffering new political blows. In the new sharply defined racial grouping of South Africans, the peaceful coloured community had suddenly become the centre of heated discussion. It concerned their franchise.

The South Africa Act of 1909 contained an entrenched clause protecting the right of coloured men in the Natal and Cape provinces to vote, provided they fulfilled certain educational and property requirements. This clause could be altered only by the two-thirds majority of a joint sitting of both Houses of Parliament. In 1951, shortly after the National Party came into power, D F Malan introduced a Bill to put the coloureds on a separate voters' roll where their votes, traditionally giving solid support to the Opposition, would have no real effect. For five years the government tried to get the Bill through parliament without the two-thirds majority until in early 1956, shortly after J G Strijdom followed D F Malan as prime minister, it succeeded by increasing the Senate from 48 to 87 nominated members.

This five-year legal struggle had aroused many South Africans to resistance while a unanimous Appeal Court had twice ruled the measures taken null and void. To no avail. While many people from Bessie's circle of contacts vowed never to trust or support the white man again and a few became active in the resistance movement, Bessie herself observed but could not really identify with this cause. She was learning to manage her new situation, and when she did begin to look outwards, it was in an entirely different direction.

She quickly settled into teaching an infant class but soon began to find the afternoons and evenings dull. Most girls of her age would have found themselves a boyfriend. She did meet someone who was interested in her. Years later she recalled the man she might have married when she was eighteen. He was desperately poor but he laughed all day long. Had she married him she would have spent her life in a Durban slum, quite possibly the mother of a large family.[39] Bessie was very attractive and innocent; but she also had a good deal of common sense. Once again she chose books.

She could not afford to buy them but at St Monica's this had never been a problem. She had always been able to borrow them. The Durban municipal library had a 'Slegs Blankes' sign outside it. One of the teachers at St Monica's, knowing that her pupils would run into trouble here, had told them about the M L Sultan Library. This was a library that had been donated to the Indians of the city by one of their own wealthy merchants but was open to anyone interested in reading. She joined it.

Naturally there were large sections devoted to Hinduism. Bessie was curious and found the literature absorbing. Hinduism's all-embracing philosophy was diametrically opposed to the strict and narrow version of Christianity on which she had been fed for seven years. Its vast conglomerate of beliefs, making it tolerant of other religions and not compelling its followers to adopt any particular rites or sacraments, appealed to her strong individualism. To some it can appear an extrovert religion: of spectacle; of mythology; of the worship of the cow; of, even, the consistent practice of non-violence. But for others it is a religion of the introvert, the travelling of the paths of spiritual progress, the search for liberation, the belief in renunciation. Besides its wealth of sacred writings such as the Vedas, Hinduism is also a social system. Life is regarded as a rite. There is no clear division between the secular and the religious, and the caste system is believed to be a way of living out a divine ordination. To break out of one's caste is to break *dharma,* or the order of things transformed into moral obligation. Some Hindus may profess not to believe in any god, but all Hindus believe in the caste system.

Some of the other most generally held concepts are the pantheistic belief that all is God and therefore that all life is sacred; that the god Vishnu returns to earth in various guises from time to time to help and guide his followers; and that man himself is a soul in perpetual transmigration, bound to his wheel of fate and striving to live this life better than his last so that he can advance along the road towards spiritual perfection and union with the principle of the Absolute.

Hinduism was very visible in Durban. There were temples, with their distinctive domes, surrounded by sacred trees. There were the frequent religious processions and public trance ceremonies that struck terror into the African population. There were the large number of ritual objects such as holy ash and incense sticks for sale in the market place, and the religious literature including pictures of four-armed gods, in bookstalls. Bessie observed all these things, but they did not attract her. It was the philosophy that did.

There was also a more direct reason for Hinduism to appeal to Bessie. Among the people she now began to meet, she found that Mahatma Gandhi was greatly admired, indeed almost idolised. He had lived in South Africa from 1893 to 1915, during which time he had established the Natal Indian Congress and taught the Natal Indian community to combat discriminatory laws with non-violent resistance. That they had not cast off his influence they demonstrated very effectively in 1946 in their two-year resistance to the Asiatic Land Tenure and Indian Land Tenure Bill, intended to prevent wealthy Indian merchants from buying land in 'white' areas. When India launched an attack on South Africa during the first session of the newly established United Nations on account of this very issue, it was a humiliating blow to Smuts. It may well have weakened his position sufficiently in South Africa for him to be ousted in the general elections of 1948. Of far greater immediate tragedy for the Durban Indians, however, was the fact that the Mahatma had been assassinated earlier that same year.

Several aspects of the Gandhi story inspired Bessie. Gandhi himself was both of the world, an astute political bargainer, and yet not of it. But what amazed her most was the realisation that this great Hindu also believed in Allah and Christ, and was admired by both Muslims and Christians for his teachings. This illustrated the inclusive nature of Hinduism as opposed to Christianity's exclusiveness. Many years later she was to say:

Never have I read anything that aroused my feelings like his [Gandhi's] political statements. There was a simple and astonishing clarity in the way he summarised political truths, there was an appalling [sic] tenderness and firmness in the man. I paused every now and then over his paper, almost swooning with worship because I recognised that this could only be God as man. He drove the Indian masses mad with devotion. He was their first and only spokesman, he was a peculiar combination of India's ideal, the truly religious man and astonishingly, a practical man of the world.[40]

All these impressions crowded in on the young girl. Once more she turned her back on Christianity. Many years later she expressed it thus:

I had no need to go to church from the age of 18 but I was in church almost every day before that at the mission school. There I read widely and also became very familiar with the Bible. I do view it as a history of the Jews, nothing more. There were things done, teaching put over to me that I viewed with horror. Whole areas of the world were blanked out on geography maps as heathendom, especially India. It was impossible for missionaries to convert India. They had a long tradition of enquiring into the things of the spirit. It was a way of life there and something very beautiful ... So you could say I moved straight from Christianity, which I found stifling to Hinduism which I found was very rich and deep in concepts.[41]

Bessie could also sense in this group of people a political awareness and cultural identity that she had never experienced in her home or among Nellie Heathcote's friends. She soon became friendly with a thin, ascetic follower of Ramakrishna, one of the leading Hindu teachers of the nineteenth century, whose main emphasis was on mysticism and a form of theocracy. Later she joined the sect. This led to trouble with her coloured landlady, who put up a notice on the bathroom door: 'People who go in for devil's business must not use this bathroom!'[42]

Bessie weighed this up against what her new friend told her: 'You wouldn't have come here unless you had been a Hindu in many of your previous births', and chose Hinduism. She then found lodgings with an Indian family. No longer for her the sheltered mission life. Bessie's new landlady, named Rose, kept her regaled with intimate details of her love life. She had once loved a man, very effeminate in his ways and given to quoting Shakespeare, who left her when she became pregnant. She later married 'a man as handsomely and vigorously male as Marlon Brando and as gigantic in his tendernesses and generousities [sic]'.[43] But Rose did not appreciate him. She spurned his love-making but told Bessie all about it anyway while longing for the 'man who got away'.

Going home to visit the family in Pietermaritzburg, Bessie tried to initiate Veronica Samuel into her new interest. There was a Hindu temple in William Street, quite close to their old home, and Bessie took Veronica there.[44] Carefully removing their shoes, they went into the cool interior, with the heady smell of incense hanging in the air. They stared round curiously at the elaborate and beautifully wrought statues and decorations. Bessie never believed in hiding things, so on returning home, she immediately told Nellie Heathcote where they had been. With the years Nellie Heathcote had grown to accept what Bessie did. She was now a woman of such achievement that her every action was approved. And that very day she had demonstrated her affluence by buying Veronica Samuel a pair of shoes.

It was a year of intense intellectual growth for Bessie. She assimilated especially Hinduism's pantheistic concepts and the idea of the sanctity of the common man, and in the years to come gradually gave them her own touch. But the process had been far too rapid; it brought her to the brink of a breakdown. This, in turn, forced her to abandon these ideas for the time being: 'I forced myself into a way of life and thought that was completely foreign to my upbringing. I couldn't see it at the time but I do now. I don't regret what was wrong or unwise that I did, because it gave me the ability to discriminate that truth from what is a waste of time.'[45] The experience brought on a time of 'mental disturbance that I doubt I could ever stand again'. When she says that 'those two years after I left St Monica's were the most awful in my life,' the statement is, unfortunately, only relative.

In this mental state, it was impossible for Bessie to manage her teaching. Though she was anxious to impart knowledge to the children in her class, knowing all too well that it was only through education that they could hope to escape from the dreary poverty of their homes, she could not get the response she wanted from them. She felt that they did not appreciate what she was trying to do for them. Discipline was an important element in the school, and she found it very hard to make her pupils sit, stand and keep silent at her commands. When she showed them friendship, they responded by becoming unsettled and unruly. Then she had the headmaster at her door, looking concerned. Going to work each morning became more and more of a burden for her. In June 1958 she resigned from her job. 'I was sure and still feel that teaching is not for me. Perhaps I just imagined that it was driving me out of my mind but I thought so at the time,'[46] she wrote three months afterwards.

Back she went to St Monica's and told Margaret Cadmore that she had given up teaching and was going to Cape Town. Margaret Cadmore was shocked. She had nothing against people taking up new challenges but, to her, Bessie's decision seemed foolhardy. The girl had very little money, no prospective job, nowhere to live and no friends to stay with. She feared for her safety in a big city. When Margaret Cadmore tried to dissuade her, however, Bessie broke down, cried hysterically and rushed away.[47]

Once again she returned to Pietermaritzburg for a holiday. On 7 July 1958 she turned twenty-one: this event was celebrated with a little party. But though Nellie

Heathcote also tried to dissuade Bessie from going away, she had made up her mind. She had money for the train fare and could manage for some weeks on what she had saved up. She was determined to get herself a job as a reporter. At the end of July she left home for good, heading for the Cape.

Journalism in Cape Town & Johannesburg, 1958–1960

Bessie Head had never been much interested in history, because, as she later realised, it was not *her* history, but the white man's. Nonetheless when she arrived in Cape Town, she responded immediately to its gracious old buildings and huge, sheltering oak trees. Here was visible history as she had never experienced it.

The fact that Cape Town is the oldest white settlement in Southern Africa makes itself apparent everywhere. There are traces of its origins as a 'halfway house' to the East Indies, established by the Dutch in 1652. There are many reminders of its time as a thriving colony of free burghers, before Holland had to see it taken over by the British during the Napoleonic Wars. And the remnants of British influence at the Cape are also easily discernible. The resentment and bitterness sown then between the Dutch and British survived the next century and a half. The only thing the two groups could agree on was 'the native question', as they appropriated more and more land once occupied by the country's original inhabitants.

Bessie had the address of a hostel, the Stakesby Lewis, in District Six, the coloured quarter sprawling up the slope of the mountain and stretching down to the docks. It was run by a Christian organisation and was the centre to which all poor travellers gravitated on arriving in Cape Town. The warden asked for £10 in advance for the month of August and advised her to go down to the office of *Drum* and *Golden City Post* in Hanover Street, if she wanted a job as a reporter.

Bessie knew the tabloid *Golden City Post* well, having often read it in Durban. It was a weekly, given to sensational reports. It appeared in three editions, one in Johannesburg, aimed at attracting the African population, one in Durban, adapted to Indians' taste, and one in Cape Town for the Cape coloureds. It seemed to offer the better possibility for a job. The monthly magazine *Drum* also addressed a black public, but through its short stories and articles, often capturing the vitality of township life in brisk colloquial prose, it had already become the mouthpiece of urban Africans. It had quite a reputation for a hard, direct style. It would not be interested in a beginner, and a young woman at that.

The day after her arrival in Cape Town, she went to see the editor of the *Golden City Post,* Dennis Kiley. He remembers this first encounter well: how very nervous Bessie Emery was. Tears welled up into her eyes inadvertently as she tried to persuade him to give her a chance on his paper. He could not refuse. She looked so young and vulnerable. Her large, expressive eyes radiated intelligence and sensitivity. Her hair was short as it had always been, and she was slightly plump. As always too, her dress, though somewhat worn and the only one she possessed, was freshly washed and ironed. But how to help her? Bessie had to prove her worth. She was taken on as a freelance reporter, to be paid at the rate of three shillings per inch for her copy, for a three-month trial period.

Dennis Kiley started by sending her to the courts to listen to cases and follow up their human-interest aspect. The editor accepted her articles, which grew longer week by week. The only trouble was that she was almost penniless. Living alone in a big city is expensive, and Bessie's savings disappeared rapidly. Dennis Kiley could see that she was struggling and helped her financially where he could. She even tried to submit short stories to another local newspaper and the *Reader's Digest,* but was unsuccessful.

More than a month after starting work, she had still received no payment from the *Golden City Post.* Bessie was desperate. As it was, she stood in debt to Dennis Kiley and the warden of Stakesby Lewis Hostel, who was allowing her to stay on there and pay at a later date. Her foster-mother, Nellie Heathcote, was too poor. Her mother substitute, Margaret Cadmore, was disappointed in her. Her natural mother Bessie Amelia Emery . . . suddenly Bessie remembered her inheritance. There was not much left in the fund, she knew, but she had nothing.

On 10 September she sat down and wrote to Margaret Cadmore, explaining her situation without over-dramatising it. 'So far they haven't paid me for August and I've existed on no money. I have not cried as I made the decision.' She then asked if she might have the remains of her inheritance from her mother. 'At a wild guess' she thought that there was about £12 in the Guardian Fund for her. 'I have been wicked to get into this poverty. Don't lecture too much as I'm sorry,' she added in a postscript.

The letter was not written in a cringing, begging tone. Much of its five pages was given to lively descriptions of her working conditions. The most direct cry for help came at the very conclusion of the letter: '[B]ut I am desperately poor. Please help me.'[1]

Margaret Cadmore responded instantly. On 20 September she sent £20 to Bessie, who wrote a long letter of thanks which is unique in the light it sheds on her emotional and professional state in these early years of her career:

You must know that you are an amazing person to grasp a situation so quickly and send help, post haste. Do you know what somebody else would have said: 'Oh she wants money eh? Blast the girl! I can't do anything. Besides how do I know what she is doing over there!' But you are different. I always suspected you were a genius and your trust and belief in me is just too wonderful. I will never let you have cause not to trust me.

She proceeded to talk about her state of mind (peaceful), Mr Kiley (mercurial), and the coloured people she was meeting: 'The people here are more worried about their political rights and daily bread than my friends in Durban were worried about an eternity. So my mind has rest from problems that cannot be solved and is also awakened to a world of helpless and enslaved people.'[2]

What Bessie was describing was more than a budding social and political awareness. It was her first conscious confrontation with her own identity within a group. To have grown up as a coloured in Natal was a very different experience from coming to the world in District Six, Cape Town. The Natal coloureds were a poorly defined minority group. In an unjust society where privileges were connected with being white, they clung to the notion that they were almost white and saw this as their only chance of improving their material state. They defined themselves as much by what they were not as by what they were.

This was not the case with the Cape coloureds. They were descended from the original Khoikhoi inhabitants of the Cape and the imported slave population. Company records from 1671 show that three-quarters of the children born to slave mothers were mulattos. By 1795 there were over 25000 privately owned slaves at the Cape. Dutch burghers could not marry freed slaves, but could marry freed mixed-race slaves. Until the end of the eighteenth century, religious considerations determined the social pattern of the colony so that the distinction was made between Christian and heathen, rather than between white and mixed-race or black. Nonetheless, a stratifying of society was beginning to occur because the whites were commercially stronger. Under them was an intermediate group consisting of free blacks, emancipated slaves and mixed-race, while slaves and landless Khoikhoi, now forced into labour, formed the lowest stratum.

In 1828 after the Cape had become a British colony, all subjects of the Crown were given legal equality. Unfortunately it did not go hand in hand with social equality. This meant coloureds were poorer than whites because they had less remunerative jobs, but they still had a clear sense of their own worth. Capetonian society remained cosmopolitan and whites there retained a tolerant attitude to non-whites generally and the coloured population in particular. These people were almost totally westernised, spoke Afrikaans and kept their own traditions in their own areas, the best known and most central of which was District Six.

It was in District Six that Bessie lived and was to work. She was the only woman reporter. This meant that she was always being given stories connected with women and children, 'while the men reporters get murders and politics to do. One day I should like to get hold of a good murder.' The truth of it was that sordid court cases and scandalous incidents were not Bessie's forte at all. Both Dennis Kiley and Ken Mackenzie, who as the Cape Town editor of *Drum* shared the Hanover Street office, realised this. Dennis Kiley did his best to teach her the ropes. Her version: 'I have a habit of knocking on his door and asking "Are you busy Mr Kiley" and inevitably "Yes I'm always busy." Then I timidly hand in my story. "Hmm this is good but can't you make it more lively?" I have a passion for dry statements but our newspaper is a sob paper. He seems to think I'll get the style soon.'[3]

His version:

Being a court reporter was a very rough job, not the environment for her at all. But she got round that. I remember once she was just walking along, somewhere in District Six, when she got talking to a little old coloured lady who invited her in for a cup of tea. She started to reminisce about her simple pleasant life, how they used to go to places like Hout

Bay for a day out on a Sunday. Bessie wrote a sensitive little piece. Not at all typical of that sensationalist newspaper. But I said to the editor, 'Look, publish this.' That little piece was much more typical of the things she was capable of doing and would wish to do than what she wrote otherwise.[4]

In her letter to Margaret Cadmore, Bessie described how the paper had launched a series of articles entitled 'Making Your Dreams Come True'. When she was sent out to write the first, her first mission was no easy one. She had to go and help two old bachelors to find wives. The next week she had to take three crippled children by cable car to the top of Table Mountain and describe the outing. 'I can see myself doing strange things as I fear people's dreams could be extraordinary,'[5] she wrote of this assignment. It would seem, though, that it was Bessie who was doing the dreaming. There are no records of this series of articles in the *Golden City Post* at that time.[6] And of course, on closer consideration it becomes clear that such assignments would have gone to the top reporters, not a green beginner. Bessie was doing her best to convince Margaret Cadmore that she was managing. Long afterwards she told a friend that during her early years as a reporter in Cape Town she had typed out cookery recipes and done other hack jobs, as well as covering immorality cases in the courts – a much more realistic picture of the scope of her work. About three years later she was to use some of her experiences as a reporter to provide the colourful and disturbing background for her first novel, *The Cardinals*.

Moving in and out of so many people's lives made Bessie aware of social injustice and human worth in an entirely new way. 'This type of work leaves no time for mind troubles or frustrations or hysterics. One is always listening to other people's troubles.'[7] However, she also came across another form of discrimination that surprised her:

The life of the Coloured people here is quaint and bewildering. There is a rigid caste system; the upper class who are very fair and cultured; the middle class who are factory workers and the no goods who are so poor that they have degenerated morally . . . I have walked into some houses where the reception has been very cold. They seemed to pick out immediately that I had no class and sophistication, which is associated with being fair . . . I was very amused that people could be so childish, just because I'm a shade darker. I have never thought of belonging to any particular class of society but most probably I belong to the low class because I feel so happy in their carefree unsnobbish society that I already have many friends among them. I like degenerate people. They are sometimes pathetic, very shrewd, and often trying to better themselves. They are fun too. Life is one big joke to them as they are rough and live amidst violence. The middle class are inclined to ape the upper class so I do not worry with them.[8]

Bessie's method of coming to terms with snobbery was to retreat from it into the world of the intellect:

I detest snobbery but maybe I'm a mental snob . . . I search avidly for anyone really intelligent. With intelligent people one forgets such shameful matters as the colour of one's skin and facial features which seem to matter so much in South Africa. Heavens! I will not ape anybody. I am an individual. No one shall make me ashamed of what I am!⁹

Such noble protestations must have warmed Margaret Cadmore's heart. She nonetheless wrote a very concerned letter to Dennis Kiley. What with Bessie's humorous and affectionate descriptions of him, she felt that he would certainly be willing to help her. She asked him to do something about paying her more – 'we don't want her to end up destitute in the streets'. Dennis Kiley could write back that though times were hard for Bessie she was not destitute and she was showing progress in her work. And sure enough, after her three-month trial period was over, she was made a staff reporter and began to earn a better wage.

Meanwhile apartheid was being enforced more and more widely. People not classified as white were steadily being removed from urban areas; schooling was controlled; a much more comprehensive pass system was introduced; and in 1957 the Extension of University Education Act established 'tribal' colleges for each racial group.

Resistance to these laws increased. Following the Defiance Campaign, the African National Congress had convened a Congress of the People at Kliptown, near Johannesburg, in 1955, where the Freedom Charter was adopted. This attracted people of all races to stand up and declare that 'South Africa belongs to all who live in it, black and white, and . . . no government can justly claim authority unless it is based on the will of the people.' The following year, the government had collected sufficient 'evidence' to arrest 156 people and accuse them of high treason, a capital offence, for their connections with the Freedom Charter, which was now considered a communist document. They were brought to court in a trial that lasted until 1961.

Other kinds of resistance also made themselves felt. There was active opposition to the fact that African women were now also being forced to carry 'reference books'. Unrest was breaking out in the western Transvaal and Pondoland over the Tribal Authorities and over Bantu education and the new 'tribal colleges'. In June 1959 there was unrest in the townships outside Durban. Dennis Kiley was transferred there and covered the explosion in January 1960, when angry Africans murdered seven policemen involved in a liquor raid in Cato Manor, near Durban. This meant the outbreak of a new period of rioting, unrest and severe police repression.

In April 1959 Bessie decided to move away from Cape Town. There was a chance for her to get a job on the *Golden City Post* in Johannesburg and she took it. From living on the periphery of events, Bessie was now caught up and swirled into the centre.

It was not her new job, however, that caused this change. In fact she moved from *Golden City Post* to *Home Post*, a weekend tabloid supplement. Here she took over a column designed for young people consisting of a newsletter entitled 'Dear Gang' and an advice column called 'Hiya Teenagers'. After a fortnight she introduced herself:

I want to tell you a little about myself. I haven't really introduced myself so you hardly know anything about me. I think I am an adventurous sort of person and because of that

I am always getting into trouble. When I was small I often got a good box on the ear because I was forever going down to the river near my home when I should have been in the back-yard playing with dolls. Agh! I just hated dolls. I wanted to know all about boxing and race horses and everything a girl shouldn't know about and I loved lots and lots of ice cream ... The things I don't like are getting up early in the morning and sewing.[10]

Journalistically this work could hardly have been as interesting as her Cape Town assignments. But it carried with it the assurance of a steady income. Furthermore, it is surprising how quickly Bessie's personal style became evident in her column. She soon suggested starting a Gang Club and asked her readers to write a letter to a boy who had rheumatic fever. She called for suggestions for a club motto. She introduced a handwriting competition and asked for riddles. She apparently received a warm response. And there were appreciative comments: 'I think you are wonderful'. Club Motto: 'There's no one but Bessie for us.' Though she used trite phrases – 'she was quite a pet of a girl' – and glossy non-truths – 'when I got home that evening Mum and Garridge were the best of friends'[11] – her approach obviously appealed to young people. Dramatic journalism it was not.

As in Cape Town, *Golden City Post* and *Drum* magazine shared the same offices in Johannesburg. Amongst others, Bessie got to know Lewis Nkosi, Can Themba and Dennis Brutus. They were all journalists of considerable reputation, men who were 'supposed to exhibit a unique intellectual style, usually urbane, ironic, morally tough and detached'.[12] As a *Drum* reporter, it was assumed that 'one couldn't deal professionally with urban African life unless one had descended to its very depths as well as climbed to its heights'. Neither could be considered part of Bessie's life. She did not find the contact with her new colleagues fearsome, if we are to believe her column, 'I've Been Happy':

It hardly seems possible that at one time I had qualms and second thoughts about taking over this page from Sharon. I arrived from Cape Town one wet Monday morning feeling as I looked miserable ... But my funny feelings left almost immediately I entered the office. (Don't let anybody tell you that newspaper people are hard-boiled and intimidating!) Within a week I had made friends with almost everybody on the staff. And now, after six months, I have made more friends than I ever had.[13]

Sometime shortly after she moved to Johannesburg, Bessie and a friend went down to Pietermaritzburg for a few days. It was her last visit to her childhood home and her last contact with her adopted mother. Nellie Heathcote's heart condition had become more serious and she died in hospital shortly afterwards. Bessie could not attend the funeral, which Rhona arranged. Veronica went to live with her parents and she lost touch completely with her Aunt Bessie. Two years later she married and returned to Pietermaritzburg.

In Johannesburg the opposition to apartheid at that time drew its support from people of all races. In 1955, in a clear negation of the government's insistence on the separation of races, representatives of all the major extra-parliamentary groups met in a Congress of the People and adopted the Freedom Charter, which announced, 'South Africa belongs to all who live in it, black and white'. However, there had been growing discontent expressed within the African National Congress by a group who called themselves the Africanists, and whose motto was 'Africa for the Africans'. In November 1958 at the ANC Transvaal provincial congress there was open confrontation between ANC leaders and the Africanists and the latter were forced to leave the gathering. In March 1959 this breakaway group founded the Pan Africanist Congress with Robert Sobukwe as its chairman. It was the question of multiracialism which divided them. The Africanists felt that the struggle for equal rights was the black man's struggle. They opposed the ANC's policy of multiracial alliances, arguing that others, whites in particular, could be sympathetic to the struggle but could not be involved in the same way as blacks.

Robert Sobukwe was born in Graaff-Reinet in the Cape. His father was of Sotho descent and his mother was a Xhosa, both staunch Methodists who valued education for their children. Because of his undoubted promise, Robert had been sent to Healdtown, the Methodist mission school near Fort Beaufort in the Eastern Cape, then on to the South African Native College at Fort Hare, near Alice. As well as showing academic brilliance, Sobukwe rapidly developed a political awareness and demonstrated natural talents of leadership. As president of the Students Representative Council, he rallied his fellow students and stunned some of the staff by declaring in his final speech that 'we are what we are because the God of Africa made us so. We dare not compromise, nor dare we use moderate language in the course of our freedom . . . Africa will not equivocate! And she will be heard! REMEMBER AFRICA!'[14] The year was 1949.

With such promising young men as Nelson Mandela and Walter Sisulu, he joined the Youth League of the African National Congress. He was inspired by the principle of non-violence, and became involved in the Defiance Campaign and other protest actions of those years. Gradually, however, the new trend towards multiracialism within the ANC made him uneasy. He regarded it as a betrayal of the African cause. Minority groups of whites and Asians were gaining key positions within the liberation movement, and he felt that the old forms of manipulation had simply taken on a new character.

Everyone who knew Robert Sobukwe was impressed by him. In 1954 his fine academic record and quiet-spoken, courteous manner had gained him the rare position of language assistant at one of the country's leading white liberal universities, the University of the Witwatersrand. Though the university practised academic non-segregation amongst its students until 1959, the staff was almost wholly white. Only a handful of black academics were appointed as language assistants in the Department of Bantu Languages.[15] Gradually Sobukwe's integrity, dedication and deep concern for others drove him from the introspective life of a scholar into politics, where he combined these qualities with extraordinary powers of oratory. He proved to be a born leader.

The Pan-Africanists began to make their presence felt. It was especially their attitude to whites that gave rise to a great deal of discussion. Sobukwe himself was not a racist but many members of the organisation did feel intense animosity towards whites. And Sobukwe made his view of white liberals abundantly clear when, in an important speech in May 1959, he said that every time the ANC had started a campaign, the liberals had come creeping in. 'The PAC says there will be no compromise with anybody who is not an African,' he added.[16] This attitude was hurtful to those whites who were deeply committed to the black struggle. One of them, Patrick van Rensburg, secretary of the Liberal Party and later to play such an important role in Bessie's life, replied by saying: 'I will not stop fighting because Mr Sobukwe does not like the colour of my skin. The sooner people in this country stop thinking about skin colour the better.' Sobukwe did try to calm ruffled feelings by continually rejecting the concept of race and stressing instead the unifying idea of one human race. The PAC's unequivocal refusal to co-operate with non-Africans was modified by a clause in their official statement of policy maintaining that anyone who accepted Africa as his home was accepted as an African.[17] But many people found the PAC's attitude confusing.

Pan-Africanism attracted Bessie. Through Matthew Nkoana, a reporter on *Drum* with whom she became friendly, she was inspired to cast off her role of spectator. For the first time ever, she involved herself in politics.

But why Pan-Africanism? one may ask. What was Bessie doing in an organisation which was creating so much stir over the question of colour? Could she even feel that she was welcome there? The second question is easy to answer. The PAC, after some fierce arguments, had agreed to include coloureds in their definition of 'African'. They too were indigenous to the continent and suffered under white oppression. This policy statement was made at the end of May 1959,[18] shortly after Bessie arrived in Johannesburg. This may well have been what attracted her to the movement. Here was somewhere where she could be accepted as she was, on an equal footing with all other members, her racial affiliations examined, then forgotten in the struggle for greater human equality.

As with her foray into Hinduism, it was the discovery of the philosophy behind the Africanist concept that attracted her. The great African continent had long been involved in a process to re-establish its own identity. Various strains were making themselves felt. There was the influence of the black American intellectual William Du Bois, who believed that Africa was the spiritual and cultural centre for all blacks. His influence extended to the writers and poets of the 1920s Harlem Renaissance, for whom Africa became an almost obsessional, unifying image. There was the growth of the Négritude movement in the French-speaking colonies, a recognition of the African personality on its own terms and a return to cultural values that lay beneath the superimposed European norms. This concept of the 'African personality' was also the inspirational principle behind the political movement for African emancipation found in Pan-Africanism. Ideologically various in origin, these concepts nonetheless represented a fundamental unity of African thought that was inspiring some of Africa's leading statesmen of the late fifties. Thus Kwame Nkrumah, Prime Minister of Ghana since 1957 and about to become the first President of the Republic of Ghana in 1960, was greatly influenced by Du Bois's teaching.

Of even more immediate influence on South African Africanists were the writings of George Padmore. Born in Trinidad and educated in the United States of America, Padmore joined the Communist Party and began an important international career as a journalist connected with the Trade Union for Negro

Workers. When he became disillusioned with communism, he developed instead a Pan-Africanist philosophy published in 1956 as *Pan-Africanism or Communism: The Coming Struggle for Africa*. The next year he was appointed Ghana's African Affairs Adviser by Nkrumah and met and influenced many of the young and promising African statesmen. In 1959, the year Bessie began to show an interest in his works, he died in Ghana, his death creating added interest in his writings.

In an introduction written in 1972 to Padmore's second edition of *Africa and World Peace*, W M Warren says that 'the appeal of Pan-Africanism was its linking of socialism with nationalism, nationalism with international co-operation and imperialist exploitation with black chauvinism'.[19] Bessie, however, found his ideas revolutionary when she began to read Padmore in late 1959:

After reading George Padmore's book my whole manner of speaking and thinking and walking changed. It totally unsuited me for living in such a climate and environment as South Africa. It gave me a new skin and a new life that was totally unacceptable to conditions down there ... George Padmore is a prophet to me. Over and above that he was the initiator, the liberator of Africa; he was too a kind of John the Baptist crying in the wilderness – make ready the way ... What else does the liberation of Africa mean to me but this inner awakening and alertness – as though from some direction I may be given a hint, a clue and eagerly pass on this small grain of truth to some other seeker to question, examine and add his grain.[20]

Bessie was working on her writing as well. Early in 1960 Dennis Kiley was transferred from Durban to the *Post* head office in Johannesburg and he bumped into Bessie on the pavement outside their office one day. He could see at once that she had changed. She seemed much more determined and much less anxious. She told him she was writing a play. Indeed she dug into her bag and produced a manuscript, pushing it at him. Standing in the busy throng of pedestrians, he could only glance at it superficially. 'It's set in District Six, I can see,' he said to her. 'What sort of accent will the actors use – the District Six accent?' She was utterly scornful as she snatched back the play. 'Of course! Of course they will use that accent. It deals with those people.' She had a very clear idea of what she wanted and seemed confident that she would make a success of her writing. But that play never advanced beyond the draft stage. Perhaps she put some of her ideas into the short pieces she wrote a year or two later.

With her teenager column, Bessie continued to reach out to young people. Whether the theme was spaceships, pets or books and reading – 'Calling all Bookworms' was the name of that particular column – she almost always ended by asking for some response from her readers. And she received it. The letters poured in. In March 1960 she abandoned the advice column, addressing 'Hiya Teenagers' to the slightly older group of young people and writing on a specific subject. The article that first week proved to be of no little historic significance. She began by asking:

Remember those complaints I received that you teenagers don't appreciate anything and are generally as 'dumb as mules'? Well, it's always good news when someone says:

'Teenagers, they are just wonderful.' That is exactly what I heard a few days ago when talking to a jazz musician.[21]

This musician, a member of Kippie Moeketsi's band, the Jazz Epistles Verse 1, was Dollar Brand, then about to embark on an international career as a jazz pianist. In Cape Town and now in Johannesburg, the Jazz Epistles were arranging concerts for young people and Bessie gave them both praise and support in her article. The response from her young readers had been encouraging. 'If young people like jazz, which is really great music, then these young people are just great too,' said Dollar Brand. The same week Bessie had an informative article about the habits of ants for the 'Dear Gang' age group.

In December 1959 the PAC executive revealed its plan for a campaign against the pass laws. The oppressive system whereby Africans – women as well as men now – had instantly to produce their pass whenever they were accosted by a policeman, had perpetrated great suffering and distress. All anti-apartheid organisations had been protesting to no avail. The PAC now decided on a non-violent campaign whereby blacks would invite arrest in their thousands by not carrying passes. The new element was that PAC leaders would be at the front of the protest marches, thus becoming the first to be arrested. They and their supporters would flood the jails and embarrass the courts, for their motto was 'No bail, no defence, no fine'. The ANC was also planning a massive Anti-Pass Demonstration on 31 March 1960, linked with a national campaign for a minimum wage of one pound a day.

Sobukwe was more than aware of the pressure on him. If he was to have a chance to show what the new organisation stood for, their campaign would have to precede that of the ANC or be swamped. Every ounce of the executive's organising talent and energy went into planning a protest action for 21 March 1960.

It was during the weeks preceding this fateful date that Bessie finally joined the Pan Africanist Congress. She was fired with enthusiasm and embarked on a fundraising project for the party. It was in March, too, that Matthew Nkoana introduced her to Sobukwe.

They met at a political gathering and launched straight into a lively discussion. Sobukwe had just been reading about land reform in China.[22] He was considering the strange factors that could impede the progress of a revolution. In China Mao Tse-tung could not get peasants in certain areas to cultivate the land he had finally acquired for them because their ancestors were buried there. 'I've seen people do the same in the Eastern Cape where I come from,' said Sobukwe. 'There was hardly any land left to cultivate but people would rather die of starvation than plough on the land where their ancestors were buried.'[23]

Sobukwe wrote to her twelve years later: 'You were very intellectual and sceptical the day we met – quite suspicious, as many of our intellectuals were of the Africanism we propounded which, I admit, did have some racialist undertones then.'[24] Some of Bessie's apparent stand-offishness might have been plain shyness. Sobukwe made an indelible impression on her.

Though the campaign had not received the wide publicity it needed and attendance at some meetings was disappointing, Sobukwe decided not to delay it. On 21 March he and other PAC leaders walked from their homes to Orlando police station, the largest police station in Soweto. Just after eight in the morning, when a crowd of about 150 to 200 people had gathered, Robert Sobukwe, Potlako Leballo and other prominent PAC men went into the charge office and asked to be arrested because they were not carrying their passes. They were told that they would have to wait: the white officer in charge was busy. Thus it was that the little gathering sprawled outside in the sun. Women living nearby served them coffee. The leaders chatted to their followers. Bessie Head was also there, having arrived early. Whether she intended to be arrested or was simply offering moral support is not known. She was extremely nervous. She spoke to Sobukwe that day too, though apparently not very articulately. Years later she described her state of mind to him thus:

Then the next time I met you was the morning at Orlando police station where someone had tried to run away to Swaziland . . . and everything was turning upside down. Indeed, at that time I was not functioning so well, if I ever really do. I am extremely prone to having emotional storms and a very turbulent destiny. It hardly remains on [an] even keel. So the best I might have done at that time was stutter very badly so I think you might not remember me.[25]

She was there to witness Sobukwe's arrest when it finally occurred. The confused station captain had sent out a call for help. At about eleven o'clock, three security policemen arrived and went into the police station, to emerge shortly afterwards and read out a list of ten names. It was a list of the entire PAC leadership, with Sobukwe's name heading it. They all went inside and asked to be arrested for not carrying passes. They were told they were being arrested for incitement, a much more serious charge. The crowd outside was told to disperse, but they remained there, also requesting arrest. Finally they too were taken into custody. It all happened peaceably. By that time Bessie had gone home.

Non-violence was met with police non-violence in most places. The major exception was at Sharpeville. Here a larger crowd had gathered and demanded to be arrested. The police maintained later that their position was threatened but the evidence shows a now notorious lack of restraint on their part. With the murders at Cato Manor fresh in their minds, they fired repeatedly on the defenceless crowd, killing 68 and injuring 186. At Langa near Cape Town two people were killed in a similar police attack. A new chapter in South African history had begun.

There were shocked condemnations of the shootings from other anti-apartheid organisations; stay-at-home actions in many townships proved successful. The PAC achieved one limited victory when the government agreed to suspend pass arrests for a month in order to get a crowd of demonstrators in Cape Town to disperse. The government banned public meetings, and ordered massive arrests. At first Prime Minister Verwoerd thought that he had simply another internal crisis to contend with but during the next few weeks, as the truth about the Sharpeville massacre emerged, such concerted international condemnation of the police action flooded into the country that he realised he had a greater problem on his hands.

Undeterred, the government hastened to ban the ANC and the PAC. After a massive stay-at-home demonstration on 28 March, declared a Day of Mourning by Albert Luthuli, President General of the ANC, over a thousand were arrested in dawn raids. Some were released without trial but over five thousand were later convicted and sentenced.[26] On 30 March, a state of emergency was declared in almost half the country's magisterial districts. On 9 April National Party supporters had to sustain a new shock when an attempt was made to assassinate their leader, Hendrik Verwoerd. It turned out that a white man with no obvious political motive was responsible, and by this time the government, though clearly shaken by the impressive demonstration of black resistance, had once more gained the upper hand. It remained to punish the offenders and apply more advanced forms of repression.

Bessie's column dated 27 March was obviously inspired by the events of the preceding days. It was entitled 'It Takes Guts to be a Rebel' but was not overtly political. Instead she discussed the need for teenagers to rebel against their parents. She reported a psychologist as saying that the teenager who rebels against his parents is normal and the teenager who does not is tragic. And she agreed: 'To my mind a rebel is no tame weakling filled with self-pity, but a person with a lot of guts. Someone who is willing to fight and learns quickly the great value of being independent and standing on his own two feet.' She went on to describe a young friend of hers named Buddy who got the reputation of being a 'ducktail', local slang for a youth with longish hair, because he was so anxious to live independently. 'We don't have to be the extreme kind of rebel that Buddy is. We can learn independence and thoughtfulness by just being true to ourselves, and thereby finding that we can look at life truthfully also. We test everything before we accept it. We become explorers and adventurers in mind.'[27]

Sobukwe and the other PAC leaders were brought to trial in the Johannesburg Regional Court and Bessie sat in the packed 'non-European' section of the court, listening as all the accused refused to plead. Sobukwe in his usual courteous and serious manner explained:

We refuse to plead, because our contention is that the law under which we are charged is a law made exclusively by the white man, specifically for the oppression and suppression of the blacks, and the officers who administer the law are themselves white, and in this whole drama only the accused is black and we don't feel that justice can be done under the circumstances and we therefore refuse to plead.[28]

Either at the trial itself or on the two previous occasions when they had appeared briefly in court to be remanded in custody, she had had some contact with the accused men, handing over newspapers and exchanging a few words with them. On 4 May 1960 Sobukwe was sentenced to three years' imprisonment for inciting others to commit an offence as a protest against the pass laws. Other PAC leaders were given shorter sentences. Once more Sobukwe used the trial to propagate his belief that he and his friends were contributing to the ongoing struggle of the human race for the removal of mental, moral and spiritual oppression. 'If we are sent to jail there will always be others to take our place. We are not afraid to face the consequences of our action, and it is not our intention to plead for mercy.'29

Bessie was also scooped up in one of the many raids of this time. Years later she explained that because of the thousands of men who had been arrested during the pass campaigns, there were many women and children even more destitute than usual:

So an Asian man and I collected huge sums of money together and handed it over to the party headquarters. The few men there immediately took that money and went off on a huge womanising spree. When the police raided me they found a letter from the Asian man in my handbag expressing complete disillusion with the situation.30

Despite this negative attitude to the PAC, they were both charged with furthering the aims of a banned organisation. The case was finally dismissed but not before it had gone to the High Court.

It would appear, however, that Bessie had earned her freedom. She had turned state witness: 'I was a state witness in 1960 about a case in which a letter had been found in my possession',31 she wrote in 1967. Very little can be traced about this trial. It seems that the court records have been destroyed or dispersed, and none of Bessie's associates of the time have been able to throw any further light on the affair. There is, however, a reference in an article written just before she died which might have relevance: 'I have such a delicate nervous balance that when faced with danger or secret activity I tremble violently. The spies of the Boers would have long found me out and sent me the parcel bomb.'32 She here indirectly acknowledges an inability to withstand violent treatment. She made one other indirect reference to the incident – in a letter she wrote to Robert Sobukwe in 1972. She told him that 'a long winding story leads from the morning I last said goodbye to you at Orlando police station. Not very long after that I tried to commit suicide. It was caused by many things.'33 That she should refer to a suicide attempt so cryptically to Sobukwe may well have been her way of telling him that if she had betrayed his trust in her, she had also tried to expiate her action.

Another of the 'many things' which overwhelmed her now may well have been her first sexual encounter, a violent and unwelcome one forced upon her by someone she had admired but for whom she entertained an inexplicably violent dislike much later in her life. If this is true, and she told the story to a reliable source,34 then it casts much light on Bessie Emery's later attitude to sex.

It was at the end of April that Bessie seems to have been desperate enough to try to take her own life: 'I one morning swallowed 50 sleeping tablets and was forcefully brought back to life; by doctors. The process was so painful that nothing ever broke me again because there is nothing so awful as being pulled back to life with stomach pumps and drips,' she admitted to a friend eleven years later.35 Her name disappeared from the teenage column quite abruptly. On 1 May 1960, Sharon, the reporter from whom she had taken over the previous year, resumed editorship. She immediately re-introduced the advice column and never explained what had happened to Bessie.

Political & Emotional Involvement
1960–1964
The Cardinals

Once more Bessie had tried to relate her life to the South African context. She had wished to reach out beyond herself. Instead, perhaps because she over-reached, she had completely lost her balance. Her interest in Hinduism had been abandoned in hysterical outbursts and flight. Her first serious contact with politics had ended in humiliating capitulation to the oppressor; her resultant remorse had driven her to a suicide attempt.

Bessie was volatile by nature. Moments of great elation could be followed by periods of deep depression. This was the period of her life where the two opposing sides of her nature began to manifest themselves. She was both pragmatist and dreamer. From childhood she had been practical and helpful. Throughout her schooling she had done what was expected of her and responded to reason. But the mystical dreamer in her needed an outlet. In her philosophical quest and her political involvement she thought she could reconcile her two sides. Like many before her and since, she longed to translate her dreams for the betterment of mankind into sensible actions. And she believed she had found a method. The process of unleashing her imaginative powers, which was actually what was happening here, overwhelmed her to such a degree that there was no possibility of tempering the experience with reason. In each case she had been dashed and disillusioned to an alarming degree. She believed that she was through with religion; through with politics. Gradually, however, her resilient common sense showed her that she was wrong.

After a period in hospital, Bessie left Johannesburg and returned to Cape Town. Her job on the *Golden City Post* was waiting for her. She tried to work. For two months she tried. But she could not throw off the depression she had had in Johannesburg. She had to resign from her job. Very little is known of her movements during the next year.

The political scene gave no cause for optimism. All the leading Pan-Africanists were jailed. The organisation, now forced underground, was floundering. Leading ANC men had also gone underground or fled the country.

On 31 May 1961 South Africa was declared a Republic. The government thus broke the remaining bonds with Britain that the Nationalist government so hated. It also had to withdraw from the British Commonwealth, with its economic advantages, because of the animosity of other member states. Nelson Mandela, as leader of a new National Action Council, organised a general strike to coincide with the inauguration of the Republic, but did not gain the hoped-for support. Mandela, too, went underground shortly afterwards. He and other resistance leaders now took a historic step: they abandoned their principle of total non-violence. As the only possible counter to the government's increasingly harsh methods, they established a military wing of the ANC, uMkhonto weSizwe (Spear of the Nation). About the same time Poqo (We Go It Alone), with PAC connections and more overtly in favour of violence, was also established.

During this period of unemployment Bessie was befriended by a German woman, Cordelia Günther, who had lived through the 'trauma of the Hitler era'.[1] This was when she first gained some insight into the horrors of the Holocaust which would later become part of the nightmarish world of her third novel. Through the stories Cordelia Günther told, she began to realise how close to the Nazi persecution of the Jews the South African form of racialism was, containing the same elements of irrational and unprovoked attacks by the ruling class, the same demoralised, cringing response from the victims. At this time too, she also 'straightened out' her approach to men – 'always look at a man with a proper stare, never a come-hither stare'. Her German friend 'cast her eyes at anything in pants and suffered terrible frights on this account'.[2]

Bessie's routine with men, to judge from her own accounts, was never very successful. As well as a deep diffidence, a good measure of mission-school prudery and a wistful romanticism, her practical no-nonsense approach could well have concealed the hurtful nature of her first experience of sex which she rarely mentioned. She related best to men with whom she could engage in an intellectual discussion. When she told Margaret Cadmore in 1958 that she detested snobbery but was perhaps 'a mental snob' herself, she added: 'I flourish in the company of an intellectual but there are very few really intellectual people here. I was lately introduced to a French proffessor [sic] of theology; a brilliant man. We had a discussion for three hours and I felt happy for days.'[3] It is likely that she retained much of this attitude for many years.

As she gradually recovered from her breakdown, she began to look around for friends. And where else than in political circles? As she remarked in 1963, 'Every and any man, woman who ever thinks in this country gravitates to some political party. Outside this you may have friends but none that you could carry on a reasonable or intelligent conversation with'.[4] She soon became part of a 'large circle of political activists and writers'[5] to which Randolph Vigne, an active member of the Liberal Party and her friend and mentor at a later stage of her life, also belonged.

This may well have been her most active period as what she later described as 'B Head, great pan-Africanist on a soap-box'.[6] Randolph Vigne remembers her attending Liberal Party meetings, yet giving the impression of being very much on the periphery of their group. She would sit there glowering, her eyes flashing disparagement. People found her unnerving. 'I never joined fund-raising campaigns because I can't ask for money. I never paid at fund-raising parties because I was always broke and yet drank as much wine as I could and talked as loud as I could and quarrelled with the whites who were there.' Nor did she take kindly to any form of patronising from white liberals: 'The "liberal" whites seemed to like one to fight because they always provoked the arguments ... and always laughed at offensive remarks.'[7]

Because of her reputation as the only coloured woman journalist in Cape Town, she was a popular figure among the young men of District Six, who were keen on testing out their political ideas. She had taken up smoking and drinking by this stage and she would often sit on the edge of the pavement in the warm afternoon sun, the inevitable cigarette dangling elegantly from the tips of her fingers, discussing any number of political issues with her 'followers'. This is how another of her good friends remembers her. He was a fisherman himself, ten years older than Bessie. His name was Amin Mohammed, but most people called him Zoot. Though they did not agree altogether on politics – Bessie was still a warm supporter of the PAC – he found her fiery enthusiasm appealing and they became friends.

She had also embarked on an original form of journalism. She began writing her own paper, which she called *The Citizen*. It was nothing more than a double-sided cyclostyled sheet in which she took up local issues, questioning the justice of the laws and highlighting the absurdities of the apartheid system. It was strongly pro-Africanist. She would go to the Stakesby Lewis Hostel, which as an influx centre for people from many parts of the country was always busy, and try to sell her newspaper.

In about July 1961, a young man, newly arrived from Pretoria, and staying with an uncle, went to the Stakesby Lewis to meet a friend. There he suddenly found himself face to face with Bessie Emery, anxious to sell him a copy of *The Citizen*. Harold Head, for that was his name, was 24 years old, about six months older than Bessie, short and good-looking. He was immediately attracted to the verve with which this young woman addressed herself to her highly improbable task. She was slim and neat of build but what he noticed were her eyes. They were large and dark and the luminous milky film covering them made them at once expressive and unfathomable. Harold Head, charming and friendly by nature, had found himself a job as caretaker of the Bloemhof Community Centre, but like Bessie, he was interested in reading, journalism and politics. He was a member of the Liberal Party and already friendly with Randolph Vigne and was soon to launch out into the precarious existence of a freelance journalist.

For some weeks the two young people were often bumping into each other. Then one evening as Harold was locking up the community centre, Bessie arrived to see him. She accompanied him on his round and in the main activity room, with the windows closed and the lights extinguished, she suddenly took off all her clothes and confronted him, naked. Harold, surprised and moved by the beauty of her naked body bathed in the moonlight coming in through the windows, told her that she was beautiful and that she had better get dressed again. Later that evening they made love for the first time. This marked the beginning of an intense love affair. When they decided to get married some weeks later, they were horrified to discover that they would have to wait several weeks to get a marriage licence in Cape Town. Instead, on 1 September 1961, accompanied by Cordelia Günther and another friend, they took the train along the coast to

Simonstown, in False Bay. It was a picturesque ride and the little party of four were in high spirits, enjoying the views of fishing villages in the fresh sunlight of a spring day as they passed on their way. In Simonstown they were married.

For a time they lived at the Tafelberg Hotel, in Upper Constitution Street. Soon afterwards Harold was given a job helping with the production of the liberal fortnightly news magazine, *Contact*, edited by Patrick Duncan and, about the same time, they moved into a rooming house in William Street, in the heart of District Six. Families shared a kitchen and cooking facilities. The conditions were not good and the Heads were very poor. However, Bessie livened up the room with colourful magazine pictures on the walls and kept their few belongings spick and span. To her great delight, she soon discovered that she was pregnant, though this meant that another problem loomed ahead of them.

Caroline Head, Harold's sister, arrived to visit them early in 1962. Bessie and Harold met her at the station. Caroline took in Bessie's warm, intelligent eyes and short figure, now filling out, and liked her. As they were leaving the station, the road was blocked by a minor traffic collision. The implicated drivers were shouting at each other; by-standers were contributing to the general discord. Out of nowhere a young white policeman appeared. Suddenly Bessie's clear voice, with an accent that was the product of her Natal and especially English missionary background, rose above the hubbub. 'Isn't that just typical of the British! They always arrive.' The young policeman looked totally nonplussed and Caroline, to whom the remark was addressed, did not understand what she was getting at either. 'Yes,' she said with a stately little flourish, 'I mean they're always on the scene.' Caroline realised that she had acquired a highly individualistic sister-in-law.

Bessie had taken in a stray cat just before Caroline arrived. She showered attention on it and was obviously very attached to it. Their budget was so tight, though, that they could not afford to feed it. Bessie decided to have it put down and contacted the SPCA. When she had to part with it she wept copiously for most of the day.[8] From the days when she had cared for Nellie Heathcote's fowls and poured out her affection on Miss Thomsett's dog Penny, to the last 'man' in her life, her faithful dog Pa, Bessie had a deep and special relationship with animals.

Caroline found Bessie a difficult person to live with. Her changes of mood were sudden and often alarming. However, she and Harold seemed very fond of each other and he accepted her temperamental behaviour calmly. Bessie referred to Harold only once in her published writing. In one of her early pieces, describing their life in William Street, she said that whereas she was constantly fuming and exploding at the behaviour of her landlady, with her husband 'there was never a note of discord. He is naturally tactful and a skilful negotiator of human relationships. They adored him.'[9] There is much to suggest that the first year of her marriage, at least, was a sociable, active, even happy time for Bessie. Her husband certainly remembers it like this. They had not told each other important details from their past. Bessie had never mentioned the suicide attempt. Harold had never told about a spell he had spent in jail. All the more surprising that Bessie should have later implied that it was this fact that had made her fall in love with him: he had taken the rap for other members of his gang.[10] Years afterwards she was to sum up her marriage in very negative terms:

My husband, Harold Head, came along at a time when there was nobody else. I had begun to think that I would never marry or have children. I think he came at a time when I wanted those things. He appeared to like books – the life of the mind. So I agreed to marry him and have regretted it ever since.[11]

Both Bessie and Harold were trying to find an outlet for their articles. In January 1962 Randolph Vigne and some friends launched a new monthly journal, the *New African*. At a time when independent African states were emerging, it was intended, as the title suggests, to traverse political and cultural frontiers in Africa. It was Harold who broke into print here first. In the May 1962 issue, a highly satirical article called 'Three Views of South Africa's Pinko Question' appeared. One section of this article purported to be written by a 'Dr the Hon Paul Makatini, Minister of Pinko Administration and previously professor of Pinko Anthropology at the Nkrumah University in Lutuliville'.[12]

Harold was also responsible for the journal's circulation, which gave him a small income. He was a competent administrator.[13] Bessie recalled later how she helped with the typing of articles for the *New African* while she was expecting the baby. Howard was born on 15 May 1962. Bessie was reading *The Fountainhead* by Ayn Rand at the time and Howard was called after the protagonist, Howard, based on the famous American architect, Frank Lloyd Wright.[14]

Bessie's first contribution to the journal appeared in July 1962. It was to be the only poem she ever published, 'Things I Don't Like'. It expressed the raw pain of being oppressed, victimised and patronised because 'Hot sun and the geographical set-up / Made me Black.' She rejected them all – the 'Good, bad and sympathisers' – and vowed that 'Today is my day/ Going to get back, tit-for-tat / All you stole.'[15]

This was obviously a deeply painful period of her life. Someone who met her only once, in March 1962, just before Howard was born, wrote to her later: 'You made a strong impression on me because of your deep inner anger which I could do nothing about.'[16] The frustration and hate expressed in her poem was seldom again as evident in her writing, though the emotions did surface later in a short piece from 1963: 'Every white face that you see passing by churns you up until you could just cry to be delivered from this unceasing torment of hate, hate, hate. You wonder if that fat, smug complacent white matronly face was the one who wrote the letter in last night's paper ... "We have people in our midst who have just recently emerged from savagery ...." '[17] In the first novel she wrote outside South Africa, she gave her protagonist just such a burden of hate to take with him when he fled from that country.

The next piece to appear in the *New African*, in September 1962, was characterised by the conciliatory and generous view of life that she was later to be admired for. It is called 'Let Me Tell a Story Now ...', and has the rambling, colloquial style of many of her later pieces. Like them, too, it is very personal. The quaint twist she gives to the piece – describing the story that she says she wants to write but cannot – makes her concluding paragraph poignantly convincing. 'When I think of writing any single thing I panic and go dead inside. Perhaps it's because I have my ear too keenly attuned to the political lumberjacks who are busy making capital on human lives. Perhaps I'm just having nightmares. Whatever my manifold disorders are, I hope to get them sorted out pretty soon, because I've just got to tell a story.'

It is here we are given an insight into her hitherto unsuccessful writing career: 'I have two unpublished manuscripts. One got lost in the post. The other got lost among the rubble of a publisher's desk.' People probably did not believe her when she said this, though it was true. She made no effort to sound convincing, however, because she was not interested in letting people read what she had written. 'It was a hotch-potch of under-done ideas, and, monotonous in the extreme . . . If I had to write one day I would just like to say people is people and not damn white, damn black. Perhaps if I was a good enough writer I could still write damn White, damn Black and still make people live. Make them real. Make you love them, not because of the colour of their skin but because they are important as human beings.'[18]

She had been working on one of these early manuscripts during 1961 and 1962. Then called *Where the Wind Don't Blow*,[19] this probably is the one that surfaced about thirty years later. She had given it to a friend in return for his help; and it proved far less 'under-done' than she had considered it. Now called *The Cardinals*, this novella also fills in considerable autobiographical detail about Bessie Head's state of mind at the time. In the tortured figure of Mouse, the illegitimate half-caste waif, who has 'a beautiful soul that was nurtured on a dung heap'[20] but is so maimed by life that she cannot experience any form of emotion, Bessie is clearly presenting a view of herself. There are recurrent references to insanity and 'the looney bin' yet it is in the figure of Johnny, the outspoken, rebellious womaniser who falls inexplicably in love with the unimposing and inhibited Mouse, that we see most clearly the problem that Bessie was grappling with then: the lack of a father figure in her life. Johnny, probably the least romanticised of Bessie Head's male protagonists, turns out to be Mouse's father and the complexity of the relationship between the lovers is depicted with fine insight. In concluding at the point where they are to embark on an incestuous relationship – though neither is aware of this – the novella moves daringly, though somewhat ineptly, into an area of taboo. However, the most powerful message of *The Cardinals*, meaning those who herald change, is found in Mouse's struggle, first to attain literacy, then to master the art of writing. Creativity does appear to be released as a result of love, but Johnny's final warning remark 'that life is a treacherous quicksand with no guarantee of safety anywhere' seems to apply as much to art as to human relationships.

With her marriage, Bessie's identification with District Six became more complete. She had been somewhat itinerant until then: moving in; moving out; living in a hostel; living with a friend. The couple's straitened circumstances meant that they threw in their lot completely with the other inhabitants of William Street and the District.

No one has much of a private life in District Six. The neighbours make it their business to know all about you and they don't mind what your sins are. In fact, if it comes to the push they'll defend you even if the law considers you in the wrong ... We are the real good and jolly neighbours, minding each other's business the way neighbours should. We can't help it because we're all piled up on each other.[21]

Caroline Head recalls that she was surprised at the crowded living conditions in the Heads' tenement. Though the second of a family of seven (Harold was the eldest) and the daughter of a poor seamstress, she had never experienced that kind of slum living before. Writing two years later, Bessie remembered the 'crowded four-roomed house' into which they moved, and gratefully too, the housing situation being what it was. She also recalls the 'storm-filled atmosphere' with a landlord who was 'forever threatening us with bodily assault, ably abetted by our landlady who alternately suffered from fits of wild generosity and wild anger'.[22]

Richard Rive, another South African writer who grew up in District Six and whom Bessie and Harold Head knew, wrote about his childhood in realistic terms. He said that 'the slum was damp, dirty and dank. As children we ran around bare-footed in patched clothes, howling at drunks and shouting obscene encouragement at barechested street fighters.' His is a vivid picture of the area, describing the way the streets of District Six sloped down 'perilously' towards the harbour. William Street was somewhat higher up the mountain than Hanover Street, where the office of the *Golden City Post* was situated. 'Around us were squalid alleys, refuse-filled streets and mean lanes called by such fancy names as Seven Steps, Horstley Street and Rotten Row.' He recalls the various shops he had known: Velkes Wonder Shop; the Fish and Chip shop 'with saw-dust on the floor and the plate-glass windows steamed over with cooking oil'. He remembers 'Langman's musty Indian store smelling of butterpits and masala'.[23]

Bessie did not romanticise her life there either, but, like Rive, she captured the atmosphere. For example, it inspired her first description of a sunset, showing her budding resolve to observe and record accurately:

Always the still Autumn air controls the earth's scent with a nostalgic sweetness that is unlike any other season of the year. Sharp and distinct, these scents blend with the yellow-gold sky as it imperceptibly changes to a powdery mauve and then a vivid, splashy orange-red that pulsates and pulsates. Two children pass by, barefoot, absorbed, with comic red-painted sunset faces. Suddenly the sharp black silhouette of rooftops appears outlined against the glowing sky.[24]

Like Rive too, Bessie recognised the most important element of life in District Six: the sense of community. From this awareness arose the few words of praise she ever spared for South Africa. Her friends had warned her that Cape Town would weave a spell around her. If she went away, they said, she would always want to come back again. Their words proved true. She had returned to it, not knowing what drew her. 'Now I do know. I love the Cape because it can give me, a writer, a fierce individualist – a warmth, a love, a sense of something that is the opposite of isolation, a sense of belonging, if not to the country, at least to the human race. I have found all this among the Coloured community in the Cape,'[25] she wrote in 1963.

Bessie was a realist. She observed with distress the way in which many coloured people, who might be semi-literate or illiterate, had become 'trapped in a round of misery, poverty and week-end drunkenness'. The average coloured person was a 'timid God-fearing law abiding citizen of his own particular hell'.26 These comments are astute observations on the effects of poverty. They are also her defence of a people who were allowing themselves to be caught up in the latest apartheid restrictions without sufficient resistance. She even felt that they were being misled by some of their own leaders.

She was referring particularly to the transfer of coloured education to the Coloured Affairs Department. After Cape coloured voters were struck from the common roll in 1956, a Coloured Affairs Department was established in 1959. In 1962 there was talk of centralising coloured education and the Coloured Persons' Education Act was passed in 1963, establishing an Education Council which consisted of eight people appointed by the State President to supervise the educational programme of coloured children.

What concerned Bessie in 1963 was that 'with unashamed determination' the coloured people were 'handing over the education of their children to the Coloured Affairs Department'. She criticised 'the fat pompous principals' and others who were 'running over each other to lend an ear to the government and its good boys'. And she exonerated the ordinary people, asking: 'Have they been conditioned like dogs to accept whatever comes to them? Have they lived too long in abysmal poverty and hopelessness so that nothing matters anyway?' She argued that in order to break away from this vicious circle, the children desperately needed 'a truthful, normal education', not one that was going to 'grind them back into muck'.27

Later that year she wrote another article entitled 'The Gentle People. The Warm, Uncommitted "Coloureds" of the Cape'. Culture, she says, is not the preserve of white westerners in Africa.

Culture, in its truest sense, in its universal sense is the expression of the personality of a people. The Cape Coloured has this personality and he expresses it in little gestures and habits that are unique ... He adapts and grows and absorbs, adding to himself all the time. He welcomes strangers, is curious and interested in them and with a quick wit and jolly humour puts on a bit of their garments ... In a cold and loveless country like South Africa his warmth of heart and genuine friendliness is like a great roaring fire on the white icy wastes of the Antarctic.

But, as Bessie saw it, he had one definite weakness:

[H]e is that infuriating character – the uncommitted man. He has given his loyalty to no one ... The Coloured man knows ... his oppressor. He of all oppressed groups in South Africa fears his oppressor most because he is closer to him and really understands the ruthless nature of his power. So, he complies. He is obsequious, just so long as everybody leaves him in peace. Instead he would rather expend his hidden rage and frustration in drink and acts of violence on his own people or else try to outwit and make fun of you with his shrewd sense of humour.28

'Snowball', a fellow lodger in their rooming house about whom she was to write some years later, was one such person whom she found too passive and peace-loving. He allowed life to knock him around far too much. When Bessie expressed her sense of frustration over his inability to defend himself, she revealed her desire to protect him from all the unwarranted blows that rained down upon his scarred face. Her vignette captures the man's strange blend of simple goodness and non-categorical belief 'wherein science and spiritualism and all other contradictory ideas could live in chaotic happiness'.[29]

In all these pieces about her Capetonian acquaintances, Bessie showed how she understood and responded to their problems. In affectionate irritation over the Cape coloured's passive acceptance of his fate, she took on the role of champion, perhaps even mentor. However, it is interesting to note that the personal pronoun remained in the third person: 'he' never became 'we'. Bessie understood but could not identify. She remained the observer.

In about September 1962 the Heads moved to Port Elizabeth. Harold Head had been given a job on the progressive daily, *Evening Post*, the second black reporter ever to be employed there. After a while, they found a small house in the Korsten area. Harold embarked on the demanding job of a newspaper reporter, covering cultural and political events and often being met with rudeness and downright aggression for being there at all. His credentials and the reputation of the *Post* usually saved the situation. He often also covered the many tragic and violent incidents being treated at Livingstone hospital, very close to where they lived.

While in Port Elizabeth Bessie and Howard Head renewed their friendship with the poet Dennis Brutus, whom they had met in Cape Town and greatly admired. After being imprisoned in Johannesburg, he had been banned to Port Elizabeth, which meant that he was confined to his house and could not receive more than one visitor at a time. This last restriction tended to be disregarded. Brutus was deeply concerned about the predicament of black sports people and the fact that they had no possibility of participating in the Olympic Games, a sports event built around ideas of human equality. In 1958 he had established the South African Sports Association, which later became SANROC, the South African Non-Racial Olympic Committee, with Brutus as president.

In this capacity he corresponded with Ira Emery, the General Secretary of the South African Olympic Committee. Since his days as a star athlete, Emery's career as an administrator in the world of sport had blossomed. He had managed the South African team to the British Empire Games in Australia in 1938, and after the war, in his capacity as general secretary, headed the South African Olympic teams to the Games in London in 1948, Helsinki in 1952 and Melbourne in 1956.[30]

Dennis Brutus once approached Emery personally to discuss the position of black sportsmen. However, Emery could not see that Brutus had any reason to feel discriminated against: in his eyes there were no black sportsmen worth considering for the Olympics. The few who had won athletic events, for example, had been awarded watches, thus technically becoming professionals. In the idiom of the time, Ira Emery addressed Brutus as 'my boy'; and, as the law demanded,

Brutus accepted the designation passively. However, as he was leaving, his mission a total failure, he said quietly: 'One day soon we are going to get South Africa excluded from the Olympic Games'. Whether shocked or purely affronted, the tall, blustery man seemed to deflate before Brutus's eyes.[31] The prophecy was soon to be fulfilled.

In 1960, when the Sharpeville massacre had provoked global indignation, South African sport came under the spotlight and it was demanded that South Africa eliminate racial discrimination from its Olympic team, or withdraw from the next Games. Prime Minister Verwoerd refused to consider the ultimatum, with the result that from 1964 (until 1992) South Africa was excluded from the Olympic Games, a bitter blow for Emery, who had retired in 1961. He had dedicated many years of his life to a specific cause, and made a niche for himself in South African sports history, expending all his energy on furthering international understanding through sport, while nonetheless strengthening the bastions of racial discrimination.

Bessie and Harold, taking a close interest in all these negotiations, did register the fact that 'Emery' had also been her maiden name, little realising that Bessie was at that moment extremely close to uncovering the mystery of her identity.[32] Any investigation of Ira Emery's background would have revealed the name of his first wife: Bessie Amelia Emery. The key to Bessie's own life history, which her mother had insisted on stretching out to her in the form of the shared name, was there for the taking. But Bessie did not realise it.

At the beginning of 1963 Harold Head was offered the editorship of *Contact* and with it the chance for more serious journalism and a regular monthly salary. This was because, as yet another assault on the liberal opposition, Patrick Duncan had been banned and had decided to leave the country. Harold returned to Cape Town in about April, staying at the Tafelberg Hotel again, while Bessie and Howard remained in Port Elizabeth. They spent some weeks with Dennis Brutus and his wife while Harold once again tried to find somewhere for them to live.

Even if Bessie could have continued to return again and again to Cape Town – and her chances for doing that were fast running out – it would not have been to the Cape Town that she loved. Winds colder than the blustery south-easter for which the region is known were buffeting the coloured community. The Group Areas Act was making itself felt. Plans were already being made to declare District Six a white area and move the coloureds out to the desolate Cape Flats where prices were high, accommodation difficult to get and transport bad. By 1966 the first houses were being evacuated. The next year the Coon Carnival, a highly popular New Year procession of song and dance, was declared a 'traffic threat' and forbidden. Dollar Brand composed his 'Blues for District Six'. Finally the bulldozers came in and razed the remains of the country's most distinctive slum to the ground. Bessie, having left the country, would only hear of this later. Word may or may not have reached her of the strange unhealed scar on the slope of the mountain; the prime real estate area that was never rebuilt; the rubble-strewn acres that by some strange unspoken agreement remained to mark the site of District Six.

Life was hard enough without the troubles of the future to weigh her down. Bessie became more shrewish. Harold found more and more outside interests. According to her, fidelity had never been his strong point. The political situation was becoming increasingly threatening. The old sense of camaraderie in political circles was disappearing. With her growing sense of alienation from the country as a whole came a distancing from political activity.

In March 1961, the Treason Trial which had begun with the arrest of 156 people in December 1956 was finally concluded. The remaining 30 people involved were all acquitted: yet another example of government abuse of authority. The arrests and long-drawn-out trial had provided a check on anti-apartheid activities while the police, especially the Special Branch, improved its skills.

In August 1962 Nelson Mandela was arrested. The following July other leaders of uMkhonto weSizwe were surprised by the police at their headquarters at Rivonia in the Transvaal. They were sentenced to life imprisonment and uMkhonto's power was broken. Mandela was to spend the next 28 years in prison, mainly on the notorious Robben Island.

In November 1962 there was unrest in Paarl in the Cape. Though the original cause was an outbreak of violence by African migrant workers, suffering under harsh residential laws corruptly enforced, the riots developed into a show of power by Poqo, the underground movement loosely associated with the PAC. When Bessie heard that coloured women who had been living with African migrant workers had been murdered in a horrible fashion by members of Poqo, she began to feel disillusioned with the PAC as well.[33]

In 1963 Dennis Brutus was arrested. He escaped from prison, was recaptured and then re-imprisoned on Robben Island. In 1966 he left the country on an exit permit. During their time in Port Elizabeth and afterwards, Bessie had shown him some of her writing. In assessing her work, he had tried to combine honest criticism with encouragement, and this she appreciated. In an article entitled 'For a friend, "D.B."' which was printed in the East African journal *Transition*, in November 1963, Bessie bemoaned the fact that she was 'constantly losing friends these days'. She remarked that D.B. did not want to leave and would be very unhappy wherever he was then. For those left behind life was

lonelier and intensely isolated. South Africa is an intensely lonely, intensely sad country. It must have always been, but you only begin to notice the loneliness and sadness when all your friends are gone. Friendship is like the part of you that is not very brave; and, if you have friends you find yourself rising to extraordinary heights of strength. You get up to crazy schemes; you talk crazy and it is as though with your friends you will fix up all the wrongs in the world. Suddenly that happy, warm laughing world is shattered and you are left alone to face a horror too terrible to contemplate.

In these sentences there was a growing sense of desperation. When you lose your friends, she wrote, you lose your sense of humour and there is nothing 'quite as painful as not being able to laugh; sometimes'. You are overcome by 'an apathy and passiveness ... You cannot think. You cannot live ... Maybe I am going to pieces.' This was her second period of intense hatred of white people. 'You can't think straight about anything if you're hating all the time. You even get scared to write because everything has turned cock-eyed and sour.'[34]

Harold Head had finally found rooms for his family in a house in Hanover Street. Towards the end of the year they moved, again, to 31 Dixon Street, in the Muslim quarter below Lion's Head. Whereas Bessie had managed to get along with the neighbours most of the time in their other abodes, in Dixon Street she was constantly clashing with people. By November 1963, when the Dennis Brutus article was published, she was feeling that her whole life was a failure. She decided to take Howard and stay with her mother-in-law in the township of Atteridgeville, outside Pretoria.

An article published in the *New African* in February 1964 depicts her new environment. The township lay in a valley surrounded by rolling hills, so isolated that it was almost an island community. In the myriad of ' doll-like houses' lived families with the uniformity of attitudes and 'close fellowship' of such a community. Most children had their hair straightened with 'cold straight' only to discover that the chemicals also destroyed hair cells and caused bald patches. Young girls produced babies outside marriage because most young men were considered 'criminal' by their parents. Young men became 'criminal' because they chose unemployment rather than the trials and hazards of going to work. They became restless, frustrated and violent.

Everyone struggled with the transport problems. Atteridgeville's setting was disastrous for its inhabitants because the only work to be found was in Pretoria. Bus and train connections were miserably inadequate.

People in the township used to say that they were 'good at following funerals but not so good at following politicians'. That is why they did not give much support to 'a fierce political individualist' whom Bessie calls 'Boeta L'. Apparently he rushed up to the Secretary General of the United Nations, Dag Hammarskjöld, who was visiting South Africa at the time, and shouted 'Take back your Bible, White Man. This is an eye-blind. You tell us to go to church while you are in the battle-field.' Afterwards the people reproached him for his action: 'Boeta, you must not do such things. They will put you in jail. Besides, Dag Hammarskjöld did not invent the Bible.' Apparently the only political action the people ever performed was to get rid of the police security post at the entrance to the township by smashing it up so thoroughly that it was never re-established. 'Today the "Watchboys" office is a curious and deserted outpost that cannot help but give one a twitch of amusement as one passes by.'[35]

Again Bessie's picture of a section of the South African coloured community includes an implicit reproach. Their lack of commitment is especially clear in the title, 'The Isolation of Boeta L'. As this piece hardly rises above the purely descriptive, its interest is biographical rather than literary and it probably represents an attempt to break what was now becoming a chronic writer's block for her – and to earn some money.

Relationships with her mother-in-law were deteriorating rapidly. One day when Caroline came to visit the family on her day off from the hospital where she now had a job as a nursing sister, she found to her amazement that Bessie had moved in with the neighbour and that she and her mother-in-law were hardly communicating.

By February 1964 Bessie was desperately unhappy. Something prompted her to send out a cry for help to someone she had met fleetingly in Cape Town and liked, Patrick Cullinan. A poet, he also farmed and ran a sawmill in the Eastern Transvaal. In her letter she explained that she had been trying to get a teaching post somewhere in Africa, and in fact both she and Harold had often talked about leaving the country. Nigeria had been named. Now she was determined to leave, both because she was not happy in her marriage and because she hoped that in a free African country she would find new inspiration for her writing. She had even applied for a passport. On the day that she wrote the desperate letter to Patrick Cullinan, however, she had been told that the South African authorities would not grant her one, perhaps because of her brief membership of the PAC. Her one chance would be to try and get an exit permit, which would mean that she could never return to the country. But this could take six months to be granted and once again she could risk a refusal.

Patrick Cullinan and his wife Wendy wasted no time in responding to her letter. They drove to Pretoria and met her, on Bessie's insistence, at the Zoo. The appearance of two whites in the township of Atteridgeville would have attracted too much attention and Bessie feared that it would lead to harassment by the Special Branch. Patrick promised to help her.[36]

Meanwhile Bessie had seen that Bechuanaland, the huge semi-desert British Protectorate lying west of the Transvaal border, was advertising for teachers. She sent off an application and was offered a teaching post in a village called Serowe. 'Serowe? Where's that?' she asked as she searched for an atlas. Her knowledge of Bechuanaland was very limited. She found Serowe on the eastern side of the country, quite near a station on the only railway line through the country, and this was vaguely reassuring.

Patrick Cullinan provided swift and effective help. He contacted a civil rights lawyer he knew and within a few weeks Bessie had an exit permit. By early March she had accepted the post in Serowe. Once more she packed her belongings, including Howard's pushchair, and a few months before her little son turned two, they embarked on the most significant journey of Bessie's life.

Botswana
A Fresh Start 1964–1977

Bessie with Howard in Port Elizabeth, 1963 (courtesy Khama Memorial Museum)

5

Teaching in Serowe
1964

And so Bessie Head left South Africa behind her and turned her face resolutely towards Bechuanaland. Her knowledge of the country's geography was sketchy; its rich history was not to unfold to her for a long time. Only its political climate was familiar to her.

For the year was 1964 and the countdown had begun for the independence not many had believed Bechuanaland would ever achieve. The huge country of approximately 600 300 square kilometres, with its barren interior and poverty-stricken population of only 600 000 people, had very little to recommend it. It was hemmed in by Southern Rhodesia, Angola, South West Africa and South Africa, all under white minority rule. In many ways its position had predetermined its development. It had been a British Protectorate since 1885 but it was a burdensome possession. Had Cecil Rhodes had his way, it would have been incorporated into the territory controlled by the British South Africa Company, later Rhodesia. Though this attempt was thwarted, by the middle decades of the twentieth century there was again the pronounced feeling that the territory, like Basutoland and Swaziland, belonged geographically and historically to the Union of South Africa and should be added to it. There was an increasing hostility in South Africa to the presence of British influence on its borders, but the whites who lived there led the same privileged lives as those in South Africa. They controlled the country's main source of income, the production and sale of cattle to South Africa. They ran the trading stores with supplies imported mainly from South Africa. Bechuanaland was part of the South African customs and monetary union. Nevertheless, there apartheid was implied; in South Africa from 1948 onwards it was enforced by law.

As first Hendrik Verwoerd, then John Vorster, tried to introduce the idea of separate Bantustans or 'native homelands' for the black inhabitants of South Africa, the idea of annexing the High Commission Territories, as the three protectorates were called, became more and more appealing. This had been allowed for in the Act of Union of 1909. They could be added to the country as three huge new homelands and thus raise the proportion of land available to blacks from 13 to 47 per cent of South Africa's total area. The Tomlinson Commission had pointed out in 1955 that Africans expelled from white areas could be accommodated in this new territory. These plans alarmed Britain, and as South Africa's racial policies became more and more of an anathema to the outside world, Britain had to revise the idea of incorporation and think in terms of independence instead.

Prospects looked bleak for Bechuanaland as an independent state. The Kalahari Desert makes up much of the country, which meant that the population was sparse and scattered. Right up to the eve of independence, the administrative capital of the Protectorate was located in Mafeking, South Africa. The infrastructure had been sadly neglected, so there was no industrial development. There was a catastrophic lack of educational facilities.[1]

In Bechuanaland the power of the chiefs was well established. As the eight major Setswana-speaking tribes were ruled by their paramount chiefs, tribal culture to some degree co-existed with British control. It was the chiefs and the powerful families related to them who were the main cattle owners in the tribal areas.

In the 1950s the British finally decided to grant the country independence, and a series of preparatory steps had to be taken to introduce the idea of democracy to the people. In 1959 and 1960 the first political parties were established. In 1961 a Legislative Council, with separate voters' rolls and direct representation for whites, indirect for blacks, was set up. Two years later, Bechuanaland moved towards a form of self-government prior to complete independence. A Select Committee was established to eliminate racial discrimination in the country; the provision of better educational facilities was given high priority; the population was registered in a nationwide census.

It was when preparations for this census were in their final stages that Bessie arrived in Serowe, a village on the escarpment that sharply defines the Kalahari Desert's eastern edge. She had no way of envisaging its extreme remoteness. From Mafeking she and Howard took a train to Palapye, one of the stations on the railway line linking South Africa with Southern Rhodesia through Bechuanaland. This was a journey lasting over twelve hours. From Palapye there was little public transport to Serowe, some forty-eight kilometres to the west. Perhaps they walked some of the way or were given a lift on a truck. Around her stretched a flat, barren landscape every bit as forbidding as that she had passed through in the western Transvaal. And here there were even fewer signs of life along the way.

Then finally Serowe. Its sheer extent surprised her. It straggled on and on, about thirteen kilometres in circumference, she later discovered. To the west a broken escarpment provided the natural rim to the hollow pan in which the village had grown up. It was, and is, one of the largest African villages south of the Sahara, with a population of about 30 000 people in 1964. Calling it a 'village' is in many ways misleading; merely an indication that it is neither town nor city.

Who can be prepared for the intricate complexity of such a place? There is a comforting smell of smoke from the many outdoor fires, lying over it like a collective blanket. Yet it consists of an almost endless number of family units: five or six mud-walled grass-thatched huts clustered behind a picket of cut thornbushes or a large, strangely green succulent hedge often referred to as the rubber hedge. These compounds, headed by a senior male member of the family, are linked by a network of stony paths, a group of related family compounds constituting a ward. Flocks of hens with scraggy chicks, each bossed by an ostentatious rooster, are busy on their endless search for food; and yellow-eyed goats are everywhere, scavenging paper and rubbish and turning it into flesh and milk. The only thing they avoid is the rubber hedge. This hardy transplant to the village, named *tlhare-setala*, meaning the 'green tree', has proved very adaptable, surviving because its waxy leaves prevent almost all evaporation and its bitter sap makes it unattractive even to goats.

Most people, Bessie was soon to find out, had more than one home. In the summer they could move out to their fields outside the village to cultivate maize and sorghum. The men and boys might spend months living out on their cattle-posts, even further away, tending their cattle. Meat export was at the time one of the country's important sources of income and the transition from the traditional Tswana way of life, with a subsistence economy, to an economy based on cash sales was a topic of constant discussion in the early sixties. In a good season, with rain and plentiful grazing, cattle meant money for the family. However, there were not many good seasons. In fact when Bessie arrived, the country was in the grip of a drought that grew worse each year and was to stretch over a ten-year period. Sometimes the only rain they would get would fall during one week in November, sometimes on one day.

The natural centre of Serowe, near one of the largest and most beautiful trees in the village, was the open space in front of the former residence of the chief, still used when the elders of the tribe met for council meetings and referred to as the *kgotla*. Now the Bamangwato Tribal Administration buildings and the offices of the Central District Council were established near at hand. For Serowe was and still is Khama country. It was here that the Bamangwato, by far the largest social and political group of the Tswana nation, had settled about sixty years before under the leadership of their important paramount chief, Khama III. Rising up behind the *kgotla* is a large, steep outcrop of rock, called Serowe Hill. Here the royal burial ground, the Khama Memorial, is to be found. A fenced-off sanctuary among the rust-red rocks harbours the graves of Khama III and his successors. Khama III's grave is marked with a bronze *phuti*, the small antelope which is the emblem of the Bamangwato. From this elevated stand the royal tombs survey the sweep of the plain below with its endless cluster of huts.

There were also signs of western civilisation in the village: the British flag flying over the District Commissioner's office; the ramshackle post office; the trading stores; a welfare centre; a health centre; school buildings; a library. A local landmark was the London Missionary Church, built of brown sandstone. Until 1956 it was almost regarded as the state church in Khama country. Khama, himself deeply religious, had given this society the monopoly that prevented other denominations or sects from establishing themselves in his territory. When the decision was finally reversed, others were welcomed provided they built schools and hospitals. Amongst others, Anglicans, Roman Catholics and Congregationalists had since established themselves. There were also a great number of pentecostal churches, established by the local inhabitants for their own people and allowing 'ancient African customs to be observed side by side with Christianity'.[2]

Accommodation was not easy to find in the village. When Bessie appeared at the Tribal Administration office, as all newcomers to the village were expected to do, she was shown to the teachers' hostel. It was a building that had originally been the local library, so it was long and narrow and devoid of furniture, but it gave Bessie and Howard a roof over their heads. Later they moved into a pleasant rondavel next door to another teacher from the school, Mma-Jennings by name. This was in one of the oldest wards of the village, the Sebina ward.

She was soon forced to fathom something of the complicated political background of the place. Serowe was also the unofficial headquarters of the newly established Botswana Democratic Party. Tribal and family loyalties were very important and explained the villagers' special regard for the party's young leading politician. His name was Seretse Khama.

Seretse Khama was of royal birth, the heir to the chieftainship of the Bamangwato. A single event had prevented him from taking over his hereditary position. He had married a white Englishwoman.

The young man had an impressive background. He was the grandson of Khama III. He had hardly known his father, Sekgoma II, who had died in 1925, when he was four years old. His uncle, Tshekedi Khama, himself only twenty, was called home from his studies at Lovedale in South Africa and appointed regent.

Tshekedi Khama was a remarkable man. During his regency, true enough, he made some enemies, people who regarded him as truculent and stubborn, but he also had many friends. They appreciated his courage and magnanimity. But conflicts with the British were unavoidable. The best-known incident occurred in 1933. The Resident Commissioner, always at loggerheads with Tshekedi Khama, saw his chance to get rid of him when he heard that he had had a white man flogged. The man had chosen to live under tribal law and the *kgotla* had meted out the punishment, but a force of 200 marines from the Royal Navy base at Simonstown near Cape Town was summoned to remove Tshekedi Khama from the chieftainship for exceeding the limits of his authority. The farcical nature of this incident amused the British press: 'Join the Navy and see the Kalahari' as one cartoon put it.[3] Tshekedi gained much sympathy in Britain. The next year, as part of the ongoing conflict, which had now developed into a threat to incorporate the whole of Bechuanaland into South Africa, he published statements in England alerting people there to the fact that the racial inequalities existing in South Africa would then also become law in Bechuanaland. This was probably a major factor in preventing all three High Commission Territories from being handed over to South Africa at this time.

These were the events which shaped the young Seretse Khama's childhood. While he was growing up, he had before him the example of a courageous and dedicated man; someone he admired deeply and regarded as a father. All the more tragic was the schism that developed between them.

Having spent so many years protecting his people and his tribe's land from encroaching white men, Tshekedi Khama realised more than most people how important it was for his ward to have a good education. Seretse Khama was sent to England. After a year at Balliol College, Oxford, in 1945, he transferred to the Inner Temple in London to study law. While there he met, fell in love with, and married Ruth Williams. It was a courageous act that produced more opposition than even the young couple could have foreseen.

They had considered the personal opposition. Tshekedi Khama and the elders of the tribe were shocked. The choice of a wife for the future chief was a choice that had to be approved, if not made, by the tribe itself. Tshekedi Khama used every means within his power to stop the marriage, as did Ruth Williams's parents.

The opposition from official quarters was less expected. The dramatic division of the tribe into two factions meant that the British government intervened for reasons of 'internal security'. Both men went into banishment, Tshekedi Khama voluntarily rather than meet Seretse Khama's wife and Seretse Khama unwillingly, tricked by the British authorities, who invited him to England for talks and then refused to let him return to Serowe. Popular opinion both in Serowe and England had by this time swung round in favour of Seretse Khama. But to no avail. The British (Labour) government remained adamantly opposed to him. There is apparently only one explanation for this unbending attitude. The South African Prime Minister, D F Malan, demanded it in return for the uranium Britain so desperately wanted from them.[4]

Uncle and nephew eventually became reconciled and Tshekedi Khama worked tirelessly to get both his own and Seretse Khama's ban lifted. Tshekedi Khama himself was permitted to return to Bamangwato territory in 1952, settling not in Serowe but in Pilikwe. But it was not until 1956 that Seretse Khama was finally allowed to return to Bechuanaland as a private citizen. He had to renounce his and his heirs' rights to the chieftainship. This he did because his years in England, observing the wind of change blowing over Africa, had convinced him that the future of his country lay not with the decisions of the chiefs but with western democratic procedures. Seretse Khama's training for statesmanship had been hard but, as it proved, effective.

Shortly after his return, the first political parties appeared in the Protectorate. Though the powerful chiefs resisted them as a threat to their own authority, the clock could not be turned back. In 1960 the Bechuanaland People's Party, advocating 'one man, one vote' was formed, with clear links to both the ANC and PAC. Two years later Seretse Khama established the Bechuanaland Democratic Party. Its stated aim was to consider the needs and problems particular to the people of Bechuanaland in a spirit of moderation and compromise, rather than copy the structure of parties from other regions of Africa. That he was of royal blood himself, and thus combined democratic principles with the traditional pattern of chieftainship, was a distinct advantage for the party.

When Bessie arrived there in early 1964, Serowe was astir with an awakening political consciousness. That a man of international repute lived in and moved about the remote African village, loved and respected by the local people, was not something she had expected. Everywhere there were signs of intense political activity. Every Motswana was suddenly being drawn into the remarkable changes that were sweeping over the country. The men understood the significance of contributing an opinion and reaching a common decision. This was the practice from earlier times: the chief would call them to a *kgotla*, or council meeting, and together they would solve whatever problem had arisen. But voters' rolls? And for women too? Not that everyone was enthusiastic, as Bessie reported in a short story: '"Miracles are happening these days", they [the old people] say, unhappily.'[5] Many of her short pieces from the period refer in passing to political gatherings and the issues of the campaign. The political turmoil of the period, however, is always subservient to the personal turmoil of her adjustment to village life. This involved adapting to her job as a teacher; getting used to the living conditions and climate of Serowe; and finding some way of relating to its inhabitants – foreigners as well as the villagers themselves.

Bessie's teaching contract was with the Tshekedi Memorial School. The advertisement to which she had responded had been part of the concerted drive on the part of the government to recruit teachers from elsewhere to improve the educational standards and combat the teacher shortage in the Protectorate. The Select Committee appointed to scrutinise the country's laws for racial discrimination had found education particularly infested. From early 1964 countermeasures were taken. Schools which had previously been only for the white traders' children had to be opened up to children of all races. Though feelings about this never ran high in Serowe, in the western part of the country there was an organised protest when the white community of Afrikaner farmers had to relinquish their monopoly to an air-conditioned school with swimming pool; a protest that was to no avail.

Education had always been valued in Serowe. Originally the London Missionary Society had provided schooling for the children of the more wealthy members of the community. During Khama III's reign, promising students were sent to South Africa to complete their education. Tshekedi Khama's aim was to make elementary schooling available to all the children, as well as providing some secondary and technical education. Work regiments, each consisting of men of about the same age, were allotted specific tasks by the regent. Building schools was one of them. So by 1966 the village was equipped with about nine or ten schools, as well as the impressive Moeng College. This was partly a technical school, providing secondary education as well as training in agriculture and domestic science for both sexes. It had been built and financed entirely by the Bamangwato under Tshekedi Khama's instigation and completed just before the clash with Seretse Khama occurred.

As schools went, the Tshekedi Memorial School was one of the better ones, bearing witness again to Tshekedi Khama's foresight and ambitions for his people. The buildings were reasonable but the equipment was poor. Bessie was to find that whether she had to teach her class about the structure of the human skin or the tropical rainforests of Africa, she would have to rely on her own knowledge to do so, reference books being a luxury the school simply could not afford.

Bessie knew that she had a daunting task ahead of her. Not only had she been away from the classroom for six years, but when she had last faced a roomful of children, a confident girl of only eighteen, the class had been somewhat more homogeneous than the present one. And somewhat better fed. Coloured children in segregated Durban, poor as they were, did not lack the bare essentials to the degree this class did. The hard years of drought in the area showed. She saw before her many thin, even gaunt, children. Many came to school without breakfast and by midday their mouths were white and pinched with starvation. Furthermore, while the girls were of the normal first-grade age of about six or seven years old, the boys, who had been helping their fathers at cattle posts outside the village for some years before they could be spared to go to school, were often about eleven years old. However, their desire to learn something, anything, was intense.

Though she sympathised with her pupils and hoped to brighten up the bleakness of their learning with imaginative touches, she was not a very successful teacher. Bernard Letsididi, who taught with her at the time, described her as a 'born journalist' rather than a teacher, and emphasised the fact that she had come to the school from journalism not teaching. He called her 'excitable' by nature.[6] Her teaching was later to prove the area that caused her most distress in her relationship with the local population.

For the time being, it was the climate that had to be confronted. When she arrived it was winter, which meant it became dark suddenly, almost dramatically, at half past five.The darkness frightened her. She used to keep a candle burning beside her bed until the moment she felt herself falling asleep.Then she began to discover the beauty and intensity of the stars and to describe the night with 'stars hanging large, low and glowing in a deathly silence'.[7] Summer came. It was fiercely hot. The desert landscape awoke ambivalent feelings in her. It was stark and bare and, she thought, ugly. Yet its very barrenness forced her to observe things in a new way. She saw how man and nature complemented one another, the pattern of the 'hard, dry, dark and leafless trees'[8] being repeated in the gnarled brown bodies of the old people.

Rainclouds gathered in the sky, mercifully tempering the blaze of the sun. But no rain fell. The clouds were gradually blown off again. However, that year they were lucky. Some rain did fall. In November, the extreme heat finally gave way to wild and unpredictable storms. The dry earth was suddenly covered by a fine carpet of grass. Wild flowers appeared. So did insects in abundance. 'Egypt's land, I call it. I've been invaded by swarms of flies, then swarms of scorpions and when I had killed them all there were swarms of moths the size of birds'[9] was Bessie's comment.

When the thunderstorms burst over the village, the intricate patterns with which the women had decorated their huts were washed away. Their mud porches crumbled. Their beautifully moulded mud stoves and ovens collapsed. With patience and skill the women went straight to work repairing the damage. They secured the foundations, then they mixed mud, manure and river sand in equal parts, and pounded and kneaded it before working it onto this base, continually smoothing and pressing to shape and strengthen it. Bessie watched in secret admiration as they rebuilt their mud kitchens and patiently redecorated their mud walls. She was poor too. She also lived in a hut. Gradually she felt that she too was becoming part of this mud life.[10]

'I have lived all my life in shattered little bits. Somehow, here, the shattered little bits began to come together,' she said, about a year after her arrival in Bechuanaland. 'There is a sense of wovenness; of wholeness in life here. There were things I loved that began to grow on me like patches of cloth . . . '[11] The image of the country's providing her with a new outer covering seems to have remained with her. Some years later she wrote: 'What have I said about the people of a free land, I who borrowed their clothes, their goats, their sunrises and sunsets for my books?' Although it was published both as 'Dreamer and Storyteller' and 'An African Story', her original title for this short piece was 'Borrowed Clothes'.[12]

In actual fact Serowe was not nearly as isolated from the outside world as she had supposed. Apart from its being a centre of local politics, it was also a meeting place for the steadily increasing stream of South African political refugees. There was an unofficial ANC representative, Stephen Sello, in the village and he and others, themselves former refugees, received people who had been smuggled out of South Africa on account of their political activity and organised a refugee route to get them to Dar es Salaam, if they were not successful in settling them into the community. They were largely dependent on local hospitality and the goodwill of the tribal authorities.

One such refugee using the escape route proved to be an unexpected visitor for Bessie: her husband Harold Head. He had fled most dramatically from South Africa. In August 1964, six months after Bessie had left the country, Harold Head was banned. This meant that his movements were restricted, his contact with other people limited and he had to report at the police station once a week. He did so only three times. Directly after his third appearance there, tired of being a 'still-life victim ... always conditioned', he decided to revolt. He started on the long train journey from Cape Town to Mafeking, heading for the Bechuanaland border with just one week at his disposal to cross over. He arrived at Pukwane, near the border, where he knew people who would help him across, but he was suddenly forced to rush out of the hut where he was hiding, without his coat in the freezing winter cold, and fling himself into the goat pen amongst the goats, because a police patrol car swept into the village. Finally he crossed over into safety, later remembering with gratitude and some romantic nostalgia the kindness shown him in Pukwane.[13]

This account stirred Bessie's imagination and though Harold was made only moderately welcome, she was later to use the story of his flight to good effect. Harold was to move on from Serowe to East Africa and then to the United States. He would finally settle in Canada where he acquired the passport he had so sadly lacked in South Africa. While Bessie regarded their marriage as over, he tended to think that they might be reunited as a family again and did invite his wife and son to join him in North America in 1966.

There was also another South African in Serowe. Two years before Bessie arrived, Patrick van Rensburg, a former South African diplomat, and his wife had started the project that soon was to affect the whole village. Patrick van Rensburg had been active in the Transvaal branch of the Liberal Party and was particularly hated in government circles in South Africa because he was considered a traitor to the cause, having left the South African diplomatic service in order to combat apartheid. After going into voluntary exile from South Africa and spending some time in London, he settled in Bechuanaland, determined to help improve educational facilities in the country. There was a crying need for secondary schools: at that time there were only five, all newly established, all small. He asked to be allowed to start a secondary school wherever it was most needed. The Bamangwato Tribal Administration granted him a plot of land eight kilometres outside Serowe.

Young people longed to further their education. The school could be established only if the students helped with the building. To do this they needed to learn how to build. From such a practical point of departure, the 'philosophy' behind the Swaneng project was born. Patrick van Rensburg wished to inculcate commitment to development in his students and give them the necessary knowledge and skills to be of use to others. To concentrate on traditional secondary education would benefit only the top few students. This he did not want. He wished to establish a model of secondary education that would be 'accessible to everyone', enabling 'everyone to be productive'.[14] He wanted his students to go out and fight the country's 'hunger, poverty and ignorance',[15] so he introduced a new subject, development studies, into the curriculum. It was a course intended to teach the students the aim and purpose of economic development and the way economic growth brings social change. He encouraged them to use their new knowledge by becoming involved in village affairs. This applied particularly to the organising of a consumers' cooperative which Patrick van Rensburg established about the time of Bessie's arrival; and a marketing cooperative, to enable the villagers to control the sale of their cattle, which came into existence shortly afterwards.[16]

Overseas volunteers with teaching and training skills, who shared his visions, were already arriving to help him. The first expansions in Patrick van Rensburg's programme had already taken place. He saw that there was a large group of youngsters who could never qualify for secondary education. They needed vocational training and basic schooling. He established a two-year training course which was to be self-supporting so that everyone could afford it. He named his new scheme the Brigades and established the Builders' Brigade first. With this scheme in its infancy and demanding all Patrick van Rensburg's energy, he spent little time in the village and did not get to know Bessie when she first arrived.

During these early months in Serowe, Bessie was fortunate to find a friend who could stretch her intellect greatly. Jane Kerina, a black American, was based there, working with her husband, Mburumba Kerina, on a project to help refugees from South West Africa. He had been one of the first petitioners to address the United Nations Security Council on the question of the South West African mandate. As Bessie portrays her, Jane Kerina was a woman of unsettling individuality, much more politically enlightened than Bessie. According to the apparently autobiographical account of the friendship given by Bessie Head in two different pieces from this period, the two women had fiery political discussions. 'You're full of contrived confusion! You're an escapist! You're an exhibitionist!' were some of Jane Kerina's accusatory epithets. Bessie would answer: 'I couldn't possibly be an exhibitionist. I am lonely and loneliness does not boost the ego.'[17] The American would be totally unimpressed and pound on, intent on giving Bessie the rudiments of a political education. She also tried to get her to read books to 'dispel a bit of that fog in thy cranium'.[18]

The educating process would have been easier had Bessie totally lacked ideas of her own. But this was not the case. She still believed in Pan-Africanism and her admiration for George Padmore's writing was still intact. She saw him as some John the Baptist, crying in the wilderness to prepare the way. To her the liberation of Africa meant an intellectual and spiritual revival, an 'inner awakening and alertness'.[19] In her friend's view she needed to be more politically committed to the struggle for Africa. However, Bessie did feel herself an African in Africa, and felt deeply hurt when it was implied that she was not.

In a very early article from Bechuanaland, Bessie gave two reasons for this lack of involvement. Just as there are some people who are temperamentally unsuited to become stockbrokers, she said, because they are 'unable to sustain the shock of the rise and fall of the stock market', so there are others, herself included, who felt a nightmarish terror when admitted to political circles. According to this version, she lacked courage.[20]

In fact the explanation was more complex. She was beginning to recognise the fact that her isolation was partly the result of her own choice. She would have liked to please her American friend by accepting her faith. She had also disappointed other people because of her lack of political commitment. But she had to be 'free mentally to take off in any direction' she chose. 'To choose freedom is also to choose loneliness,'[21] she said. Nevertheless, she chose freedom. It was to be a choice that would flavour all her writings.

She was soon to validate her choice in a remarkable way. In a flush of inspiration and amusement, she sat down and wrote another short piece about Jane Kerina. She had already described her political involvement. Now she captured her friend's disregard for authority, her spontaneity and physical vitality. She shrewdly depicted village attitudes – subdued and mean – and against this background, the American woman's exuberance. 'From her I learnt this lovely swear word – goddam!!'[22] said Bessie. She showed how she was also busy 'as women the world over about things women always entangle themselves in – a man, children, a home'. Bessie recognised her as a 'new kind of American or even maybe . . . a new kind of African'.[23] She called her piece 'The Woman from America'.

Bessie was eager to become part of village life. Perhaps here at last was a place where she could settle and build up a life for herself and Howard based on freedom and a respect for human rights. What brought disasters showering down on her head was her disregard for human frailty. She was naive enough to believe that because she was making an effort to integrate herself into village life, the villagers wanted her to become integrated, with herself dictating the terms.

Bessie was now twenty-six years old, quite slim and calmly attractive. She had an open face with large gentle eyes and a generous mouth reflecting little of the hardship she had already experienced. During her first months in Serowe she was probably subdued and desperately lonely. Then she began to open up. She began to respond to a society that seemed to function well, allowing personal dignity to its members. Gradually, however, the inbuilt disadvantages of village life also began to appear.

Bessie had been plunged into a world where everyone's behaviour was a source of common concern. Here was someone who pushed her child round in a pushchair when every other mother bound her child to her back. Here was someone whose pleasant appearance and whose elusive quality, half dignity, half reserve, attracted an attention she had never expected and did not altogether enjoy. As was her way, though, she responded eagerly and with much enthusiasm to any chance she had to engage in a good discussion.

Agreeably surprised to find people who were well educated and articulate amongst those with whom she now came into contact, she would tend to launch into one of her enthusiastic conversational advances, eager to explore with someone else her own complicated thought processes. That the educated and articulate were as usual mainly men gave the contact an extra flavour. Men found her interesting and different, free and friendly.

Reflecting a few years later on her own conception and her own mother's fate, she wrote to her friend from Cape Town days, Randolph Vigne:

She must have been as mad and impulsive as I. She must have loved going at a man and grabbing him around the neck and found white men too stiff for that game. You can only do that to a black man. He just loves it when you go at him and grab him around the neck. I am just like her. I like to do things to men and say all kinds of horrible things and be very provocative.[24]

Not surprisingly, such behaviour would have caused confusion. Signals would be misinterpreted. For in Bessie's breast there still beat a heart that believed in true and lasting love and eternal fidelity. Men wishing to settle for less, encouraged by provocative rufflings, would meet an unexpected opposition. And this brought on trouble. She antagonised some of the influential men in the village. Worse than that, she antagonised their wives.

In Bamangwato society there has been a long tradition of treating visitors with courtesy and hospitality. Several tribal subgroups, who had moved down from the north some generations earlier because they had received protection from Khama III and a place in Serowe, were shown tolerance and acceptance, probably because their assimilation had been a long, gradual process and they conformed to Bamangwato behaviour patterns. However, elements of the old closed hierarchical system still remained. The remnants of the San people, found mainly on the agricultural lands and at the cattle-posts, were an isolated group working as serfs or labourers. And a small community of coloured people near Serowe, though they spoke Setswana as their mother tongue, never became part of the Bamangwato.

In her enthusiasm to establish herself and become accepted, Bessie was insensitive to the norms of village life. It gave rise to a tremendous backlash later. What is more, she complicated the whole process by falling in love. Most often these events, which coloured her life – and especially her writing – in the years to come, are referred to obliquely. However, a short article from this period, almost certainly autobiographical although she calls it a 'long wrangling diatribe about an imaginary love affair'[25] and only published seven years after her death, reveals the intensity of her feelings and her confusion. There are references to the proud, reserved nature of the man she loves. There are references to being overwhelmed, engulfed, swept along. There are references to the 'chasm of terror' separating them, even after 'months of careful approach'. But when the chasm is finally crossed, the darkness becomes a 'living, moving force of deep earth-harmony' and she knows herself to be a meaningful part of life 'so that the rain-wind and the sun-wind of Africa beat about my face, arms, legs and the earth-pull is strong in my body which is vividly, intensely alive'. The poignant conclusion is very powerful, in which she recognises that for her this man is 'the beginning point and a centre around which revolves a vast gulf of peace and tenderness', and that she 'cannot let go of him' though she has had to bind herself to promises of secrecy and acknowledgement of the temporary nature of the affair to get him at all.[26]

Several of Bessie Head's other early writings, probably also largely autobiographical, refer to an aloof young politician who was a gifted orator. 'He was an artist, using words and plain statistics to project his own inner turmoil making earth and heaven, destiny and independence, vivid and real and alive because they are all bound up in the life of man ... Such a man, with evil intentions, could cause wreckage and disaster.'[27] In another working of the same incident, Bessie considers it fortunate for the British and the chiefs that they had him on their side. Had he been on the side of the Pan-Africanists or the communists, 'he would have swayed the vote their way ... He could be dramatic, tragic, emotional ... endearingly charming ... just doing as he pleased with vigorous masculine abandon.'[28]

She was clearly attracted to the man, but also terrified of him. He is sometimes described as an outsider, like herself, the henchman of the important politicians. This could account for the traces of pain, sorrow, and rage etched in the harsh lines of his face. His fierce expression and the way he stared right through her unnerved her. She felt herself caught up in something she could not fathom, once even experiencing a form of telepathic communication with him. She was one day possessed of an inexplicable restlessness. She paced about her rondavel muttering, 'Don't worry! It does not matter!' for no apparent reason. Later she heard from a friend that at that moment some of the young man's political opponents had been making such a slanderous attack on him at a political meeting that he had had to leave 'amid much ribald laughter'.[29]

References to being in danger of engulfment and thus obliteration are again present in these descriptions. She compares her state to that of a mouse sitting on the wall of a newly built dam wall, swept into 'a terrible unfathomable mystery' when the water floods in. She felt a power outside herself 'controlling and yet uncontrolled by me. That is why I prefer to believe I am insane.'[30]

The mysterious lover, or lovers, are never named. She sometimes hints that she has inadvertently become involved with important people in the village: '[O]ne of the V.I.P.s of the "royal" family got big eyes for me too. Not much to the liking of his female. There was talk of doing me in last year, she said so, so he cooled off making eyes at me.'[31] And she sometimes suggests that she is not to blame: 'One of the most painful moments of my life came when a Batswana woman said to me, with actual hatred: "What do you want running after the Batswanas?" No one acknowledged the fact that the man looked at me first. I would never have noticed him.'[32]

There is no doubt, however, that much of the material for *Maru* can be traced back to Bessie Head's experiences during these early months in the village. She could have had a sporadic affair with one person while cherishing the brief and beautiful memory of the other, her 'true' love. Whatever construction is put on the events, it is abundantly clear that she antagonised the villagers by her behaviour.

In October 1965 she said that 'the women don't love me. They think I'm playing a new game to their disadvantage. The men are vicious brutes when they can't get a woman to bed.'[33] Four years later, she wrote:

I know about the triumphant cohesiveness [of African people] from having loved an African man. You can nearly get killed. The story travels from place to place along the unseen grape-vine and you are tightly surrounded by a net-work of spies. Your every move and word is closely watched and reported. People are deadly faithful to their own, not to you, the outsiders.[34]

Navigating a course between the melodramatic, the highly romantic and reality itself is not always easy in trying to assess these events. Sometimes, however, when the going seems hard, Bessie Head provides a refreshingly prosaic comment about herself: 'I'm a hell of an ugly woman – I don't know why I'm in so much trouble. It's never happened to me before. Not the kind of woman men take a second look at but HERE I've created chaos and confusion – even to the point of having my sanity threatened.'[35]

It was at school that the various pressures building up against her finally exploded in October 1965. The cause appears to have been a case of sexual harassment. The principal 'thought he could get started to sleep' with her. When he did not succeed here, he turned on Bessie, according to herself, and twisted her arm, 'manhandling' her in front of the schoolchildren. Whereupon Bessie bit his arm to free herself and fled from the school, screaming. The headmaster sent the police to take her to the charge office, declaring that she had gone out of her mind. This dramatic flight appears to be the second Bessie had made from the school. She referred once to a previous occasion when the School Committee had held an emergency meeting and had forced her to return to school.[36]

This time there was no way back. The sense of persecution was growing:

Such tremendous pressure has built up against me in this little village and I shall get no help from the police if my life is in danger . . . The authorities have made no bones about the fact that they don't want me here . . . I'm not exactly loved by the Batswanas here. I shouldn't really care – there's only a kind of rat-race, royalty, society you can revolve in anyway.[37]

The School Committee required that Bessie undergo a medical examination to test her sanity. No one could have imagined how this would terrify her. Nor did she divulge to anyone the full horror of a situation in which echoes of her childhood were sounding in her ears. 'God knows what I am' [sane or insane], she wrote three weeks after biting the headmaster. 'Expect only myself just holding on,'[38] she added. She was in a very serious plight.

This is where two friends from her South African days began to play an important role in her life. She had kept in touch with Patrick Cullinan all the time she had been in Serowe. He it was who knew 'every single detail'[39] of how things had been piling up against her. Randolph Vigne came back into her life when she wrote to him shortly after she fled from the school. 'I don't know if you might remember me – BESSIE Head.'[40] They now began to give her moral support and practical help both in coping with her daily life and in her writing.

She refused to allow herself to be tested for insanity. She looked on such a test as totally humiliating; she could not understand why the authorities should want to break her when she was anxious to leave the country anyway and they would be rid of her; but most of all she feared some damning certificate which would prevent her getting work in any other African country.

For the next two months she felt herself intensely threatened. 'It's going to be God's own miracle if I get out of here alive,' she wrote, commenting on the way every event in a village is common knowledge: 'in an African village it's goddam deep and dangerous.'[41]

After the first confused reeling, though, she once more rallied in a manner indicating a surprising grasp of the situation. 'Pull strings that side like hell for me Randolph, please. I intend to stay alive. There are useful things to do on this earth and I don't intend busting up anybody's show. Just surprised people want so desperately to bust me up. Got to find a level of survival.'[42] At the end of December she received notification from the Department of Education of the Bamangwato Tribal Administration that she had been blacklisted from teaching for having deserted her post. Even before then she knew she had jettisoned her chances of getting another teaching post, which made it all the more imperative for her to make her writing pay.

And indeed it was when Patrick Cullinan and Randolph Vigne both directed her energies towards writing that she began to gain control of her fear. On Christmas Eve, 1965, she wrote to Randolph Vigne that she could 'hang on here' if she could get busy right away with shaping up her stories for publication. The first of what she later was to call her 'Botswana and me' crises had been weathered.

Earlier in 1965 Bessie had written such short pieces as 'For "Napoleon Bonaparte", Jenny and Kate', 'The Green Tree', 'Summer Sun', 'The Old Woman', 'Sorrow Food' and 'The Woman from America'. These and other descriptive articles, some to remain unpublished till long after her death, she had sent to Patrick Cullinan. Bessie was handicapped by having no typewriter of her own so Patrick Cullinan had some pieces typed out and copies sent to her. The idea was now for Randolph Vigne to try and find a market for her stories in London.

However, it was *Transition*, the East African journal, which first published a Serowe piece, in September 1964. It was the short story called 'The Green Tree',[43] the title referring to the widely-used succulent rubber hedge. This is the first time Bessie presents the scene that she had borrowed and learnt to love: the paper-dry parched grass, the minute clusters of green leaves, the strange unproductive green tree which appears to have adapted itself to local conditions but which is actually concerned like everything else with the silent fight for survival. She links this tree with a stranger to the village, a woman who, like it, has seemed to adapt herself to conditions there but who underneath is still strange and therefore disturbing to the protagonist, a man who finds his life unsettled by her arrival. In 'Tao', which appeared in 1967 but was probably written much earlier, the same theme of an ill-matched love affair is examined from the woman's viewpoint. Seen in conjunction with the rambling piece, 'For "Napoleon Bonaparte", Jenny and Kate' and 'Where is the Hour of the Beautiful Dancing of Birds in the Sun-Wind?',[44] which both give more explicit accounts of the disruptive passion of a stranger for a man in a powerful position, these four early pieces could be said to represent draft versions of *Maru*. Furthermore, the long title 'Where is the Hour of the Beautiful Dancing of Birds in the Sun-Wind?' is taken from a poem called 'The Poet's Post' by Harold N. Telemaque, which she had read in *Transition*, and changed the quotation into a rhetorical question. From Telemaque's image of the Sun-Wind comes Bessie Head's idea of the Rain Wind, used here for the first time, and explained much later.[45]

There is another short piece from about this period, 'A Personal View of the Survival of the Unfittest'. Considering some of the same ideas as those found in the rambling 'Napoleon Bonaparte', this personal statement, in which Bessie again draws clear parallels between the 'convulsion of change in Africa' and the 'corresponding convulsion in my own life', is clear and moving:

There is not a single church I care to enter. Though I do not know what I am doing, or where I am going, I would rather weave the strength of my backbone into the fabric of my life. It makes me tolerant, receptive, sensitive. There is nothing pessimistic or neurotic about a backbone. It is the jauntiest, gayest thing in the world, forever driving the body, mind and soul forward in this ceaseless urge to live, live, live. It is the last thing I have left.

Again she refuses to be coerced into accepting dogma of any sort, religious or political. Though she says that she does not fear death, she does not want to 'face a sudden and violent ending' as a result of having every part of her life controlled by politicians. And again she emphasises her own individuality, the fact that she is a

private person, with an intense, private obsession, consumed with curiosity at the riddle of my own life. Why have I been abruptly placed, abandoned, in a crazy wilderness with an almost unbearable load of inner urges that are either the test of my self-control, or the root and cause of degradation, downfall and self-destruction?[46]

She seldom later expressed her views on individuality with such clarity and coherence.

While this piece, along with 'Sun-Wind' and 'For "Napoleon Bonaparte", Jenny and Kate' were only published posthumously, 'For Serowe: A Village in Africa' appeared in the *New African* in December 1965. This is a purely descriptive piece, precise and vivid:

Summertime in Serowe is an intensely beautiful experience. It rains unpredictably, fiercely, violently in November, December, January . . . The earth and sky heaves [sic] alive and there is magic everywhere. The sky takes on a majestic individuality and becomes a huge backdrop for the play of the rain.[47]

Besides conveying the harsh beauty of the village, Bessie also captures the tough survival instinct of its population and of herself, a woman of Southern Africa. Not a black woman, just 'an ordinary and wryly humble woman'.

Another short story from her early months in Serowe was published in *Transition* in the April/May 1967 number. Laced with irony and humour, 'Sorrow Food' is the story of Boshwa, a promising young politician, who is educated in New York before returning to 'this stinking Job's country' at 'a critical stage in the history of Africa'. He backs the wrong horse. While other 'guys cut it smart, kissing the tribal stool', he chooses Pan-Africanism though he should have known that it would 'never hit this goddam tribal backwater'. Boshwa has a set of moral values that allow 'a hell of a broad space between conscience and honesty', and when he is caught out, he has to eat sorrow food and 'stick around in politics as the only representative of Pan Africanism in this critical stage in the development of Africa'.[48] Though Bessie later disclaimed any ties with the writers of the *Drum* school and their tough, taut style, she did use the technique a couple of times herself, as 'Sorrow Food' illustrates.[49]

The series of sketches which she entitled 'Village People' includes 'The Old Woman' and 'Summer Sun'. Here the drought, and the starvation which comes with it, are her concern. In each case Bessie shows the people's resigned passivity, their ability to survive on next to nothing 'in a permanently drought stricken country'. These pieces are a tribute to the ordinary people of Serowe, with whom she here identifies. Indeed she takes on the role of intermediary, reminding the gods 'somewhere' that in case they have overlooked 'desert and semi-desert places ... there are people here too who need taking care of'.[50] Poverty and suffering were states Bessie understood. This is also very evident in the short story 'Looking for a Rain God', a poignant account of starvation, desperation and the ritual murder of two small girls by their father and grandfather.[51]

Of the assortment of stories and descriptive pieces she had collected together by the end of 1965, there was one that was to have unexpected success. This was 'The Woman from America'. It was accepted for publication in the influential British paper, the *New Statesman*, and appeared in August 1966.

While directing her thoughts towards her writing had probably helped Bessie regain her mental equilibrium, it had certainly done nothing to improve her immediate financial situation. She was no longer earning a monthly salary, but, even while she had, her pay packet of R32 (£16) had not been enough to cover her expenses, and she had incurred a debt of R104. She asked Randolph Vigne to help her to find scholarships to apply for, explaining that she could not ask for more help from Pat Cullinan. He was doing so much already.[52] Randolph Vigne referred her to Patrick van Rensburg and wrote to him himself.

Bessie made her own feverish plans, determined to leave Bechuanaland as soon as she could. A friend gave her name to the Canadian Union of Students where she applied for a scholarship, and she began to investigate the possibility of a United Nations grant to join a training programme.[53] She had been corresponding with a German man ever since she had lived with Cordelia Günther in Cape Town, and she now told Harold Head that she was planning to emigrate to Germany and marry him. However, the idea was dropped along with the friendship.[54] Meanwhile Patrick van Rensburg gave her R50 on which to live and Randolph Vigne decided that she should have an agent in London. He arranged for David Machin, from A P Watt Authors' Agency, to act for her.

Bessie spent Christmas Day 1965 with the Van Rensburgs. This gave her the chance to get to know them better. Patrick van Rensburg was a soft-spoken man, peering at the world in a slightly puzzled way from behind his spectacles. It was only on further acquaintance that it became clear that behind his apparent diffidence lay an iron determination; that the dreamer's eyes were combined with a fair measure of practicality; and that this reserved man would risk a great deal to help people in need. It transpired that he could lend her a typewriter, which delighted her. All the same, the visit left her in a depressed state of mind. 'I must say Pat van Rensburg gave me a hell of a drubbing. He said I should not have exploded like that . . . I don't feel so good too – rather an awful failure.' Obviously her experiences during the past months had chastened her. 'Maybe I'm paranoid and all that and an unpleasant person but I try to avoid upsetting my fellow men. I try to live as consciously alone as possible and it gets easier every day.'[55]

Bessie now lived in a small hut four metres square. Any writing she did was done at night, balancing a candle on her knee. Though the hostility she had felt earlier had subsided, there were still people who thought 'I should have got it more than I did',[56] and she still felt spied on. There is no doubt that she had been deeply shaken by the concerted dislike she had been shown. 'I'll never forget the hell and terror of that month . . . They nearly killed me here and I'll never forget it. I must protect myself.'[57]

Bessie's terror could have been partly justified. Village jealousy and retribution are probably underestimated as behaviour-regulating forces in a rural society. In his sociological study of self-identity among the Tswana of Southern Africa, Hoyt Alverson recognises the presence of 'invidious envy' in the society and refers to the *dikgaba* many of his informants told him about. It is not so much regarded as the curse of evil itself as the evil 'one man wishes on another because the former envies or resents the latter's attainments'.[58] One informant said: 'The hot blood of envy can force families to break up',[59] and another: 'I fear *dikgaba* – the (malevolent) envy of others in this community, which can cause me to be overcome in my work.'[60] A psychiatrist, David Ben-Tovim, who spent three years in Botswana working on a mental health programme, has also commented: 'I have always felt that the role of envy in the regulation of life in small-scale communities has been underestimated. We saw it all the time professionally.'[61]

At the Van Rensburgs' Christmas gathering, Bessie suddenly saw a possible way out of her predicament. She met an agriculturist, Vernon Gibberd, who had been appointed by the Bamangwato Tribal Authorities to run an experimental farm, the Radisele Development Association farm, which had been started by Tshekedi Khama with the aim of improving the farming methods of his people. Vernon Gibberd was convinced that the disadvantages of drought and poor soil could be counteracted scientifically, that even under drought conditions good crops could be produced. This was the kind of parable from real life Bessie needed to believe in.

She asked Martin and Mary Kibblewhite, some of Patrick van Rensburg's first expatriate helpers on the Swaneng project, for their assistance. She wanted to go to the farm, doing whatever menial work was needed in return for somewhere to live and some time to write. As personal friends, the Kibblewhites obtained Vernon Gibberd's support, after which Bessie applied to the tribal authorities for permission to go to Radisele. At the end of January, to her great surprise, it was granted. These men worked closely with the people who had blacklisted her from teaching.

In February 1966 she packed up her belongings and left Serowe. Patrick van Rensburg once more offered practical help. He had applied to Canon John Collins, the founder of the International Defence and Aid Fund, which was to provide so much support to victims of the apartheid system in the years to come, and received some money to help Bessie settle her debts in the village. He did more than this. He collected R400 for her before she left and paid it out to her in portions of R6 a week for the next ten months.[62]

Bessie was optimistic about the future. She realised that the hostility she had experienced had strengthened her in some way. She had acquired 'an inner self-assurance that was lacking before . . . All this works well for me to think things out; to write.'[63] One of her parting remarks in a letter to Randolph has an almost prophetic ring:

I could learn a lot [on the farm]. Bechuanaland is entirely an agricultural country. I need that kind of background; all of its battle is against the elements and people are different – their selfishness, greed and hatreds are odd and different because of this tremendous battle to survive against overwhelming odds. I could get all I needed on this farm in concentrated form . . . A good book, published, may be an open sesame to more creative, constructive work.[64]

6

Radisele & Francistown
1966–1969

When Rain Clouds Gather

The Bamangwato Development Association farm at Radisele was about 80 kilometres south of Serowe. It was very isolated, its only contact with civilisation being a railway siding: the nearest shop was 40 kilometres away. 'Serowe is like Manhattan compared to it,'[1] wrote Bessie. Originally Tshekedi Khama had appointed an Englishman, Guy Clutton-Brock, to run the farm, but he had moved to Rhodesia and Vernon Gibberd, who came there in 1963, had taken over. The farm manager, Rasiduelo Montshiwa, was married to one of Khama's relations, and thus had royal connections. While Gibberd felt he and the manager had a good rapport, the BDA Secretary and some of the committee members sometimes opposed his improvement plans. This friction Bessie registered.

Vernon Gibberd's research was mainly centred on water and irrigation. Water being such a scarce commodity, especially during the drought-ridden years from 1958 to 1966, his concern was to help the local population to collect and conserve it, using methods related to their way of life and economic situation. He developed the 'flood-spreading' method of cultivation, whereby narrow strips of cultivated land alternate with bare strips which served as watersheds, feeding any available water into the cultivated furrows. Gibberd had worked out the method by observing that the deep ruts in a dry road could sprout with fresh grass. When Bessie arrived at Radisele, one of the worst droughts the country had known was taking its toll of cattle and other animals. The only available water was being used on the cattle ranch, which meant that no vegetables could be grown.

Conditions were primitive and the financial situation was 'pretty, pretty desperate'.[2] Bessie and Howard were settled into the visitors' rondavel and very soon she was being given typing jobs. Vernon also found ways for her to help on the farm. He was experimenting with Turkish tobacco, which he hoped could become a cash crop – something that would bring money into a society whose economy was based mainly on subsistence and bartering. Bessie was put to harvesting this, and also to 'test-smoking' the crop, as Gibberd himself was an inveterate non-smoker.[3]

Bessie quickly began to make plans. She found the agricultural activities extremely interesting. Memories of her childhood passion for growing things in Nellie Heathcote's garden and her many years of obligatory gardening at St Monica's came back to her. She decided to try and get a grant of money that would enable her to do a two-year course in agriculture at the development farm. There was a fair chance that she would succeed. She had been in touch with Lars-Gunnar Eriksson, the director of the International University Exchange Fund, and he had spoken about trying to raise about R600 for her.

No grant was forthcoming, however. As Bessie had already realised in the preceding months and was often going to be reminded later, she was not actually qualified for higher education courses. She had only a Junior Certificate, which was all that was required of coloured students to qualify for a teacher-training course. Her teacher's diploma was thus inferior. She could not get a teaching post in England with these qualifications, for example, and an application for a scholarship to India about this time was not successful.[4] To be accepted for any course of university standard, she needed two years' extra schooling and the resultant Senior Certificate with matriculation exemption, often referred to as a 'matric'.[5] This was yet another reminder of the discriminatory refinements of the apartheid system.

At the same time, the awareness that she was a stateless person was beginning to haunt her. Rather desperately, she also began considering leaving Bechuanaland and settling wherever she could acquire citizenship. She considered Kenya. Then India. India was becoming representative of all good and tolerant values, for Bessie's religious fervour had suddenly surfaced again.

The encounter with Vernon Gibberd may have precipitated this. There is no doubt that she found the combination of brilliance and dedication which she observed in him a source of great inspiration. After the depths to which she had recently plunged because she felt herself totally alienated from other people's values, here was someone who apparently believed in the same things as she did and was putting his beliefs into practice. 'He makes you feel the world can be changed overnight,'[6] she wrote a month after arriving at Radisele. However, the general context of her remarks makes it clear that she had already distanced herself from such innocent idealism. 'He is just like my blood brother only an innocent person full of glowing idealism . . . It's one thing to be an idealist but fatal to be so innocent. He can't even see that people hate him because he's brilliant and they're not and his brilliance offends them.'[7] It was apparently the Secretary to whom she was referring.

In May she told Randolph that at the risk of making him think that adversity had unhinged her mind, she had to tell him of a change she had experienced. 'I've suddenly got the firm conviction that something like the equivalent of God is around in Southern Africa.' She wrote of 'the strangest revelations' she had been having. 'I even said to myself: "B. Head, take care. You've been sitting alone for three months in the desolate wilderness, that's why you've started 'seeing' things."'[8]

But the experience left her exhilarated. 'Figure it out – I might have really gone round the bend. I mean people who get visions and see a gigantic light descend on them from the sky can't be all there but if so I feel mighty happy. If one is happy and cracked it's much better than being unhappy and sane.'[9]

Another theme appeared in the same letter. She was now totally committed to a belief in reincarnation. She was convinced that she had an important role in the spiritual development of the universe; that her strange birth and existence were important pieces in the puzzle of life: 'Actually I'm not the kind of person that's just born for being born sake. It's very significant that I've been born in Southern Africa. All these years I've been trying to find the purpose in it and true enough there's smoke all around but bless me if I can find the fire.' It was here that she referred directly to India as her spiritual home. 'Quite a lot of my previous incarnations were spent in India . . . I'd . . . ask for citizenship [there]. It's one of the most tolerant countries on earth.' Bessie's soaring prophecy – 'I'm not quite gone round the bend yet, Randolph, but one of two things will happen: – 1. the unexpected . . . or 2. I'll soon get an opening in India'[10] – ends on such an anti-climax that Randolph Vigne was no doubt torn between laughter and tears.

With these disturbing signs of mental instability had come the upward surge of Bessie's spirits that had been evident ever since she began to think seriously about the short stories she had produced. There was also the new resolve that her real effort was now to be channelled into a full-length book. 'Here [in Radisele] I could get a goddam good saga written – a saga about the elements with dramatic, tormented monologues delivered to the elements. There'd just never be a book like it written before,' she wrote a month after she went to Radisele. 'The place is desolate, lonely and I need hours of ruthless solitude to get written the kind of book I want to write . . . I want a novel so that I can take off as me in it . . . I just want a kind of ocean roar all the time.'[11] Bessie reviewed some books for the June 1966 issue of the *New African*, but apart from that did not get down to serious writing at Radisele. Nonetheless it was on the wave of some of this energy that her first novel was to be produced.

Trouble began to brew at the development farm. Some of the people at the settlement had expected Bessie to support them and not the white man, Vernon Gibberd. But Bessie would not do this. 'I liked the ideas of the man . . . and how he had fitted himself into the position of very poor people.'[12] By May she was once more making bitter remarks about the 'violent cross currents of hate and fear', about 'obstructionists and they're black people mind you' and about the need to be 'sharply alert' in order to tell a friend from a foe. She ended the letter to her long-suffering, 'everlasting friend' Randolph even more dramatically: 'There's quite a likelihood I might be popped off too. This letter will be opened and read and it's anybody's guess what the openers-of-letters have in mind.'[13]

At the end of June, five months after arriving there, she left the farm hurriedly. The committee who ran it had had many complaints about the fact that she and Howard were living in the visitors' rondavel. A confrontation resulted and Bessie was thrown out. This time there was no one to whom she could turn. She took the bus as far as Palapye. With her bundles and boxes, she settled down on the steps of the little post office. Her four-year-old boy, tired and bewildered, pressed himself against her.

She was homeless and desperate. Sitting there, Bessie penned a plea to Randolph to help her in whatever way he could. 'It would be a relief to be free of malice, intrigue and unfathomable, weird, weird people who are shockingly cruel,' she said in her short note. But she was not completely broken, for she concluded: 'I'm holding on.'[14] Thus Randolph Vigne heard of her plight some weeks later when the tardy Bechuanaland post finally reached London. It was not easy for him to find a way of helping her this time.

The lady who worked in the local telephone exchange was better able to do that. She took pity on the two stranded figures on the post office steps and offered them a room. It was probably through her that the chance of a new job suddenly came up for Bessie.

Just over two weeks after arriving in Palapye, she started as a typist for the construction firm which had been commissioned to build the road between there and Serowe. They needed someone who wrote intelligible English to type the firm's important correspondence. 'Typing is bad but hope I'll learn. Job is GOOD. Oh God, relief to be employed.'[15]

For two months Bessie enjoyed the swashbuckling life of the only woman staff member on a construction site. She relished it. Work went on day and night in order to get the 50 kilometres of gravel road laid in time. This was part of the burst of effort to improve the country's infrastructure – two other key stretches of road had also just been started – for independence was scheduled for the end of September 1966.

There was a rough crowd of about two hundred men from all over Southern Africa working there. There were many fights. There was much swearing. Bessie had no trouble adapting. Thanks to the spicy vocabulary garnered from her mission school headmistress, Margaret Cadmore, further laced with a good number of 'goddams' acquired from her American friend in Serowe, she was well equipped to meet any swearing man on equal terms: 'I really fit in and am just thinking how I can organise myself in future so that I spend the rest of my life with rough loud swearing men. I don't like hypocrisy and pretence and malice and there's really none of it here. Everybody works hard and they're travellers.'[16]

The pay was bad, R30 per month, though no worse than what she had been earning as a teacher in Serowe. She was not a qualified typist and her work involved reams of figures. But she worked hard and managed, grateful for what she was earning and the prospect of at least a year's work.

On the instructions of an old friend from Johannesburg days, Matthew Nkoana, then in Cairo, the unofficial PAC representative in Francistown contacted her. He told Bessie that he could arrange for her to get a work permit while in Bechuanaland and could also help her to leave and go to Zambia. Bessie was very interested in doing this. She was still afraid of what could happen to her: 'I somewhat underestimated my enemies and I think I'm not liked because perhaps people do not want to be truthful about their aims.'[17]

In early August she was told by her agent David Machin that the *New Statesman* had accepted 'The Woman from America'. The £30 they were paying for it represented two months' salary for her and it was probably from this angle that she considered the news, not being particularly aware of the literary and political standing of this weekly. But following publication, she began to receive many responses to her article. In fact this event was to change her life.

Her address was no longer 'Serowe, Bechuanaland, Africa'. Nor by the time the article appeared was it 'Palapye', for at the end of August Bessie was fired. The circumstances were 'very sordid. Seems if I decide to sleep with every Tom, Dick and Harry – I'll keep a job.' The incident made her once more determined to leave Africa because she feared that she would never be allowed to live there without 'being hounded by unscrupulous men who think women are cheap'.[18]

It was natural for Bessie to move on from Palapye to Francistown. Without work, without a work permit and without any money, she had only one choice: the refugee settlement there. Again, she contacted Solly Ndlovu, the PAC representative, and was registered as a non-political refugee wishing to go to Zambia. She and Howard once more packed their belongings and took the hot, slow train to Francistown.

Francistown was a frontier town. Tucked up in the northeast corner of Bechuanaland, it was about 65 kilometres from the Rhodesian border town Plumtree, on the railway line linking Salisbury and Bulawayo to Cape Town via Mafeking. It was then an outpost of British colonialism, with the British District Commissioner and the local police keeping the wheels of administration oiled, while the white traders and local farmers gathered each evening at the better of the town's two hotels to settle the problems of Africa over a couple of lagers. The daily arrival of the steam trains, one going north, the other going south, regulated the activities of the town. Francistown was very dependent on its railway line.

And on its airstrip. The town was an important recruitment centre for the South African mining industry. Here WENELA, the Witwatersrand Native Labour Association, collected together black workers from the northern parts of Bechuanaland and from Angola and flew them to Johannesburg. The link to South Africa was thus just as important as the link to Rhodesia, though there was no road. The eroded and desolate area, bordered by the Shashe River which divided the Francistown district from South Africa, was forbidding countryside, as fleeing refugees would also know.

Francistown had become something of a refugee centre by the time Bessie arrived there. Its position made it a natural goal for people wanting to get into Zambia, for the Bechuanaland and Zambian borders touched for a hundred metres at one important point: in the middle of the Zambezi River where the western wedge of Rhodesia almost met the Caprivi Strip, that narrow appendage to South West Africa originally intended to give its German colonisers access to the Zambezi River. Here at Kazungula there was a ferry across the Zambezi from Bechuanaland to Zambia, with the Victoria Falls and Livingstone only about 50 kilometres further east. Refugees called it the Freedom Ferry.

By 1966 there was a steady stream of people fleeing from the South African regime into Bechuanaland. Not only had police methods in South Africa become harsher; the fact that Bechuanaland was on the verge of becoming a free African state made it seem an attainable haven. No longer was it possible to attempt to integrate refugees into the community as Stephen Sello had done earlier in Serowe. The numbers were too large; their backgrounds too diverse.

Basically there were three groups of people: young men from the liberation movements, the so-called freedom fighters, who escaped from South Africa and Rhodesia and sought training at an organisation camp in one of the free African states; those escaping either from political prison sentences or police persecution – called political refugees – or from generally intolerable conditions – the non-political refugees; while the third group consisted of the village refugees, whole groups of people moving into northern Bechuanaland from Angola or the Caprivi Strip because of South African police harassment. They crossed what were in fact artificial borders to settle into villages with relations or family members. These caused least upset to the status quo. According to the 1951 United Nations Convention on the Status of Refugees, Bechuanaland was obliged to offer asylum to any refugees crossing its borders from South Africa because it was the only available first country of asylum. Though the territory was often regarded as merely a stopping place on the way to the north, refugees found that it was not as easy as they had hoped to move on to other free African countries, as these did not have the same obligation to accept them. The movement north was slow.

In Bechuanaland in this period there were between 90 and 120 transit refugees. The authorities faced a dilemma. To restrict the movements of these people and keep them together could give rise to pockets of smouldering discontent; but to allow them to move around freely would threaten the precarious unemployment situation and perhaps allow spies to infiltrate the country.

It was decided to collect them together in certain towns. Francistown was one of them. What to the authorities appeared a natural precaution was felt by the refugees to be unnecessarily restrictive treatment. They found it frustrating to live in isolation with others with whom they might have very little in common. Unofficial representatives of both the ANC and the PAC soon appeared in the refugee centre. They were never officially recognised by the government, but they were accepted as being valuable mediators and organisers of what the authorities most wished for as regards the refugees: to keep them moving, birds of passage on their way to settle somewhere else.

Refugees were not always popular with the local population. They were often sophisticated urban dwellers, some reasonably educated, some in possession of a number of skills. This alone tended to alienate them from the villagers. They were also generally not related, in terms of tribal groupings, to the Tswana, so it was more difficult for them to be absorbed into the rural communities. Furthermore, as the whole problem became more regulated, they were given small cash handouts to exist on. This struck the local people as unfair. They had to work for their food.

When Bessie arrived in Francistown, she made her way to the refugee camp. Francistown itself, in a pattern adopted from South Africa, actually consisted of two towns. There was the white area: the railway station, the two hotels, the post office and trading stores, some of a better standard than others. A wide straggling piece of dry, dusty, no-man's-land separated this from the African township, where the camp was situated. The term 'refugee camp' was something of a misnomer. The refugees lived in a large double-storied house, the 'White House', with a big yard. There was a communal room where young freedom fighters slept while waiting to be sent north. Families could occupy a whole room or share it with one or two single people. Cooking was done in the yard, sometimes on a communal fire, sometimes on one fire per family. Not all the refugees lived there but it was the common contact point and information centre.

Bessie's one aim was to get out of Bechuanaland as quickly as possible. While still in Serowe she had chewed over the problem. 'How do I get away from here?' she then asked. 'I have no travel papers. I'm a non-political refugee. It's a relay system. Political refugees in Dar-es-Salaam vouch for those coming on behind. Then you get an identification paper that lets you through Zambia. It's very top level like a V.I.P. I'm just an ordinary person.'[19]

But since then she had acquired contacts with one of the two official resistance groups. There had been talk of travel documents. It was with a certain optimism that she greeted her fellow members of the PAC at the camp.

The camaraderie did not last long. We have only her version of what happened and it has a familiar ring. One of the men tried to force her 'by the hair' to sleep with him. As well as that, he took on her political education. He tried to 'stuff some idiotic literature and attitudes down my throat. I let him have a piece of my mind and ever since then I have been treated as a spy or something untouchable.' She was denounced as a 'PAC adventurer and a useless person in the struggle,'[20] which meant that clearance from the Zambian government was likely to be a long time coming.

Fortunately for Bessie, she found somewhere else to live. It was a humble two-roomed wooden cottage – a 'shack in the bush' she called it – with corrugated-iron roof and large veranda. It lay in the sandy no-man's-land between the black township and Francistown itself. Though she did not realise it when she rented it, the house was supposed to be haunted. This meant that many of the local inhabitants preferred to take the road into town, although it was much longer, rather than cut across the dried-out river bed and thus pass Bessie's house. At night no one dared use the shortcut to town.[21] When she heard the stories connected with her house, Bessie was quite unaffected. Gratefully beginning to collect some pieces of furniture and basic utensils, she started to make a home for herself and Howard. She slept and worked in the living room and put him in the other room. He needed a place to call his own as much as she did.

While Bessie was taking on the ideology of the PAC and in Francistown everyone was talking of the independence celebrations, South Africa was plunged into official mourning. Dr Verwoerd, the Prime Minister, had been assassinated on 6 September 1966, one of the central pillars of the apartheid structure thus being removed by a mentally unstable parliamentary messenger. Not many in Bechuanaland felt the urge to offer their condolences.

At midnight on 29 September, at all official posts in the country, the British flag was lowered for the last time and the blue, white and black striped flag of the new republic was hoisted. No longer would the name Bechuanaland apply; no longer would Her Majesty's Commissioner, Sir Hugh Norman-Walker, represent the highest authority in the country.

At one stage independence had seemed almost unachievable and even now the mere changing of official insignia was not in itself enough to ensure the new state a successful future. Botswana's position as regards its neighbours was not secure. Only Zambia was independent. To the west, South West Africa was chafing for freedom from South African occupation. Angola, across the Caprivi Strip, was in the early stages of a guerrilla war against its Portuguese colonisers. Its neighbour to the northeast, Rhodesia, the former British colony, had issued a unilateral declaration of independence the previous year, under the leadership of its Prime Minister, Ian Smith. When Smith would not accept the British demand that the government should begin a process of handing over power to the blacks, he broke away, retaining white minority rule in a country where the whites were outnumbered by twenty to one. The United Nations imposed economic sanctions against Rhodesia at about the time of Botswana's independence, but years passed before their effect was felt. Instead, in 1966, there was a feeling of optimism among the ultraconservatives of the Rhodesian Front Party, who believed that they had saved their way of life. They also felt a corresponding distrust of the newly-independent state. Botswana's main railway line was part of the Rhodesia–South African railway system, and the new nation shared a long stretch of boundary with Rhodesia.

As always, though, it was the relationship with South Africa which loomed largest. Botswana, while being dependent on its powerful neighbour for economic support, rejected its politics. The country's main export, cattle, went through South Africa, which in turn supplied such important commodities as oil and foodstuffs. In the coming years, Botswana would have to take a stand against South Africa or make a mockery of the term 'independent'. And the country's economic prospects seemed disastrous. True enough, copper had been discovered the year before; but copper is a notoriously unstable economic commodity. The feeble economy was, however, to be given an unexpected boost. The year after independence, a substantial diamond deposit was discovered near Orapa, 225 kilometres west of Francistown.

The political leadership of the country seemed to promise stability. Seretse Khama, as leader of the party which had won an overriding majority, 28 out of 31 seats in the general election of March 1965, was sworn in as the first president of the Republic. He and his party were determined to create a society with equal opportunities for all. He had recently reiterated in New York what had been his deep conviction since he returned to Africa: 'I cannot contemplate a future for Bechuanaland with separate representation for different racial groups . . . Not by such a system could be created a unified nation in Bechuanaland.'[22] He was also anxious to replace many of the white officials or expatriates in the civil service with local candidates. But he believed there was a place for whites in his country and now his vision of *kagisanyo* – unity, peace, harmony and a sense of community – looked as if it stood a good chance of materialising.

Bessie described the coming of independence in a piece called 'Chibuku Beer and Independence'. Randolph Vigne had asked her for something on independence and she had grudgingly obliged. 'I don't think I could write about Bechuanaland Independence. I hate it temporarily,'[23] she said before doing so. The article appeared in the November 1966 issue of the *New African*.

To mark the occasion, Rhodesia sent tankloads of free Chibuku beer to Francistown. To six young students, Rhodesian refugees, this was almost like 'news from home' and Bessie went along with them to the celebrations, armed with her water bucket. The law of the jungle prevailed at the beer distribution centre, but they 'drank in peace and comfort' by virtue of their strength of numbers. There was no feverish excitement, nor violent emotional outbursts; 'just a raggle-taggle crowd of poor people wandering about aimlessly and uncertainly'.[24]

Someone who attended the midnight ceremony described how the British flag was lowered in dead silence. When a single voice shouted 'Hooray' and another 'Burn it', the onlookers turned round to stare in amazement. One old man said that such outbursts embarrassed everyone, especially the white people present.

But the refugees did not feel the same respect for the British. On hearing about the ceremony, they laughed uproariously. Having fled night and day through wild country, expecting death or violent confrontation all the time, these students had a tense, over-excited air about them. They felt baffled to be 'at the dead calm centre of the storm that rages over the whole of Southern Africa'. And here Bessie used for the first time an image that would continue to fascinate her in the years ahead.

Though she had only vague and ambivalent feelings about independence herself, Bessie finally dissociated herself from the students' ribaldry. She sensed something good in the event. 'Perhaps it is the rags and tatters of poverty that are worn with an upright posture and pathetic dignity. What ever it is I say it is good because you feel it in your heart as peace.'[25] She surprised herself with so positive an attitude to the country. 'I have noticed that I've often said things unconsciously and then come to feel deeply about them at a later date,'[26] she explained to Randolph over a year later.

After independence began the long process of trying to find somewhere for Bessie to resettle. During the next two years the New York office of the UN High Commission for Refugees[27] applied to twelve different countries in Africa to get her resettled. But to no avail.

Thus started Bessie's second 'Botswana and me' crisis. Officially she was designated a stateless person: she had to report to the police station every Monday morning, a practice she was to keep up for thirteen more years. No refugee could be given employment through official channels. This meant that she had to find some form of self-employment. A writing career would be the perfect answer to this.

And Bessie was fired as never before with the desire to write.

I shall just have to get SOMETHING written. While I am here. And I'm prepared to strain every nerve, day and night to write the best, I've ever written. There is no alternative. After that I might be in a position to by-pass ANY circumstance; any revolution in Africa where the individual is an expendable commodity ... But I can't be shoved around by pompous fools. I haven't a vendetta of hate. Quite the opposite.[28]

Bessie's isolated house provided her with a place to write. But she was desperately poor. The refugee dole, R40 per month for two people, probably barely covered her rent. She spent her days finding food for Howard and herself. Sometimes she would give whatever there was to Howard and go without herself. Sometimes she would shoplift a cabbage, some mealie meal or samp, to keep starvation at bay.[29] At night she tried to write, if she could afford a candle. Yet she was not alone in her misery. All the refugees were equally poor. Often some of the young ones would gather on the porch of her house. Many were students, keeping up their studies in the hope that they could move on to some place where they could complete their university degrees. They'd shout and argue and scream at each other for being sell-outs and in it all I was some oddity of a half-caste who was the exception and could be made acceptable in the Africa they were going to rule.'30

And Bessie was having a patch of good luck. Ever since she had come to Francistown, she had been receiving letters in response to her article in the *New Statesman* from people telling her of their interest in African development or pointing out how ignorant she was. One of these became a regular correspondent. An aspiring writer, her name was Nini Ettlinger. Bessie enjoyed writing letters. She was soon telling Nini Ettlinger about her many difficulties and her great ambitions. The most pressing practical difficulty was that she had no typewriter and very little prospect of ever being able to buy one. Posthaste came a cheque for R50 with instructions to buy a typewriter and repay the money when convenient. Bessie did so gratefully. The two women kept up a lively correspondence and in its early stages this friendship gave Bessie much pleasure.

Another friend who was standing by with support and advice was the well-known novelist Naomi Mitchison. She had had her first novel published in 1923 and had been writing steadily ever since. She married a Labour politician and from 1945 to 1965 was herself a member of the Argyll County Council, Scotland, where they lived. After meeting Linchwe Kgafela, the young chief-elect of the Bakgatla, one of Botswana's important tribal groups, while he was studying in England, she became so involved with the welfare of the Bakgatla that she travelled to Botswana, staying at Mochudi, the tribal capital, for long periods of time and being made Tribal Adviser and Mother to the Bakgatla in 1963. She felt that there were strong similarities between an African tribe and the once-existing Scottish clans and she placed her vast store of knowledge of politics and local government, of farming and crop production methods, at the disposal of Linchwe Kgafela. Perhaps Bessie and Naomi Mitchison had met at Patrick van Rensburg's the previous Christmas. Perhaps Vernon Gibberd introduced them while Bessie was at Radisele. Perhaps it was Naomi Mitchison's didactic little reply to Bessie's article on Serowe that brought them together. This appeared in the *New African* three months after Bessie's, putting her right on a few points. Bessie had written that 'there isn't anything in this village that an historian might care to write about' and Naomi Mitchison had hastened to reveal the rich historical background of Serowe and the Bamangwato.31 She seemed to have missed the real point of what Bessie was saying: that historians 'do not write about people and how strange and beautiful they are – just living'.32 Bessie had not intended to shine the cold light of logic onto the dreamy mood she had created.

They began to correspond. Bessie later went to Mochudi and visited Naomi Mitchison. A friendship developed at a time when Bessie was crying out for love and affection. One of Naomi Mitchison's great interests at Mochudi was the improvement of crop production, especially the output of *mabele* (sorghum), given the poor soil and lack of rain. Since her time at Radisele, Bessie had also been very interested in this question and they exchanged tips on seed types and gardening methods throughout the years of their correspondence. Perhaps it was she who was responsible for a thawing in Bessie's attitude to Botswana. '[S]he loves me to love Botswana,'[33] Bessie wrote in 1968. And in her dedication to Naomi in her first novel, Bessie wrote: 'and for Naomi Mitchison, who loves Botswana'.

It was another 'woman from America' who gave Bessie Head her first real break. The now famous article had been read with interest by one of the editors at Simon & Schuster. Her name was Jean Highland. She wrote to Bessie asking for more of the same sort of writing. Was she working on a novel? Bessie replied that she was longing to write down some of the ideas she had in her head, but she was so poor she could barely afford to buy a pencil, let alone the necessary paper. Jean Highland immediately sent her a ream. More important, she persuaded the publishers to invest in Bessie's talent. In December 1966 Simon & Schuster sent her a cheque for $80, the advance on a book they wanted her to write.

Bessie wasted no time. By mid-January 1967 she had the first two chapters written and the title chosen. Her novel was to be called *When Rain Clouds Gather*. Its setting was the development project where she had worked. David Machin thought the first chapters were 'very good indeed'. Bessie feared that she could get herself into a fix 'because it has people in it quite identifiable'.[34]

Bessie had learnt to write by the trial and error method. Patrick Cullinan tried to steer her away from what he called the 'flights of fancy'.[35] He liked it when she analysed the commonplace. 'No factual meat', he wrote as a comment to one of her short stories, 'out of touch with physical reality'.[36] Bessie loved the flights of fancy: 'in spite of what dear Pat says I desperately want to take off on one long goddam vivid flight from physical reality'.[37] Nevertheless she tried hard to 'EXTERNALISE'.[38]

Randolph, too, tried to discipline her pen. For him it was simply to ensure communication. Evidently her accounts of visions and gigantic lights in early 1966 had made him uneasy. He asked her to stick more to facts and write less about 'Life with a capital L'. Bessie replied: 'I'm sorry if I wrote L life letters but I think I've been so miserable that everything's been going round and round in my head ... Well I hope this letter has been FACTUAL enough.'[39]

Nini Ettlinger also tried to teach her the art of writing. When Bessie sent her a short story as a gift after receiving the money for the typewriter, it was returned heavily corrected. Nini Ettlinger told her that she could not hold an emotion at a climax. She paid too little attention to 'painting in a scene'.[40] Bessie knew that Nini Ettlinger was right and tried to learn from her. As she said, she was short of new approaches. Later Nini Etttlinger told Bessie: 'You really must not write with your heart on fire. It's not literature. I really mean it.'[41] This caused Bessie to blow up. Despite serious entreaties and heartfelt apologies from Nini, Bessie never wrote to her again. When she had some spare money, she repaid the loan for the typewriter and cut Nini Ettlinger out of her life. 'She thinks I am inferior to her, intellectually, what do I do? She is good in her own right. I have to write at my level.'[42]

Thus it was that when Jean Highland and two other editors from Simon &

Schuster, Pat Read and Bob Gottlieb, took Bessie by the hand, as she called it, to help her shape *When Rain Clouds Gather* into a novel, they were taking on someone who enjoyed having support in her writing but could certainly also become temperamental. Throughout 1967 they worked at it. Section upon section of the manuscript was sent backwards and forwards; suggestions made; improvements found. Bessie did not take exception to their criticisms.

In fact, during this long process, a friendship grew up between Jean Highland and Bessie which was to last many years. 'Jean and Pat gave me more affection than I have ever had in my life. There was also the beautiful editing Pat did on the book,'[43] she wrote to David Machin three years later.

It was a year when Bessie had a great need for love and affection. Probably nobody realised how poor she had become. A year later she confessed to Randolph:

I have had to discipline myself to stay a week on end without food. And yet somehow hold my mind together. There have been days and days when I've had to give all the food to my son and then sit up the whole night typing my book. Now and then Naomi sent me ten pounds ... There's nothing like outright hunger over a prolonged period to make you lie back and stare deeply at life. I thought I should grasp this for the future.[44]

By November 1967 she had the main draft of her novel complete.

Local officials had long felt that the refugee question in Botswana was becoming more than they could cope with. In March 1968 the United Nations High Commission for Refugees and the World Council of Churches sent a two-man mission to Botswana to help regulate the position of the refugees and to get the government to adopt the United Nations Convention on the Status of Refugees. This meant getting them to accept an obligation not to deport people and to be willing for some settlement of refugees in what was, for all of them, their country of first asylum.

Terence Finley, a welfare officer, was part of this mission. An energetic and earnest young man, he arrived in Francistown in March 1968, after two years in Rhodesia working for Amnesty International. His first job was to interview all the refugees, collect relevant information about them and send it to the office in Gaborone, the capital. In Francistown he met Bessie and was aware from the start that she was an unusual person. His flat lay on the outskirts of the white area and it was easy for him to cut across the sandy stretch of land near Bessie's house on his way to the refugee camp. Though Terence Finley did have transport, he was loath to arrive at the poorly equipped camp in a flashy green truck. So at first he walked out there. In the blazing heat, he often gave in to the temptation to call on Bessie as he passed her house.

Bessie was always sprucely dressed and her home neatly kept. She was always welcoming and hospitable, often making tea for him and serving it with due ceremony. Though he was an official and white, and he soon learnt Bessie's views of both these specimens, she never seemed to regard him as either. Once temperatures and pressure of work had sent him into the driver's seat of his truck, he often gave her lifts or helped her in practical ways. For eighteen months he was a good friend and an impartial observer.

His work was exacting and often thankless. There were many obstacles to be overcome for every single refugee that he sent on to a more settled existence. Meanwhile he tried to keep up the morale of those waiting. Every so often he would invite them to a discussion evening at his flat. He bought in a good supply of beer and let things take their course. Tempers flared up easily and the discussions became very heated. Inevitably they became political. When Bessie came, she certainly had her say. She had very strong views and she did not go along willingly with anyone else. Though the other refugees seemed to accept her fiery retorts quite calmly, she was difficult to have at that sort of discussion: there was a point beyond which communication could not proceed. After attending two or three gatherings, she seemed to realise this too and kept away.[45]

Though she could be annoyingly domineering in such a situation, Bessie seemed to Terence to be a very private person. She was wary of men and afraid of any physical involvement. Nor did she ever appear to flirt or encourage advances. Terence's observations here correspond very much with what Bessie said about her 'routine with men' which was never to give them a 'come-hither stare'. What then had caused all her trouble with them wherever she had been? Not Bessie. Though she behaved foolishly and naively in Serowe, she paid a high price for it. It is doubtful that she made the same mistake twice. She can be blamed for many of the difficulties she got herself into and many of the friendships she lost but, as regards men, she was a victim of the Southern African sexual pattern of the sixties. In it, a man took for granted that a woman who was not decorously keeping house for her husband would only achieve whatever aims she had through his bed. 'It's pretty terrible ... for a woman to be alone in Africa. Men treat women as the cheapest commodity,'[46] is how Bessie put it. Despite her colourful language and extraordinary theological ideas, she had very strict, even narrow, moral values. But apart from that, she felt very strongly that she had a right to live her life as she chose.

Though he shared many of her financial worries, Terence Finley was never really aware of Bessie's writing activities. He saw her typewriter when he visited her and knew that she was 'working on a book' but by the time he arrived in Francistown the worst was over. Bessie was proofreading, but this she kept very much to herself. Only when he was presented with one of the very first copies of her novel to reach Botswana early in 1969, did the magnitude of what she had achieved, sitting night after night at her typewriter with her candles beside her, really come home to him.

When Rain Clouds Gather proved to be a natural extension of the talents Bessie had been developing. Her short pieces, articles and stories had shown her preference for observing, recording and dreaming; her appreciation of the unpredictable. At last she had her chance to tell a story. Now she could say that 'people is people' and even prove that she was a good enough writer to 'write damn White, damn Black and still make people live'.[47] She chose a development project in a village in independent Africa as her setting. Her theme was the way changes in traditional family patterns, crop production and political status affect the lives of the people, especially the women, and the traditional distribution of power.

She needed a protagonist who was disillusioned: someone who had grown up within the stifling framework of South African racism and had fled from this, now to be confronted with these new forms of cooperation. Her husband came to mind: his struggle against the system, his determination to escape it, his exciting flight across the border into Bechuanaland. She used his accounts of this in her introductory chapter.[48]

Harold Head's adventure was thus used in Bessie Head's first novel, giving him a long aversion to it. Another incident inspired her as well. One morning she found a young man standing quietly on her porch when she returned from shopping. 'Do you mind if I study here?' he asked. Gradually her 'whole mind swayed towards him'. He talked about tribalism and its ills. He looked at her with some of the sunlight from the window filling his eyes, 'smiling, amused, lofty, majestic'.[49] He gesticulated slowly as he talked and he promised her the whole continent of Africa because he liked her. In return she made him the protagonist of her first novel.

She sensed both the young man's pain and his vision. It is this blend that gives her novel its freshness and originality. She tells her tale: a South African political prisoner, Makhaya Maseko, flees across the border to Botswana to escape a banning order and is befriended by an old man from the village of Golema Mmidi who tells him of the great changes taking place in the village. A white agriculturist, by name Gilbert Balfour, has been trying to introduce cooperative farming methods which have proved surprisingly promising, because Balfour has considered the needs of the villagers and lives like them himself. He has gained the old man Dinorego as his ally and finally succeeds in gaining the self-contained and beautiful Maria, Dinorego's daughter, as his wife. His success, when it comes, is largely due to the arrival and help of Makhaya, who is much better than he is at instructing the village women. They, as the main working force, need to be won over. Makhaya also finds fulfilment and a wife in Golema Mmidi. The emphasis on cash crops, boreholes and new types of grass changes the future perspective of the villagers and they in turn band together and rid themselves of a tyrannical chief, symbol of the rigidities of tribalism.

However, it is more than a simple tale with a happy ending. Colonial and urban values are given an ironic twist. A young urban dweller, despite his inherent distrust of 'tribalism', chooses a rural existence instead of seeking the bright lights of the city. A white man chooses to live by black rural standards. A poorly educated black woman dominates a giant of an English agriculturist. Whites and blacks exchange innermost thoughts. The emphasis on the practical details of crop cultivation sometimes threatens to obscure the narrative entirely.

There is much of Bessie herself in the complex Makhaya. This is not seen so much in his idealism, his belief that he has reached 'the crossroads of life ... One road might lead to fame and importance, and another might lead to peace of mind. It's the road of peace of mind that I'm seeking' (p. 20), as in his inner turmoil and sense of human isolation. He calls himself the Black Dog because he has been so mistreated by the rest of mankind that he sees life only as 'torture and torment ... an abysmal betrayal, a howling inferno' (p. 128). In his inner being he hates the white man, 'a powerful accumulation of years and years and centuries and centuries of silence. It was as though, in all this silence, black men had not lived nor allowed themselves an expression of feeling. But they had watched their lives overrun and everything taken away' (p. 133).

The healing process begins slowly when one of the village women, Mma-Millipede, shows him that 'generosity of mind and soul' are real. He feels then that 'the hatred might fall away from him like old scabs' (p. 132). Two incidents serve to detonate the pent-up violence within him. As he blasts rock to make the dams that will bring water to Golema Mmidi, he is struck by the irony of his action: not so very long before he had been in jail for wanting to 'use this very dynamite against the enemies of human dignity' (p. 137). And after his angry confrontation with Chief Matenge, when he vows in all seriousness to kill him, it is later his lot to enter Matenge's palatial residence and cut the chief's body down from the rafter after his suicide. '[T]he God with no shoes, with his queer, inverted reasoning, had brought Makhaya, a real and potential murderer, face to face with the body of Matenge just hanging there and hanging there. "Don't you see?" he said softly. "Murder is small-minded business" (p. 178). Makhaya voices Bessie's own confusion most particularly when, while recognising his own background of persecution in Africa, he still feels distaste for the 'hate-making political ideologies' (p. 80) intended to counter this persecution.

Gilbert, the other main character, is not portrayed in the same depth. He remains a dedicated idealist, a peripatetic handbook on agricultural methods. His touching love for Maria, his eccentric proposal to her and hints of the scars he carries from his childhood are the only glimpses the reader is given into the recesses of his personality.

The village people grouped around Makhaya and Gilbert provide a varied and colourful background. Because the economy has been based on cattle-farming and the men are thus away at the cattle-posts for long periods of time, it has always been the women and children who populate the village:

No men ever worked harder than Botswana women, for the whole burden of providing food for big families rested with them. It was their sticks that thrashed the corn at harvesting time and their winnowing baskets that filled the air for miles and miles around with the dust of husks, and they often, in addition to broadcasting the seed when the early rains fell, took over the tasks of the men and also ploughed the land with oxen. (p. 104)

In creating self-reliant women like Maria, Paulina and Mma-Millipede, Bessie Head presents their hardships and triumphs, and those of their sisters, in a sharply realistic light. Traditional norms no longer exist and it is the women who suffer. Perhaps the husbands have had to go much further afield in search of work; perhaps there never was a husband, for 'a love affair resulting in pregnancy was one sure way of driving a man away, and it was a country of fatherless children now'. Men have become so used to being superior in the eyes of the law that they have become morally degenerate. They feel no responsibility for a family and the women are left caught in a 'trap of loneliness'. Paulina, noting the interest that Makhaya shows in children, thinks that 'perhaps this man still had tribal customs which forced him to care about children' (p. 119). Because they feel neglected by their men, there is a strong communal feeling among the women. They work together on the new projects with delight, offering each other support, companionship or banter.

Most of Bessie's comments on the plight of the village women are unequivocally critical of male attitudes, but she also uses humour to cast light on the relationship between the sexes. The most delightful example of this is where she uses the fire-making process to illustrate qualities essentially male and female. A fire built by a man is a mathematically precise entity, each stick slowly placed in the correct position after considered thought. It serves only the purpose it has been intended for, burning clear and smokelessly and then dying. To a woman a fire is 'only a ragbag'. It has to meet a number of demands, as quickly as possible, so she throws firewood into it in 'haphazard confusion'. It boils water, it cooks a stew, it makes a pot of tea, smoking 'like mad' all the time. 'But would people ever eat and stay alive if housework was so precise and calculated like this bright, smokeless, quick-burning fire?' (p. 140)

Tribalism is to a large degree considered responsible for the inferior status of women: one of the first changes Makhaya had introduced in his previous life in South Africa after he became head of the family on his father's death was the rule that his sisters were to call him by his first name and associate with him as an equal; he could be no part of the 'clinging, ancestral, tribal belief that a man was nothing more than a grovelling sex organ' (p. 15). Though many women of Mma-Millipede's generation have had some schooling, it has not been sufficient to develop their independence, for they remain 'their same old tribal selves, docile and inferior' (p. 68).

Tribalism is thus set up as an antithesis to progress. The chiefs and politicians such as Matenge, Joas Tsepe and even Chief Sekoto remain epitomes of evil, corruption and moral lethargy. Bessie, in discussing tribalism, disregards the complexities that she has recognised in other human situations. The plight of the women with their fatherless children is the result of the collapse of tribalism, for example, and the virtues of sharing and common concern are virtues of the older generation too. She allows Dinorego and Paulina to attribute positive traditional attitudes to Makhaya without commenting on the irony of this; and all in all takes the easy way out by allowing tribalism, and Matenge in particular, to become the villain of the piece.

Much attention is given to the country's newly evolving political system. It has recently acquired self-government and the party in power consists of sons of chiefs, representing a moderate line in politics. The opposition consists of four or five liberation parties aligned to the Pan African movement, 'with little or no membership among the people but many undersecretary generals' (p. 46). Joas Tsepe, Matenge's only friend and supporter in Golema Mmidi, is the under secretary general of the Botswana National Liberation Party. At first the aim of this party is to liberate the people from British colonialism. After the general elections, however, it sets about liberating the people from its elected government, claiming that the election has been rigged and that the government is simply an extension of the power of the chiefs. However, when the party discovers that the sons of chiefs have an anti-chief policy, the party quickly declares itself pro-chief.

'To many,' says Bessie, airing a favourite view, 'Pan-Africanism is an almost sacred dream, but like all dreams it also has its nightmare side, and the little men like Joas Tsepe ... are the nightmare. If they have any power at all it is the power to plunge the African continent into an era of chaos and bloody murder' (p. 47).

The problem of refugee status is also considered. Gilbert's arrival in the village and his establishment of a cattle cooperative diminishes the chief's income made through cattle speculation, so when he sees a chance to throw Gilbert out by attacking Makhaya, he wastes no time in doing so. Gilbert has no right to harbour a refugee. 'If there was anything the new government disliked, it was a refugee, and because of this, no man in his right senses would harbour or employ one' (p. 48). Once again, though, a twist of fate, an act of human goodness, thwarts the evil intentions of the chief. The police inspector, George Appleby-Smith, sticks 'his neck out' for Makhaya (p. 73), thus losing his chances of promotion for another few years, and arranges a residence permit, which comes through in record time.

If Bessie has failed to grasp sufficiently the complicated traditional structure of village life in Botswana, the vitality and aptness of her descriptions of the environment indicate her intense appreciation of this. From the start Makhaya is associated with the sun. In a description which begins to signal Bessie Head's importance for African writing as a whole, she depicts him walking alone in the bush on his first morning in the new country:

It was just his own self, his footsteps and the winding footpath. Even the sunrise took him by surprise. Somehow he had always imagined the sun above hills, shining down into valleys and waking them up. But here the land was quite flat, and the sunshine crept along the ground in long shafts of gold light. It kept on pushing back the darkness that clung around the trees, and always the huge splash of gold was split into shafts by the trees. Suddenly, the sun sprang clear of all entanglements, a single white pulsating ball, dashing out with one blow the last traces of the night. (p. 16)

After this Makhaya is often linked to the sun. It is therapeutic in contrast to the 'shut-away worlds where the sunlight never penetrated, haunted worlds, full of mistrust and hate' (p. 81) and the 'grey graveyard' (p. 158) in which Makhaya usually lives.

All the more poignant then that the same sun should blaze down destruction in the worst drought the country has experienced. 'The sky had lost that dense blue look of the winter days and spread itself out into a whitish film, through which the sun poured out molten heat in pulsating waves from dawn to dusk.' Corpses of cattle and wild animals are strewn indiscriminately over the parched landscape. In this desolation, the vultures reign supreme. They gather on the ground in huge flocks and hold 'important discussions in hoarse, rough voices' flapping their 'long, soppy brown feathers in imperious indignation' (p. 159).

Throughout the novel the narrative is sustained with images taken from the life of the village. Perhaps some are hardly more than clichés, as that of a little girl moving 'like a wind-blown leaf' (p. 138). But there is accurate observation behind

Bessie's description of an old man whose reasoning ability is always there 'at the forefront, like a cool waterfall on his thoughts' (p. 85); or of a woman whose thoughts are 'as uncertain and intangible as the blue smoke of the fires which unfurled into the still winter air and disappeared like vapour' (p. 94); or of evening mists that shiver 'like homeless dogs' and slyly creep 'into the hedged yard for a bit of warmth' (p. 140).

Bessie's honesty and involvement, her optimism grounded in an awesome realism, are attributes the reader recognises and appreciates in her first novel. She accepts and respects the multiplicity of human relationships and the complexity of human nature. This means that there is a tentative, questioning, uncertain linkage of event to event and character to character. Makhaya's world, especially, is wavering, ambiguous.

In the final chapter Bessie muses at some length about the nature of God and the kind of God that could be beneficial to the African continent. That Makhaya begins to refer to himself as God, though he also professes to be, and wishes to remain, an ordinary man, adds to the theological confusion. Bessie does not resolve the issue. But, as the future will show, she certainly does not abandon it.

Bessie had admitted quite early that some characters were easily identifiable[50] and that there was a clearly autobiographical element in *When Rain Clouds Gather*. Because she had to consider the problem of defamatory or libellous material prior to the novel's appearing in England, we are given a little insight into this question. For example, she listed the characters for her agent and discussed their resemblance to living people:

Paulina and Makhaya are on the whole myself and much of what I'd say and do. Mma-Millipede, Dinorego and Paramount Chief are complete inventions. There are three characters likely to be identified with any number of people in Botswana, Gilbert, Matenge and Joas Tsepe.

She said that Naomi Mitchison recognised Joas Tsepe as a 'certain politician' but in fact

there are any number of Joas Tsepes here and they all talk, walk and do the same foolish things . . . Then again with Gilbert. Most of the volunteers walk around in short khaki pants and great hob-nailed boots . . . As for Matenge, he is again like at least half a dozen chiefs . . . Each one will howl yet they all do the same things to people and persecute the poor.[51]

Naomi Mitchison agreed with her that none of the main characters was recognisable or that there could be any question of libel. She did think that Gilbert seemed like Vernon Gibberd but that he would not sue her.[52]

Bessie got much of her background information for the agricultural details from Oxfam, the famine relief organisation. It had done research in Botswana in connection with help given during the 1965 drought. An agricultural officer checked everything she wrote.

Another concluding task, and one in which she took much pleasure, was deciding to whom she was going to dedicate the novel. Her final choice of wording was: 'FOR Pat and Wendy Cullinan, Pat and Liz van Rensburg, "HOORAY!" and U-Shaka, and for Naomi Mitchison, who loves Botswana'. 'Hooray' was Bessie's name for Jean Highland. 'U-Shaka' was an unexpected and puzzling addition. Bessie had developed a sudden fascination for the famous Zulu chieftain, a fascination that was to have interesting future consequences.

Howard's sixth birthday, 15 May 1968, in Francistown; Howard second from left (courtesy Khama Memorial Museum)

7

Serowe Again, 1969

Maru

❄

After *When Rain Clouds Gather* had been dispatched, Bessie was apprehensive and restless, knowing that Bob Gottlieb and Jean Highland were already waiting to see what she could produce next. She wrote: 'You've no idea what shaky legs a person can have. Now I could not attempt another unless, this time, I convinced myself that it was really going to be great – for my own sake, for my own life, for the struggles in me.'[1]

During the process of writing her novel, Bessie's attitude to Botswana had changed. She no longer wanted to leave the country; not when so much of her 'life and thought had gone into it'. She had begun to find things that she valued and did not want to lose:

I like the way I am just a nonentity, a nobody. I like the silence and all the hours I turn to study books or study myself. I like the way I have to walk miles for water and carry it home on my head. And I just like the Batswanas, not the big shots, but all the people who walk around with no shoes.[2]

As well as the natural sympathy she had always had for the poor and the down-trodden, she was now also of the opinion that suffering makes a land holy and that ordinary people would be the ones to conquer evil because they would soon 'pull down the mighty from their seats'.[3] She said that the 'whole world has had enough of the bloody bastards who can only rule by preventive detention, blood, greed, caste, class, spies and the secret service'.[4] She was surprised that she could feel love for Botswana, after the people had called her insane; but the very fact that she could seemed to prove to her that her love was real, something endur-ing that had grown out of rejection. She made a decision:

I'm going to bloody well adopt this country as my own, by force. I am going to take it as my own family. Then since my ambitions are high I am going to put what I think is finest and noblest in Africa in Botswana and show it as having the best of tribal culture . . . I've also got a feeling, something queer and laughable that I can catch hold of God for Africa.[5]

In April 1968 she quickly produced an article for the *New African*. It was orig-inally called 'Africa and Revolutions' but was published as 'God and the Underdog. Thoughts on the Rise of Africa'. It is rambling and subjective, sometimes rising to a disturbing note of hysteria. Her view that God is a 'Nigra' woman is intertwined with a belief in African liberation. The article also includes further interesting recollections of her god-like African-American friend from the Serowe days, with 'her big, flashing black eyes and her universal compassion for the Sudra or underdogs of the world'. However, Bessie now provides a new angle on the friendship by saying that she is often filled with 'hot resentment at the battering and bashing she gave me'. The problem of her own lack of identity is clearly both-ering her, for one of the things she finds hardest to take is her friend's insistence that she is not a genuine African. Gradually she realises that though she 'might not be a genuine African' she is 'most certainly a genuine Sudra' because for the greater part of her life she has 'only lived in the slums of South Africa' where she had been born.[6]

She might lay claim to an African identity through a birthright of poverty, but during the next months she was forced back to thoughts of her mother and her own strange birth; forced to examine the significance of her hybrid heritage. In October 1968 she wrote to Randolph Vigne that though she had once been 'a hot rod black nationalist', as he well remembered, she soon grew out of that phase because many people pointed out to her that she was 'not black enough'.

She realised that her destiny was leading her 'along other paths', that she was going to have to opt for 'mankind as a whole'. She concludes: 'You know, my friend, a combination such as I of two nations finally establishes the human race.'[7] In the same letter she relates to Randolph Vigne the story of her concep-tion:

I don't think I told you this but my mother's family locked her up in a mental asylum for sleeping with a black man. I feel they did this to save the family name from scandal and she was in the asylum by the time I was born. I carried this with me for a long time. There is a terrible depth of loneliness in supposed or even evident insanity. There is more. A birth such as I had links me to her in a very deep way and makes her belong to that unending wail of the human heart ... I feel she belongs to me in a special way and that there is no world as yet for what she has done. She left me to figure it out.

Bessie was becoming more and more explicit about the special role she believed that she had to play in the future of Africa. In a letter to Jean Highland, from about the same time, her sense of historic destiny is clearly stated and she refers directly to the Saviour of Africa:

The lovers and helpers of mankind are not born in a day. It has taken me thirty-one years to know who I am. It has taken my God 47 years. The two of us finally knew each other in these past four or five weeks, though when he was born in Botswana a number of prophecies were made about him. I was included in them because the two of us have always been a team together. That is, when he was Jesus, I was Paul. When he was Ramakrishna, I was Vivekananda.[8]

Bessie believed completely in her visions. Once earlier she had said that she knew 'that something like the equivalent of God is around in Southern Africa'.[9] Now she seems to have been in contact with him. A man who was 47 in 1968 would have been born in 1921. What god-like personality on the local scene would be that age? She seemed to be referring to the President of the Republic.

Bessie had admired Seretse Khama from the early Serowe days: 'Seretse Khama is the surprise of Africa . . . During those years of being in the background he made the most experiments in farming in Botswana.'[10] . . . 'Seretse is really a towering personality . . . '[11]

During this time Bessie had become acquainted with his cousin, close friend and political helpmate, Lenyeletse Seretse. Lenyeletse Seretse and Seretse Khama's grandfathers were brothers. Traditionally it was the custom for children to take the name of the paternal grandfather as a surname, so there was no fixed family name, though this custom is changing.[12] The two boys played together and Tshekedi Khama, Seretse's guardian, took a liking to Lenyeletse Seretse and sent him off to school at Tiger Kloof College in South Africa with Seretse Khama and some other chosen boys. Later, Lenyeletse Seretse was given the demanding task of taking part in the building of Moeng College, intended to provide the Bamangwato with secondary and vocational education. He was a popular man, known for his humanity, a 'soft friendly, amiable personality' as Bessie described him, but sometimes also showing the 'closed reserved face' of someone who knows too much and is not telling.[13] As Central District Council Secretary, Lenyeletse Seretse had been involved in finding Bessie accommodation on her arrival in Serowe and through him she had undoubtedly been aware of Seretse Khama in his capacity as tribal secretary. Later she said that she had only stood face to face with the President once, at a public meeting, where she had asked about the position of refugees in Botswana. 'He answered quite steadily and quietly and in a friendly manner.'[14]

Through Terence Finley and his contacts with a large number of official institutions, it had been arranged for Bessie to do a correspondence course in tropical agriculture. She would receive a monthly payment from a United Nations fund for the duration of the course, which was to last until July 1969, thus providing her with a source of income until then.

In the many fluctuations that made up her life there was one constant point: her love for her son. People who knew her at this time all remember her genuine concern for him and his affectionately independent manner towards her: 'A child will often behave to people in general the way his parent treats him. I began to notice that he would do to other children what I did to him at home, that is he unconsciously puts his arm round the neck of a friend and speaks to him most tenderly.'[15]

Not that Bessie constantly referred to Howard in her correspondence. Her writing activities were often so intense that it is sometimes hard to imagine where he fitted into the picture. But he was a quiet little boy by nature and very self-contained. He lived his own life, played his own games with his friends, then returned home to his strange mother, who would be bashing away feverishly at the keys of her typewriter or wandering backwards and forwards distractedly as she repeated newly composed phrases to herself.

For some reason Bessie Head never learnt Setswana herself, not even of a rudimentary sort. Howard, being so young when they arrived there, never considered himself anything other than a Motswana. While they were in Serowe, he often spoke to Patrick van Rensburg's children in Setswana because that was the language the children used. Though he, like her, had no official status in the country, Bessie must have often felt relieved that Howard had become socially integrated into a society that had given her so many adjustment problems.

In January 1968 he began to go to school in Francistown. He was almost six years old. Here it was that older children began to tell him he was not a Motswana, he was coloured. He used often to complain about this, to Bessie's great distress. 'I used to break out into a sweat not knowing what to say because I started it in the first place. I don't think he understands words like human being and mankind.' The children seemed to regard Howard as an impostor. 'Apparently being a Motswana is a very exclusive thing.'[16]

One Saturday in August little boys walked round the streets of Francistown distributing what she was told were 'religious pictures': a family scene of a tall man sitting in a chair, a short woman standing beside him and a little boy beside her. Bessie saw one picture briefly but refused to take it from the child, to her later regret. Shortly afterwards she was inside the house when she saw four sixteen-year-old boys approach Howard where he was playing in their own yard. She heard one of them shout 'I don't care. I won't do anything for you', as they hurled stones at Howard. She rushed to the door and the boys fled. Howard was naturally deeply unhappy about the incident, which neither mother nor son could find any explanation for.[17] A few days later, he came home from school once again puzzled and distressed because his playmates had told him that he and his mother were going to be Bamangwato royalty. In some way Bessie felt that the so-called religious pictures were responsible for the attack.

In a letter to Jean Highland close to the strange incident, she made several references to a forthcoming 'gigantic event' and a 'new world', where people would have their 'spiritual vision awakened', and she would play her part.[18] On a more mundane level, however, she apparently felt seriously threatened by the event. So much so that she suddenly removed Howard from school and decided to teach him herself, a more difficult proposition than she had thought. She told Randolph Vigne that it 'was much easier to let him go to school and only play at teaching at home, which was what I had to do. Now I have had to put drill and sweat into it. I know mean humanity around here is rubbing their hands with glee.'[19]

This last sentence reflects another aspect of Bessie's state: an increasing sense of victimisation. During her time in Serowe, she felt she had suffered under the raw disapproval of the villagers. The situation seemed to repeat itself in Radisele and Palapye; in each case Bessie believing that she was being persecuted unfairly. The pattern was set. Bessie's feeling of paranoia lasted the rest of her life. 'I have never known people being anything but horrible and enjoying the mental torture of another,' she continued in the same letter to Randolph.

As well as the immediate problem of teaching Howard herself, she now faced the more serious one of finding somewhere else to send him to school. Encouraged by Randolph Vigne, she began to consider returning to Serowe. She knew that Patrick van Rensburg's school at Swaneng could offer Howard a good education in a less parochial atmosphere than any other school in the area. Van Rensburg's educational experiments were attracting volunteer helpers from all over the world. For Howard, then, this would be the obvious solution.

For Bessie, however, the decision to move was not all that easy. She was more than aware of the enemies she had made while there before. She feared the hostility of the villagers. Terence Finley saw her regularly and tried to advise her. He, too, favoured contacting Patrick van Rensburg and finally she did, embarrassing though she found it. Once again she would have to ask his help to extricate her from a mess. And as she explained to Randolph, 'I have suffered such torture of mind that I do not like to refer to the matter.'[20] Patrick van Rensburg helped her immediately by promising to take Howard at Swaneng primary school.

In December, with a host of other unexpected problems crowding into her life, she was still strangely elated about her new vision of God. She wrote to David Machin – as indeed she had also written to Jean Highland – that she believed that people would not suffer oppression for very long and that they had realised this: 'If people reach a sudden illumination where they respect each other regardless of the skin colour or the shape of the nose etc. then the way is open for the brotherhood of man and the removal of poverty and suffering . . . God is a living person and a person who will change the world.'[21]

Bessie had to leave her good friends Maria and Zoot Mohammed, her little house in which she had written her first novel, and worst of all her dog Spot. She found a reasonably good solution to these problems by letting the Mohammeds take over her house and her dog. Maria had just had another baby and they needed better accommodation than they had, though their circumstances were as straitened as those of all the other refugees.

Just ten days before she was due to leave, Bessie received her first advance copy of *When Rain Clouds Gather*. With this in her hands, she could surmount the insurmountable. 'God, God, God but it looks terrific. I feel this way because it is only a first baby. I am going out of my mind. I am going out of my head.'[22] Her fortunes had been given a sudden lift but she was still a refugee. And armies of confused thoughts were marshalling themselves for a confrontation in her mind.

Bessie returned to Serowe at the end of January 1969. The move went more smoothly than she had dared to hope. Maria and Zoot Mohammed helped with the packing and Terence Finley provided the transport. She knew that accommodation was difficult to find but a friend lent her a small house on a very temporary basis as he was intending to sell it. She hoped that he would let her stay there for a few months. Howard, proudly equipped with a new pair of shoes, started school on 30 January. He was relieved to be among playmates again.

Much had happened at Swaneng since Bessie had last been in Serowe. Students and staff at the school had worked regularly during weekends and holidays to help construct the classrooms and laboratories needed. But their community service did not end here. They had also built extra classrooms for local primary schools and during holiday work-camps had helped construct the

Shashe River School, based on the same cost-covering secondary-school principles as Swaneng school. As well as this, they travelled to Molepolole, 350 kilometres away, to build classrooms there.[23]

The Brigade movement had expanded considerably. In 1965 the Builders' Brigade had been established and proved very successful. With a programme consisting of four days in production and one day at school learning English, mathematics and the theory of building, the young trainees were getting enough contracts to cover their costs. In 1967 nineteen out of an original class of forty passed their trade test.[24] Similar trainings in other trades, which could provide further options and thus further opportunities for young people, were now also needed.

The Farmers' Brigade started next, taking in a huge new area of land and establishing itself with sheds, farm buildings and houses for the instructors. As well as this, Textile, Carpenters' and Mechanical Trades Brigades were also launched. Teachers taught both at the school and in the Brigades. Together Swaneng School's secondary education and the vocational model of the Brigades provided a comprehensive educational system encompassing a large number of skills. Swaneng Complex, as it now became known, had a large staff of volunteer teachers and though there tended to be a rapid turnover, many dedicated and talented people attached themselves to the school for long periods of time and helped shape its future. The villagers and others further afield watched with a mixture of admiration and scepticism as the 'brightly-shirted hirsute young men' pursued 'their somewhat pink ideas with aggressive enthusiasm',[25] as an Establishment principal once put it to Vernon Gibberd, now settled in Serowe and deeply involved in the Farmers' Brigade.

There were many people with whom Bessie had much in common. The only trouble was that Swaneng Hill was eight kilometres away from the centre of the village where Bessie was living. There was no bus system but there were some private taxis, which packed their vehicles and cruised around on established routes, and this is how Howard got to school.

In the village itself there were also many new developments. A shopping area, very grandly named the Mall, had been laid out, further down the main road from the *kgotla*, thus shifting the centre of gravity of the village. A new post office was being erected here; several of the well-established trading stores were already in the same area, as was the consumers' cooperative built a few years before as part of the Swaneng project. In time two banks and a butchery appeared. And a number of other retail stores and general dealers were established on the edges of the Mall, while vendors selling a variety of things from vegetables to clothing settled down outside the stores.

There was only one disadvantage with the new precinct. The dried-out bed of a stream formed part of the wide expanse of open ground around which the buildings were clustered. During the usual drought, the whole area was dry and stony, the cinnamon-coloured powdery soil swirling up in little dust-devils or sweeping across it in gusts of sand. Such were the contrasts of the place, however, that torrential rain could transform the Mall into a fierce stream of water. Then shoppers needed to take off their shoes and wade across from one set of shops to the other.[26] Eventually a culvert was built to channel the stormwater and a footbridge erected over it. But almost a decade was to elapse before this happened.

Another ambitious building activity was later begun on a raised outcrop of rock which was part of Serowe Hill, close to the Mall. Just as the new consumers' and marketing cooperatives were breaking the monopoly of the retail and cattle traders, so plans were being made under Patrick van Rensburg's guidance to establish a hotel. It was intended as a low-price alternative to the only other hotel in the village, the expensive Serowe Hotel, established some years before by an important South African brewery company. In providing beds at a reasonable rate, rather than rooms, it was to be more of a hostel than a hotel. The excellent quality of its food soon made it as much a valuable alternative eating-place for villagers as a hostelry for visitors. It was built in natural sandstone in modules: a dining room, a kitchen, individual rooms with three to four beds, and an ablution block. As more accommodation was needed, further buildings went up, spread out on the slope of the hill and connected by pathways. From the terrace in front of the dining room visitors could enjoy a view of the village. It was the good turnover from the cooperative store that financed the building of the Tshwaragano Hotel, as it was called, and it too was run as a cooperative.

Returning to Serowe proved every bit as difficult as Bessie had feared. She had the feeling that everyone was watching her and talking about her behind her back. Several people asked her what had happened to the child she had given birth to in Francistown. A shopkeeper refused to serve her when she asked for some cheese in a perfectly normal voice, because she was not treating them 'with respect'.[27] Her most humiliating experience was having a young man urinate in her direction, outside her own door. 'The gesture was the abyss of male filth but that young man did not think so. He stood there laughing insolently in my face ... I learned to see evil face to face and it is something I will never forget. It hurt me very badly,' she wrote ten years later, on one of the very few occasions she ever mentioned this incident.[28] Gradually she began to understand what people were gossiping about. She had no visible source of income but, because she was still receiving money from the United Nations for her course in tropical agriculture as well as her refugee dole, there she was with money to buy food. Rumour had it that she was being supported by some lover who visited her secretly. He was presumably father to the child she was supposed to have given birth to after leaving Serowe two years earlier. This child she had murdered and thrown down a pit toilet. As the extent of the gossip and its spiteful nature became known to her, she was crushed. Such actions as getting rid of a baby horrified her; they were 'far removed'[29] from her own life. And no one would be able to produce the lover because there was not one – 'not one of them is ever going to see my sex organs'.[30]

Gone were all her noble plans to love Botswana and the Batswana even if they hated her. 'There is not one sane person in this village ... my mind is distracted with intense dislike for the people of this country. I am beginning to really loathe them,'[31] she now wrote to Randolph Vigne.

Shortly after she moved into the house, it was sold. The new owner was not interested in helping Bessie. He demanded that she vacate the place immediately but she refused. She had absolutely nowhere to go and she was determined to make it as difficult as possible for the new owner, David Maganu, to evict her. On 13 March she was taken to court. She lost the case and was ordered to vacate the house forthwith.[32]

Bessie was not cowed. She asked the Van Rensburgs to take care of Howard for some days. While he moved in with them, she demonstrably camped out with her belongings in the yard outside the house. She was only there a few days. The Council Secretary, Lenyeletse Seretse, came to her rescue. There was a small hut empty in the middle of the village near the *kgotla* and Bessie was allowed to rent this.

Terence Finley was in Serowe on business shortly after this incident. He was shaken by Bessie's behaviour. He spent all his time trying to find niches for the refugees, some way that they could be absorbed into Botswana society and begin to live meaningful lives again, and he knew how important it was not to provoke the authorities. Bessie now seemed to be jeopardising all her chances of starting a new life. Compared with many, she was fortunate in getting away from Francistown and finding a better school environment for Howard. Not only did he tell her all this, he wrote to her soon afterwards repeating what he had said. He stressed that the onus was on her not to spoil her chances of being issued with a residence permit, even if provoked, and to consider her long-term future and that of Howard.[33] Without a residence permit, there was every possibility of a refugee's being moved to an entirely different part of the country if he or she gave trouble.

With Terence Finley, whom she admired and respected, taking such a firm stand with her, Bessie must have realised that she needed to be careful. However, she was in such a nervous state by this time that she could no longer act with caution or indeed with rationality. She was suffering from severe insomnia, a condition that was to become chronic in later years. Her head ached. Words like 'Dog, filth, Bushman dog' churned round in it, like some gramophone record stuck in a groove. And more than this self-hatred, a violent dislike for all black people filled her. 'I sometimes can't look at the face of a black man or woman without at the same time thinking that they are the epitome of all that is grasping, greedy, cruel, back stabbing and a betrayal of all that is good in mankind.'[34] A whirring and hissing noise accompanied all her confused thoughts.

In late March, when the Easter holidays had just begun, she took Howard with her and went shopping. Her night had been plagued by nightmares. She was confused and hysterical. After buying a transistor radio for which she had little use, she had to go into the office at the back of the shop to have it registered for a licence. As she looked at the three men in the office she could only think how much she disliked them, how much she disliked all Africans, their hair, their noses ... Suddenly she began trembling and broke out in a cold sweat. 'You bloody bastards,'[35] she shouted.

Then she started to scream. High-pitched and never-ending. People rushed to prevent her murdering someone. As they grabbed hold of her roughly, they realised that she was bathed in perspiration and shaking like a leaf. The police bustled in officiously, but everyone agreed that what they needed was an ambulance. Howard stood regarding his mother with large, speculative eyes. There was no doubt about it, she was not her usual self, had not been ever since she had cried hysterically at home because he would not eat his porridge. He crouched down and began to play with his car. Someone took him over to the Van Rensburgs and he moved in there again. The Gibberds also helped care for him.

Bessie was admitted to hospital in a serious state. She was drugged and slept for fifteen hours. The screaming, the hospitalisation, the chance to sleep, but most of all the verbalising of her forbidden inmost thoughts had had a cathartic effect on her. She overcame her hatred. 'Once I said I hate the black man, it just passed from my mind the same as it is difficult, after writing all those blood curdling items on the white man to remember what it is I hate him for. It gets lost once you spit it out.'[36] Thus it was that she made a surprising recovery, and with the hospital staff still fearing that she was close to death, she woke up bright and cheerful and determined to go home.

Bessie's breakdown brought a change in her life in Serowe. In a most dramatic way she had shown the villagers that she was crazy. The doctor and hospital had endorsed it. It was much more forgivable to be a crazy woman than a loose-living one. Crazy people were allowed to move around unobstructed. They were a part of the village scene. If not accepted, Bessie was now tolerated. The gossip subsided. About this time she had a dream in which she heard a group of black people discussing her. They said that this time she had exploded of her own accord; no one had been harming her. One of them suggested that she needed treatment but another thought that this was not necessary. All she needed was for someone to put Vaseline on her behind and then throw her out of the window![37] Though she awoke terrified, her interpretation later is interesting: she felt that the people talking were ashamed of themselves for having caused her trouble and she seemed to accept their 'apology'.

Yet a hard core of disillusionment gradually led Bessie to believe that she had been just as much the victim of racial prejudice as her son. 'Perhaps I did not realise how much, what is known as a mixed breed, is really deeply hated by African people,'[38] she confessed to Randolph Vigne. Some months later she said that 'everything went wrong from the time Howard was assaulted. I never seemed to recover and the nightmare was so persistent and inward-turning, in my own mind that nothing seems to wash away the horror of this racial business.'[39]

Not only had she railed against black people; she had also railed against God. In a letter to Randolph Vigne about six weeks after she came out of hospital, she said that 'something has died in me ... maybe God is just as evil and malicious as these people and long planned my destruction. Only he was waiting until I was finally broken, like now.'[40] An even more disturbing dream where she heard someone crying 'in a terrible voice' and where she searched anxiously for the person, while a white woman of the idealistic type she admired pursed her mouth in disapproval, led her to assume that it was God who was crying because she had called him 'malicious'. She asked Vigne, in case he was 'managing some of the affairs of God', to 'put matters right for me'. In these ways she tried to pull herself out of her nervous breakdown.

On 11 March 1969, about the same time as these events, the first hardback edition of *When Rain Clouds Gather* was officially published in New York. The book sold well and Simon & Schuster soon brought out another hardback edition. Meanwhile it appeared in London, published by Gollancz, on 15 May 1969.

The reviews began to stream in. They were very encouraging. The *Times Literary Supplement* called it an 'intelligent and moving novel'.[41] The *New Statesman*, however, found its 'naked sociological commentary' overdone: 'There is too much undiluted sociological and agricultural textbook language, but the book is justified by loving and humorous descriptions of African land and people, by powerful, generous feeling and passionate analysis of the position of the black African.'[42] The only review Bessie liked was one which appeared in the *Illustrated London News*. Dominic Le Foe said: 'Her book is not only a fine literary performance, it is a remarkable service performed for her race. Its publication may well be remembered as a moment of significance in the evolution of modern Africa and her relationship with the rest of the world. It deserves that distinction.'[43] She thought that most critics misread the book, 'each according to his particular prejudice'.[44] One comment must have amused her: '*When Rain Clouds Gather* represents the only serious imaginative writing in English on Botswana – I discount the sentimental effusions of Naomi Mitchison . . . '[45]

When Rain Clouds Gather opened up new horizons for Bessie. In 1969 she made three important new friends. In fact they were pen-friends, though the description hardly covers the intensity and extent of some of the correspondence they exchanged any more than it covers Randolph Vigne's written form of persistent encouragement and support for Bessie through thick and thin. The first was Giles Gordon, her editor at Gollancz. He was a Scot with writing ambitions of his own, who took on Bessie's professional development and often her personal concerns. The second friend was an American, Tom Carvlin, a news editor at the *Chicago Tribune* and father of eight children. When 'The Woman from America', after appearing in *Classic*, the South African quarterly in 1968, was reprinted in an American journal called *Atlas*, in March 1969, Tom Carvlin and his wife, committed Christians intent on doing their share to lessen the gap between the 'haves' and the 'have-nots' of our world[46] read it. They were inspired by the story and responded instantly by writing to the address given. The third new friend was the freelance journalist and writer, Paddy Kitchen, living in London. She wrote a review of *When Rain Clouds Gather*[47] for a London periodical and then contacted Bessie to ask her whether she could conduct an interview by post with her for the *Times Educational Supplement*. While Tom Carvlin and Bessie soon got on to discussing theological questions, Bessie and Paddy Kitchen found they had a common interest in gardening, and sons of about the same age. Tom Carvlin was soon sending her money to support her projects and Paddy Kitchen was sending her books. They took her problems very seriously, trying to help and encourage her in whatever way they could. Wendy Cullinan also contacted Bessie after the novel appeared to thank her for dedicating it to them. 'I very much like the way in which the racial politics are integrated into, and thus become just another aspect of, the ordinary day to day domestic politics,'[48] she wrote. After that, the Cullinans seemed to glide out of her life for some years.

American philanthropy also spilled over onto Bessie's friends. Through Terence Finley, Bessie was able to put a friend of Tom Carvlin's, Betty Ulrich, in touch with Zoot and Maria Mohammed. 'I . . . leave it to the two to feed each other's souls. Because love and help must never be a one-sided affair. I have several times observed how Mr Mohammed and his wife fed my soul and their capacity for friendship and loyalty and many other things,'[49] Bessie wrote. Betty Ulrich was anxious to give the Mohammeds some support, financial as well as moral.

Bessie was in close touch with Terence Finley (who was hospitalised in Serowe around this time, and read his presentation copy of *Rain Clouds* while there) and corresponded frequently with the Mohammeds, which helped her to keep a firm grip on everyday life. Zoot Mohammed kept her informed about Spot. He proved a lively addition to their household, though his fondness for meat was an expensive habit. When Bessie wrote to the family, he would smell that the letter was from her, and become so excited that Zoot Mohammed would have to tell him to quieten down. 'After all, old fellow, I went to school not you so give me a chance to read it.' Then Spot would growl as if to say, 'Okay, but make it quick and tell me what she says.'[50]

Borne on a wave of encouragement and sympathy and released temporarily from destructive obsessions, Bessie suddenly found herself bursting with creativity. An editor from Simon & Schuster's department for children's books, Ann Stephenson, had asked her if she could write a book for young people in the *Catcher in the Rye* tradition. Bessie doubted whether she could consciously do that. Just as she had earlier written about wanting to be able to 'take off as me' in a novel and wanting 'a kind of ocean roar all the time'[51] while she was writing, she here once more stressed the importance of a creative state that is intuitive rather than planned. 'For one thing', she said, 'I write best if I can hear the thunder behind my ears.'[52] Nevertheless, in June she promised to write a short novel, something half the length of *Rain Clouds*, as she seemed to have got bogged down with the plans for her second book.

Because she and Howard had felt the full effects of racial prejudice, she had been sent to her 'roots and sources', as she put it. Suddenly things began to fit into patterns in her mind; the ocean roared, the thunder echoed. Without relying on rough drafts, she sat down at the typewriter and began on a new novel. It was as if the book were 'writing itself'.[53] It was to deal with racial prejudice. She called it *Maru, maru* being a Setswana word meaning 'clouds', 'the weather' or, in a figurative usage, the elements.

While writing *Rain Clouds* Bessie had begun a correspondence which developed along unexpected lines:

I owe all my information of the oppression of the Masarwa or Bushmen people to an English Agricultural officer named George Macpherson. I first wrote to him for some agricultural information about a remote area of Botswana, but instead two little Masarwa named Leshelwa and Tshebe dominated the correspondence we had for almost a year. More than that, he came as close as anyone will ever get, in humanity and affection, for one of the most downtrodden and despised of all black people. I absorbed from him, then just as if destiny slapped me in the face, my son started school and during the mid-year was assaulted on the grounds of his looking like a Masarwa or Bushman. Hence the material for *Maru*.[54]

She later acknowledged her indebtedness to this 'terrific white man with a heart the shape of the universe itself,[55] dedicating her new novel to 'George Macpherson, Leshelwa, Tshebe and my son'.[56]

Bessie worked at full pressure throughout the next three months though her accommodation could hardly be called sumptuous. She told David Machin that her house in Francistown 'was a palace compared to what I have here'. She described her mud hut as being a small circular room in which she had to cook, wash and eat. 'There is no space to spread out my files, notes and working materials without their becoming covered with layers and layers of dust. Many insects also make their abode in the grass thatching and calmly submit their droppings all over the place.'[57]

Inquisitive goats would wander in and out as if they owned the place while she was typing. She had an old gramophone and her favourite record at the time was one by the South African singer, Miriam Makeba: 'I've written some smashing pieces by humming on a favourite love song. When writing *Maru* for instance I was mad about a number "When I've Passed On".'[58] The lyrics, written by Bill Salter, captured her imagination. The idea of not having any markings for a grave, of at some stage transcending the stress of living and standing stripped and free, which was expressed in the song, appealed to her. She said that she accepted it as her 'own rigid soul doctrine'. She thought that 'Makeba interprets it beautifully and I can only think that he [Bill Salter] must have been stirred by her own achievements to hand over such gems of soaring magnificence and abysmal humility.'[59] Later she told Wendy Cullinan that she 'ran the record right flat down to its groove and then put that classic rhythm and majesty into *Maru*'.[60]

When she was not listening to Miriam Makeba, she was reading Boris Pasternak. It was at about this time that she finally outgrew D H Lawrence and turned to Pasternak. She acquired a copy of *Doctor Zhivago*; also a thin volume of his poetry, probably Lydia Pasternak Slater's translation, *Poems by Boris Pasternak*, which appeared in 1958. She absorbed his lyrical descriptions of the changing seasons, the poignancy of his love poems and his increasingly outspoken condemnation of the communist regime. She told a friend in 1974 that she had read *Doctor Zhivago* 'solidly for five years' and she kept going back to it. 'He waited sixty years and then recorded the catastrophe, slowly, patiently, and damned, I'm afraid, communism, forever. People haven't found the perfect formula for life on this earth. I work at that too because I have suffered so much.'[61] Some years later she was to say that he had remained 'forever and a day . . . a steady light in my life'.[62]

By September she had completed her novel and sent it off, calling it a 'masterpiece, but certainly not for little children'.[63] It was turned down by Simon & Schuster, but Bessie had no time to feel disconsolate. David Machin, her agent, very enthusiastic about it himself, sent it to Gollancz and in November Giles

Gordon accepted it. She was proud of herself. 'They would not have done this had it not been damn, blasted good.'[64] For the second time running, a novel had been almost snatched out of her hands by a publisher. As yet, she did not realise what an achievement this was.

Many elements from Bessie's own life were incorporated into *Maru*. It had been easy for her to acknowledge the biographical influences in *Rain Clouds*, easily identifiable in the cooperative farming project under the auspices of the enterprising young Englishman. The generally positive interracial relationships portrayed there, however, are in no way a reflection of Bessie's own early experiences in Botswana. In *Maru* she rectifies this. It proves painful and unsettling but this is what she had meant when she said that her next novel 'was really going to be great – for my own sake, for my own life, for the struggles in me'. As a protest against racism, the novel has obviously grown directly out of Howard's experiences at school and the protracted and somewhat inexplicable hostility she had felt in Serowe. The incidents have been filtered, her own first shrill reactions tempered. This makes her message restrained, serious and moving.

Maru is the name of the paramount chief elect of an African people living in a remote village, Dilepe, in Botswana. A new teacher is sent there. Her name is Margaret Cadmore. She has a brilliant academic record and proves to be cultivated and quiet. Nonetheless her arrival causes extreme agitation. This is because she is a Masarwa. 'Masarwa' is the local term for 'Bushman' and, since independence increasingly recognised as a derogatory designation for the San people. From the first moment Maru sets eyes on Margaret, he makes up his mind to marry her; and he does. He renounces his high position for her sake and moves away with a few faithful friends to start a new life in complete obscurity.

Presented like this, *Maru* sounds like a romantic re-working of a western folktale. However, such a summary of the plot takes no account of the urgent social message, the complex inner conflicts, and the unresolved ambiguities which form the core of this unusual novel. Though it is apparently a love story which concludes with Maru marrying Margaret, it appears that she cannot return his love completely. She has fallen irrevocably in love with Moleka, Maru's best friend, and he with her. Nonetheless, Maru manipulates Moleka into marrying his sister Dikeledi.

And the love element is only one of the novel's contrapuntal themes. Sometimes the theme of racial prejudice seems all-pervading and *Maru* could appear to be a political statement. Sometimes it is the realm of *Maru's* strange gods, secret kingdoms and esoteric human relationships that dominates. And underpinning, linking and illuminating these are Bessie Head's views on human creativity.

Margaret Cadmore's strange background is described sparingly but vividly. Her appearance stamps her as an outcast. This she has inherited from her San mother who wore a filthy loose-hanging shift over her stick-thin legs, and died in childbirth on the outskirts of some distant village. The baby is destined to be spurned, by adults and children alike: 'They spat on you. They pinched you. They danced a wild jiggle, with tin cans rattling: "Bushman! Low Breed! Bastard!"'(pp. 10–11).

Margaret's education and rich inner resources come from her adoptive mother, the missionary, Margaret Cadmore senior. This woman's abundant energy and common sense, her irascibility and tendency to vituperative language, her hopes and genuine concern for her adopted daughter, provide Margaret with the ballast to face the inhuman treatment to which she is often subjected. She learns to take control of 'the only part of life' that is hers, 'her mind and soul' (p. 16), for nothing can 'un-Bushman her' (p. 18).

She accustoms herself to observe, from a vantage point, the behaviour of her persecutors. 'What did it really mean when another child walked up to her and, looking so angry, said: "You are just a Bushman"? In their minds it meant so much' (p. 17). She accustoms herself to keep silent, suppress emotion and accept the isolation and lack of human communication that is her lot even throughout the teacher-training course she does so well in.

Her self-respect remains intact. This is what causes the eruptions when she arrives in Dilepe. When people ask her whether she is a coloured, she replies 'I am a Masarwa.' She is unconcerned by the fact that Dilepe is 'the stronghold of some of the most powerful and wealthy chiefs in the country', all of whom own 'innumerable Masarwa as slaves' (p. 24).

Dikeledi, Moleka and Maru each give Margaret support in his or her own way. Through their combined efforts, she survives the intrigues of the headmaster to oust her. Maru's skilful use of 'witchcraft' amusingly sends him and his scoundrel friends packing. It remains for the villagers to come to terms with their prejudice: 'Something they liked as Africans to pretend themselves incapable of was being exposed to oppression and prejudice. They always knew it was there but no oppressor believes in his oppression' (p. 48) ... '"The eye is a deceitful thing," they said. "If a Masarwa combs his hair and wears modern dress, he looks just like a Coloured. There is no difference"' ... 'They were trying to accustom their hearts to their children being taught by a Masarwa. They said: "Prejudice is like the old skin of a snake. It has to be removed bit by bit"' (p. 53).

Margaret quietly accepts her role as outsider and settles down to enjoy the rhythm of sunrise and sunset in the village, having long reconciled herself to 'being permanently unwanted by society in general' (p. 94). Her calm equanimity provides in itself a powerful comment on racial discrimination.

Dikeledi finds it annoying. When one of the schoolchildren asks Margaret: 'Since when is a Bushy a teacher?', the room starts heaving for Margaret and the children's faces blank out. 'Why did you keep quiet?' Dikeledi asks after saving the situation. '"I was surprised," she replied, quietly. "They used to do it to me when I was a child but I never felt angry"'(p. 47).

Though Margaret does seem cowed and often instinctively raises her hand as if to ward off blows, Dikeledi recognises this as a device to hide 'another personality of great vigour and vitality ... You were never sure whether she was greater than you or inferior, because of this constant flux and interchange between her two images' (p. 71). Margaret's rich inner universe proves stronger than prejudice. Thus it is that the theme of personal relationships absorbs that of racialism. And in this world Maru reigns supreme.

In the prologue which serves as an epilogue and contains what one critic calls 'sealed orders',[65] we are already aware that Maru is a man who never doubts 'the voices of the gods in his heart' (p. 8); a man who acts out 'his own, strange inner perceptions independent of the praise or blame of men' (p. 6); who 'has a vision of a new world' that slowly allows 'one dream to dominate his life' (p. 7). He is a powerful force for good. All the visions and vivid imagery he is subjected to direct his footsteps 'along a straight road – that of eternal, deathless, gentle goodness' (p. 37). For Maru it is perfectly natural to read people's hearts and superhumanly manipulate their actions. He is able to tap dream images. He can project his dreams onto reality and thus make them real.

Despite extraordinary powers, he is still a human being with human weaknesses. He makes mistakes in his choice of mistresses though he falls genuinely in love with the women he chooses. He deplores the misuse of power yet seems responsible for causing the ill health and even insanity of these women, whom he says he has 'killed'. Furthermore he employs a network of spies to get his own way in everything.

Margaret Cadmore has a great untapped talent. She is an artist. Her drawings provide the faceless oppressed with human qualities. They open up her kingdom to Maru:

She chose her themes from ordinary, common happenings in the village as though those themes were the best expression of her own vitality. The women carried water buckets up and down the hill but the eye was thrown, almost by force, towards the powerful curve of a leg muscle, resilience in the back and neck, and the animated expressions and gestures of the water carriers as they stopped to gossip. They carried a message to his own heart: Look! Don't you see! We are the people who have the strength to build a new world! And his heart agreed (pp. 107–108).

This insight into the true worth of ordinary people complements Maru's ability to see and hear people's thoughts and deeds, 'even their bloodstreams and the beating of their hearts' (p. 7), an experience he sometimes finds sickening; and his meddling concern with the inner lives of the spiritually elite group who have 'kingdoms of their own'. Margaret's creative powers are translated into paintings. Maru's rich creativity is used to manipulate both those he loves and those he fears to ensure the coming of the new order. He creates situations. He stages the downfall of his rival to the last detail, though ensuring him a very satisfactory compensation in the shape of Dikeledi. All the same he shows again that he is not an omnipotent deity because he does fear that he may have misjudged Moleka. Dark shadows can mar his happiness with Margaret, as can her desperate tears when she dreams of a wounded and broken Moleka.

Yet by his act of marrying Margaret, Maru has identified himself with 'the many wrongs of mankind' (p. 8) and opened the dark, airless room in which the souls of the Masarwa have been imprisoned, to set them free.

The convincing way in which Bessie Head arranges her strange material is impressive. The villagers' treatment of Margaret is full of local colour and comic touches but its universal relevance is always clear. And the complicated interrelationships of people living on many more levels than the physical, which she describes so directly, could on one level be considered as African elements in the tale – witchcraft, hidden terrors of darkness, archaic remnants of a time before materialism triumphed – while on another they could relate to aspects of modern parapsychology, finding resonance among countless Westerners.

Her account of the younger Margaret Cadmore's childhood is also a lively tribute to two of her mothers. (She once conceded that she had had three mother figures – her biological mother, her foster mother, Nellie Heathcote, and her teacher, Margaret Cadmore, without any mothering.)[66] Her greatest heritage from her biological mother was her name. In *Maru* she recognises this while also paying official tribute to the most important influence of her girlhood, Margaret Cadmore of St Monica's, by combining her name with the namesake idea. Unfortunately Margaret Cadmore did not live to read it. However, one of the real Margaret's childhood friends contacted Bessie when *Maru* appeared, intrigued by the mention of her name.[67]

In *Maru* the tragic San woman is given special recognition. Margaret Cadmore treasures a sketch of her dead mother on which she writes: 'She looks like a Goddess' (p. 15). Bessie Head once said that she regarded her biological mother as a goddess: 'My mother is my private goddess. I alone adore her.'[68] And she also admits that her own 'complete mental identification' with the young Margaret stretches out to embrace 'an oppressed people'.[69]

Throughout the novel Bessie refers to these people as either the 'Bushmen' or the 'Basarwa'. Some years later she was to explain that 'that word Sarwa is very suspect. It's an offensive word and sticks in my throat as does Bushman. I suspect that they were refugees of the Mfecane and lost all their cattle. Or they had no property and bonded themselves to the Batswana for a livelihood.'[70] As she was to discover when she began her historical research, the San people were not direct victims of the Mfecane, not being herdsmen but hunters, later attached to Tswana tribes as bond-slaves. When Khama III became chief he found both Bushmen and Sarwa in the tribe. Though Bessie had heard that he gave them the right to own property, the question of whether he liberated them from serfdom is still open to dispute. If he did, it proved to be only a temporary measure because they became a subjugated people again.

There is a postscript to this aspect of the novel. A young American anthropologist, Megan Biesele, found *Maru* so inspiring that she spent years living with a group of San people in one of the desert regions of the country. When she had learnt their language, she read to them, chapter by chapter. They responded by making Bessie a necklace of shells, seeds and grass straws and sending it to her with their thanks for what she had written. She was very touched by this gesture but unfortunately the necklace was later lost.[71]

The romantic element in *Maru* has interested many critics and one at least has referred to its 'King Cophetua-like plot'.[72] Bessie had no need to go so far afield to seek her inspiration. Had she not in her own village a handsome young chief-elect who had suffered banishment and all manner of indignities because he had married someone whom society could not accept – a young English girl? It is a brilliant twist to give the story an even more exaggerated racial dimension. And of course to give herself the heroine's role. It is undoubtedly Seretse Khama and his childhood friend, Lenyeletse Seretse, who inspired the characters of the two young men. Seretse's sister, Naledi, who went into exile with her brother and his family and returned a qualified nurse, would have been an inspiring model for the 'drastic revolutionary', Dikeledi, the first wealthy woman in the area to put her education 'to useful purpose' (p. 25). She later married Lenyeletse Seretse. Margaret's teaching experiences can also be seen as a romanticised version of Bessie's own. Here she makes use of some comic touches to turn the tables on her real-life persecutors.

Then there is the question of names. Giles Gordon had suggested that the title was too foreign an element for a British or American reading public. Furthermore, so many names beginning with 'M' was confusing. He had asked whether some could be changed. Bessie would not hear of it. All the names, she insisted, had been carefully chosen and could not be changed: 'Moleka', pronounced 'Moleeka', means 'close companion' or 'playmate' and 'is a very common and tender address here. I do not write only for white people!!'[73] 'Margaret Cadmore' was her 'tribute' to the memory of her teacher, whom she imagined to be dead. But most of all, 'Maru, pronounced "M-a-r-u" with no stress anywhere'[74] and the nearest Setswana equivalent to the black brooding storm she depicts in the opening lines of the novel, had to be kept as the name of her male hero. 'God help me, it would kill me to change the title . . . the whole goddam book is Maru and he is a giant.' She pointed out how Maru, like Makhaya from *When Rain Clouds Gather*, was a combination of 'feminine sensitivity and borrowed maleness . . . The endless, outer, caressing snapshots are a trick to direct the eye of the reader inwards.'[75]

The strange personality of Maru is in many ways an extension and elaboration of Makhaya. Bessie looks again at the somewhat incomprehensible view of God she aired in *When Rain Clouds Gather*. In *Maru* Makhaya's statement, 'sometimes I think I am God'[76] is examined. Maru is a human being with superior moral values and highly developed intuitive and perceptive powers, in Bessie Head's terminology a god – 'by gods I mean people who are humble, unpretentious and who, when presented with those two roads, prefer the good'.[77] Both Maru and Moleka consciously choose new roads and both are clearly 'gods' but the distinctions in the soul values of Moleka and Maru and Maru's own fallibility are tentative attempts at showing that people are not 'two-dimensional – they are universes, stars and suns and planets and energy'.[78] The references to power, and its destructive misuse, are interesting in this connection.

D H Lawrence, like Bessie, found no contradiction in referring both to God and to his 'gods' and may quite possibly have inspired some of the phraseology in *Maru*. The realm of his 'dark gods' was never an area Bessie ventured into, but a sentence like 'They did not bother to greet one another because their bloodstreams were one' (p. 50), repeated six pages later as 'They did not greet one another. Their bloodstreams were one' (p. 56), has a distinctly Lawrentian ring. When Bessie had spoken earlier about wanting to 'catch hold of God for Africa', she added that she wanted 'this God to be something like D H Lawrence imagined him, loving women. And taking into account that machinery, agriculture, progress go hand in hand with spiritual knowledge.' More significant was perhaps the fact that reading Lawrence's highly autobiographical works, where he fearlessly tries to capture the flux of the inner life and the confusing imbroglio of human relationships, had given Bessie the courage to treat her very different set of human circumstances in a similar way. A leading critic once placed Lawrence in line with William Blake by calling him a 'poet without a mask'.[79] Bessie was on the way to becoming a writer without a mask.

Above: *Bessie's second house in Serowe, with Mma-Jennings in front*

Below: *Swaneng Hill School, Serowe*

Putting Down Roots, 1970

A Question of Power

In August 1969 Terence Finley left Botswana for Zambia and thereafter for England, a rather abrupt conclusion to his period in Africa. Bessie in Serowe, like the other refugees in Francistown, missed him. He had worked hard for all of them and had at least one minor triumph to his credit: in February 1969 he had organised the airlift of 25 Namibians (belonging to the liberation organisation SWAPO) from Francistown to Nkumbi College in Zambia. He had chartered a plane with UN aid from Lusaka, negotiated the complicated red tape involved and finally encouraged, goaded and pushed his refugee friends on board the aircraft in Francistown. One, a huge stolid Namibian they called the General, could hardly be persuaded to leave the camp which had become his home. Bessie was later to use his nickname, though not his personality, in a short story she wrote.[1]

At the farewell party that the refugees gave Terence Finley in Francistown, they expressed their appreciation of his steady concern for their lives. A year later he wrote to them all, a pastoral letter to his little flock, reminding them that in the final instance it was only they themselves who could resolve their lives and bring about the changes necessary for all of them.[2]

With Terence Finley gone, Bessie relied even more on her 'pen-friends'. Her correspondence, especially with Paddy Kitchen, Tom Carvlin and Randolph Vigne, was lively and prolific. Nor did she have any doubts about her own gifts in this direction: 'Forgive the vanity, but few people equal my letter-writing ability!!'[3] In a semi-humorous vein, she began to build up a family for herself. Randolph Vigne had long been designated the father. She was constantly reminding him of this and sometimes quoting her version of his homilies to her: 'Don't be bigoted. Don't swear at God . . . Don't show off. Keep your mouth shut while important people are talking. Have a social conscience . . . When have your efforts to make me respectable EVER succeeded?'[4] Randolph Vigne was not enamoured of the designation, being only ten years older than Bessie, but she said that he would simply have to put up with being her imaginary father – there was no one else suited for the job.[5] Later she told him that if he should by chance 'turn up as my real father next time . . . encourage me to study biology . . . You're sure to recognise me, in the household, for creating tempests.'[6] She once paid him a compliment which, considering Bessie's views on that subject, is worth reflecting on: 'Next to God', she wrote, 'you are my favourite person.'[7] Tom Carvlin and his wife were given the titles of 'grandfather' and 'grandmother', though they were not often used.

In a more serious vein, she told Randolph Vigne that family mattered less to her than friends. She wondered how

such sanity asserted itself, considering what we were faced with in SA . . . I hardly think one's greatest loves are to be found firstly in a family circle and certainly not in colour compartments. To have the time and the place to choose great friendships seems to me, the nearest thing to heaven on earth. There is something about some people (I found a handful) that makes you say: 'They are eternal in my life,' . . . any kind of betrayal of those affections seems to me the end of the world itself, so great an ideal to me is the word: Friend. I also meant that you belonged among the elect.[8]

This ideal state was not one she always lived up to. In fact she would terminate a number of friendships abruptly and arbitrarily through the years.

Jean Highland had left Simon & Schuster and moved to Bantam Books as an editor. At her suggestion, this important publishing house bought the paperback rights to *When Rain Clouds Gather*. For Bessie this meant £1000 from an unexpected source. Her dream of leaving her cramped one-room shed and getting a small house of her own suddenly lay within reach.

Patrick van Rensburg was once more consulted. Once again he came to the rescue. There was a small plot of land adjoining the land he had been allocated for his Swaneng Hill School project. He began negotiations with the tribal authorities to try and have it transferred to Bessie. He offered the help of the Builders' Brigade to build a small house for which she could pay cash.

In October the grant of land was arranged and building could begin. The house was to consist of two bedrooms, a toilet, bathroom and kitchen. It would cost about £700. *The house is minute but the pride is overwhelming. It is the first brick thing I shall ever own. The cause of the bedlam is that I keep on getting under the feet of the builders to see how the bricks go up,*[9] she wrote. She enjoyed observing the calm way the Motswana instructor taught the young students the necessary skills as they worked on the house. 'Change that to a continuous join,' he would quietly call out. 'Very little talk, only work and a murmured correction now and then.' In contrast, the shrill voice of the Danish instructor working with the students at the Farmers' Brigade would shatter the calm atmosphere with disparaging comments: 'They don't know anything. They are so lazy. Phenyo, don't leave the manure on top of the garden bed. The nitrogen evaporates.'[10]

November brought the excitement of moving into the house. There were not many possessions: two beds, a table and two chairs for the kitchen, and a writing desk and bookcase for Bessie's room. There was no electricity. She continued to write by candlelight, but now she had gas rings fed by a portable cylinder installed in the kitchen. This was a luxury, as was the running water. Not for sixteen years was she to own a refrigerator, despite the heat of the country. She never owned a telephone. Emergency calls had to be made from the post office, Swaneng Hill

School or the Farmers' Brigade. The house was to be called 'Rain Clouds', and the name, on a carved nameplate, was displayed on the door.

About the time Bessie moved into her new house, Patrick van Rensburg started another alternative rural development project. At an early stage Bessie became involved. It was intended to involve a new group of people, the poor, unemployed adults, giving training as well as employment to people who needed both. The project was named Boiteko, 'self-help'. A group of about one hundred self-employed producers was established, whose aim was to exchange products through an internal bartering system whereby no one earned a wage, yet everyone's needs were met; and with it a variety of sub-groups: spinning, weaving, gardening, tanning and leatherwork, pottery, brewing, building, brickmaking, carpentry and thatching. Once more several hectares of land in Serowe's Newtown ward near Swaneng were allotted by the tribal authorities. The members of Boiteko were to fence the area, build the necessary workshops for each group and establish what was to be the organising centre, the cooperative store.

Bessie became the instructor of the gardening group. She had valuable gardening knowledge to pass on: how to plant in deep trench beds with sixty centimetres of loose, cultivated and manured soil with which to work; how to grow seedlings in plastic bags to avoid damaging roots during the critical transplanting process, when the high evaporation rate in the dry climate usually claims many small plants; how to irrigate effectively. Some she had learnt at Radisele and some from her course on tropical agriculture, completed a few months earlier.

She started off with much enthusiasm. The first essential was to fence the garden area and this was very hard work. The ground was dry and stony and the fencing had to be solid and effective to keep goats and cattle out. The gardeners were almost all women. The weather was very hot and support from the other members waned. Often Bessie and one other member, Bosele Sianana, worked on alone. Bosele was quiet by nature. She spoke very little English and Bessie did not speak Setswana but they established some emotional link all the same and worked away side by side in silence, each anticipating the other's needs.

Bosele Sianana was struggling to understand English, absorbing it silently and then coming out with an unexpected sentence or two. Bessie was her language teacher as well as her agricultural adviser and she was to become one of Bessie's most loyal and long-suffering friends. Later Bessie described the progress like this:

Then the fence came out of it. And today long, neat rows of vegetable beds. Somewhere between the fence and the vegetable beds I was entirely swamped by the internal storm. But today I look at the garden almost as an evolution in the relationship between the woman and I . . . Something remained of the early effort; the pioneer struggle.[11]

Bessie's long friendship with Bosele Sianana was unique in another way: it was her only true companionship among the local villagers. Other than Bosele, Bessie's Serowe friends were almost always either South African exiles like herself or white expatriate volunteers.

Within months Bessie was engaging Tom Carvlin's support. He started sending her seeds, though at first he had difficulty in finding what she wanted. In reply he received highly entertaining and informative letters on the progress of the garden.

Bessie described the scene when the ladies in her group heard that she had received seeds from America. First 'Miss Bosele' arrived. Bessie told her that she had received seeds from America. Bosele was the silent type; she took the packet, examined it, smiled and made no further comment. But as soon as 'old Mrs Snow' shuffled up, she said: 'Mma-Heady has got seeds from America.' (Mma-Heady means 'The mother of the boy called Head'.) As the long-legged Mrs Tshitego swung gaily up to the group, she got the same information. She burst out laughing. She did that often. And the loud and critical Annah K was also told. She raised imposing eyebrows. Considered the matter in silence. Then delivered the terrible judgement: 'We are not clever enough to write letters to America.' Bessie squirmed, 'not knowing how to interpret this, most of all because all the jab, jab that was going on was in Setswana, with so much "Mma-Heady" flung around.'[12]

She also told Tom Carvlin about her seedlings; how a certain type of cabbage germinated in three days and grew nearly five inches in the first month. Her transplanting method was so good that she could guarantee the survival of every single cabbage. They were also growing sweet peppers and experimenting with broccoli. And Bessie was very enthusiastic about the Cape gooseberry, which had adapted very well to conditions in Botswana and which she was planning to use for jam-making. The Carvlins continued to send seeds and money to help the gardening project while Bessie was engaged with it.

About this time Bessie made another new friend. Tom Holzinger was a young American draft-resister who had moved to Serowe in 1967. Having read *When Rain Clouds Gather* and being inspired by it, he sought Bessie out when she arrived in Serowe and was something of a match for her in ideas and enthusiasm. Perhaps there was some physical attraction as well, but she gave the friendship a platonic direction by pointing out that she was nearly ten years older than him and calling him her son. '"My son,"' she said, '"will you take care of me?" So he said, intensely: "Willingly."'[13]

Tom became important in Bessie's life when they were still struggling with the fencing. He was energetic and strong, and wasted no time in joining the work gang. His help was gratefully received. In fact Bessie was quite euphoric one evening. She knelt down and put her head on the ground where the fence had been erected. 'Thank you, God Tom,' she said. 'Oh, I have acquired the most beautiful son in the universe.'[14]

Gradually the various workshops and centres were erected. It was decided to build in natural stone from the Serowe hills, using local sand, lime and wooden supports, and erecting well-built permanent square or round buildings with thatched roofs, at very reasonable cost, provided everyone helped. The cooperative store was given priority and work vouchers, called *Dirufo*, meaning 'sharing', were printed. There were three values. A Boiteko was worth ten shillings, a Dirufo was worth one shilling and a Serufo was worth one penny.[15] Later this was altered to make a Serufo equal to six hours of work.[16] The plan was for the economy to be self-sufficient. Imports were not to exceed exports.

Bessie and Howard settled into their new home. She did not regard herself as a strict mother, but there were certain basic family rules. For example, she insisted that Howard take a bath every day. He was not really cooperative. This was not something his friends were subjected to. One day, after being newly washed and got ready for bed, he withdrew into her bedroom where things were very quiet. Curious, she went in to find him sitting on the mat, laboriously rubbing Vaseline all over himself. His Batswana friends did not bath in water. They used Vaseline to make their skins glow.[17] So Howard was getting the best of both worlds. His friends also took the oddities of his mother with equanimity, and one of them recalls how they accepted without question the fact that Howard seemed to be subjected to rules that were incomprehensible to them.[18]

The great joy for both mother and son was the evening bedtime story. Paddy Kitchen sent Howard a gift of several of the 'William' books by Richmal Crompton. Bessie was delighted. She embarked on *William the Bad*, having enjoyed every minute of the Pooh stories, as well as *Alice in Wonderland*. William had a special place in Bessie's heart: 'He's a GIANT among children.' She discovered that both she and Paddy had read every William book they could get in their childhood. 'Funny how we did all the SAME things!!' In a more serious vein, she discussed with her the problem of children's books on Africa.

They are produced by American and British publishers, with the rule in mind – children there want to know how children in Africa live. They are so dull, they stun the mind. The children go dutifully to school. Then they come home and dig the garden, herd the cattle, eat porridge from a wooden basin . . . no fun, no veering, reeling imagination in fun and mischief and adventure . . . The public there [in Europe] is drilled into caring about poverty . . . What I am trying to put over is that children are fascinating, anywhere and beautiful things can be written about them, for them, because they are as important as adults, perhaps even more.[19]

Bessie later told Paddy Kitchen about how their bedtime story was once interrupted by a violent thunderstorm. She had to shout out each word to be heard. She kept telling Howard that she couldn't hear what she was saying; he kept replying that he could hear perfectly well and just keep on reading. Suddenly there was a shout, 'Open the door, open the door.' It was a young volunteer from the Brewers' Brigade. He lived in a mud hut with no windows and he and a girlfriend wanted to come in and watch the storm from one of Bessie's windows, but they could not penetrate either the noise of the storm or the Bessie-and-Howard shouting match: 'I thought: "Phew, that lets me off the hook with that pest, Howard." We had a tea party and had to shout at each other to get heard above the roar of a magnificent storm.'[20]

Bessie was beginning to gain weight. She and Paddy Kitchen had a joke about Bessie's waistline and her age keeping pace: 'age 30 years old – waistline 30; 31 years old – waistline 31; 32 years old – waistline 32'. But when she turned 33 on 7 July 1970, she was exultant. 'Bang went the order this year! Age 33 – waistline 31½' There was a reason for this. She had acquired a bicycle. From then on it was her habit to cycle into town each day to see to her post. It gave her life an added zest. 'There's a blue sky overhead and little pathways and the wind in my hair. What a life! That's why the lady is a tramp.'[21]

In her most optimistic moods, she still hoped to find a new husband. She confided to Betty Ulrich that she would really like a daughter, so she would have someone to care for her when she got old 'because my son will be fixing all those mechanical things which I don't understand and I thought that a little girl might like to be a writer like me. Therefore I am looking for another husband just now.'[22] Bessie had her dreams but she was also a realist. So to Randolph Vigne she confessed, shortly afterwards, that she was 'unapproachable by any man. They are petrified by the rush of words as though it makes them impotent. Also I have a fearful aversion for men unless they are of good character. I nearly killed Harold and I could not endure such an experience again.'[23]

Some years later she was to admit ruefully that 'actual romantic longings tend to fall away as one gets older'. She did not miss the romance or even the physical companionship of a 'sunset walk'. But her mind missed something: 'It's a good collaborator. I miss some man who is my equal and with whom I could work and talk to and plan with. I've had such a shitty life that I kept on hoping that the last patch would be better.'[24] He never appeared.

Bessie often complained about her eyesight. As a child she had worn spectacles but seems to have abandoned them when she left school. But it was actually Randolph's handwriting that caused her distress. This was a standing joke between them. He often dashed off letters to her in the train, in what she called his illegible scrawl, and she repeatedly begged him to type his letters to her: 'Or do you really like your letters to go half-read? . . . One day you will have such top secret information to disclose and no one will understand.' She said that he would probably be the cause of her wearing glasses, which would certainly make her look noble and dignified 'but look at all I'm going to miss seeing – like handsome gents.'[25] In June 1970 she acquired bifocal spectacles, which was just as well as the 'Chinese special' he sent her at that time was 'hard to beat'.[26]

In early 1970 the Swaneng Hill Secondary School project began to cause Patrick van Rensburg a great deal of frustration. He was finding it a strain keeping the students involved in the practical activities connected with the building up and running of the school. Because there was so little secondary education available, Swaneng School and its untraditional methods was actually a second choice for many of its students; and the brigades would be a third choice.[27] Many were from wealthy homes and did not really relish the idea that students should also take on some of the menial work at the school. The senior ones especially became more and more reluctant to work. Despite the noble principles on which it was founded, Swaneng School was becoming an elitist educational centre and the distinctions between the Swaneng School students and those enrolled in the brigade programme were more marked. The Farmers' Brigade trainees, especially, had to work very hard to develop their farm and they resented the fact that the secondary school students did so little manual work in comparison. These students were often the most critical of the system, while every day reaping one of its important achievements: fresh food produced by the Farmers' Brigade trainees. Except by applying constant pressure on the students to help more, Van

Rensburg did not know how he could improve the situation. He made an unexpected move. Driven to a state of extreme exhaustion, he confronted all the discontented students with a list of his complaints. This was in the form of a 'big character poster' like those used in the Cultural Revolution then taking place in China and much admired in Serowe, which he put up in a classroom. His action was what he called 'a personal campaign against elitist students'.[28] He also resigned his post as headmaster of Swaneng School, from then on concentrating his attention on the Brigade movement. Another principal for Swaneng School had to be found.

This was a dramatic confrontation and the atmosphere at the school was electric. Bessie Head, knowing all those involved and living so close to the school herself, was drawn into events. Patrick van Rensburg was ill after the showdown and had to go away for some weeks to recuperate. That his ambitious project was now threatening his health worried Bessie very much. Tom Holzinger, also there at the time, sees Patrick van Rensburg's use of a poster as a possible source of inspiration for one of Bessie's most notorious actions some months later.

Though her letters were often still spiced with lively comment, Bessie's mental health was deteriorating once more. Sometimes she would be lying inert on her bed when Bosele came to fetch her to work in the garden. Bosele would look at her somewhat severely and ask whether she was coming to work. Bessie would mutter something about having the flu, drag herself up, and trudge off down the dusty road behind Bosele.[29] But after some hours of hard physical labour her mental problems often seemed more bearable. What is more, neither her gardening activities nor her variable health interfered with her writing.

Shortly after finishing *Maru*, she wrote a short piece for the *New African* entitled 'Makeba Music'. It seemed a fitting tribute after the way she had been absorbing Miriam Makeba's 'weaving, difficult rhythms'[30] while writing her novel, together with the last chapters of *Doctor Zhivago* and Pasternak's poems. This is when she began to discern a similarity between Pasternak's writing and Makeba's music.

That two unlike artists like Pasternak and Makeba eventually said the same, eternal, everlasting things to my heart, appears to me that they travelled a similar road where everything was a mass of pain, confusion, loss and human stupidity. They recorded it all with silent eyes, possessively keeping the beauty in their hearts to themselves.[31]

Bessie told Randolph Vigne how she had once been sent to interview Miriam Makeba when she worked as a reporter in Johannesburg. They were supposed to have lunch together, but Miriam regarded her with still, black eyes and refused to speak to her. Bessie had to go away again. Puzzled and annoyed, she asked a friend, 'What gives with that woman?' and he replied, 'She doesn't like coloureds.' For a while after that it cost her something of an effort to like Makeba's music: 'Then the feeling wore away. I would have lost a lot. That's half the reason why I don't like anyone shut up or turned down.'[32]

In the same number of the *New African*, Bessie also had a review of *African Religions and Philosophy* by J S Mbiti. She had taken an instant liking to the book. Mbiti's views of religion in Africa reinforced some of her own and gave her food for further thought. She is clearly in agreement with his 'wide and generous' view that takes in not only African people but the humble everywhere 'who shall, one day, unexpectedly, inherit the earth. It is hard to imagine a heaven where the Pope officiates, because so many people would have to be excluded, but it is easy to imagine a universe and a people instantly immersed in a religious way of life.'[33] She talks about a feeling of 'at-oneness with all living things' which is the basis of 'African traditional life', and a very original God there, quietly managing affairs 'behind the scenes', in what Mbiti calls a type of transfused religion. Bessie sees this as the thought process of a people rejected by others, lacking the means and education to find God 'in a posh place'. These people, and she includes herself, have to make do with whatever is at hand 'and if God is a subconscious process in our minds, he is perhaps that much more dignified and respected. He is not exclusive either.' Finally she points out the emphasis placed on the cooperative element in African life. This need for help and cooperation might also eventually include God, who might unashamedly admit 'that he is unable to manage the enormous job of being God all by himself. That old man So-and-So with no teeth, but a good heart, gave him a helping hand, so that it is just anybody's heaven, where each person can feel that he matters infinitely and is loved, infinitely.'[34]

In a work such as Mbiti's, Bessie found unexpected support for her own attempts at presenting the concept of God in more egalitarian terms than the traditional ones, by removing the hierarchical and authoritarian elements associated with the Christian and Jewish traditions, and rejecting God as the ultimate in (white) male authority. Though she was totally out of touch with the newly emerging feminist movement, her own original thought processes had brought her very close to the religious revolution that feminists in Western countries were advocating in the seventies.[35] Though Bessie would have hooted with laughter at the idea of re-translating the Bible to rid it of patriarchal language and the male experience, she was involved in a much more radical confrontation with organised religion. While her criticism encompassed forms of sexist discrimination, she also went beyond this. Her message was directed at all people and her doctrine was the doctrine of the Ordinary.

In 1967 she had written that a 'person is reduced to finding his own God, when he finds himself surrounded by SO MANY false gods. Now, because I treasure my God so much I had to broaden him out. I could not have him narrow-minded or bigoted.'[36] The idea of a poor man's God had been with her since she wrote *When Rain Clouds Gather*. In June 1969 she told Randolph Vigne she simply wanted

God in mankind instead of up in the sky. Put him inside a man and a man is obliged to live a noble life, where other people can depend on him to be truthful in his dealings. People brought up on Christianity think God has nothing to do with them . . . They just go on shitting up the world and feel no responsibility for their character or anything they do.[37]

About the same time that she reviewed *African Religions and Philosophy*, she wrote a short story entitled 'Jacob: The Story of a Faith-Healing Priest'. Of Jacob she said:

It was never quite clear to those who loved Prophet Jacob just who his God was. At times he would refer to him as Jesus. At times his God, in moments of inspiration, appeared to be the width and depth of his own suffering. This in turn he called the Voice which had come to him at all the turning points of his life, forcing him into strange and incomprehensible acts.[38]

More and more she seemed to feel that what made people gods was a sense of worship for all life, an inner joy. And this was a state that it was not easy for people in powerful positions to achieve.

If Man with his human frailties is God, then God is both good and evil. But this had never been a problem for Bessie:

The Hindus faced a broader concept of God than that presented by Christianity and had it [Hinduism] not absorbed me at one stage I might not have survived so long. They say: 'We know of a God of both good and evil, the saint struggling against the sinner until the saint dominates.'[39]

She could in no way accept the Christian doctrine of man becoming godlike through the forgiveness of sins:

I don't go along with any God who has the power to remove the sins of the world. I only accept that each soul is responsible for its own actions and that all souls, whether God or the devil walk the razor's edge ... that the pure and noble of today may be the demons of tomorrow. I throw the accent heavily on self-responsibility.[40]

In Bessie's system of thought, the spiritual strivings of ordinary people were elevated to the status of God. Similarly she regarded evil as a living force both inside and outside humanity. In the months after writing *Maru*, there was a growing tone of hysteria in her references to evil. In one of her early letters to Tom Carvlin, on whom she mainly tested these ideas, she wrote rather matter-of-factly that she had met the Devil. Evil, she said, is a force with a

propelling and almost eternal motion. To meet, in the flesh, a transmitter of this force is no joke. He's very similar to God, with his all-seeing eye and very attractive to weaker people because the power motive is THE thing with him ... His company is not play time. I took one look at him and ran as fast as my legs could carry me.[41]

She longed to be released from the 'overpowering malice and viciousness' which pursued her. 'It is that I hate, the eternal propelling motion of the evil I have seen, as though it is such a sweet, horrific sensation, evil, that it can never be entirely done away with.'[42] More and more it became clear that she was living in a world of visions or hallucinations, peopled by a host of characters who reappeared in new situations like actors in a long-drawn-out melodrama. Nor were they entirely imaginary; they were dream images of people in the village, people Bessie had encountered or knew slightly. More and more she saw herself combating evil, messing up the major demons' show 'before they could start a new hell run in Africa'. On Judgement Day she intended to get hold of some of these major demons and say, 'Look here, there's going to be no more nonsense from you.'[43] Clearly these experiences were not new. They had started shortly after she arrived in Botswana, intensifying during the time she was at Radisele. What was new was Bessie's detailed description of them.

She felt herself to be part of a soul drama, a new act of the eternal conflict between good and evil. She believed her strange birth and destiny to be part of a larger pattern of things. Behind everything she described was her underlying belief in reincarnation. In this life she was meeting up with spiritual giants who had been her friends or foes in previous incarnations. As an indication of the direction her thoughts were taking, she had sent a desperate letter to Jean Highland as early as June 1969 asking her to try and get her a copy of *The Gospel of Sri Ramakrishna*. This was sent back to her posthaste.[44] Ramakrishna was the founder of the Hindu sect to which Bessie had been attached in Durban about fifteen years earlier. One of his most important disciples, Vivekananda, was one of the first Oriental swamis to travel to Western countries to spread his gospel. A Ramakrishna–Vivekananda centre was established in New York, which Bessie obtained information about. At this time, too, she acquired a book entitled *The Master As I Saw Him*, describing a Western convert's life with her guru, Vivekananda.[45] Bessie believed herself to have been this swami in a previous incarnation and that she had also lived at other important points in history.

In 1968 she sent a short piece entitled 'Patterns, Pictures, Impressions'[46] to Jean Highland in which it became apparent that she also thought of herself as the biblical King David. Here she referred to a person whom she called Long Profile. He could, she said, make 'these abrupt breaks into my life on an entirely mental plane', and there was 'definite and easy communication' between them. Then there was another man, Gilbert, whose soul was suddenly round her ears 'like a violent wind'. Finally, she mentioned two other characters – a man named Deep Ridge and a woman named Dan. Bessie imagined herself very much in love with Deep Ridge, she later told Tom Carvlin. In fact the three of them – Dan, Bessie and Deep Ridge – were 'reliving a strange complicated drama'. Bessie believed that in a previous incarnation she had killed Deep Ridge's wife and her present experiences allowed her to pull out, look at and re-run 'a crime committed ages ago which backs up in a strange way, other parts of the drama'. She then explained: 'Not to mince matters, I was the David of the Bible, who slaughtered Uriah to get his wife Bathsheba. This Bathsheba turned up in the form of the man "Deep Ridge" and the present wife was the great old general Uriah.' She also described the way the other man, Long Profile, manipulated her, 'for his own horrific ends, the swine'.[47] 'Patterns, Pictures, Impressions' produced a concerned reaction from Jean Highland, not improved by the fact that early in 1970 Bessie sent her a closely-written three-page piece entitled 'Bothwell', the next version of the drama. It is the earliest comprehensive statement of Bessie's obsessional thinking. Now she believed herself to have been Mary Queen of Scots in a previous life, and that the drama between her, Bothwell and Elizabeth I was once more unfolding. In Botswana she had been re-united with Bothwell:

Everything else was there, the violent dominating energy, that rushing sound, the fearful power, the certainty with which he communicated with my soul: 'Ah, so it is you again! Ah, Comrade! I throw my soul into your soul with reckless speed. I trust you. I trust you.' . . . Those . . . words and all his responses were the result of centuries of endeavour between us, and it was the endeavour, the sheer uphill push, the endless deaths and disaster that made him such a sure and certain inhabitant of my soul.[48]

For some unclear reason the goodness of her soul was to be subjected to tremendous evil pressures this time round. Bothwell, now in the person of the man Gilbert, did not defend her as she had expected. Instead he 'bowed out early in the drama', unmanned by an 'effeminate slob' she called 'S', in the evil role that had previously been Elizabeth I's. Nonetheless she was totally loyal to her Bothwell/Gilbert soul-mate: 'For your sake, I do not care if they make me die a thousand more deaths because I cannot live in a world without your qualities of nobility, truthfulness, sacrifice and manly dignity.'

If she here resorted to clichés, there is a poignant intensity in the section where she describes the tortures 'S' inflicted on her: 'For two years he beamed a straight hell at me: "You are the dog of the Africans. You are filth." . . . I was allowed no rest night or day to live with my mixed breed appearance . . . I could not bear to look at myself in the mirror for real terror that I was some unnameable horror.'[49]

Such glimpses of her sense of sexual and racial inferiority are extremely disturbing and show the apparently light-hearted references she often made about her appearance in a new light: 'I am not photogenic, though in some of my other incarnations I used to be. This thought of the other prettier incarnations makes me very shy of having my face published,'[50] she wrote in early 1969. And when Randolph Vigne replied that she was young, attractive and brilliant, she was quite nonplussed: 'I read your letter . . . then I went to look at myself in the mirror, (a very rare event). I can't believe I am, as you say, young, attractive and brilliant . . . suddenly you say something so nice, quite out of touch with reality as one has to live it.'[51]

There were also a number of references to sexual profligacy and corruption in 'Bothwell'. She contrasted her 'beautiful' love with the way others think of love 'only with their sex organs'. She referred to 'S' and 'his dolls and prostitutes'. She talked about falling in love and only thinking that one's emotions were important. People 'don't stop to check up on their souls, whether their souls crawl with worms and how unpleasant it is to embrace evil. Such people simply force themselves on you: "You must go to bed with me because I want you."' She despised 'S' for his sexual behaviour, but at the end of the piece it was also apparent that she felt betrayed or let down:

I used to say he was my friend and other beautiful things – I said it for the times I had worked with him as a monk, because as a monk I knew that his standards were as rigid as my lover's. But I don't know this pervert and I am ashamed of the word 'friend' now. It is degraded.[52]

These three elements – the grandeur of her destiny, the inexplicable cruelty and evil of her torturer and her distaste for sexual corruption – constitute the main themes of all Bessie Head's writing on this subject prior to the publication of her third novel.

Although all these spiritual phenomena were completely real to Bessie, her mental confusion was not so great at this stage that she could not distinguish between the various levels on which she lived her life. She had no actual communication on a physical level with these people who made 'abrupt breaks' into her life 'on a mental plane'. The person who broke into her mind with his soul 'like a violent wind' around her ears appeared 'totally unaware of all the things he had so urgently communicated' to her. She seemed to undergo some sort of initiation, and she saw how her soul moved forward rapidly in revelations accompanied by 'fires and highly fearful physical sensations', yet as she survived this fire, she kept quite silent, 'proceeding with life quite normally'.[53] And she was wily enough never to reveal the exact names of the earthly forms of her spiritual mentors or antagonists to any of her correspondents. She might drop a clue here and there, as she did once when writing to Paddy: 'Sorry, a running battle is going on here with the devil. His name is S......'[54] (with six dots to indicate the number of letters in the word) followed by 'Satan' in parenthesis. But of course 'Satan' is only a five-letter word.

Nor did she ever go into any detail to Randolph about any of her visions. She knew his reaction and could suddenly become mockingly amusing in the midst of all her misery: 'The times I mentioned God to you, you wrote back very reproving letters. You said: "Your version of God addles my wits. Don't presume to lipread God. Be very careful not to swear at God . . . " and so on.'[55] All the same Randolph Vigne was given a mild reproach once because he did not treat what she wrote to him seriously enough. 'You ought to pay attention to a few things, though, especially my views on the universe. Some of them are prophecies. Or did you not know that I am a prophet of some kind, huh? My sense of humour might fool you into thinking that some of my most noble conclusions "addle your wits".'[56]

In 1974, after the publication of her third novel, she made one more attempt to describe these experiences in what to her seemed a logical sequence. This time she focused on the behaviour of the man she had called 'S' or Long Profile and mainly considered events relating to her physical or external reality. After she had been three months in Botswana, things, as she said, 'began to go wrong'.[57] She began to have visions of a monk who visited her. She called it 'a slowly unfolding story, that was twisting and turning this way and that'. But she did not say anything about it because she 'was absolutely sure something profound and meaningful was happening and that one day all would be clear' to her. This, she saw later, was her 'undoing'. Parallel with these visions ran a series of strange remarks from villagers she hardly knew, telling her that people were waiting for something important to happen, asking her whether she would like to be an important person, and saying that they shared a big secret. When she moved to Francistown the strange incident occurred of the distribution of the 'religious pictures'. It was as a result of these pictures, she later believed, that Howard was attacked while playing quietly in their own yard. Bessie, convinced that a momentous revelation was about to be made, for a while longer continued to live in a world in which she felt light constantly flooding into her mind. Then things changed. The visions became terrifying and perverted and she knew that she was being forced to view the source of all the evil in the world. At the same time, especially after her return to Serowe, she felt that people victimised her more and more.

Accompanying the increasing intensity of her descriptions of her spiritual experiences, came increasingly frequent references to bad health. She often said that her 'whole nervous system was shattered . . . Sudden and terrible headaches descend on me. I live on a huge assortment of tablets.' She said that the doctor was not able to help and Howard suffered as she was harsh and irritable. 'If I swallow a tranquilizer tablet 3 times a day he gets by without a good beating.'[58] A few months later she said: 'What a nightmare I have been through, as though I were being slowly choked to death. It's been going on the whole of 1969, and I nearly died during the last spell.' She added that Tom Carvlin wanted to 'scalp' anything that harmed her, 'but how do you scalp depression?'[59] Tom Holzinger, who visited her almost daily, trudging across the veld from his rondavel in Newtown ward nearby, insists that some of these references are exaggerations, the metaphors of a born writer, and do not accurately reflect her actual daily life at that time.[60]

About nine months after Bessie started on the gardening project she was 'thrown off': 'Village people did not want me, regardless of the fact that much was achieved . . . .You'd ask why? Then read *Maru*. To Africans I am a Bushman, filthy, tainted, half-breed.'[61]

So there it was again. This 'racial business'. That many of the clashes were clashes of personality, and not racial, is also part of the picture. Pat van Rensburg's comments on this occasion, as reported by Bessie, were: 'Trouble really revolves around you. You aren't easy to get on with.'[62]

In fact this proved a temporary conflict. Bessie withdrew from the garden project but continued to produce seedlings in her own garden and supply them to the Boiteko garden. Later she returned to working there one day a week.[63] Before this solution was found, though, the confrontation brought on yet another period of depression. 'My mind has temporarily snapped,'[64] she wrote.

She was plagued by fears of her own death. Statements like 'you feel your hold on life is getting so slack, you might not be there the next day'[65] were not uncommon. In contrast to many other situations, she might well have underplayed her death moods and suicidal tendencies. Sometimes, though, she could refer to them in a humorous vein. She could write that she was forever troubling Death as she was forever troubling her friends. She suspected that her friends could sigh and say, 'There she goes again' and perhaps Death too did not take her very seriously.[66]

But from early 1970 she began to make plans for either Tom Carvlin or Randolph to adopt Howard should it be necessary. That she duplicated her appeals and caused confusion makes them appear less authentic. Then she modified her instructions so that Randolph was to ensure that Howard was sent to Tom Carvlin in America. Randolph Vigne told her that she could rest assured that Howard would be cared for should that be necessary, but that she was being excessively gloomy all the same.[67] Some years later a new set of adoptive parents were chosen for the boy.

Bessie's confused and confusing plans for Howard should anything happen to her were a very real expression of her love and concern for him. She once told Randolph Vigne how nicely Howard was turning out. She felt that she had tried to teach him so much but he adopted only two of her admonitions. 'He's damn scared to mention any prejudice. He'll say it but apprehensively as though I am about to blow him into the sky. The other thing was – don't take without giving something in return.' One day he returned home from school fascinated to have heard about Jesus, for Bessie gave him no religious instruction at home. 'Can I make a present for Jesus?'[68] he asked. Later he also wanted to give something to Father Christmas, considering all the things he gave away.

Tom Carvlin, father of eight, was naturally worried about how Howard survived the fluctuations of life with Bessie. She admitted that she was appalled at what he had endured:

There are only the two of us. We are travelling companions. There were a number of blows I had to take and since he was forced by destiny to be there at that time, he got some of the hind end of them. It is more terrible for him because he is more than just a little boy. He is an appendage of my soul . . . There's no other child I know who has so much stamina and could have endured so much hell . . . The truth is, I was not born for a coddled life and the Organiser behind it all made quite sure that I did not have a wilting snowball with me but some kind of fierce soul, the type who was always in the front line of the battle field wielding an axe with blood-curdling yells.[69]

Whatever the explanation, Bessie's hysterical outbursts and deep fits of depression seemed to pass Howard by, but he peered out rather anxiously at life and knew how to remove himself from the direct line of fire.

For Bessie 1970 had been a year of productive physical and social activity, though this did not outweigh the emotional and spiritual torture she also suffered. It was driving her to the brink of mental collapse. Meanwhile, *Maru* was shaping up: the editing under Giles Gordon's careful guidance, the galley proofs, and finally publication in February 1971.

9

Ripping Up the Young Plant, 1971–72

A Question of Power

❄

The Christmas of 1970 found Bessie seriously ill. She lay in bed for weeks. Was this the year when she heard heavenly choirs singing 'Glory be to God on high and on earth peace to mankind?'[1] Was this when she wandered outside in her nightdress to listen to the sound of it, distraught with fear that she might have been blaspheming against a God 'up there' after all? Did she place some cake and tasty bits on the floor beside Howard's toys on Christmas Day and creep back to bed, leaving him to manage as best he could?[2] This is probably one of the scenes transferred from her own existence to her next novel. She talks about periods of 'complete blanks'.

How unreal it must have seemed to her that *Maru* was published on 21 January 1971. She had received some advance copies a week or so before that date and was so delighted with the new novel that she kept holding it to her heart. '[I]t is a goddam beautiful book, like nothing else on earth,' she said with a brief surge of enthusiasm, and added that it was a hard look at racial oppression but written 'with a real glow'.[3] The news from Giles was that it was selling well and that the reviews were favourable. Unfortunately she barely registered any of this.

At Christmas time Bessie became obsessed with the idea that the Vice-President, Dr Quett Masire, had been assassinated by a young Peace Corps volunteer. No one would acknowledge the fact. The President, Sir Seretse Khama, was doing everything to keep it a secret. For three weeks Bessie tried to find out what was actually happening. The conspiracy seemed enormous. Even the newspapers wrote as if he were alive. She became desperate, determined to disclose the frightful affair.

Why, one may ask, should someone who had always lived so isolated a life and who felt more and more despised by the Botswana population suddenly concern herself for the country's politic? The first answer that comes to mind is that she was deranged. And this is true. She had by this stage lost her last tenuous grasp on reality. Even in this state, though, there was an extraordinary inner logic about her behaviour patterns. In concerning herself about Masire, she may have been recalling her very early days in Serowe when she had fallen overwhelmingly in love with a young politician with phenomenal oratorical powers. Quett Masire had been in Serowe at that stage,[4] helping to organise the Bechuanaland Democratic Party. He would fit Bessie's description of the unnamed aloof young man, brilliant, ambitious, but outside the immediate circle of the local VIPs. Now she believed this first love to be dead, a victim of the same web of intrigue Seretse Khama had been spinning around her life for the last four years. The news that Seretse's daughter was in hospital had also been circulating in the village for some time. He was the cause of this also, she felt. Here was yet another indication of his evil powers.

Bessie was confined to bed. 'Somewhere at the back of my mind I am broken totally,' she told Paddy in mid-January.[5] She was not exaggerating. Tom Holzinger, one of her closest friends, was away from the village from July 1970 to February 1971, during which time he and a group of about eight students who had recently completed their training at the Farmers' Brigade were trying to establish a market garden in Selebi-Pikwe, the site of the recently opened copper mine. Living as settlers and struggling constantly with the lack of a secure water supply, Tom Holzinger and his group had little contact with Serowe.

People at Swaneng were worried about Bessie. There was, for example, an elderly woman named Joan Blackmore with whom Bessie was friendly. She and her husband lived quite close, across the road and down the hill, at the Swaneng Hill School. Their daughter was running the primary school and they were very involved in all the communal activities. Joan Blackmore had a conventional Christian faith in God and tried to live a life of service and friendliness. Her views irritated Bessie and provoked long, pointless arguments. Her slightly pious, simplistic phrases would probably have taken Bessie directly back to Nellie Heathcote and her childhood, an unfortunate association. Mrs Blackmore believed that she could relieve some of the suffering of the world by visiting the sick and this she did very conscientiously while Bessie was ill.

On one such visit Bessie was up but deeply depressed and she refused to let Mrs Blackmore into the house. Undeterred, the kindly old woman said confidentially: 'I'll pray for you Bessie,' to which Bessie replied in a thundering outburst of exasperation, 'It depends on which God you're praying to',[6] and slammed the door violently. She staggered around for most of the day. Howard, who lived his own life with friends and came home in the evening to get some food and go to bed, was relieved to see that she was up when he came in. 'Will you read me a story?' he pleaded and she promised to do so before he went to bed. Evening came. Thoughts of Seretse Khama and the way he had invaded her inner life, the villagers' dislike of her, her own feeling of being an unwanted outcast, the 'murder' of Masire, and the interference of Mrs Blackmore churned round in her head. She could not concentrate, not even on the pleasant task of reading a favourite bedtime story to Howard. She stopped in mid-sentence, pushed the book to one side and rose hastily. Howard let out a wail of protest. She could not do this to him, leave him in the middle of a story. But his mother neither saw nor heard him. She found a torch, for it was pitch dark, and rushed towards the door. 'Where are you going?' he now cried. For a moment Bessie registered where she was. 'Oh, Howard . . . look, I have to go and see Mrs Blackmore. I'll come home soon.'[7]

She ran along the rough path, down to Swaneng School and in at the school gate. Joan Blackmore was just outside her house. She had been visiting a friend.

She heard someone approaching quickly and her torch lighted up Bessie and her wild, distracted face. 'Bessie, what on earth is the matter,' she began anxiously, running towards her. Bessie lifted her hand and struck the elderly woman on the side of her face, sending her torch flying. Then she called her any number of abusive names in an uncontrolled outburst. Joan Blackmore crouched back, horrified and stunned. Others heard the outcry and came running. Then Bessie began to scream and scream, heading towards the gate. Footsteps pursued her. She turned round, challenging her pursuers with more violent language, then hurried home and locked the door. She could hear anxious voices where her friends had gathered at the gate, trying to decide what they should do.

Perhaps she had desperate plans to kill Howard, then herself. But he came towards her calmly, asking her what was the matter, telling her how she frightened him with all her talking to herself in the night. She pulled herself together sufficiently to reassure him and put him to bed. She could not manage to read the rest of the story. Throughout the night she agonised over the fact that Seretse Khama had seemed like God to her but was now also acting like the devil. Could he be God and the devil at once, making use of other personified forces of evil to bring about her death? She would have to kill him before he killed her. She would have to expose his evil ways. It was apparently during this night that she also wrote a memorable letter to Randolph Vigne. It is a euphoric but sane description of her reactions to the advance copy of *Maru*, in which she also refers to her own bad health and makes a cryptic remark about 'knocking' a 'certain old lady who had it coming to her' soundly on the head with her fists.[8]

The next morning they were both up early. 'We're going into town,' said Bessie. Howard was uneasy. She seemed to be acting strangely, even for her. The Mall was almost deserted when they got there. Perhaps it was the letter she had brought with her to post that directed her steps towards the post office. Perhaps she had already chosen for her purpose the low wall on which people used to put up notices about village activities. For she had with her a notice, a 'character poster' perhaps, saying that Seretse Khama had committed incest with his daughter and suppressed the news of the assassination of his Vice-President. This libel was fully signed: 'Bessie Head'. Howard stood regarding her with deep concern as she pasted it up on the wall. He knew his mother was not like other people and he knew she did things other mothers did not do. This he accepted implicitly. Though he did not really understand what she had written on the notice, he felt that this time he should warn her, beg her to take it down again. But he did nothing. He watched her put it up, then he took her hand as they started on the long walk home.

Bessie was very calm and determined. She made herself a cup of tea when they got home and sat down. She seemed to be waiting. Very soon the police arrived. There were peremptory knocks on the door and two young policemen asked her if she was Bessie Head and if she had written the notice they had with them. She answered defiantly that she had. 'Then we must ask you to come with us,' they said. She drew away from them and they grabbed her. She began to struggle, then scream. 'My son,' she said, 'I can't leave him alone.'

'He will be taken care of,' said one of the policemen. They pushed her into the back of the truck and, with Bessie sobbing and wailing, they drove off to the police station. She was put into a prison cell. Later she appeared in court and was asked to explain her action. She said that she was the only person who dared to make a public outcry over Masire.9 No one understood what she was saying. Everyone kept assuring her that Dr Masire was alive. Her other accusations against the President were even more grave. The magistrate ignored them and tried to pacify her, for now she was raving uncontrollably about the President being both the Devil and God. He had her admitted to hospital once more.

She was put into the same ward as before. This time induced sleep did not help her. In fact it intensified her nightmares. It was when she closed her eyes that the worst horrors of her inner world unfolded.

The doctor began to realise that she was terrified of sleeping and he could see that this was too complicated a mental state to cure with sedation and sympathy. At the end of March they decided to send her to the country's only mental hospital, at Lobatse in the south-east corner of Botswana. In a letter to Terence Finley dated 25 March, she wrote at length about the Masire conspiracy then added: 'I hope to be in England soon. I'm trying to arrange things with my publishers.'10 These sentences have a disturbing familiarity about them. Did not her mother write in a similarly totally unrealistic vein from her mental hospital in Pretoria in 1934 about taking her son on a holiday to England?

At Lobatse the patients were kept in locked wards and the treatment was often harsh. The staff were surprised to have someone like Bessie there. She was aggressive, and swore constantly. She refused to cooperate and showered scorn on the Italian doctor, the only psychiatrist in the country. Conditions were stark. Bessie was supposed to help clean the ward and do the hospital laundry but she refused. After that, she was given a sedative three times a day and left very much to herself.

Her breakdown had caused great distress in Serowe. First of all, Howard had to be cared for. He was taken in by Margaret and Stan Moore. They worked at Swaneng and Margaret Moore especially had got to know Bessie when she bought vegetables from the Boiteko garden. Howard was showered with affection and taken on many outings. In May they celebrated his ninth birthday with a party for the whole class and a birthday cake in the shape of a football field. He became an independent and even more vigorous young boy during the three months he was with them.

Patrick van Rensburg had the awkward job of placating the President. However, Seretse Khama was understanding and generous, winning sympathy by the way he handled the situation and making people generally more tolerant of Bessie's behaviour. Van Rensburg and the Moores also had to circulate news of her to her concerned friends abroad. They soon learnt that her condition was serious and the treatment could well take several years.

According to her own accounts, she also sent off highly distressed letters to Tom Carvlin, Jean Highland and Naomi Mitchison, describing the evil with which she was surrounded and saying that she was being victimised unfairly. 'At that time I sent [Naomi] a wild and incoherent letter,' Bessie wrote later to Giles Gordon. 'I was just hitting out in the air to relieve myself of a terrible inner torture and nothing I said at the time made sense to anyone.'[11] Jean Highland and Naomi Mitchison wrote giving her support each in her way. Naomi Mitchison's letter stated categorically that Quett Masire was alive, that she had just spoken to him. Tom Carvlin prayed for her.

After a period of total apathy during which she lay on her bed all day, she realised vaguely that she had to get out of Lobatse. She forced herself to get up; she became helpful and friendly, flattering the psychiatrist by showing an interest in his children and swallowing his racial views without a protest; she did some careful reading of Darwin's *Origin of Species*; and while her friends were trying to adjust themselves to the possibility of her being confined there for several years, the news suddenly came through that she had been released and was now perfectly well. She was sent home with the strict injunction that if she mentioned 'so-and-so's name again' the police would take her back to 'the loony bin'.[12]

She arrived back in Serowe at the end of June. The Van Rensburgs and Naomi Mitchison were convinced that she ought to go to England immediately, perhaps because they had the best insight into local affairs. Naomi Mitchison wrote in mid-July that she simply had to go into an English mental hospital when she arrived there and let them help her disentangle fantasy from reality. But, she added encouragingly, many writers had been in that position, 'half way between one life and another'.[13] It did not take Bessie long to realise that she simply did not have the mental or physical stamina to arrange such a move and the idea was dropped. This mention of leaving Botswana did, however, herald the first faint strains of what might be called one of the leitmotifs of the seventies.

Bessie was far from well. Willing herself out of the mental hospital, however, was probably what helped her most along the road to recovery. The first three weeks at home were the most critical. On 15 July she concluded her letter to Randolph by saying: 'There is only one human nobility left in me. I am not afraid to die.' And to Paddy, a week later: 'There's a pain between me and everything I'm doing just now and I am not really concentrating because it is so awful. It just hangs over my chest area like a permanent and persistent clamour.'[14] Even more poignant were her closing remarks in another letter three days later: 'I was like a millionaire who was forced to surrender his wealth at gunpoint and start all over from scratch with nothing ... God knows how I suffer at present ... I'm not such a tough guy like Al Capone. I'm crying.'[15] Paddy told her that it seemed unfair that many artists and natural visionaries had to pay the price she was paying for their talents and genius. 'One feels the world should be able to house them more gently.'[16]

Bessie had once called Howard the 'appendage' of her soul.[17] Her departure for Lobatse had given him a sudden emotional freedom. His classmates told him his mother was mad, but he took that calmly. 'I like mothers' was all he said when Bessie told him he could go and live with someone who was not mad if that worried him. He had friends around him. They enjoyed coming into his yard and playing football with him.[18] Football was his passion and Bessie had promised him a brand new ball. Having his lively presence near her now helped her through her darkest days.

Her other 'son', Tom, did his share by visiting and encouraging her. And everyone who knew her was so concerned about her health that she was deeply touched by the kindness she was shown. She went over to the Blackmores and apologised for striking Joan Blackmore. She 'forgave me so quickly and her old man too, I stared at their faces in disbelief. There was something there I had not seen for a long time, the normal, the friendly, with a soft kind glow about the eyes.'[19] She kept asking herself whether this was the real world, where people forgave in a kind way. She had not been used to that 'internally'.

Gradually the painful process of evaluating the experience could commence. To Jean Highland, Bessie said that 'the things troubling me seemed to have a coherence of their own but not when spoken out loud'.[20]

I seem to have taken a strange journey into hell and darkness. It was the darkness I did not grasp because at the same time I saw the light. There seemed to be a heaven in many human souls with a stillness and perfection complete within itself. I felt . . . the same completeness in myself . . . I thought that an inner heaven could make a heaven on earth.[21]

But while she was trying to write about this ideal state she was being caught up in an inner world which was 'a raging torment'.

In a letter to Terence Finley she sounded a note which would reappear often. She said that '[t]here is a strange thing about this country and its people. It is a natural teacher, especially on how to learn humility.'[22] This was the greatest blow to Bessie's self-respect: the fact that she had hit out at people who were innocent. 'I made a terrible mess of everything and it is so awful, the things I said and did that it seems no repairs are possible.'[23]

She said much the same to Paddy Kitchen, retracting many of her strange remarks in the letters she had written the previous year. 'The most important thing is that society did not treat me badly, especially since I came back from hospital. The trouble was where my mind was travelling. It was horrible territory full of evil images.' With this new vulnerability came a new note of uncertainty. She was still thinking about Satan, but now she began to wonder whether she had 'a long history of evil' behind her. She also felt that her temperament had changed. Her violent temper had become subdued.[24] She felt 'lost in a sorrow too deep for words . . . Did I really have to learn so much . . . I must have been an unusually stupid person to have so many bombs thrown at me.'[25] Her friends also noted with some sadness that she was 'painfully humiliated and apologetic'.[26]

But Bessie was beginning to speak in riddles again, revealing snippets of her complicated inner perceptions to one friend and edited versions of events to another. Randolph Vigne was told that 'it was one man, then another man, then another man and weird versions of love in the air, accompanied by abnormal sights'.[27] To Paddy Kitchen she described the drama of her arrest by saying that she had told several people that 'so and so has been killed by so and so'.[28]

By the middle of August she was apparently beginning to pull out of her breakdown. She had already admitted that she had begun to write down notes and ideas. They were the tentative start to her third book. But what was really helping her back to sanity was her gardening activities. In the six months she had been ill, buildings had been going up near the garden. The cooperative shop, pottery workshop and brewery were now complete. The garden was also flourishing. 'I suddenly wake up and find my village of Golema Mmidi right on my doorstep. People are just busy doing EVERYTHING.'[29] They were bringing their home-made articles to the shop and these were then exchanged for other wares, using the Dirufo voucher system that had been devised. There were also some bags of sorghum, mealie meal, sugar, tea, candles, products bought with aid money to supplement the home-produced wares. Bessie explained to Paddy how she was now responsible for making gooseberry jam every Saturday morning at her house, where a group of ladies gathered to help her; she also spent one day planting out seedlings in the Boiteko garden; and prepared seedlings in her own garden for transplanting. For doing this she earned three Boiteko (about R3) a week.[30]

The gooseberry bushes in Bessie's own garden were yielding prolifically, ten pounds of fruit a week. She paid Howard and his football friends a few cents for helping her to pick them every Friday afternoon. She was very good at informing the village women on the nutritional value of the vegetables and fruit they pro-duced. She also impressed on them that gooseberries were rich in vitamin C and this was an additional reason for the successful sale of their jam. Sometimes people passing by her yard when she was outside working would remark 'Cape gooseberry' and smile to show that they had understood her sales propaganda. 1971 was a summer with good rains. This meant that everything in the garden thrived. Cabbages and onions were sold in a twinkling. Later a particularly destructive beetle, the *sebokolodi*, seldom seen in the area, descended on the lush vegetables, destroying them. The hazards of market gardening are many![31]

Bessie bought a string bag and necklace for Paddy from the shop and sent them off. She had become very friendly with Christine and Peter Hawes, who started up the Boiteko pottery project, and she tried to build up a collection of pottery articles with her work vouchers. The pottery was thick and chunky and looked beautiful on the table, with 'designs on them invented by the students. This is the most exciting thing about the Boiteko project – that it has the poten-tial to make people inventors and is a cross between people's own skills and the skills of the volunteers at the school.'[32]

Unfortunately the scheme in its ideal form did not last very long. The trouble arose because the cost of the bought goods far exceeded the income of the cooperative. It was soon discovered that there was a bill for R2000 for imports. The Dirufo system was dropped. It failed, in Patrick van Rensburg's words, because he succumbed to the temptation to provide 'a wider range of goods in the store than we had produced or in fact could afford'.[33] The Boiteko mem-bership fell to forty people, but the idea from then on was to share the earnings equally among the members. It was indeed a fortunate thing that this experiment was at its best just when Bessie had most need of feeling success in a communi-ty venture.

Earlier Paddy Kitchen had sent Bessie the three novels she had written and Bessie had responded with very detailed notes and comments on the first one, *Lying-In*. Some months after returning from Lobatse, she embarked on another long discussion about the novel, which she admired greatly: 'The writing is a piece of music. It grips the heart . . . You just never forget the lines, the tense, vivid, squeezed out descriptions.'[34] Bessie was very conscious of the sound of sentences. She reacted emotionally to them. Passages could be prosaic, or soaring, phrases rebounding. 'Each person knows their working materials – I think the shoemaker knows his sandals are coming out right – so with the first line of a book.'[35] She worked by instinct and she trusted it.

She was beginning on her third novel, afraid that she would soon be running out of money unless she sold something more. She told Paddy that she was working on something called *Summer Flowers*. The protagonist, Theophilus, started out by being a man who was having two love affairs at once, but was then changed into a 'good man tabbing Satan' and handling 'the undying evil in Satan with a sense of humour'.[36] While her letters and her general behaviour seemed to suggest a large degree of recovery from about August onwards, one occasionally has glimpses in letters of indications that she may still have been struggling with inner demons into November,[37] just as she had struggled silently for years beforehand.

In October Bessie heard that *Maru* had been bought by a film man in New York. She called it a 'damn blessing' as the money coming in from that would keep her going for about a year. She could not imagine, though, how *Maru* could be made into a film; its drama is internal. As it happened, nothing came of the film project.

Towards the end of the year Bessie became friendly with Tony Hall and his wife Nouannah. He was an English agriculturist attached to the Farmers' Brigade and his wife was Shona. They had met and fallen in love in Rhodesia, which was her home, and after much heart-searching decided to get married. They had to move to Botswana to do so. Tony was a deeply religious person who spent hours listening and talking to Bessie. 'Our minds aren't meeting,' he said, in the same way Tom Carvlin had, as he listened to her story for the first time. 'Your presentation of good and evil is something I have never heard before.' Nevertheless he stayed with her for four hours, 'pulling and pulling me out of death with a kindness I have never known in my life before'.[38]

It was with the Halls that Bessie and Howard spent Christmas. She had recovered sufficient of her old verve to write an amusing and detailed letter of the various disasters that formed part of the Christmas scene, such as their going on a picnic and Nouannah Hall forgetting the duck in the oven and Tony Hall walking home for two hours to remove it. Some of her old biting wit had also returned: 'In the old days I would have found an excuse not to join the picnic but when Tony said "We asked if you could come along too" and she said "Oh, Bessie, of course, of course". They're all supposed to say that since the poor dear darling came out of the loony bin. So I smiled quite cheerfully and said of course, of course, too. There's nothing like the loony bin to make one love one's enemies.'[39] Such hilarity helped her keep thoughts of the previous year in the background. With the Halls, Bessie acquired two new members of her 'family': Tony she called her brother, Nouannah her sister-in-law. It was unfortunate for her that they returned to England early in the new year, but she retained a very serious, though sporadic, correspondence with Tony Hall.

Because of its appearance in the middle of her breakdown, Bessie had never really had time to enjoy the reception *Maru* received. The fact is that it had been given serious and positive reviews in most of the leading papers. 'Simplicity and sophistication are the keynotes of Miss Head's style' and her story is told 'with a touch of allegory that is purely African in feeling' was how the *Daily Telegraph* reviewed it.[40] The *Times Literary Supplement* praised the 'delightful touches' in her account of the village and its institutions, but found the friendship of the two men and their different responses to love 'too often obscured by a wilful invocation of the arcane'.[41] She had not even been able to appreciate the review in the *Tribune* saying that *Maru* was not a 'quasi-fashionable myth of our time' but one of 'universal validity' with the 'quality of goodness' in Margaret Cadmore a 'source of strength and beauty'[42] in the novel. It was written by Dulan Barber, Paddy Kitchen's husband. Later in the year from America came Martin Levin's comments that Bessie Head 'depicts African life with deep personal commitment – and a lyrical flair that gives it a delightful tilt into fantasy'.[43] In December Paddy Kitchen named *Maru* as her choice of Book of the Year in the *Scotsman*.

While commenting on further British reviews just received from Giles Gordon at the beginning of 1972, Bessie provided some very revealing insights into her view of her role as a writer. She began by saying how different these reviews were from the American ones she had seen, which all tended to emphasise the fact that it was a story of black men in black Africa. Most critics 'swallowed *Maru* whole', only one remarking that he was a mixture of good and evil. Her audience seemed to need to take a writer as the 'epitome of everything African. How much I am the displaced outsider, I alone know . . . To a great extent, my preoccupations are all within.' She felt that most writers have national characteristics first, then after that they are 'universal humanity'. But her position was different. She had been given the task of portraying the man with no shoes in Africa, and she had to do it from within. Instead of Jesus or Buddha being her teacher, the ordinary people were to teach her. She embarked on the task eagerly, never anticipating the 'hair splitting truthfulness that went hand in hand with the choice . . . I was unprepared to be that unimportant, that levelled down, but at the end of it I am, through sheer terror of its opposite, the V.I.P. , the pride and arrogance and egoism of the soul.'[44]

Bessie was now working very hard on her third book. By March she had finally decided on a title: *A Question of Power* . . . 'and I throw the title line in at the end . . . "If the things of the soul are really a question of power, then anyone in possession of power of the spirit could be called Lucifer."'[45] A theme familiar from her correspondence is linked to it as David's destructive love for Bathsheba illustrates her point: 'It was planned murder, ordered by God.' The forces of hell which she now confronts 'do not concede that immense suffering is enough; they want total doom; they want the total destruction of the soul . . . I put down these things almost matter of factly as they appeared in a sort of stream of consciousness way, a kind of under-current life that proceeds side by side with real life'.[46]

By April, *A Question of Power* was finished. There was a note of extreme trepidation in the accompanying letter as she sent the typescript directly to Giles Gordon at Gollancz and the copy to her agent, Hilary Rubinstein, who had taken over her affairs at A P Watt after David Machin left in September 1970. 'There is almost despair in me. I tell an impossible story,'[47] she wrote. She was doing what she could to prepare herself for having it rejected.

In the first pages of *A Question of Power* we are presented with what could be described as a chart, drawn in clear simple, lines, and mapping out a journey. Our attention is directed to the places where important incidents occur. The landscape is blocked in in general terms; the three travellers are named and presented.

The direct style of the language notwithstanding, studying this chart fills the reader with foreboding. 'Here it was,' say the notes from our guide, 'that one of the travellers cried "Thank you! Oh God, thank you for the lever out of hell!" And here it was that another said: "Love is two people mutually feeding each other."' The landscape into which the travellers venture sounds even stranger. There are references to 'soul evolution', 'things of the soul', vast 'inner perceptions', events occurring 'at the end of each life' and love being 'freedom of heart'. The three travellers are named Sello, Dan and Elizabeth. Both men love Elizabeth. Sello and Elizabeth are 'twin souls'. Sello is described as wise, humane and loving, yet Elizabeth grows to despise him. Dan has tremendous charm and physical attraction for her, yet Elizabeth hates him too.

The purpose of the journey is revealed. Elizabeth is to be totally exposed to evil and find out what saints really mean when they make statements about it. Elizabeth's destination has already been guessed. Sello and Dan are accompanying her to hell and Dan seems intent on leaving both Elizabeth and Sello there.

This is the scenario Bessie Head presents with such apparent simplicity in *A Question of Power*. Much of the novel takes place in a realm where souls move freely, temporally and spatially, and where they are measured in moral terms, though not on the usual scale with good at one end and evil at the other. It transpires that, in return for an acceptance of her scenario, or at least some degree of suspension of disbelief, the reader is to accompany Bessie Head as she explores a nervous breakdown from within, an entirely different undertaking from analysing or discussing one.

There is a disconcerting authenticity about Bessie's inner world. What psychologists would call hallucinations, she depicts as finely gradated departures from reality. In the early stages of the breakdown she can say: 'Agh, I must be mad! That's just an intangible form' (p. 23), after she has offered a cup of tea to the white-robed monk always visible to her beside her bed. However, thereafter the landscape becomes more and more surrealistic, each subsequent encounter with Sello or Dan depicting some new facet of mental instability.

The conflict between these two characters is the other central issue of the novel. This and the closely related insanity theme – what Bessie Head had described as 'a kind of under-current life' – are welded together by the novel's outer framework, which is the story of how Elizabeth, a refugee and outcast, adapts to a rural African society and overcomes her sense of alienation through her participation in a development scheme.

To highlight the causes of the disintegration of Elizabeth's personality, Bessie uses the device of externalising, even dramatising, her psychological scars and suppressed fears and aspirations in a series of dream visions. Sello and Dan, who themselves span the gap between reality and fantasy, not only because they gradually dominate her waking life just as much as her nightmares, but because she knows them also as inhabitants of her village of Motabeng, appear as the manipulators of these manifestations.

Elizabeth's role in the unfolding drama is closely connected with suffering. She thinks about her past, her tragic childhood. She was born in South Africa. Her mother was white, her father black, an unforgivable sin in this racially segregated country in the late thirties. She bears not only the double burden of being an orphan and racial outcast, but also the stigma of possible hereditary madness, for she learns that her mother committed suicide in the mental hospital to which she had been confined after her daughter's birth. Elizabeth develops an adoring love for this woman who insisted that she bear the same name as herself; and left instructions and money for her to be given a good education. As an adult Elizabeth wonders whether this is her initiation into the sharing of suffering. Perhaps her dead mother made a silent appeal: 'Do you think I can bear the stigma of insanity alone? Share it with me' (p. 17).

One of Elizabeth's early visions is a moving encounter with the poor of Africa. People place cut and bleeding feet on Elizabeth's bed and one woman asks her,'Will you help us? We are the people who have suffered.' They have the 'still, sad, fire-washed faces . . . of people who had been killed and killed and killed again in one cause or another for the liberation of mankind'.(p31) Elizabeth knows that she must help them.

There is a constant fragmentation of the 'characters' in Elizabeth's inner universe, which increases the pressure on her mind. Sello and Elizabeth's Socratic dialogues rapidly degenerate into confused nightmares as Sello divides himself into two dissimilar personalities. Two important new apparitions appear: a bolt-throwing superwoman named the Medusa and a character called the Father, walking round in the guise of an agricultural expert in khaki shorts and hob-nailed boots. Medusa represents the destructively exclusive, 'the surface reality of African society' (p. 38). Here Elizabeth cannot belong. In the first place she is not a black woman, she is a coloured. Echoing the scorn Bessie Head's African-American friend poured on her because she was not a 'genuine African',[48] Medusa tells Elizabeth that 'Africa is troubled waters . . . You'll only drown here . . . You don't know any African languages' (p. 44). Elizabeth's philanthropic feelings are likewise worthless. Medusa says that she can do much more good in Africa than Elizabeth can: 'I am greater than you in goodness' (p. 37). Elizabeth is also made to feel a failure sexually; she can in no way experience sexual sensations comparable with the exquisite ones Medusa produces.

The Father (a new portrayal of Gilbert, from *When Rain Clouds Gather*), is introduced as one of Sello's kindred spirits, for Sello disappears into him, indicating soul identification or the raising from the personal to the universal. In this case the father figure becomes a god figure and later a hero figure: 'He remained a hero-image, to her' (p. 107). The Father is a remarkably handsome man, 'spectacular' and 'dashing'. He can raise his 'majestic head' and survey the universe 'with cold eyes and supreme indifference'. He always identifies with the poor and wears his beggar's rags with 'the stately bearing of a king in fine raiment'. The

Father is exactly what his name implies: the illegitimate Elizabeth's personified desire for a father figure who is also a noble hero. That he watches over her, warns her of great danger and then deserts her also fits into the pattern. He cannot intrude on his daughter's sexual experiences, unpleasant though she finds them. But he can and does resist Dan toughly for a long time (p. 118).

Medusa, on the other hand, is gradually debunked. Elizabeth comes to terms with those aspects of her own personality which Medusa personifies. She begins to realise the limitations of belonging to what Medusa, in her identification with African nationalism and power-lusting presidents, calls 'my people', for they can easily become mere child-like slaves dictated to by a 'mother' or 'father'. She cannot be hurt any more by being called coloured. 'Too many people the world over were becoming mixed breeds and shading themselves down to browns and yellows and creams' (p. 63). And as regards her sexuality, Elizabeth has to admit that other things, such as 'long years of prison confinements . . . death, . . . loss, suffering and sacrifice', all aspects of love too, had counted more for her.

Elizabeth accepts with resignation her own limited sexuality for the same reason that she identifies with the poor. She too has the inbuilt knowledge of extreme oppression. Compared to the eccentric Sello and the glamorous Dan, she is self-effacing, subdued, a victim. Socially she is oppressed because she is a woman and politically because she is a coloured. This theme is examined in multifarious ways by Bessie Head. Spanning the centuries, covering the continent of Africa, feelers are sent out, parallels are drawn, ironic comments made. A victim of racial oppression, for example, is really a flexible, free person, she says. 'He doesn't have to think up endless laws and endless falsehood . . . He is presented with a thousand and one hells to live through and he usually lives through them all.' The victims' faces become scarred with suffering, but the 'torturers become more hideous day by day . . . Who is the greater man – the man who cries, broken by anguish, or his scoffing, mocking, jeering oppressor?' (p. 84).

Elizabeth is a victim of spiritual oppression for reasons which she does not understand and which she cannot totally resist. As she is drawn deeper into the web of evil she finds that her resources do not suffice. Her efforts to create counter-themes of goodness are 'like the feeble flayings in the air of a beetle flung helplessly on its back' (p. 64). She says that to prefer nobility and goodness is not enough. 'There are forces who make a mockery of my preferences' (p. 85). This refers to what Elizabeth sees as yet another complicating element: her strong belief that it is Sello and later Sello and Dan who have invaded her life and are manipulating it for some purpose of their own. As she sees it, the fact that her experiences of the totally destructive nature of power are gradually uncovered through what she calls 'an entirely abnormal relationship with two men' might not be 'due to her dubious sanity' but to the 'strangeness of the men themselves' (p. 19).

Victims have subdued, reduced personalities but they also harbour strong passions. Elizabeth's consuming love for Dan only comes out in glimpses for this reason. Only gradually do we realise that the form of hell she endures with him is one where his jeering genuinely affects her. She is jealous; she does feel sexually inadequate; she does feel an outsider socially.

These dramatised internal confrontations are juxtaposed with events relating to Elizabeth's everyday life, which is concerned with starting a market gardening project in the village. There are people who help her in various ways: the 'Eugene man' who has also fled from South Africa and is involved in 'a thousand and one things at the same time' (p. 68) to improve the opportunities of the young people and illiterate villagers in Motabeng; the young Peace Corps volunteer, Tom, who is equally willing to discuss the problems of the universe with Elizabeth or help her to erect a fence around her garden; her co-worker on the gardening project, Kenosi, who doggedly hauls her back to physical labour when her mental state is desperate; and her small son Shorty, whose preoccupation with paper aeroplanes, sky jets and footballs is greatly responsible for her recovering her sanity. The activities of the newly established local-industry groups are also vividly described and there are delightful sketches of some of the international volunteers working with Eugene on his many projects.

Inextricably worked into the theme of Elizabeth's breakdown is Bessie Head's treatment of the theme of good and evil. It is the growing realisation that good need not necessarily triumph over evil and that God need not be good that originally unhinges Elizabeth's mind. First Sello is shown as a man of 'vast inner perceptions' (p. 11), a god-like figure. In terms of power, though, good cannot equal evil. Sello, we know, is 'opposed by personalities whose powers, when activated, rumbled across the heavens like thunder. He had nothing its equivalent in this war' (p 43). He has a quality of soul-power which is 'passive, inactive, impersonal'. It is linked in some way to the 'creative function, the dreamer of new dreams; and the essential ingredient in creativity is to create and let the dream fly away with a soft hand and heart' (p. 42). Sello walks, moves, thinks and lives 'like a flame on a dark night'. He holds the 'essential clues to the evolution of the soul' but he holds them tentatively (p. 41). With time this gentleness appears as weakness.

Good and evil continue to be depicted in ambiguous terms as Sello is associated with the evil Medusa and his mean-faced twin, the Sello in the brown suit. Over the centuries Sello has from his position of power perpetrated many evil actions in the name of God. Elizabeth herself has once been implicated. In one of her incarnations, as the biblical David, she has ordered the death of the innocent Uriah in order to marry his wife Bathsheba.

Just as Sello's form of goodness has become undesirable, so Dan's evil appears attractive. It is effective as compared to Sello's spinelessness (p. 43). Dan is associated with the blazing sun (p. 100), contrasting with Sello's 'flame on a dark night'. His entrance is dramatic, in 'clouds of swirling, revolving magic' (p. 102) and an explosion of red fire, again in sharp contrast to Sello's slow and humble materialisation.

Dan has control over physical feelings, deep exclusive love between two people, miracles and magic. He tells Elizabeth that he is frantically in love with her and that their souls are joined together at the roots (p. 46). After enthralling her with tender demonstrations of physical love, which make Sello's Socratic dialogues sink into insignificance, he gives her many indications of his god power. It is 'a sort of spinning, revolving, eternal motion, a sort of power behind all powers that . . . kept the stars up there . . . that made the universe revolve around the universe. Ought a person not to turn over and sleep peacefully? Everything would be taken care of' (p. 116). It gives Elizabeth a sense of false security. She can leave the shaping of her identity to someone else.

Shortly afterwards, however, the subtle exposures begin. Dan's use of power is deathly dangerous. He uses slander and insinuation to destroy people, such as the Asian man who has shaped Elizabeth's attitude to the poor (p. 120). He begins to direct his power against Elizabeth. The visions become more and more degenerate. In ways by far outdoing Medusa's realm of evil, Elizabeth is again confronted with her own sexual inadequacy and personal prejudices. Dan constantly works on the idea that she is not an African, she is not part of their show, she does not belong there and cannot react the way an African woman would to sexual advances. In a never-ending display, he parades all kinds of women before Elizabeth. At the same time he infests her days with twisted accounts of other people's perversions. He undermines the innocent and normal; everything is 'high sexual hysteria' (p. 160). Yet she cannot free herself emotionally from him. She feels like a 'rabbit trapped in helpless fascination by the powerful downward swoop of the hawk. It knows its death is near and awaits it, helplessly' (p. 160).

Dan's aim is to cause the fall of Sello. This he almost achieves. He twists and discredits Sello's ideas for a better world until Elizabeth abandons him entirely. Sello now seems to alternate between lives of sainthood and spells of debauchery. He is 'Jesus and the devil, too' (p. 175).

Yet just when she reaches this, the lowest spiritual ebb, Sello says: 'Elizabeth, love isn't like that. Love is two people mutually feeding each other, not one living on the soul of the other like a ghoul!' (p. 197). The softly spoken words from the weak Sello, diminished into insignificance before Dan's all-dominating ostentation, suddenly send shivers of renewed life through the battered Elizabeth, who is still blinded into believing that 'living on the soul of the other' is love. 'Thank you! Oh, God, thank you for the lever out of hell!' she cries in relief (p. 198).

Sello's words tip her centre of being back towards the ordinary. Everyday living with everyday kindnesses become important once more. Kenosi's loyalty and painstaking stewardship of the garden; her son's persistent trust in her; Tom's untiring efforts to help her; Mrs Jones's generosity of spirit, all confirm Elizabeth's doctrine of the ordinary: 'Ordinary people never mucked up the universe. They don't have that kind of power, wild and flaring out of proportion. They have been the victims of it' (p. 190). She sees that there is 'no God like ordinary people. You'll find Dan and Medusa in heaven and hell, but you won't find ordinary human kindness and decency there. God in heaven is too important to be decent' (p. 197). Elizabeth herself feels 'as normal and ordinary as other people, yet she had been nearly killed in this rigmarole of hell' (p. 200).

Sello's and Dan's attacks on Elizabeth frequently have her cowering; but in the final issue she is not cowed. Herein lies the strength of the victim. She is a necessary object on which power can be exerted. But when power has destroyed her persecutors, she can pick up her life and continue living. Her passivity has become her strength.

In realising how narrow the division is between good and evil, (p. 161), Elizabeth also realises that goodness cannot be enforced. If a god figure is needed to enforce goodness, then he becomes the devil: 'If the things of the soul are really a question of power, then anyone in possession of power of the spirit could be Lucifer' (p. 199). She later realises that that was what Sello was trying to demonstrate to her by taking off his vesture garments: that goodness is vulnerable and that goodness devoid of power is love.

After her first breakdown Elizabeth regains her sanity by thinking that love is many variations of one theme: humility and equality. In an image which could have been taken directly from *Maru*, Elizabeth sees love as a young girl walking down the road to meet her lover. 'And love was like a girl with wonder in her eyes. And love was like a girl with a flaming heart and impulsive arms. And love was so many things, so many variations of one theme: humility and equality – for when those men said: "Is it possible? Could you love me?", thrones and kingdoms were of no account against the power of love.' This image has about it all the exclusiveness of romantic love (p 54).

Dan's love is of this sort. He has shown it to her in the vision of the deep blue heaven where two people stand wrapped in an eternal embrace. They are surrounded by symbols of their love, grapevines with roots entwined, a roaring river symbolising powerful, all-consuming love. 'There was nothing else, no people, no sharing' (p. 108). Elizabeth's recovery has depended on her understanding this. 'She treasured the encounter with Dan. The suffering she had endured had sealed her Achilles' heel; that of the brutal murderer for love.'

With her journey to the depths of hell finally over, she once more thinks about love. Now she thinks of her love for Sello. Together, she feels, they have introduced 'a softness and tenderness into mankind's history'. They have

perfected the ideal of sharing everything and then they have perfectly shared everything with all mankind ... It was the point at which there were no private hungers to be kissed, loved, adored. And yet there was a feeling of being kissed by everything; by the air, the soft flow of life, people's smiles and friendships ... That was the essential nature of their love for each other. It had included all mankind and ... it equalized all things and all men (p. 202).

Recovery from the nervous breakdown brings gradual healing to Elizabeth's shattered nerves. She has learnt to accept herself as she is, personally, socially and politically. She has been forced to consider her own emotional life and has chosen service to others rather than self-indulgent forms of love. She has clarified her views on moral issues and acquired firm humanistic convictions. She has been able to surmount her feelings of isolation and alienation and place her hand on her land in a 'gesture of belonging'.

The abstruse subject-matter and high level of protracted desperation at which most of the novel is written are not components that lend themselves easily to being shaped into a readable form. In balancing the frenzied with the prosaic and using Elizabeth's dogged struggle to lead a normal existence to counterpoise the fierce internal struggle, Bessie Head believed that she had achieved a coherent structure for the novel. But would the reading public realise this? In the letter accompanying the manuscript she admitted that the novel was either printable or totally unprintable. It is almost autobiographical but not in the usual way. The narrator or central character Elizabeth lives more in contact with her soul than living reality . . . It is an allegorical novel. It is about God and Dante's inferno. Sello is the traditional image of God as Old Father Time, yet in no way does he give to Elizabeth a traditional explanation of God. He is doing several things at once – he is divesting himself of his vesture garments, he is partially recreating for Elizabeth the Fall of Man, he is slaying Lucifer or the killer dog power theme that has caused so much misery in human history. He goes about these activities in his own original way. Lucifer is Dan . . . He thinks as the original Lucifer did that he ought to be God, by himself, as his power impresses him . . . He cannot be God . . . unless he totally destroys both Elizabeth and Sello as they oppose power.[49]

In calling the work 'almost autobiographical', Bessie is acknowledging the process of examining or reworking her own experiences in her three novels which has been progressively intensified. Seen together they constitute a trilogy; an untraditional trilogy in that the movement is inward rather than forward. The Sello–Dan theme is recognisably an extension of the Maru–Moleka one; though less pronounced, the tainted, ambiguous quality of goodness is also present in the earlier work.

As had been the case with both *Rainclouds* and *Maru* and as her correspondence abundantly confirms, she once again transfers large areas of her everyday life directly into the novel, in this instance the Boiteko project. Important personalities she has known are included, either in symbolic form, such as the Father and Medusa, or as realistic, easily recognisable characters: the Eugene man, Kenosi, Shorty, for example, and Tom, whose name is not even changed. The 'under-current life' of *A Question of Power* moves into the area of painful personal revelations as the story of her origins comes out for the first time, revelations not to become clear until her first genuinely autobiographical pieces began to appear shortly afterwards.

The central issue of the novel, what Bessie Head calls the 'killer dog power theme', contains so many elements recognisable from her correspondence that this too must be seen as a reworking of highly personal material. For a number of years prior to her breakdown, her letters had resounded with such phrases as 'taking on Satan' or being battered by 'torrents of hatred' and her first drafts of *A Question of Power*, when she still called it *Summer Flowers*, were hardly to be distinguished from some of the descriptions of her own life she had given friends. She saw herself singled out for an incomprehensible assault of evil. She had come to the conclusion that it was necessary for the clearing of 'a lot of junk out of the soul'.[50]

She felt constrained to give her experiences universal relevance, which involved trying to pinpoint or define the forces of evil she was describing. During this process, though 'normal religious terms' were not part of her vocabulary, she was sometimes forced to admit that perhaps there was 'something in the darkness'. 'I don't think it is easy for mankind to bury its demons,' she wrote, recalling how one of Hitler's generals had reported at the Nuremberg trials that Hitler seemed to run the war on the advice 'they' gave him – voices with which he communicated. 'People on looking back decided that he had a force of evil behind him and was its victim.'[51] What is interesting with this remark is that Bessie interpreted Hitler's symptoms in religious terms – 'force of evil' – rather than in psychological ones –'hallucinations'. She explained her own experiences in the same way. Some years after her breakdown she was to say: ' What I did not expect myself was to have some of the basic riddles uncovered in a forlorn, vast, empty, drought-stricken land like Botswana.'[52] She had again had to re-think the ideas she had brought with her to Botswana. She later wrote: 'People here have told me that they have their own way of killing each other and it wasn't openly violent. This side I can definitely confirm as I encountered that force – the difference being that I wasn't brought up in the tradition . . . but that other kind of killing is very horrific – it can go on for years and aims at the inner life and is piecemeal torture. This is what I wanted to flee, I think because it horrified me so much because it was so new and difficult to deal with'.[53] To Tom Holzinger, who was probably closest of all to the situation Bessie attempted to describe in her third novel, she later said that A Question of Power might not be

the classic struggle with God and the Devil I thought it was. It might simply be local African horror and I might have put my grand and faulty imagination into something I don't understand. Because all I have left is the horror and perhaps people don't know anything about how Baloi work and how they go on and on behind the scenes. I simply thought that that brutal horror was the same thing that got hold of Hitler. It might simply be local and African and something I don't understand at all.[54]

With her reference to Baloi – which she later defined as 'those people with a bad heart'[55] – she was obviously looking at local witchcraft beliefs in a speculative way.

To the degree that the writing process can be regarded as a form of therapy, it would appear to have been successful. Elizabeth, a reflection of Bessie Head herself, does achieve healing, can banish her sense of isolation and feel that she belongs. Unfortunately, as time was to show, the autobiographical element does not apply in this vital area. Bessie could not eradicate her paranoiac concern with evil by writing about it. Similarly Elizabeth, in the novel, achieves considerable insight into the fact of its being her mixed blood which can provide her with a unique purpose in life, whereas Bessie could not at that stage retain the vision. The novel-writing process had given her a certain breathing space but from now on the most effective way for her to order her thoughts was to lie in her letter-writing.

It was Hilary Rubinstein who reacted to the typescript first. He told her that he was afraid that the new novel would not find a publisher because it was 'too dense and intractable'.[56] He added that he was absolutely convinced that she would write books again that were 'as intensely meaningful' as her previous two, if not even better. Then came the letter from Giles Gordon. In extremely carefully shaped phrases, he said that A Question of Power simply did not get across to him and that he felt that it was very much a draft of a novel, not a completed one. Bessie, he thought, had not distanced herself sufficiently from the experiences she described, there seemed to be no sort of narrative drive, the characters were difficult to grasp, and (worst of all from her point of view) the language seemed to be a 'heightened form' of prose poetry bordering 'on the meaningless'.[57] He told her gently and politely that he was sending the manuscript back to Hilary.

With the reception of these two letters ended the post-Lobatse honeymoon period. All Bessie's own doubts about her new novel were forgotten. She rose up in noble indignation at this criticism. Her scrawled margin comment on Hilary Rubinstein's letter, beside his hope that she would again write intensely meaningful books, was 'The height of patronage, B. Head', and she engraved these words, plus those of Giles about her language, on her heart and quoted them to all sorts of people for years to come.

Nor did she hesitate to express her opinion to the gentlemen in question. Though the letter to Hilary was lost in the post, we are given an idea of its nature by the fact that Bessie was later afraid that he would sue her for libel. She also explained to Paddy that she was 'mighty confused' when she sent a postcard to Giles and that she could have written 'you damn bugger' on it by mistake![58]

Paddy Kitchen unwittingly entered the fray. Giles had given her the manuscript to read. She thought that Bessie was 'half way to cracking a very big egg indeed'. In her view Bessie had not really succeeded in bringing together the practical facts of Elizabeth's life and the 'mythic influences' of Sello and Dan. She tried both to console and to encourage her, adding that one of her manuscripts had been returned twenty-three times. But she could not admit that she agreed with Giles's evaluation of the novel.[59] On Bessie's request her husband, Dulan Barber, also read the manuscript and wrote an extremely helpful and perceptive critique. But his message was the same: 'Please rewrite, Bessie.'[60]

Meanwhile Paddy's letter had crossed an overwrought one Bessie had written asking her to obtain the manuscript of *A Question of Power* from Hilary Rubinstein. She felt he had let her down by not sending it off to McCalls in America. They had published *Maru* and had recently asked whether she was working on a new book. She felt that they should at least be given the chance of seeing *A Question of Power*. She was used to someone holding her hand as Jean Highland and Pat Read had done when she prepared *Rain Clouds* for publication. This is what she felt she lacked this time. Part of the trouble was that Giles Gordon was on the point of leaving his job at Gollancz to become a literary agent at Anthony Sheil's.

She sent a desperate letter to Jean Highland, with the manuscript, asking for her opinion. Jean Highland had to give up here. She could not follow Bessie's thought-processes any longer. '*A Question of Power* scared her . . . ,'[61] said Bessie some years later. Ken Mackenzie, an old Cape Town friend who contacted her about another matter, was now drawn into the publishing dispute. He gratified Bessie by being one of the first people to appreciate the two levels on which *A Question of Power* is written and did what he could to help in London.

Bessie contacted Susan Stanford at Saturday Review Press, previously McCalls, and sent her the manuscript only to have it returned. She fired Hilary Rubinstein as her agent and hoped that Paddy would help her find another. Paddy did. She made the tentative suggestion that Bessie could ask Giles Gordon to become her agent. He wanted to take on her work. Surprisingly enough, Bessie could let bygones be bygones. She engaged Giles Gordon. As he said to her, he might not have liked *A Question of Power* from the start but he liked her other two books and had great faith in her writing. This meant that Bessie ended her association with A P Watt, and with the American counterpart, Collins-Knowlton-Wing, which was now replaced by the Anthony Sheil Associates' American agents, Julian Bach Literary Agency.

Bessie made a swift decision to let James Currey, from Heinemann's African Writers Series, which had recently published *Maru*, look at the typescript. He wrote telling her that the novel numbed him. He did not think it was really African, more part of the mainstream of Anglo-American internal writing, but he would be willing to publish it in the African Writers Series as an experiment, provided that they could find a hardback publisher.[62] He suggested that they get an editor to look at it and consider alterations that would make the book more accessible to the larger public it deserved. Bessie agreed and the manuscript was now sent to Richard Lister, whose response was the most encouraging she had had for a long time: 'I think it is a wonderful book. I feel very strongly opposed to the idea that the author should be asked to do any re-writing. The thing is superb as it stands.' He added that the book was 'a considerable achievement, a prolonged spiritual crisis seen from the inside and powerfully described.'

He admitted that small alterations were needed and set to work on them. 'It was often a matter of punctuation . . . quite often simply because the comma is in the wrong place'.[63] Punctuation had always been Bessie's vulnerable point. During the inception of *A Question of Power* she had been quoting her key sentences at her friends. In each case, meticulously, she placed a comma before Lucifer: 'If the things of the soul are really *A Question of Power*, then anyone in possession of power of the spirit could be called, Lucifer.' Later she was to refer to 'Khama, the Great' for years. 'You are not likely to come out of the encounter, alive'[64] is another example. Using 'I' in an object construction was another quirk she never straightened out – 'it gives you and I breathing space'.[65] On the other hand she was very correct about using the subject form for subject complements: – It is I, I am she, etc. 'Like' and 'as' always gave her trouble: 'She is not such a good letter writer like me.'[66]

It is actually rather amusing that *A Question of Power* should have been brought in from the cold with the help of some simple grammatical improvements. When Bessie wrote to Giles Gordon in July saying that she wished him to represent her, she added what she called a 'manifesto on how life ought to be conducted without the use of swear words'. The first point she made was that it pained her to be

continuously insulted about my misuse of the English language. I often mis-spell but spelling errors can be corrected. Some people are just like that, they can't spell. A lot of prepositions get dropped. Someone can pick them up. But the impact of the English language on the rest of mankind cannot be realised by people living in certain circles in England.

She went on to say that when people use English all over the world, they give it local colour. She remembered how Naomi Mitchison had maintained that she couldn't understand Bessie's American reviews of *Maru.* They weren't written in English at all, she had said in a bored voice. But if Naomi had had books published in America, added Bessie very wisely, she would have at least made an effort to try to understand American English. 'There's also Setswana English, Chinese English etc. and for myself I prefer to evolve my own version of English as I go along.'[67] Though it is necessary to read 'politely corrected' for 'continuously insulted', the little lecture does illuminate the independent insight Bessie showed.

In November 1972 Giles Gordon could announce that he had found a hardback publisher for *A Question of Power.* Reg Davis-Poynter had just set up his own publishing house and he had offered an excellent advance for the novel. This was good news indeed. The eight-month-long agony appeared to be over. Bessie had lost her agent, and was probably more upset than she admitted about the flare-up with Hilary Rubinstein. Luck had been with her, though, in the finding of a new one. Not only had she salvaged a friendship at the last moment; she had acquired an agent who certainly knew what he was taking on.

A Sense of Community, 1973–1974

Serowe: Village of the Rain Wind
The Collector of Treasures

Bessie could have relaxed and celebrated her success, with her controversial novel finally accepted for publishing. The euphoric upsurge seemed sadly lacking, however. The novel's stormy passage had cost her some friends, and this began to worry her as the year drew to its close: 'The personal and the impersonal causes a terrible pain in my heart. I lost so many good friends during the time a thunderstorm raged in my life. They actually got nervous breakdowns from my letters,'[1] she wrote to Giles Gordon in early December 1972. Three weeks later she put it even more plainly:

I can't carry on with any friendships just now and I am grateful to the people who no longer write to me. Human beings need a lot of love you know but those who journey into hell need love in abnormal proportions. Due to this, one gets to a stage where one rejects for a while any kind of sympathy or affection to get one's balance back. There is a sort of underlying hysteria in me that could just burst out and weep like hell on the nearest shoulder. I cannot afford it. I cannot afford to write any more of those tear-drenched letters until I see how I make out as a normal human being.[2]

Bessie had asked both Tom Carvlin and Paddy Kitchen to destroy her earlier letters. Tom Carvlin did so. So when she spoke about not writing 'tear-drenched letters' she would be intending to become more restrained in her correspondence, especially with these two friends. She and Tom Carvlin did keep in touch, but the correspondence became sporadic; and the tone of Bessie's letters to Paddy Kitchen became more factual, restrained and almost formal after her writing critically of A Question of Power. About the time that Bessie completed A Question of Power, she wrote asking Paddy Kitchen if she could dedicate the book to her, to which Paddy replied that she would be delighted and proud to have this happen. In fact Bessie gave up this idea, eventually dedicating the novel to Randolph Vigne, Christine Hawes, Ken and Myrna Mackenzie, and Bosele Sianana. In March 1973 she told Paddy Kitchen that she preferred not to write for the present because she was in the middle of one of her usual last-ditch battles with the devil.[3] Paddy was travelling to Edinburgh frequently at the time and the correspondence lapsed.

Jean Highland had also stopped corresponding after Bessie's distraught letter in May. Finally, Bessie felt that Naomi did not love her any more or rather had never loved her. She, too, had been 'rather cooled'[4] off by the letter Bessie sent her when she had her breakdown. Bessie had not taken kindly to her comments to the publishers and Hilary Rubinstein about *A Question of Power*, as she felt that this was part of the reason for Hilary's aversion to it. But Randolph Vigne continued to hear from Bessie regularly.

Tom Holzinger left Serowe abruptly. It came as a shock to everyone at Swaneng when he received an official letter informing him that his residence permit, due to expire on 1 July 1973, would not be renewed. He was a man dedicated to working in the country for a long time, speaking Setswana fluently and even applying for citizenship, though this was refused. He completely supported the alternative educational opportunities offered by the Swaneng Complex, especially the brigades, and was thus against the country's established, often elitist, educational system, a typical example being an expensive private boarding school in Gaborone. This school was within the special sphere of interest of a permanent secretary in the President's Office. So it was probably an ideological clash that resulted in the administrative manoeuvre which led to Tom Holzinger's having to pack up in haste and leave for England. This was a great loss for Bessie. Tom Holzinger knew that he, along with Bosele Sianana and Howard, belonged to the exclusive little group of people whom Bessie had accepted as part of her daily life, responding to their loyalty with like feelings.[5] Furthermore, he was one of the very few friends to whom she remained truly loyal, for the sudden shifts of mood, the sudden derogatory remarks passed about many of her other friends in the course of her extensive correspondence, were not to be Tom Holzinger's fate. She kept in touch with him as he developed his 'socialist revolutionary' ideas, his desire for blue-collar work so that he would not feel a social parasite and his plans to start a Boiteko project in the U S A. 'Friends come and go for strange reasons,'[6] Bessie could remark bitterly to Randolph Vigne.

In early 1973 Bessie wrote a short piece for Dulan Barber. He was editing a collection of articles and stories on single-parent families and in early 1973 he asked Bessie for a contribution. She promptly wrote an excellent piece entitled 'Dear Tim, Will You Come to My Birthday Party?' In it she gave particulars of her childhood for the first time in a purely autobiographical form. The forthright tone cannot disguise the underlying hurt.[7]

She began making dramatic statements again, statements revealing her deep preoccupation with death. To someone in Gaborone she said that she wished to get her son out of the country and she needed travel documents for him, but not for herself: 'Dead bodies don't need travel documents.'[8] She still felt threatened by evil. In fact she began to suggest that *A Question of Power* had only recorded half the story. Since then she had embarked on the second phase of the struggle. Recognising evil as evil had brought temporary relief and the energy necessary to write the book. But she had not exorcised the devil yet. For this reason thoughts of leaving the country occupied a great deal of her attention. In July she wrote asking Tony Hall, now living in Sussex, whether he would consider selling her a small portion of the family property where she could build a house. She had a great urge to settle in England. She asked him to talk to the other family members on this matter, but no more was heard of the scheme.[9] Meanwhile she was consulting a bank manager about how one should write a will and he gave her detailed information on this matter.[10]

In September 1973 a new friend walked into her life. As she was tending her garden, she received a telegram from the American State Department in Gaborone asking her to come to the capital. The American poet Nikki Giovanni was on a lecture tour of some African countries and as soon as she reached Botswana she asked to meet their famous writer, Bessie Head. After some embarrassed enquiries, Bessie Head was traced, contacted and fetched, with all the complications of communication and transport which this involved.

Nikki Giovanni had probably first heard about Bessie Head, the famous writer, from Harold Head. By 1966, with his status as a freedom fighter, he had been admitted to the United States and had registered on a course at the John Oliver Killen's Writers' Workshop at Fisk University, in Nashville, Tennessee. Here he met the promising young poet, Nikki Giovanni.[11] She actually wrote to Bessie shortly after *Maru* appeared in 1971. She it was who had said: 'Bessie Head always reminds me of a classmate I should have had but didn't. A girl I should have shared secrets with but didn't. A girl I would have skipped Double-Dutch with'.[12] Bessie had treasured this letter and read it many times but she had never replied. So when she held the telegram in her dirty gardening hands she was dumbfounded.

Then suddenly she was in Gaborone and coming towards her was a very ordinary looking girl, no make-up even, someone she too felt she might have gone to school with. And someone with whom she immediately felt comfortable. In no time they were chatting like old friends. For the four days that Nikki Giovanni was in Botswana, she insisted on keeping Bessie by her side. Nikki Giovanni was designated the title of 'eternal sister' and Bessie was sure she would gradually remember how they had been related in their previous incarnations. Her visit gave a wonderful lift to Bessie's life. She was totally unused to being fêted and enveloped with warmth and friendship. Bessie returned to Serowe to write some of her most inspired descriptions of her daily life and surroundings. These she sent to Nikki in an eight-page closely typed letter, which even for Bessie was impressive.

A Question of Power was published in October as planned. Shortly before its publication in England, it was sold to the American publishers Pantheon Books, and appeared there in May 1974. There was an added element of excitement attached to its appearance. Davis-Poynter had nominated it as his only entry for the prestigious Booker Prize, though by November Bessie knew that she was not short-listed. Friends in London launched the novel with a party at the Mackenzies but the guest of honour was not present. They played a taped message from Bessie.

The reviews appeared. They were often carefully worded and hesitant, rather than enthusiastic, sensing something important, yet grasping it incompletely. Paddy Kitchen, writing in the *New Statesman*, was perceptive and generous in her praise, though she did admit that it was not altogether easy 'to share the journey' Bessie Head was describing. She commented on 'the clarity of the terror' that had been rescued from the 'private muddled nightmares' of what in crude terms could be called a 'nervous breakdown'; she called the writing 'well-paced, with humour and stark information lacing the horror'. In her concluding sentence she reiterated a point Bessie herself had made, referring to people of mixed blood 'shading themselves down to browns and yellows and creams'. Paddy Kitchen said that 'a great deal has been written about black writers, but Bessie Head is surely one of the pioneers of brown literature – a literature that includes everybody'.[13] Bessie liked the review, mentioning especially how pleased she was that Paddy had called Elizabeth 'Everywoman', when she wrote to thank her. 'I wondered who would see that humility that never rose above life itself,'[14] she said. A review appearing the following April in the American journal, the *New Republic*, said that *A Question of Power* enlarged 'the geographical as well as the symbolic regions of madness' and praised the skill with which Bessie involved the reader in 'the immediacy and terror of Elizabeth's confrontations with her demons'. Bessie began a correspondence with this reviewer, Roberta Rubinstein, and her husband, Charles Larson, both American academics, during the course of which she revealed more of her own experiences of evil, the background to *A Question of Power*, as she called it.[15]

No other novel of hers had been given as much critical attention, but later she became somewhat gloomy about *A Question of Power*'s reception. She felt that the critics were against her. Any mention of 'insanity' or a 'nervous breakdown' made her dislike a review. Though she valued Roberta Rubinstein's review, for example, the fact that she had referred to Elizabeth's 'frigidity' upset her. She was hypersensitive and vulnerable and maintained solidly that the novel had been about a confrontation with God and the Devil, a soul journey to hell. Her reaction showed that she had not been able to extricate herself from the experience she had described or distance herself from her material.

Getting her novel published had been only one trial Bessie faced. The modest income from her writing had gradually dried up and by August 1972 she was broke. She went to Patrick van Rensburg with her problem. During the time she had been working at the garden she had not taken any share of the earnings because she had her royalties. Now she needed money and he agreed to pay her R20 a month to tide her over. He contacted Randolph, who once more contacted Canon Collins. Some funds were collected for her in England.

Before *A Question of Power* had even found a hardback publisher, plans were being made for Bessie's future writing. Giles Gordon encouraged her to produce articles or short pieces that could be published in English newspapers and journals, thus keeping her name before the reading public until her next novel appeared.

Very rapidly she wrote 'Borrowed Clothes', an article in which she gave free rein to her thoughts on creativity. She considered the deathly effect of being confronted with a society of extreme cruelty, such as the South African one, if you happen to be born a 'dreamer and storyteller' and wish to enrich people's lives with 'thoughts and generosities wider and freer' than anything they have. She sent it off in August and it was published in the *Listener* in November, under the title 'An African Story'.

Ken Mackenzie, who as Cape Town editor of *Drum* had given Bessie advice with her early writing, had asked her to help him do some research into the life of his great-grandfather. This was John Mackenzie, the London Missionary Society minister who worked with the Bamangwato under their great chief, Khama III. It was to be a request with far-reaching consequences. Bessie found plenty about the remarkable missionary whose book *Ten Years North of the Orange River* had an excellent chapter on Bamangwato history, but what enthralled her most was the information she found out about the Bamangwato's famous chief. 'Khama, the Great' entered Bessie's life.

She wrote an article about him too and sent it off, hoping that the *New Statesman* would take it, but admitting later that it was short on fact and free on comment. When it was rejected she gave it to the Mackenzies with the information she had found about their relative, and started anew on a Khama article.

Noting the direction of her enthusiasm, Giles came up with a new idea. Why not write a 'village' book about Serowe along the same lines as Jan Myrdal's *Report from a Chinese Village* and *Akenfield, Portrait of an English Village*, by Ronald Blythe. Bessie started to read *Akenfield* and liked the idea of writing something about Serowe. Giles Gordon impressed on her that she should feel a very strong reason for writing the book and impose her own approach on her material, otherwise the venture would never be successful.

Meanwhile she had found a couple of other stories for Giles Gordon. In September 1969 there had been discussions about combining *Maru* with two or three other short stories because it was more a novella than a novel. At that stage Bessie mentioned that she had three available: 'Jacob, The Story of a Faith Healing Priest', 'Property' and 'The Prisoner Who Wore Glasses'. However, *Maru* was published alone and the short stories went back into the drawer of Bessie's desk. She had originally written 'Jacob' because David Machin wanted something from her for a short-story collection dealing with children around the world. Both 'Jacob' and 'The Prisoner Who Wore Glasses' were longer than most magazines wanted but in November she sent them off to Giles Gordon in an optimistic frame of mind.

By this time Bessie had begun to give serious attention to her 'Serowe book'. She had decided to build it up around the lives and times of three important personalities – Khama the Great, Tshekedi Khama and Patrick van Rensburg. They reflected the three stages of the development of education in village history: the missionaries' education of a few children sitting out under a tree; the establishment of village schools making primary education available to all; the introduction of secondary and vocational education.

Much of her information she obtained by interviewing people who could tell her about the activities which had characterised village life at the various stages of its development. This she could not do on her own and she was fortunate to find help. Her friend Bosele Sianana had gradually learnt to speak English, taught by Bessie.[16] She was a valuable interpreter and guide to the village wards. Bessie would hear about an old man who could tell about the role of the *kgotla* or was one of the original pot-makers in the village and she would ask Bosele where he lived. Bosele always knew things like that and she would take Bessie there, go through the long series of introductory greetings and patiently extract the account that Bessie wanted from him. Bessie would write, listen and absorb, then hurry back to her typewriter. Afterwards, she and Bosele would return to the informant and let him or her hear (or read) what she had written as a form of verification.

She had many rich experiences, as for example when she was interviewing the very first teacher in Serowe, aged about eighty. He spoke English and was proud of it. 'But', he added with an engaging smile, 'my English may not sound quite proper to you . . . The words don't come out so well, as I have no teeth.'[17]

Sometimes she could hardly make sense of the stories she was told and felt that she was not meant to. One old man had a wealth of ancient knowledge because he was almost a hundred years old. He was frail and semi-senile and for three months Bessie and Bosele would visit him periodically in the hopes of catching him in the right frame of mind to tell them about his past. After talking for ten minutes, he would begin to wheeze and cough and could not manage any more. The next time they came, Bessie always began by recapitulating what he had said last time. This would provoke splutters of indignation and he and his equally senile cronies would deny everything: 'I never told this woman anything like that. Now is that our history, brothers?' In this way she got six different – and totally useless – versions of the way their clan, the Talaote, originated. The only way she could get her own back on 'those terrible old men having fun' at her expense was to weave the versions into a fictional story and refer to the 'confused and contradictory accounts of their origins'. She called the short story 'The Deep River'.[18]

Bessie almost met her match when she interviewed Grant Kgosi, tribal *kgotla* voluntary assessor and special observer. He was a man who belonged to the old order of things, when there was time to sit under the shady trees of the village *kgotla* and discuss at great length intricate points concerning human justice. Grant Kgosi was what Bessie called a 'supreme example of the grandeur and charm of this old world on which the sun is setting'.[19] An added touch of originality was his passion for writing official letters. Whenever he found an example of injustice or need, he wrote an official letter about it; two are included with the interview to illustrate this. He formulated each in his special way and flavoured it with flourishes such as 'I . . . have the honour to voice my views' and 'Your affectionate servant'. This gentleman saw such an advantage in knowing an extremely articulate lady who bashed away at the keys of a typewriter with ease that he often visited Bessie, and in his booming, majestic voice asked her to type out letters for him, sometimes falling asleep on her mat while she did so. He even carried the interest so far as to propose to her.[20] Little did he realise that concealed within that homely female form was a writer of official letters beside which his own would fade into insignificance.

Bessie found another unexpected ally in her search for local history. Mary Kibel, Patrick van Rensburg's sister-in-law, was spending some time in Serowe while collecting folktales for a series of sixteen story-books she was writing, for use in schools in Botswana. A traditional historian called Mokgojwa Mathware was a veritable treasure trove of tales and Mary Kibel visited him many times in Pilikwe, where he lived, to hear his stories. Bessie and Bosele went with her sometimes and Bessie used an interview and two stories connected with the Bamangwato tribe in her book.[21] Bessie later recalled their happy times together and especially their last trip to Pilikwe, 'the picnic lunch in the bush, the puddles of water and the huge din of the insects and birds in the bush, out of their minds with all the rain we had had'.[22]

The most exhilarating part was doing research into Khama's life. She would need some for the 'Serowe book', but she was also working towards a biography of Khama at a later date. She admitted to Giles Gordon that she only kept going on the book through the accidental discovery of Khama the Great. 'No matter where I turn the stuff on him I've read during my research for the book had the effect of pulling my life together.'[23]

In November 1973 Reg Davis-Poynter paid an option of £100 to have first offer of the Serowe book. This gave Bessie some badly needed cash and the spur to get it finished.

There were also disadvantages connected with the work. At the beginning of 1974 Bessie said the book was weighing heavily on her and she was exhausted. She had to chase after, or rather wait for, people who had left Serowe to go out and plough their lands and would not be back for months. Then there was the question of tactfulness. 'I always have to be very polite and people rile me a lot. They first say they like girls and then they don't like to see it in print and I began to have a block mentally through being so awfully polite . . . So I shot out and made side notes in my style, and commentary,'[24] she wrote to Nikki Giovanni. She was clearly itching to get on to something more creative. And she had the material.

In late 1973, about the time *A Question of Power* appeared, *London Magazine* published what was to prove one of her most popular short stories, 'The Prisoner Who Wore Glasses'. The idea had originated years before in Francistown where Bessie had met a short-sighted little fellow, thin with a hollow chest and nobbly knees. He had been a political prisoner in South Africa and he told the story of how he had humanised a brute of a white warder. She never forgot it. After she had completed *Rain Clouds*, she started to write the tale down. She embroidered it slightly, adding 'certain tendernesses'.

She demonstrates an unusual blend of traditional story-telling techniques and sharp social commentary. By the end of the first page it is clear that the picturesque setting described in the first lines – calm blue sky, white drifting clouds, long rows of bright green cabbages – provides the background for a prison work gang, Span One. The villainous warder poses a decidedly realistic threat with his blue eyes from which 'a simple, primitive, brutal soul gazed'.[25] When it comes, the happy ending has the same rueful blend of realism and fantasy. Getting Warder Hannetjie on to their side means that the prisoners can 'manage the long stretch ahead'[26] while they show their appreciation by stealing 'certain commodities like bags of fertilizer' for his farm.

Early in 1974 Bessie was in Gaborone with the intention of asking the United

Nations High Commission Office for Refugees to re-open her file and try to help her to find a country of resettlement somewhere in the world. She was staying with Marit Kromberg, a Norwegian doctor whom she had known in Serowe and had interviewed for her Serowe book.

'What were you doing there?' asked Marit Kromberg when Bessie had told her of her morning's activities. Bessie told her the long story of her problems as a refugee. 'Why not settle in Norway?' she then said, knowing that the Norwegian government was taking in refugees from Southern Africa. Furthermore, she knew that at the University of Oslo they needed someone whose mother tongue was English to lecture on African literature.

It did not take her long to sort out the exact requirements and Bessie was given a genuine offer to resettle in Norway. The country itself sounded frightening to someone who scuffed the red sand of Serowe against her feet each day, who knew about drought, heat and irrigation but not about ice and snow; someone who listened in bewilderment to the Setswana spoken around her and had to face the fact that she would never learn Norwegian either. But Marit Kromberg pointed out the advantages: a free plane ticket to Norway; a living allowance for eighteen months while she was adjusting to the society; the prospect of citizenship; social security; good, varied educational facilities for Howard and the chance that he could become wholly integrated into Norwegian society; much sympathetic support for her as a writer. Here, after all these years, was the break Bessie had been waiting for. She could lift them both away from the evils that plagued her in Botswana. She accepted the offer.

Bessie's life was turned upside down. She would have to move fast and be ready to leave Botswana by about August so that she could commence her new job after the summer holidays and start Howard off at school at the same time. She would have to get her house sold. She would have to pack their belongings. Then there was the problem of her writing project. The 'Serowe book' would have to be got ready to take with her. However, none of these problems could be compared to the almost insurmountable ones connected with any other form of emigration. The official side of it would be arranged by the Norwegian authorities and their transport expenses would be met. Accommodation and sufficient funds to live on would be waiting at the other side.

She had her house valued and set the sales price at P3,800. The household furniture that would be sold separately consisted of two beds, a wardrobe, a table and chairs, a writing desk, a gas stove, kitchen utensils and gardening tools. But Bessie was like the old couple going on holiday from Cape Town to Durban that she had described in her very first published piece: 'Just as the first warning bell rang he shouted with real terror in his voice: "Ma, get off. Let's go home."'[27] Three months after accepting the offer, she changed her mind. She found that she could not leave Serowe after all.

Bessie's reasons for making her decision greatly distressed Marit Kromberg. She said she had deliberately chosen death. She felt she could not live much longer, 'five years would be a miracle' and she would prefer to die in the little house she had built herself. As for Howard, he would have to make his own way in the world. And should she receive a 'deportation letter' (as she called it) such as Tom Holzinger had received, she would simply commit suicide, after sending telegrams to the Botswana government and other people to let them know.[28] Some months later, however, when she heard from a common friend how much her references to death and suicide had upset Marit, she wrote to her again: 'You can always trust me to think up desperate dramas like that! Well here I am still alive.' Then she showed that she was grateful for Marit's help. Their long talks had enabled her to gain control of the panic that used to flood over her life. She would 'spend a lot of time writing panic-stricken letters to people who could do nothing about the situation'. But Marit showed her in every way that she cared about her and Bessie needed this: '[D]eep down I just wanted someone to care; once I was sure of that, I calmed down.' She admitted that she had put her thoughts about death badly, but in fact she had faced it more realistically than ever before. People normally do not do that; it is too 'unpleasant and frightening. Once I had faced that, I simply carried on with the jobs in front of me . . . It was that particular expertise that settled my mind so one should say that you are a very good doctor!'[29] It is deeply tragic that Bessie so often felt that no one cared about her. Many people had disproved this but she sometimes had difficulty in recognising and accepting offers of help in the same simple spirit that they were given.

In some moods she apparently saw herself now living 'one of the most gruesome lives it is possible for a human being to live'.[30] On the one hand, then, she was making far-reaching plans to leave the village and Africa, while on the other she was working on the most interesting parts of the book. She had reached the stage where she was arranging her material, focusing her social history around her three central personalities, men who 'wanted to change the world. They had to make great gestures. Great gestures have an oceanic effect on society – they flood a whole town.'[31] In the section relating to Khama III, she shows how he had, with his fine sense of timing and diplomacy, led his people into Christianity without entirely disrupting traditional tribal values. After the short biographical account she collects the interviews with villagers describing such things as early education, the function of the *kgotla* and traditional skills such as hut-building, tanning, pot-making and basket-making. The second section, devoted to Tshekedi Khama, is used to show how he had used the reforms of his father to launch a programme of development activities for the Bamangwato. Schools, a hospital and a college were built by the men of the tribe, working in age regiments. This meant that when Patrick van Rensburg settled in the village, his ideas of self-help were not foreign to the people. The final section gathers together interviews describing and illustrating the development of the cooperative projects such as Swaneng School, the Brigades and Boiteko. Normally Bessie allows the interviews to stand alone, though she does intrude occasionally, as with the section on religion, where she gives a brief account of the London Missionary Society in Serowe; and the first of the two chapters called 'The End of an Era', where she pays tribute to the old men of the tribe and the 'haunting magic' that surrounds them.

The parts where she could write some of those lyrical passages 'with all the stops out on the landscape',[32] as she put it, were what she enjoyed most. The Introduction captures the atmosphere of the village with keen precision. She describes the pulsating ball of fire that suddenly breaks clear of the horizon at sunrise; the 'peculiar teasing rain' that comes so seldom; the ring of low blue hills surrounding the village: '[A]t least, they look blue, misty, from a distance. But if sunlight and shadow strike them at a certain angle, you can quite clearly see their flat and unmysterious surfaces. They look like the uncombed heads of old Batswana men, dotted here and there with the dark shapes of thorn trees.'[33] Of this passage she later said that it 'takes months of observation to write a passage like that and real love. That's the difference between chores and creation.'[34]

Her 'Epilogue – A Poem for Serowe' she had ready and waiting in a first draft. When she returned from her meeting with Nikki Giovanni the previous October, she sat down and wrote what later became this poem. The birds, pathways and sunsets, the small boys with their home-made wire cars, the winter outdoor fire-sides, the wedding parties, are all there. The description of the solitary bird-call at dawn in the Introduction is also taken directly from what she wrote that inspired day when she felt as fond of her typewriter as an old piano player would feel of his piano, 'all the keys and my fingers are so acquainted with each other'.[35]

This build-up of emotional pressure as she completed the typescript of what she had decided to call *Serowe: Village of the Rain Wind* was what made Bessie take the final decision about remaining in Serowe. She explained it thus to Giles Gordon: 'I'm going to say something very illogical now. It's a question of love for a place. I'd posted off the Serowe typescript to you then I sat up the whole night and quietly thought out my situation and by the time morning came round I had cancelled all plans about going to Norway.'

She admitted that the offer had been good, but 'I have put too much of my heart into the country'. She had been thinking of Howard's future when she decided to emigrate to Norway, but she now realised that 'one could protect a child just so far and then you have to let him fight the rest out for himself'.[36] She thought of all the energy she had put into writing the book; about the way she understood so many things in an entirely different way now. She thought of the doddering old men in the Botalaote ward with their rich heritage of oral history and their roots deep in the sand, stone and bush of the place. She thought of her bicycle rides into the village every day. The way everyone knew 'Mma-Heady' and greeted her. She thought of her own little house so carefully built and her many solitary nights at her writing desk, now to be sold. She could not leave it. When she died, she told friends, she wanted to be buried at the Botalaote cemetery.

Bessie had received a welcome letter from Patrick Cullinan in November 1973. He had only recently heard about her nervous breakdown and was concerned about her and anxious to help. In fact, he had heard such unsettling things about her unhappy life in Botswana that he was already busy raising money, with the support of people like Nadine Gordimer, to pay for air tickets for Bessie and Howard should they wish to go to England. When he and another old friend from Cape Town days, the poet James Matthews, realised that the situation was not as critical as they had feared, it was agreed that Patrick and his wife Wendy should visit her as soon as something could be arranged. They came in May, expecting to see her for the last time in Africa, but were pleased to hear that she was staying after all. It was the first time the Cullinans and Bessie had ever had the chance of sitting down and enjoying each other's company. When they had met in Cape Town and in Pretoria, when they helped her get her exit permit, things had been tense and anxious, with urgent decisions constantly looming. Now there was time for 'almost solving what keeps it all up there spinning round'. The Cullinans met many of Bessie's friends from Swaneng and were absorbed straight into the 'family', as they saw eye to eye on so many things. Patrick had given up farming and he and Lionel Abrahams, a poet too, had started a small publishing firm, Bateleur Press. He studied Bessie's 'Serowe book' with great interest. On the last evening, after too much to eat and to drink, Patrick and Bessie got into an excited argument about the way white Afrikaners had treated the blacks in South Africa. Patrick could not go along with Bessie's sweeping generalisations and damning verdicts. 'Look here Bessie, you have to keep more to

Patrick Cullinan's first visit to Serowe, 1974 (courtesy Khama Memorial Museum)

the facts than you are doing now,' he said, and felt for the first time her displeasure at being opposed. She accused him angrily of supporting evil people.[37] But they parted amicably the next day, Patrick lending her a large sum of money and six months later some more: 'You left a big glow behind you with all the people you met,' wrote Bessie to Wendy shortly afterwards.[38] Later she told Patrick that she had done some reading on the subject of their disagreement and that he was right. She gave him something as rare as a formal apology.

In early June the publisher Reg Davis-Poynter responded to the Serowe manuscript. He told Giles Gordon that he thought very highly of it, but that he was afraid it would not be easy to sell. Though his offer for the book was not very high, Giles advised Bessie to take it. It was important to have a publisher who was as enthusiastic about the book as Davis-Poynter was. However, he felt that *Serowe: Village of the Rain Wind* would be improved by about a dozen line drawings to illustrate the text. Bessie wrote back immediately, accepting Davis-Poynter's offer and mentioning a friend of Mary Kibel's, Polly Isaacsen, as an artist who did line drawings which were 'very, very good indeed'.[39] She also told Davis-Poynter that she had interviewed 94 people in connection with the project and she had promised them all a free copy each. She hoped that he would be willing to supply her with these free of charge. Davis-Poynter warned her that having to supply so many free copies would inevitably send the price of the book up. At the same time Giles Gordon sent a copy of the typescript to the American publishers Pantheon Books, in the hopes that they would accept it and thus cut the publishing expenses. By the end of July Bessie had signed the publishing contract with Davis-Poynter. She pleased Paddy Kitchen and Giles Gordon greatly by asking them if she could dedicate the book to them.

Bessie knew that she still had great reserves of unworked material, even though *Serowe: Village of the Rain Wind* was complete. A short article she had written, called 'Bamangwato Children',[40] appeared that May. But she had much more stuff that could be worked into either articles or stories. If she had left Botswana she would have had to abandon her beloved Khama and these other short stories that were beginning to form in her imagination. With the decision suddenly reversed, ideas had begun to bubble into her head.

She started straight into her *Botswana Village Tales*, as she originally called the collection. 'I'm having a real boom of ideas. I think it is because I nearly lost my home, the quiet everyday routine and all the things I love here. I look at them all, appalled by the thought that I had ever planned to give up my birds, my pathways, my sunsets!'[41] she wrote to Giles Gordon later in June.

Once more she sat at her desk far into the night, with her two or three candles lighting her papers. Howard, waking suddenly and seeing her face animated and distorted in the candlelight, would hear her chuckling to herself, or cursing, and fall asleep again to the clatter of the typewriter. 'I depend very much on magic almost. Sometimes when I am sitting at the typewriter I can almost see my hands glowing with light,' she once confided to a friend.[42] But her present task gave her ample opportunity to demonstrate what she considered her particular talent as a writer: the ability to 'stand back and wait to learn . . . letting people teach you about themselves can be a wonderful experience'.[43] She once described her own creative process like this: 'I like fiction myself, once I am going strong and in the middle of work. I don't like what happens in between, the terrible doubts and frustrations and uncertainties. In between books I always believe I can't write at all – it's that long build-up period that one goes through before one can take on something new. I think eventually one's battle with fiction is the sheer power one gets in the process of creating or drawing pictures.'[44]

Her friend Betty Sleath proved a great source of encouragement as she embarked on her new project. She had helped with the mailing of the *New African* in the old days, and as an active member of the War on Want had helped to collect money for the Boiteko project. About this time she began a regular correspondence with Bessie. Her knowledge of and interest in Botswana was extensive. She made penetrating comments and even sent Bessie some suggestions for plots. One that Bessie adopted was Betty's idea of writing a story entitled 'Kgotla'. She imagined that a gathering of the *kgotla* could not be very different from any British committee, or even parliament, with its share of 'long-winded fools' coming up with irrelevant ideas. She also asked what would happen if a Christian girl fell in love with an animist boy. Could that be made into a short story? And what about the situation of an educated Christian who still believed in witchcraft?[45] Bessie was delighted with the help, though she said that she had a story on witchcraft already: 'I can see your interest in the collection is very intense. I dare not send a report on the bad days when I wake up and say: "You know B Head, you aren't any hot shakes as a writer. Why, you haven't a bloody thought in your head." '[46]

Bessie had another friend, Gothe Kgamane, in the village, who also enjoyed discussing her work with her. She had met Bessie when she was a young girl and had gone to her house with her parents to buy seedlings. Great was her surprise when she was later given a prize at the Teachers' Training College to discover that it was a book called *When Rain Clouds Gather* written by her market gardener friend. She would often ask Bessie what she was working on or discuss some aspect of village life with her. Once she saw Bessie at a funeral. She had withdrawn from the crowd and was studying everything very quietly. 'Are you writing a story, Bessie?' asked Gothe Kgamane laughingly. 'No, not really,' said Bessie. 'But I was thinking how close birth, marriage and death are to each other in a village.'[47] She was referring to the fact that just a day or two earlier all the same people had been assembled at a wedding, where many of the same rituals had been observed. In late 1973, Bessie wrote a short piece she called 'Serowe Weddings', probably later entitled 'Snapshots of a Wedding',[48] capturing some of this atmosphere. Gothe Kgamane and Betty Sleath, Bessie's 'devoted fans' she called them, had her collection of short stories dedicated to them, when it finally appeared.

In September 1974 the writer Alice Walker contacted Bessie's American agent, Lois Wallace. She had just become an editor on the magazine *Ms* and she asked Lois Wallace if she had any short stories by Bessie Head which *Ms* could publish. The agent referred her directly to Bessie.

Bessie already knew that Alice Walker admired her writing. She had been generous with her praise of *A Question of Power* and had been quoted on the jacket of the American edition as saying that she thought that Bessie Head was one of the 'most important writers . . . I find her vision trustworthy, her wisdom there to lean on, to borrow from, and to remember.' Now the famous American writer told her personally that she was a 'deep admirer' of her work. It had helped her 'see things more clearly, to understand, to grow'.[49] She asked her for short stories.

The request could hardly have come at a more opportune time. She had seven on hand. She sent off 'The Deep River: A Story of Ancient Tribal Migration', 'Heaven is Not Closed', 'The Special One', 'Life', 'Witchcraft', 'Looking for a Rain God' and 'Hunting'. Of these six were newly written and 'Looking for a Rain God' had appeared in the *New African* in 1966. Her agent in London also received copies and a concerted effort to sell these (and the others as they arrived) to British and South African magazines was now made. Giles Gordon liked them very much though he did fear that they were too 'sober' or 'unglossy for what the majority of British magazines are publishing at present'.[50] However, some were sold individually and brought in some much-needed cash before appearing in the collection. And Alice Walker chose the pick of the bunch for *Ms*: 'Witchcraft' was published there the following November. In a biographical introduction to the short story, Bessie gave detailed particulars about her childhood for the second time. These were of great interest to her growing number of admirers. The article in Dulan Barber's *One Parent Families*, while more specific and poignant, had not reached a very wide critical audience.

Meanwhile Bessie replied to Alice Walker's letter with her usual disarming frankness: 'On my own I am just the sort of happy person who lives in leaps and bounds, but that is not the whole of life – it presents you with painful, detailed learning and what has amazed me has been the blunders I've made,' she wrote, and added: 'The suffering one endures for having no set programme, plans or ideology. I mean by all this that I don't have a grand image.'[51] This was the start of a correspondence which, in its initial stages especially, generated an exchange of ideas that both parties enjoyed.

By the end of 1974 Bessie had collected thirteen stories, including 'Jacob: The Story of a Faith-Healing Priest' which had been around for some years. Though the title of the anthology was still the rather artless *Botswana Village Tales*, it soon became clear that she had organised her material with sophisticated insight. In fact she insisted upon the stories remaining in the order in which she had them because she wanted a sense of continuity, with one story subtly linking with the next.

Together they cover just about all the major themes of village life and explore the whole spectrum of human emotions. She sets the scene with her fictionalised version of tribal history, 'The Deep River: A Story of Ancient Tribal Migration'. In a world where women are of no account, she tells of a chief who chooses a woman rather than power. In the next story, 'Heaven is Not Closed', she examines the predicament of a woman who has to choose between Christianity and the traditional views of her husband and who naively hopes that 'a compromise of tenderness could be made between two traditions opposed to each other' (p. 10). Christian values and human insincerity form the theme of the next story, where the irony of the title, 'Village Saint', emerges in the first paragraph. And so it continues: cross-references, ambivalence and ironic distance from the muddle and confusion that is life itself. Just as Galethebege in 'Heaven is Not Closed' would have been good 'under any custom, whether Setswana custom or Christian custom' (p. 8), so the truly saintly Jacob in 'Jacob: The Story of a Faith-Healing Priest' is never able to make clear to his followers who his God is. At times he would call him Jesus. At times He would appear to be 'the width and depth of his own experience and suffering' (p. 21).

Some years later Bessie, in discussing the way in which the notes and interviews relating to *Serowe: Village of the Rain Wind* had 'spilled over into two other books', said that her collection of short stories dealt 'specifically with information given to me about women and their position in society'.[52] This somewhat clinical description does no real justice to the richness and diversity of her central theme, the situation of rural women. She examines aspects of wifely devotion in such characters as Johannah in 'Jacob: The Story of a Faith-Healing Priest', Rose in 'Kgotla', Kenalepe in 'The Collector of Treasures' and Thato in 'Hunting'. But sexual promiscuity, brashness and insensitivity are equally well-covered in her descriptions of Life in the story of that name, Gaenametse in 'The Special One' and Neo in 'Snapshots of a Wedding'.

Bessie shows an impatience with so-called modern women in this anthology. Consider the description of Mma-Mompati presiding over luncheons 'just like any English lady with polished etiquette and the professional smile of the high-born' (p. 14). Or Life, a bold, free woman with brittle ways and an 'undertone of hysteria' who has 'broken all the social taboos' (p. 40), and has 'nothing inside herself' (p. 43) to cope with village life. Or Neo, 'a new kind of girl with false postures and acquired grand madame ways' (p. 78). Though Bessie did have sympathy for educated women who had moved away from traditional patterns of life, as epitomised for example in her friend Thato Matome, described in *Serowe: Village of the Rain Wind* (p. 83), she does not include any such portraits here.

She is clearly more taken up with describing what are indeed the backbone of their society, the semi-literate women who rear fatherless children in a hand-to-mouth existence, having been deserted by smart men who promised them marriage and then left the village at the first signs of pregnancy. Mma-Mabele, in 'Witchcraft', is such a woman; as is Dikeledi Mokopo in 'The Collector of Treasures'. And indeed, these two stories incorporate most effectively the central theme.

Bessie is never more outspoken in her criticism of men than in 'The Collector of Treasures' though she does recognise the fact that the three stages through which rural African society has passed during the last hundred years have in part been responsible for the shaping of most male attitudes.

Traditional custom was intended to regulate the life of the whole society and generally it succeeded. But it was the women who paid the greater price for this: they were regarded as inferior, chattels even, while the men took their superior position for granted. Then came the colonial era and with it a period of great change for the men. They were forced out of their villages to work in towns where they were humiliated with degrading treatment, and because of this, the men seemed unable to meet the challenge which the country's independence provided, 'the first occasion for family life of a new order, above the childlike discipline of custom, the degradation of colonialism'. They often proved broken wrecks, with 'no inner resources at all', engaged in a 'dizzy kind of death dance of wild destruction and dissipation' (p. 92). All too many seemed content to live 'near the animal level' and create 'misery and chaos' by being responsible for the 'complete breakdown of family life' (p. 91). Like Garesego Mokopi, many quickly lost interest in a woman who was a 'boring semi-literate traditional sort'.

Sensitive traditional women wishing to avoid further humiliation and mistreatment were still no better off than when they had been trapped by the old customs which gave men inherent privileges. Driven to total desperation, they could choose the course taken by Dikeledi in 'The Collector of Treasures'. Or they could withdraw within themselves, choosing celibacy instead. In this case they would have to be prepared to suffer the revengeful manipulations of an insulted lover. In 'Witchcraft' this is the fate of Mma-Mabele, whose moral courage and common sense are tested against tribal superstition.

It is not entirely clear how Mma-Mabele survives the evil that attacks her so unexpectedly. She uses her rational powers, her shrewd observation, to convince herself that the witchdoctor is no more omnipotent than she is herself. But this cannot cure her. She uses her Christian belief, but this becomes an invented defence to keep Lekena, the witchdoctor, at bay. Finally she concludes that 'there is no one to help the people, not even God'. So it seems that like Jacob, it is the 'width and depth' of her own suffering that pulls her through. When her friends are expecting her to die, she suddenly recovers because she is too poor to sit down and die 'and there is no one else to feed my children' (p. 56). Though the short story ostensibly derives from Bosele Sianana's experience of waking up and finding a large tuft of hair cut off her head,[53] it can also be seen as encapsulating the experience Bessie described in such detail in *A Question of Power*, based on her own life. The short story acquires a new dimension if her references to the possibility of a local evil force, witchcraft, are taken into account.[54]

In the other main story, 'The Collector of Treasures', the same inner reserves of strength enable Dikeledi Mokopi to find 'gold amidst the ash', despite the 'ashen . . . loneliness and unhappiness of her life' (p. 91). In prison she becomes part of a sisterhood of sufferers who secretly nurture each other. It is their sheer will to survive that proves these women's greatest strength. 'Our men do not think that we need tenderness and care' (p. 89), says one of the women prisoners. The vividly sketched prison scene at the start of the story might well be based on Bessie Head's own taste of prison life after her libelling of the President.[55]

Again and again we are reminded of the tangle of human relationships, the inadequate and haphazard nature of human justice. In the oldest story in the collection, 'Looking for a Rain God', the reader feels intense sympathy for the plight of the family desperately waiting for rain to fall and rescue them from starvation. But in a court of law, 'the subtle story of strain and starvation and breakdown was inadmissable [*sic*] evidence' (p. 60) and the two men are sentenced to death for their rain-making practices. Though everyone in the village is horrified by the death of the two little girls, they also know 'that only a hair's breadth' has saved them from committing an equally horrible act in their desperation for rain. In two of the other stories which involve murder, there is no clear condemnation of the murderers either. Dikeledi Moroki pays for her crime with life imprisonment, but there is no doubt in her mind or that of her fellow prisoners, that their crimes were necessary and that their husbands got their just deserts. Similarly when Lesego, the cattle-man, murders his wife Life (and only gets five years' imprisonment for his 'crime of passion') society at large justifies his action. His friend explains things by saying that there are 'good women and good men but they seldom join their lives together. It's always this mess and foolishness' (p. 46). In the story 'The Wind and the Boy', the newly rich, self-important official who has a car but neither brakes nor a driving licence, decapitates the boy Friedman in a gruesome accident and gets away with it; once more, the machinery of justice seems inadequate.

There is also much wry humour in the tales. People are very conscious of their newly independent status. Thus Garesego Mokobi and his likes have no trouble finding plenty of exciting new women. 'Independence produced marvels indeed' (p. 92). And Lekena, the witchdoctor, appalled at the strength of the evil spirits bewitching Mma-Mabele, exclaims: 'We never can tell what will happen these days, now that we have independence' (p. 55). There is also the humorous account of how the whole village memorises Mma-Mompati's divorce oration on 'God, the Church, the Bible, the Sick, . . . the Honour of an Honourable Woman', because she repeats it 'so often thereafter' (p. 15). And there is even something starkly amusing in the anti-climax of the concluding lines of 'The Collector of Treasures'. As Dikeledi stands passively beside the emasculated, blood-soaked body of her husband, awaiting the arrival of the police, her friend Paul Thebolo finds her there. For a moment he is totally dumbfounded. Then he says: 'You don't have to worry about the children . . . I'll take them as my own and give them all a secondary school education' (p. 103).

Bessie does portray some men of decency and nobility. Paul Thebolo in 'The Collector of Treasures' is one who possesses 'the power to create himself anew' (p. 93). His relationship with his wife is happy and fulfilled; their yard is always overflowing with visitors seeking out their company; and through them Dikeledi's life is enriched. The final story, 'Hunting', depicts another such man, Tholo; like Paul, he has a marriage relationship 'where the whole rhythm and happiness of their lives was tied up in their work and their involvements in the needs of people' (p. 108). Thus Bessie is able to round off her collection on a note of balanced optimism. Paul Thebolo and Tholo are added to her group of noble male figures that also includes Makhaya, Gilbert, Maru, Khama the Great, Tshekedi Khama and Patrick van Rensburg. Tholo expresses Bessie's acceptance of the unfathomable complexity of human relationships in one of the final sentences of the story: 'Nothing could sort out the world. It would always be a painful muddle' (p. 109).

1974 had been a productive year for Bessie. In early May she had sent off the typescript of *Serowe: Village of the Rain Wind*, and before the year was up, she had her *Botswana Village Tales* packed and posted off to Giles Gordon in London.

Above left: *Bessie with Liz and Patrick van Rensburg, 1974 (courtesy Khama Memorial Museum)*

Above right: *Bosele Sianana*

Below: *A Boiteko building (photographed in 1991)*

Above: *Bessie in front of 'Rain Clouds', her home in Serowe, built November 1969 from royalties from the book (photo by Susan Gardner, courtesy Veronica Samuels)*

Below: *Bessie at her desk in 'Rain Clouds' (courtesy Khama Memorial Museum)*

Above: *Bessie with her sister-in-law Caroline Head Hlaba and her children, 28 August 1977, in Lusaka (courtesy Khama Memorial Museum)*

Below: *In Iowa, December 1977 (courtesy Khama Memorial Museum)*

Left: *Bessie with Pa, the dog*
Above: *With Howard (photos courtesy Khama Memorial Museum)*
Below: *Restoring the Red House as the Khama III Memorial Museum*

Publisher Clash; Philosophical Musings, 1975

The American publishers Pantheon had been considering *Serowe: Village of the Rain Wind* for a long time. The editor working with it, Milly Daniel, had said that she liked it but thought that the third section, relating to the Swaneng project, needed more work. She felt that most of the interviews were with the older inhabitants of the village and that the interviews with younger people tended to be with what she called 'white settlers' instead of young black villagers. She felt there was a need for more balance here. Perhaps Bessie had other interviews she could put in; perhaps she would be willing to do some more? This reference to 'white settlers' made Bessie uneasy. They were of course the volunteers and Peace Corps people working on the Brigades, idealistic youngsters far removed from a 'white settler' mentality. She explained that these people were a staff of volunteers, interested in 'finding out about people's humanity and working together with them'.[1] But she admitted that parts of the book had been put together hastily and said that she was willing to make alterations within limits. Discussions about what these alterations were to involve went on, with many delays, for over four months.

By Christmas time she was thoroughly depressed. Giles Gordon wrote asking her what plans she had for her next writing project. She replied that she was ready to start on her history of Khama the Great. In fact, she had been intending to go to the National Archives in Gaborone in December, while Howard was not at school, to do some research. But as the hoped-for contract from Pantheon had not materialised, she was simply too poor to make the journey. She wrote:

I don't think I have any future with Pantheon books but I still hesitated from writing them a very bitter letter. One knows the writer is the dog's body of the publishing world but God, they rub it in! They could say they have no money, that one is a risk they can't afford but they take ages to say it, not caring that one's basic peace of mind and bills hang on that decision.[2]

He was so concerned when he read this letter, that he sent her a loan of £100.

In early January, Milly Daniel wrote outlining the changes that Pantheon would require if they were to publish, at the same time making a definite offer for the book with an advance of $3500, payable in three instalments if she agreed to the alterations. Bessie felt that the suggestions were so complicated that she did not know where to start. They did not seem related to her book at all, but to a new book that Milly Daniel envisaged.

Though Giles advised her strongly to take Pantheon's offer and agree to make the changes required – times were hard, the subject matter of the book not very 'saleable' – she had made up her mind. In February she wrote directly to Pantheon Books terminating the connection. She felt unable to take on the very extensive alterations they wanted.

'Don't hate me, Giles. Don't foam at the mouth,'[3] she begged in her appealing way. Giles Gordon had to accept the decision. However, they now needed another publisher to share the costs with Davis-Poynter Ltd. Bessie had already worked that one out. She suggested Patrick Cullinan and Bateleur Press. He had read parts of the book the previous year and had liked it very much. She was sure that he would be interested.

Reg Davis-Poynter was much against having anything to do with a South African, but on hearing of Patrick Cullinan's consistent opposition to apartheid, he agreed to meet him and discuss the proposition.

In a letter from February 1975 Giles Gordon added a sentence that threw Bessie into one of her panics: '[Y]our tax situation . . . [has] raised its head again . . . I am asked to ask you to confirm that you are paying tax in Botswana or not (as the case may be).'[4] Bessie was not. She had actually been waiting for years for the sword of Damocles to fall. When she started earning money on her writing, the Botswana government had sent her some tax forms to fill in. Instead of doing so, she wrote an indignant letter saying that as a refugee she had no security in the country and no chance of ever getting employment. She had become self-employed to counter this and she thought it was unfair that they now wanted a share of her miserable income. She was made to pay a fine of R15 from the Botswana Department of Income Tax for writing such a letter but otherwise nothing happened. No prison sentence. No tax forms. She now wrote a flamboyant explanation of all this to Giles Gordon.

However, she did know that there was a double taxation agreement between England and Botswana which meant that she did not have to pay tax in England. She had filled in a tax exemption form in 1969 (for a five-year period) and again in 1974. But the enquiry reminded her that she ought to get her tax position in Botswana straightened out, something that frightened her. It led her thoughts on to other injustices, such as the fact that she paid a 30 per cent flat tax on all her American earnings.

The problem of taxation, soon to absorb all Bessie's energy, was temporarily pushed aside by a couple of more pleasant events. Firstly, she was approached by an American researcher, Betty Fradkin, who wished to interview her.

As yet interviews were something of a novelty in her life: in fact she had only given three. She had been interviewed and photographed by John Goldblatt in Francistown in 1968, after the appearance of *Rain Clouds*. In 1970 it was Paddy Kitchen's request for an 'interview by post' which marked the start of their correspondence; and in 1972 Lindsay Mackie braved the complicated local transport system to interview her in Serowe for a London newspaper.

Betty Fradkin was in South Africa researching for a biography of Olive Schreiner, and felt that Olive Schreiner and Bessie were kindred spirits. Bessie agreed to the interview and they decided to meet in Palapye, Betty Fradkin planning to take the only connection from Gaborone that was available, the 'mixed goods train', with its combination of passenger seats and goods wagons. She was uncomfortably aware that she was to arrive at an outpost of civilisation at two in the morning. The meeting with Bessie had been planned for much later that day. As she scrambled off the train, however, she saw a stocky figure with a torch in her hand hurrying towards her. It was Bessie, face glowing. She had arrived at Palapye earlier that evening and there she was, with a sweater pulled over her nightdress, to meet her guest.

They spent the weekend at the hotel in Palapye, Bessie revelling in its simple comforts and homely meals and talking all the time. Then they went to Serowe. The stretch of road whose construction Bessie had once so enjoyed being part of for so short a time had long been completed but was still not tarred. It was quite an experience for Betty Fradkin to rattle along it in the crowded local bus. She stayed with Bessie some days and was given an insight into her daily life that few other journalists were later allowed. She was naturally initiated into all the current dramas and tragedies of Bessie's life and she grew very fond of Howard. Her interview was published as 'Conversations with Bessie'.[5]

Then secondly, with school holidays again coming up in May, Bessie did manage to spend two weeks in Gaborone. This was the first of many trips to the National Archives, where much material on Khama III was to be found. There was also a good bookstore, the Botswana Book Centre, in Gaborone, and Bessie went there often. Here she made a new friend, a retired English librarian who had been interested in Botswana for many years. Her name was Mona Pehle. From 1967 to 1970 she had worked in the National Library on a voluntary basis. Since then she had been in Swaziland; now she was back in Botswana; later she planned a trip to Lesotho. She was a Quaker, a woman of original ideas and an inquiring mind. She was interested in the influence of ancestors on the behaviour of individuals. She was a tremendous reader, knew all Bessie's books and was excited to meet her. Like Bessie, she enjoyed writing letters. The basis for one of Bessie's most fruitful friendships had been laid.

Nor did she neglect her writing. 1975 was International Women's Year and to mark the event the London newspaper, *The Times*, had made a weekly column available to women to write on whatever subject they chose. Giles Gordon suggested that Bessie write an article. She reacted immediately and sent one entitled 'The Historical Emancipation of Women in Botswana'. It was published in August as 'Despite broken bondage, Botswana women are still unloved'. As the title suggests, she examines in more detail the custom of the bride-price, or *bogadi*, and its abolition which she had touched on in the first section of *Serowe: Village of the Rain Wind*. Her concluding paragraph considers the strange fact that present-day Botswana is 'experiencing an almost complete breakdown of family life . . . No one can account for it. It just happened somewhere along the line.' Though a woman is no longer bound as a slave to the yard of her mother-in-law and votes alongside the men, she is as 'unloved outside the restrictions of custom, as she was, within it'.[6] It was a clear but sad conclusion.

She also sent off a short story she had written some time earlier. She called it

'Chip Chop' and later changed the title to 'Oranges and Lemons'. It is the only story Bessie ever wrote which was set in a black township near Johannesburg. It describes the evils of life there and especially the ruthless way in which a 'gangsters' moll' named Daphne Matsulaka selects one of the township's few decent family men as her lover and systematically ruins his life. It has a cynical hard-boiled tone, another of her attempts at the '*Drum*' idiom, and is only concerned in passing with white oppression as the worst, inevitable evil. It was published in *London Magazine*[7] and reprinted in *London Magazine Stories 10* the next year.

Meanwhile the plans to find a publisher to replace Pantheon were being pursued. In September Patrick Cullinan went to London, where he met Giles Gordon and Reg Davis-Poynter. Giles Gordon could afterwards write in a very optimistic vein to Bessie about their agreement. It was a complicated one. Davis-Poynter was happy for Cullinan to bring out both *Serowe* and *Botswana Village Tales* on the South African market. The suggestion was that he would be supplied with camera-ready copy of the type, and the line drawings already collected for the *Serowe* book. He would make film from them and print from them. Thereupon he would supply Davis-Poynter with the number of copies he needed. As regards *Village Tales*, Patrick Cullinan's Bateleur Press would design, set and print the book and sell copies to Davis-Poynter. This arrangement would keep costs at a minimum and prevent Bessie from being 'taxed out of existence'. It would make Bateleur Press primary publisher of both books with sub-leases to Reg Davis-Poynter and possibly Heinemann Educational Books, because James Currey was very interested in *Village Tales*. Giles Gordon emphasised Davis-Poynter's 'dedication to your work and preparedness to co-operate in every way to see that you receive as much money for your work as possible'.[8]

Then Giles added a fateful sentence: 'As far as your earnings here are concerned, there would appear to be no way round the tax problem because of the lack of a double taxation agreement between Botswana and Britain.' He added: 'I hope you'll agree things look much, much brighter than they did.' Bessie, of course, knew that there was a double taxation agreement. She did not agree about the brighter prospects.

After the meeting, Patrick Cullinan went on to America feeling confident that between them they had worked out an excellent way to 'do the right thing for Bessie Head', as he had expressed it to Giles Gordon.[9] No one could have expected the letter that arrived at Davis-Poynter Ltd in late September.

It was from Bessie. She wrote saying that she had received so strange a letter from her literary agent that she was a little doubtful as to whether Davis-Poynter had in fact met Cullinan. It continued: 'I do not intend to have Patrick Cullinan act as my secret agent and collect money for me in dubious ways.'

She said that she was writing a number of letters to settle the present disorder in her affairs. She was investigating the taxation problem personally and her ultimate decision would depend on the reply she received from a letter she had addressed to the British High Commission in Botswana. However, she simply wished to assure both Davis-Poynter and Patrick Cullinan that once she had established the truth, business would proceed as usual 'without anyone feeling degraded or humiliated by a dubious literary agent . . . He has such a bad taste in my mouth just now that I could vomit and spew all over at the thought of him.'[10]

To Giles, some days later, she wrote that she did not find the business proposals relevant to her. What she did find relevant was the sentence about Britain not having a double-taxation agreement with Botswana. She said that he had sent her a new version of her tax problem in each letter since June and this was the last version she was going to take. 'I'm having no more of your monkey tricks.' The rest of the letter was an unpleasant attack on his creative writing. Since April, when she had sent him some apparently very frank notes on his latest book, they had been conducting a private correspondence on this matter. Bessie felt that he had sacrificed his personal integrity in the new type of anti-novel he had been writing and had been mucking around with 'sychrophantic [*sic*] flatterers and liars'.[11] Now this, together with the tax problem, became the reason why she totally rejected the proposed publishing arrangement. In a second letter shortly afterwards she said that she no longer wished him to represent her, adding what must be the prime sentence of the whole unhappy affair: 'I'd go stark raving mad if I received another letter from you . . . '[12] For the second time, exit Giles Gordon.

He was not prepared to be thrown out without stating his case. He pointed out that her tax affairs had really been confusing and that he had reported faithfully what he had been told. It was only when Reg Davis-Poynter had asked an influential friend about her affairs and he had taken them to the highest level 'that the light began to be seen by the tax authorities'. This coincided with Patrick Cullinan's visit to England, which meant that they also felt that they had straightened out that point at their meeting. He said that he had spent a great deal of time in discussions with his colleagues, trying to find a way of getting Bessie's royalties through to her without unreasonable taxation. He said that he believed that he had acted professionally on her behalf throughout. He admitted that he had not communicated clearly to her as regards the tax position, but the reason for that lay in the very nature of the case.

'Bessie, I am not angry, I am sad. I admire you as a human being enormously. As a writer you are unique and unexcelled.' He concluded his letter by saying that if she insisted on throwing him over, that was her decision. 'But in all truth you must not pretend that what isn't is.'[13]

Patrick Cullinan, returning from America in October, was shocked. He stormed up to Serowe. There he heard Bessie's version of the story and told her to her face, 'You're having a nervous breakdown, Bessie.'[14] In her opinion, he had driven to see her to check whether she 'was pulling faces or walking around without my clothes on'. She maintained that he was furious because she had seen through his ambitious plans to rise to fame as primary publisher of her fine books. 'He was very angry at being deprived of his dream by me. Deprive him I did.'[15] While he was there, Bessie made him write a letter to Davis-Poynter relinquishing the primary publishing rights to him but stating that he would be willing to publish *Village Tales* in paperback.

With Bateleur Press driven back in confusion and Giles fired, Davis-Poynter faced Bessie and her problems alone. Within the frame of her own universe, she felt her behaviour perfectly justified. She had begun to suspect that Giles Gordon was cheating her, so Giles Gordon had to go. Perhaps she also felt put out that Davis-Poynter was being relegated to a secondary role in the publishing process. But most probably she had simply not understood the complicated details in Giles's letter and had reacted to the only sentence she could understand fully and reject totally, the one in which he stated that England had no double taxation agreement with Botswana. This she knew to be untrue.

Even before this crisis Bessie had decided to take on the Botswana tax authorities. She addressed her complaints to the United Nations High Commissioner for Refugees, Poul Hartling, explaining the background for her tax problem in great detail. She emphasised the unfairness, as she saw it, of paying taxes in a country where one has no official status: 'Do we just pay tax simply because we live in a country?' She complained about the fact that 30 per cent of all her American earnings were deducted in tax. In true Bessie spirit, she embarked on discussions of subjects which she felt were relevant but which she understood imperfectly, such as the Botswana government's preferential treatment of Angolan refugees. She spiced her four-page letters with such sentences as 'I haven't the emotional resources left to go through another Botswana and me crisis' and 'Nothing on earth will persuade me to sign another tax exemption form with the British government or another book contract for those two countries. I have one last contract I signed in England and that book I donate to both those appalling governments and I hope it damns them, the greedy exploiters.'16

After reading this letter in Gaborone, an influential American friend of hers, who was mediating in the affair, sent her some of the frankest advice she was ever given. He told her that she should call a halt to mailing off letters full of 'vituperative statements that take in the whole world'. If she felt she had to write them then he would not stop her doing that but mailing them – 'NO!'17 His advice went unheeded. Within a fortnight she was busy on the most extraordinary letter she ever wrote.

It was addressed to the country's President, Seretse Khama. He too was told the story of her tax problems, clearly and unemotionally, though once more sentences like the following raised the tone of the letter well above officialese: 'People, in refugee situations, which can often be terrifying, like to have their questions answered and whether governments would offer them certain services and securities in exchange for paying tax. So I sort of hung on awaiting further word from your government.' She promised to lay all particulars of her earnings before a tax assessment officer. She then launched into a discussion of the problem of South African and Rhodesian refugees (as opposed to the Angolans). The final paragraph was the extraordinary one.

She said that there was something else she had had to live with in Botswana as well as refugeeism. She did not know what to call this 'horrific' experience, so she called it Satan. She recorded it in *A Question of Power*. She said that she was complaining to Lenyeletse Seretse one day that she was afflicted by the company of Satan and he said, 'Who started it?' She continued: 'Who started that vast, endless, horrific dialogue with hell? We both had you in mind ... It started with you. I'd be relieved if Satan could get off my back.' She also said that she regretted very much putting the notice up at the post office in Serowe. 'I am extremely sorry for it and had no intention of dying with such a crime against my name.'[18] She said that she used *A Question of Power* to pull the notice down. As Bessie herself maintained, there was an astounding inner logic and consistency in her obsessions.

Bessie later wrote proudly to Randolph Vigne: 'Nothing ever sorts out Botswana, but this letter straightened out my tax here.'[19] Davis-Poynter helped by sending her the necessary British tax-exemption forms and she revoked her curse on the greedy, exploiting British tax system. As it turned out, she had seldom earned enough to have to pay tax anyway. The third 'Botswana and me' crisis had been weathered, but further trouble of a different nature was also brewing.

Reg Davis-Poynter did not communicate with Bessie between November 1975 and February 1976. She heard that *Serowe: Village of the Rain Wind* was in galleys at the publisher's, but it was taking a long time. He had still not decided whether he wanted to accept the short stories. His silence upset Bessie. Finally he wrote, telling her that he wished to contract for *Village Tales*. This she agreed to.

However, at the end of May she changed her mind. She wrote telling Davis-Poynter that she did not wish to sign the contract after all. She interpreted his long silence as a threat to her survival and she did not believe that it was because he had been investigating the exact position concerning her tax. Furthermore, she thought the advance he offered, which was what had earlier been agreed on, was too little. 'With the exchange rate here . . . it is absolutely useless to me.'[20] She felt that 'too long hidden and unstated evils have destroyed every effort I made to rectify my affairs'. She said that Randolph Vigne would collect the manuscript for her.

Reg Davis-Poynter's reply was prompt. He said that her wild and sweeping statements were untrue, as their files could demonstrate. Since Bessie had decided that he was cheating her and lying to her, he did not wish to publish *Serowe* after all. Both manuscripts could be collected.

Relentlessly, brick by brick, Bessie had been pulling down the framework for all her creative expression. Now the whole structure was crashing round her ears. Though she did not see it like that, there was no one to blame but herself.

Since her clash with Giles Gordon, she had been represented at the agency by Anthony Sheil himself. He made several references to not understanding her affairs the way Giles Gordon had. He was also heavily loaded with work, having obligations to a long list of authors of his own. When *Serowe: Village of the Rain Wind* was suddenly released, he felt that he could not take it on. He could not suggest any other course of action than that Bessie should find another agency. She was thus also without an agent in either London or New York because the American branch of the agency withdrew automatically.

Patrick Cullinan tried to save the pieces by offering to publish *Serowe* as well as *Village Tales* in paperback. But the little publishing firm was hard pressed and he told Bessie that he was somewhat piqued with the whole affair. He said that if she had agreed to the arrangement he had put forward the previous year, then both books would be in print now and the royalties beginning to flow in. As it was, he certainly did not know how things stood and in fact their publishing firm closed down without publishing either book.

In 1977 David Philip, from Cape Town, another of the band of independent publishers who, with Patrick Cullinan and Ad Donker from Johannesburg, were willing to take risks to provide Southern African writers with a local platform, was finally to bring out *The Collector of Treasures and Other Botswana Village Tales*, as it came to be called, in hardback. Bessie Head changed the title in November 1976[21] because she was afraid that her original one made the collection sound like a children's anthology. James Currey at Heinemann Educational Books published the paperback edition at the same time. As regards the 'Serowe book', it was sent backwards and forwards to many publishers; many suggestions for revision, rewriting and reshaping were discussed at various times before it finally found a publisher.

Bessie was in the habit of writing Nikki Giovanni long philosophical letters but she often received rather short replies. Bessie complained and Nikki Giovanni apologised. She was sent little homilies on the art of letter-writing: 'It is hard for me to write a full and coherent letter to someone who only sends short scrawls because I don't know if you cared about all my latest speculations.' Bessie also described her method of writing letters: 'I pace them very sensitively against the person to whom I am communicating because it is something outside of what you can buy and sell. And it is intended to give happiness to the recipient. It is something that is for free.'[22]

Nikki Giovanni's comment was that Bessie was a 'really arrogant African lady'[23] and that she apologised as usual. She pointed out that she did not come from a culture that valued letter-writing and that if Bessie had lived where there was a telephone she would often have called her for a chat. As it happened she had written more letters to her than she had ever written to her family.

Bessie's letters began to take on a sarcastic tone: 'Indeed, I am appalled at the heaviness of your routine and something I certainly don't have to deal with is fan mail. I am also puzzled and honoured at the effort you exert to keep in touch with me.'[24] Three months later she exploded fiercely, peppering her letter with expletives and saying that they had nothing in common any longer – 'no human communication, no friendly chit-chat, NOTHING' – and adding: 'I tell you we call it a day from now on.'[25] This was written the day after she fired Giles Gordon.

These outbursts of violent and irrational behaviour can of course be seen as symptoms of her unstable mental state; in this instance, triggered off by her fear of the tax authorities: 'Each time I came to the post office and opened a letter from [Giles Gordon] my head reeled in confusion. I became ill and was reduced to a state of collapse,'[26] she explained to Patrick Cullinan. But Bessie herself recognised her volatility as an essential part of her creativity. 'Don't be upset if I quarrel with everyone. I enjoy raising hell. If there's no hell to raise I get out of style,'[27] she could say. And she often believed that her frank condemnations of others were for their own good: 'I am sure it does not kill anyone to tell the truth exactly as it is.'[28] She could be honest about her weaknesses, providing no one else pointed them out to her. She would admit that she was 'inclined to be very turbulent and hysterical',[29] or that she would 'always think in obsessive terms and later find that particular obsession quite useless'.[30] Strangely foreshadowing her later behaviour, she wrote to Nikki Giovanni in her first letter: 'I tend to get so angry all at once that people wonder what they have done to upset me so when for a long time I seemed to get along with them.'[31] She did not blame her vacillating moods on her unhappy childhood: 'No my childhood has not driven me crazy. Most human beings survive under all kinds of circumstances. It is something else I battled with.'[32] Nonetheless, when Bessie's emotional barometer suddenly heralded foul weather, then only heaven could help those exposed to the storm.

Only a few select friends were initiated into all the evil behaviour of the villain or villains in Bessie's involved publishing conflict. 'Are there two villains?' asked Betty Fradkin, struggling to keep track of events. 'The drama has gone on for so long that you have the characters on the stage mixed up,'[33] Bessie replied. To most people she said that her publisher had returned the *Serowe* manuscript after keeping it for two years and that it was inflation hitting the book industry that had led to the cancellation of the contract. Regardless of Giles Gordon's request not to 'pretend that what isn't is', she soon came to believe this herself. It was hard for some of her village informants to hear of the publishing delays. Having their names appear in print was to be a major event in their lives and they were eagerly awaiting the complimentary copy of her book which Bessie had promised them. Some did not live to receive it.

She paid a heavy price financially for her decisions. By late 1975 she was so heavily in debt that one local shopkeeper refused to greet her any more. This information distressed Betty Fradkin so much that she sent Bessie a large sum of money to settle her debts and persuaded her to accept a monthly 'loan' as well until her affairs improved: ' . . . and don't say it's compassion – it's more like participation.'[34]

Bessie was left very much to her own devices as regards the publishing of her two completed works. She began to rely heavily on help from friends. Alice Walker had been instrumental in publishing 'Witchcraft' and later 'The Collector of Treasures' in *Ms*. In 1972 Random House, New York, had included Bessie Head's short story, 'The Green Tree', in an anthology entitled *Contemporary African Literature*. Early in 1976, after she had fired Giles Gordon, Bessie approached Random House again. She called her letter 'a probe in the dark as the boat of my literary career has sunk'[35] and she hoped that she could salvage some of the wreckage by writing to people she had had dealings with before. The writer, Toni Morrison, was an editor there and thus Bessie began a correspondence with yet another of the important American women writers. Toni Morrison was very interested in seeing her work. She kept *Botswana Village Tales* and later the *Serowe* book for a long time, but because she thought that they were more suitable for young adults, she had both typescripts circulating in the juvenile department. This upset Bessie and she eventually recalled them.

Bessie's daily pattern of life was now very quiet. Many of her friends from amongst the volunteer staff at Swaneng Hill School had left the country again. Christine and Peter Hawes left in the middle of 1974. Christine, especially, had been an important person in Bessie's life, as the dedication in *A Question of*

Power reflected. But there was a new wave of trouble at the school in November the same year, which led to a further exodus. The students had gone on strike, demanding that one of the teachers be made to leave the school premises straightaway. The principal, Thato Matome, negotiated with them for five days, but they refused to attend classes. Then the school board closed the school temporarily. The teacher in question was reinstated and gradually the trouble subsided. At a meeting of the school board, it was suggested that the school ought not to employ so many volunteer teachers as they supported student unrest. This resulted in the resignation of 19 members of staff.[36] Margaret and Stanley Moore, who had taken care of Howard while Bessie was in Lobatse, left; as did Hugh Pearce, who had been teaching Development Studies at the school. He and Mmatsela Ditshego, a Boiteko potter,[37] moved to Lesotho where they married and settled.

Bessie's own connections with Boiteko had gradually become limited to her seedling work. In fact she said that she had 'dedicated' herself 'to staying away from Boiteko'.[38] She had a young boy to help her take care of her seedlings and she paid him for the work he did. 'Why did he not eat at the table with us?' asked Betty Fradkin, after her visit to Bessie. Bessie gave a long explanation, including references to previous helpers, who had been given much and stolen more. She ended with the comment: 'All my writing is about ordinary people and my relationships with them. They don't work out perfectly in real life.'[39]

In January 1976 Bessie was asked by Pat van Rensburg to return to the Boiteko project. They were trying to get the garden established again and he wanted her to work with a group of young women. After they had had a period of training it was hoped that they would be able to grow enough vegetables to realise the old aim of Boiteko: to provide a balance between production and consumption without the payment of wages. As well as working on their 'own' project, they would also be required to do work on the communal project. This communal work was to be done during the weekends.

Bessie agreed and started out with thirteen young women whom she called 'very bright'. She said that she 'had only to give them one demonstration on each subject and they immediately took control of the work in hand.' Three weeks after the project started, the workers were beginning to feel the strain of the long weekend hours as well as the long weekdays. Bessie spoke to the supervisor and he said that there had been several meetings about it but no decision had yet been reached. Pending this decision, Bessie gave her group the weekend off to get their shopping and personal affairs seen to.

She had hardly arrived home when Patrick van Rensburg and another leader of the project arrived at her house. They felt she was undermining the idea of communal work by sending her group home. She explained her reasons, which in fact were only one aspect of her irritation with the Boiteko plan. She felt, as she had done so often earlier, that it was wrong not to receive payment for work done, or to make the garden a paying affair by selling the produce and sharing the profits. She decided to resign, to the disappointment of her group of workers. Once more demonstrating that she actually had little sympathy for the co-operative ideas which she had praised in her writing, she withdrew with a flourish, typing out a paper which stated the 'List of Complaints Against Pat van Rensburg, Kopano and Boiteko Management: Drawn up by Bessie Head'. She concluded by saying that the two men were 'TOO IMPORTANT to listen to people's preferences'. Why did Van Rensburg

ask the poor, who have to meet school fees, and many household needs, to come to Boiteko and work for no salary? . . . If there is no money to help subsidise projects, Boiteko ought to close down. It is a cruel and evil farce. I have behind me four years of back-breaking labour for nothing for Boiteko and I know it leads to misery and starvation. I am sick of the farce and I will not delude 13 bright girls into believing that Boiteko offers them anything in its present form. It offers them nothing but poverty, hard work and starvation and I am not going to be a part of this evil game any more.[40]

Bosele Sianana stayed on this time too, as she had earlier. She had no alternative source of income, as Bessie had. Their friendship continued its rather erratic course. Bessie would call out a greeting to her as she passed the Boiteko gardens on her way to the village. Or Bosele would trudge up the hill to 'Rain Clouds' after work to drink a cup of tea with her. If Bessie was irritable or depressed, Bosele would go off again without a word and leave her alone for a while.[41]

With the years Howard had developed an extraordinary resilience as regards his mother's mental crises, and to this day remembers Bessie's most serious breakdown as only starting the evening she went down to Joan Blackmore's.[42] All the same, 1972 had been a bad year for him at school, ending up with a bad school report. After that his school career was chequered. Betty Fradkin won his gratitude by sending him the biography of Mohammed Ali, the boxer. He read it reverently and tied it up with string each evening to keep it from getting spoiled. Bessie suggested that he write a letter to Mohammed Ali but this he would not dream of doing. 'When did a grovelling idolater ever write to God? But he runs up the road every day and oh groan! he's going to be a world heavy weight boxing champion,'[43] she reported to Betty Fradkin.

A friend from Francistown days with whom Bessie still corresponded, Henry Klein, told her that she spoiled Howard. This surprised her greatly. 'I just looked after him, and quite casually too. Most of his upbringing was done by Batswana women for whom he had a great respect. He was an only child and moved out of the house to look for other children to play with.'[44] She said, adding her voice to the universal maternal dirge, that he had two ways of living. When he was with Batswana he was polite and respectful. When he came home he was quarrelsome and difficult.

She did worry a lot about Howard, as she worried about their common future. He was not a citizen of the country, of course, and this could have a great influence on the type of employment available to him. Bessie spent whatever spare money they had on him. He was always well turned out and had plenty of clothes, whereas it was almost a joke that Bessie had only two dresses which she washed in turn. Since her waistline continued to increase along with her age, she wore loose-hanging homemade shifts.

In April 1976, a month prior to her strange attack on Davis-Poynter, two important events occurred. She presented her first paper at an academic gathering and she met a celebrity. The invitation to attend the first Writers' Workshop to be arranged by the University of Botswana had come some months earlier and she had accepted it. Her friend Mona Pehle had mentioned that the writer Mary Benson was also in Gaborone for some months. She was due to address the Botswana Society on the subject of her famous biography, Tshekedi Khama. Bessie knew and admired the book.

Much to her surprise, Mary Benson sought her out at the Botswana Training Centre where she was staying and overwhelmed her with her friendliness. Bessie found her extremely beautiful; she was also very talkative, very knowledgeable about Bessie's books and very generous. Bessie suddenly found herself the owner of a sunshine-yellow cape of soft, lightweight wool. It was one Mary Benson had been given, which she now passed on to Bessie. The weather was cool and rainy and Bessie spent the next few days enveloped in this cape.

Such a gift did much to boost her ego, for she still regarded herself as very ugly. It came out sometimes when there was the need for a photograph. 'One can be the ugliest hag on earth, like me,'[45] she would remark in passing. The pre-breakdown years had taken a tremendous toll on her health. Her hair, for example, suddenly turned grey. At first she kept thinking that she had some dust on her head but that grey shimmer could not be washed off. That she had also started on the menopause, aged thirty-five, did not make matters easier.[46] Though she was generous in her appreciation of beauty in others, in this case Mary Benson, she did not see any in her own large expressive eyes and personal exuberance. However, she never regarded beauty as important. Instead she valued finding a soul attuned to hers, as she now did. Bessie considered Mary 'the most lovely person in the world to meet'.[47] They exchanged views on all life's deep and important subjects. Their friendship was to last five or six years.

The purpose of the Writers' Workshop was to gather young writers from South Africa, Botswana and Zambia together. The University was very new, the campus still in the process of being established. Stephen Gray, a South African lecturer and writer who had corresponded with Bessie two years earlier, when he wished to include 'The Prisoner Who Wore Glasses' in a South African anthology entitled On the Edge of the World, was there; and the promising South African poet Sipho Sepamla, and writer Mbulelo Mzamane. Bessie's paper was entitled 'Some Notes on Novel Writing'. In a fine combination of autobiographical particulars and wide philosophical observations, she presented her reasons for writing and her visions of the future. Here it was that she said for the first time that the novel form is 'like a large rag-bag into which one can stuff anything – all one's philosophical, social and romantic speculations.' She indicated her development as a writer by referring to her first effort, When Rain Clouds Gather, as harmless and amateurish and her present role as that of a 'pioneer blazing a new trail into the future'.[48]

Bessie sent Mona Pehle an account of her performance. She said that she had been short of time because the speakers were allocated an hour each but the Zambian guest speakers had taken more than their share: 'I jumped up at the last minute and said everything I had to say ... My notes were run off anyway ... Phew! Wasn't that fabulous for me!'[49] Stephen Gray has supplied some of the background to the 'Phew!' This was in fact the first time Bessie had addressed a university audience and she was very nervous. Muffled in her yellow cape, and with tears streaming down her face 'from hyperthermia and deep disorientation', she 'could only whisper ... thank you, thank you in the meekest, little girl voice'.[50] She was thereafter referred to as the 'artist with the "crying voice".' But, Gray added, Bessie was 'nobody's fool' and her paper was excellent.

One evening Stephen Gray took her to the most luxurious hotel in town, the Holiday Inn, where she should have stayed except that it was booked out because of the Trans-Kalahari Motor Race. In no time at all Bessie had singled out the elegant black prostitutes circulating in the foyer and was exhorting them to 'give up this white man's game on the spot'.[51] In the adjoining casino she created quite a commotion with her loud and indignant comments, until Gray, delving into her cape, drew out a hand and gently led her away. Bessie, meanwhile, was probably seeing herself as a reincarnated Socrates and, in fact, getting right to the crux of the matter: 'I was amazed at the way money dehumanised people ... They quietly put down the race hates and class and everything and did not look at anything but the money tables. It wasn't as exciting as Socrates' tables of money changers; where he learnt to question life so thoroughly.'[52] She had found it rather boring except for the activities of the prostitutes, she said. Presumably Bessie's one regret was that she had not engaged them in a question-and-answer dialogue.

Mbulelo Mzamane introduced Bessie to Sol Plaatje's *Mhudi* and Gray later sent her a copy of the book, to her great delight. In 1973 another South African scholar, Tim Couzens, had introduced her to Plaatje and she remained an admirer throughout her life. Not only did his style inspire her, but his material in *Mhudi* was very relevant for her Khama research. On the other hand, a book by Peter Abrahams which she had borrowed earned the comment: 'I am amazed that he's such a bad writer.'[53]

This was Bessie's first contact with black South Africans for years. They brought accounts of the increasing repression of black people but also of a build-up of angry opposition, especially among young black students. Dr Verwoerd's Extension of University Education Act of 1959, whereby the universities became segregated and ethnic colleges were established for the various black groups, had backfired in exactly the way its critics had warned that it would. Isolated and disgruntled, black students rejected all the previous generation's forms of cooperation with whites and turned instead to a new kind of Africanism. The movement to be called Black Consciousness was developing, its ideas were eloquently expressed by Steve Biko, a young medical student at Natal University's non-white medical school. He wished to help young blacks to rediscover their self-respect and build up a meaningful opposition to the powerful regime which had reduced them all to shells and shadows. From the universities the ideas spread to the black schools.

Meanwhile, in 1975, an instruction issued by the Department of Bantu Education, intended to tighten its grip further on black education, stated that in all secondary schools two subjects, Arithmetic and Social Studies, had to be taught through the medium of Afrikaans. To black students, Afrikaans had become a symbol of the apartheid regime and their own oppression. A protest sent to the Deputy Minister of Bantu Affairs, Dr Andries Treurnicht, was ignored. The language issue was part of a wider background of frustration and resentment which in June 1976 erupted into one of the country's most serious outbursts of violence ever. About 15 000 secondary school students, carrying cardboard banners with such slogans as 'To Hell with Afrikaans' and 'Beware, Afrikaans is the Most Dangerous Drug for our Future', demonstrated in Soweto. A force of hastily assembled policemen used tear gas; then guns. At least one student, Hector Petersen, was killed. The demonstration turned into an uprising as the children swept through the streets, throwing stones and killing two white officials. Many more children were killed. The unrest spread to other townships as the students refused to go back to school. The Prime Minister, B J Vorster, warned on television that 'this government will not be intimidated, and instructions have been given to maintain law and order at all costs.'54 The situation did not improve.

Instead the next months saw the growth of a new force in South African politics: a radicalised generation of young Africans, hostile to whites and their own parents. A Soweto Students Representative Council was elected and its leader urged students to demonstrate, not study: 'What is there for us students when we finish our education?' he asked. 'Whatever degrees we achieve, there is no work except to sweep the white man's floor or empty his garbage cans – or face going back to rot in some underdeveloped homeland, which we kids in Soweto have never even seen.'55 Shortly afterwards violence erupted from a new quarter as a thousand Zulu mineworkers surged through Soweto slashing residents with their pangas in an upsurge of ethnic conflict. This new form of black-on-black violence shook white South Africans. 'The government's dream of apartheid died in the flames of Soweto,'56 said Colin Eglin, leader of the opposition Progressive Reform Party.

Bessie wrote to Mary Benson shortly afterwards: 'I don't know what to say to the recent shootings in South Africa, except that the Boers seemed to need to do it to quieten the people. They have always followed a pattern. They have shot people dead and kept people quiet for some time.'57 To her sister-in-law, Caroline Hlaba, she complained that it is 'all part of one's general helplessness in the face of that horror. People will never believe that a horror like South Africa can last a very long time and that no one can do anything about it.'58 She also told Mary Benson that she had reached the point where she could only suggest wild and fantastic ways of resolving the situation:

People will never be freed by ordinary warfare – their defence budget is the largest in the world and they expect anything now except the truly fantastic and that's about all I can think of – some sort of miracle that turns every Boer into a pillar of salt; then they can be picked up and sold again on the market for a profit . . . 59

The next September, Steve Biko was to die while in police detention, as a result of blows on the head he had received from his interrogators. Because of his exceptional standing as an intellectual, his death was to provoke worldwide condemnation. This event and the Soweto rising were indeed to mark a turning point in the South African attempt to enforce apartheid.

In September 1976 Bessie made two more new friends, the American chargé-d'affaires in Gaborone, Frank Alberti, and his wife Jacqueline. Jacqueline Alberti had read Bessie's books in America and was especially fond of *Maru*, so when her husband was posted to Botswana, she made a special visit to Serowe to see the famous writer. Shortly afterwards, in September 1976, she was there again, this time with Lee Nichols, an American editor and broadcaster. He was interviewing African writers for the radio station Voice of America, and Jackie Alberti was very pleased to be able to conduct him to Bessie Head. This was the first important recorded interview Bessie gave and it turned out well. Bessie later recalled Jackie sitting very quietly in the corner, eyes glowing, absorbing everything. Two years afterwards she wrote to Frank Alberti about the visit: 'she looked at me with wonder and worship. Hundreds of people pass through my life, but no one looks at me with wonder and worship . . . From the moment we met, she never once took her glance off my face . . . '[60] Jackie Alberti invited Bessie to visit them when she was in Gaborone and Bessie looked forward to doing so. Some months later, however, tragedy struck. The beautiful young woman was killed in a car accident in which one of her children was also seriously injured. Bessie was deeply distressed and when she wrote to Frank Alberti, expressing her sympathy, she asked whether she could dedicate her Serowe book to his deceased wife. Alberti was touched by the gesture and a friendship developed. He often gave her sound advice and made perceptive comments on her writing.

Despite the collapse of her relationship with her agent and publisher, the years directly after the publication of *A Question of Power* were in many ways years of growth for Bessie. The change in her marked by her conscious decision to remain in Serowe seemed to enable her to come to terms with her own identity. In 1973 she had written:

At first I made a big blunder. I was very eager to have an African identity as a writer but I did not have African values, the tendency to praise the wrong things for material gain, the wrong people because they were the open sesame to glory; the tendency to hurt life and not know they are hurting life because they just grin all the time and behind that grin hide mental cunning and evil.

This is a harsh evaluation of the situation but, she continued, she gradually learned 'that it doesn't matter where a human being lives, as long as his contribution to life is constructive, not destructive'.[61] Though written at about the same time as she was saying that 'Dead bodies don't need travel documents',[62] it does show that in her best moments she was beginning to accept the fact that she had been naïve and immature in her early attitude to the country, but that she need not leave it because she now regarded it in a new light. In fact one of her most positive statements about herself and her African identity was made to Betty Fradkin in 1975: 'Don't worry to define my race,' she wrote. 'I've defined myself thoroughly in my novels. I am a New African. I like being a pioneer, creating light and space.'[63] Her identity was not dependent on her environment. However, at that stage she had still to make the next admission: her writing was.

As her active correspondence with Mona Pehle and Tony Hall substantiated, existential questions continued to dominate her thinking. What did she mean by God and the Devil, one may ask, because she often used the term 'God' while reiterating that she did not 'believe in nor respect a God in the sky, who has power'.[64] It seems that Bessie allowed herself a Tolstoyan liberty here. She once remarked that Tolstoy thought it futile to pray to God, but nonetheless in *Anna Karenina*, 'God, a big blind broad concept is carefully inserted at the most tragic moments: As Anna throws herself under the wheels of the train she whispers: "God forgive me for everything." It is just right at that time because it stirs the heart so much (when the human situation is so cruel and unsolvable).'[65] In a similar fashion Bessie uses God as a 'big blind broad concept' at certain moments, while at others she maintains that she has taken the God-title and given it to humankind.

She was always adamant that Christianity had given the world a bad inheritance; she never forgot that they had learnt at school that India was 'heathen'. She believed that a new age of enlightenment was dawning. Hinduism seemed closest to explaining it. To Mona Pehle she outlined the two great schools of Hindu thought: the Vedanta and the Advaita. The two schools do not oppose each other. They are designed to meet man's needs.'

Vedanta view is that the whole universe is permeated by a feeling of holiness so in essence the discipline and training extends the title of God to all things ... so in effect you say: 'This cup is God. This man is God. This tree is God ... ' It is a discipline not suited to all temperaments and the Advaita is man's small ordered neat world: 'I am man. God is a thing apart from me. I worship something apart from me.' The Advaita view comes nearest to formal religion. But I like the Vedanta view: God is about the only title that can be shared so ... I recklessly dispense the title in all directions ... A great book lurks at the back of my mind, that it is right to feel a sense of worship for all life, a sense of joy.[66]

Bessie actually wrote much more about evil and suffering than she did about joy or love. Sometimes, though, she did give glimpses of her own longings. 'I don't think I have ever been in love in my life,'[67] she once said and the remark recurs in various forms throughout the years. For example she told Tony Hall, who was amazingly good at keeping her spirits up with cheerful, loving phrases containing the touch of a harmless flirt: 'Actually you are the only gentleman who is going to tell me you love me, for the right reasons. I don't even get the gentlemen saying that for the wrong reasons! No man ever told me he loved me and I never told anyone I loved them. All sorts of things have happened to me but not love.'[68]

She seemed resigned to this state; perhaps she was not going to have that experience in this life. Sometimes she said that she knew she had had 'that kind of good luck somewhere; I am sure of it.'[69]

It was very seldom that she admitted outright that she needed love and tenderness: 'The portion of myself that was born a human being had all the needs of a human being for warmth and affection and tenderness.'[70] More often she concluded her remarks about never having met love with comments such as 'I know I have an unchanging form of goodness and that is what you love',[71] or 'The only thing I am certain of is my worth in gold.'[72]

We are sometimes given glimpses of Bessie Head's need for a father figure, most clearly in her creation of 'the Father' in *A Question of Power*. In lighter vein we have her insistence on giving this title to Randolph Vigne and her belief that her father had been a powerful and important man in earlier incarnations. In 1970, for example, she expounded on this theme to Naomi Mitchison, explaining her great admiration for the Zulu chieftain Shaka: 'Not for nothing did he appear in the dedication of *Rain Clouds*. I'd just been reading Ritter and was so stirred by the book, I threw Shaka into the dedication.' She went on to say that she admired what Naomi Mitchison had recently written about him: that if you were competent, fearless and intelligent you became his friend, even though you were poor or from another tribe. She had also described him as a man of strange moods and affections, but a man of vision. Bessie continued:

After reading this, then jumping back to read it again, suddenly a missing link clicked in my mind. I thought: 'Why goddam, that's my father. Shaka, in his second or third incarnation after Shaka was my father. No wonder I loved him so much' . . . I must thank you very much for such a beautiful description of my father. Everything you said about him applies to me, except that my organisation while military – I know the right flank and left flank of my army, is not for war but for war against poverty. They would also say, like my father Shaka, . . . 'she broke the power of the chiefs . . . she was a woman of strange moods and affections . . . she had vision'.[73]

It would be tempting to use a passage like the preceding one to explain the obvious preoccupation Bessie had with creating powerful, sometimes idealised, male protagonists.

Her own best explanation, showing this view as an over-simplification, is found in a letter to Giles Gordon at the end of 1974. It was written at the time when she had begun to turn her attention to a full-length project on Khama III: 'My plan of work was simply that I was after Khama, the Great in novel form. *Mother Winter* the novel is called and it was his austere praise poem name. He was a stern ascetic if ever there was one.' She explained that she had half the plan worked out because she had already 'worked him over several times already – his character type, the multi-sized big quiet man'. She then went on to explain her interest in male protagonists. She said that some of her thinking was 'so forceful' that she 'couldn't create female characters to carry' it. That is why she was in essence both Makhaya and Maru

. . . and it was only in Elizabeth that I broke free and created a feminine vehicle for my thoughts, exactly as I wanted to express them. But that quiet rhythm of deep feeling which so often builds up in me is so powerfully masculine that I was forced to create powerful males to bear the tide of it. Some one said to me: 'Oh, your men are so powerful. You are sadly a woman out of touch with woman's lib. You are very male orientated . . . '

Then she added a frank comment:

No, few or no men can stand me. It's simply my personality. I can't express myself as female. I can't stop thinking outside female bounds, in broad horizon terms, like a man. I did it to Elizabeth, showed myself more or less and that is one of the most attacked characters by reviewers – there's nothing wrong with the woman but she is not thinking like a woman; her generosity and thought processes are male . . . I know my head is male and I simply accept that.[74]

She sometimes also described herself as a man with a skirt on.

It was to be some years before Bessie made a conscious effort to formulate her views on feminism, yet what she wrote here was in no way as provocatively anti-feminist as she appeared to think. In her usual original manner, she was pushing aside the fetters of traditional so-called female thought-patterns. All the more amusing, then, that she remained an incurable romantic as regards sex and marriage.

Bessie gradually became more outspoken about her attitude to these subjects: 'for me sex is at the extreme end of it. I found that if one was ever physically attracted to someone the sensation could end in three days. But it is like economics and politics – a permanent muddle. I can't control politics but I can control love.'[75] She was against having anything to do with any of the local men: 'It is almost out for me, any sort of relationship with a black man. I need something very steady and deep and they are incapable of providing it.'[76] The idea of something 'permanent and deep' was of utmost importance in a relationship. 'I need permanent partnership, over a very long period. To use a crude term, love is a billion dollar business with me, something I really work at, something I build up a complete store of knowledge about, something I am absolutely sure is holy.'[77] Her expositions often involve a strange mixture of popular love-song phrases and religious terms:

I'd sort of refer to a man I might love as God but I mean by that that love is basically worship of another person. I think I don't know any other kind of love, that's my problem. I accept nothing less. I also know what it is like for me to evoke worship in someone, so I mean a very even sort of balance when I talk like that, something that is dispersed among men and women. I carry this to extremes. I mean, if I were kissed by someone I worshipped; that sort of kissed [sic] would last me an eternity and I'd need nothing else.[78]

One wonders on reading such a passage whether Bessie had in fact advanced emotionally from her view of love as she used to depict it in the weekly love story she wrote in the *Post* in Johannesburg. She gave her attitude a certain authority by saying that she would 'accept nothing less'. But she did also admit for a moment that she didn't 'know any other kind of love, that's my problem'. The trouble was that she not only applied these standards to her own life, she sometimes expected them to apply to her friends' marriages as well. On more than one occasion she took an intuitive liking to a friend's husband, made him into a god in her imagination, and then broke up with the friend because she did not show her husband the worship that was his due.

The unusual love triangles described in both *Maru* and *A Question of Power* have many elements which could suggest that they have grown out of Bessie's own experience; but the truth may be that they are imaginative workings of relatively innocent situations. There is, however, one undated piece of paper entitled 'Some notes on love and relationships between men and women' which says that, in her long life, only one man fell in love with her. He was, she said, 'disturbed and attracted' by *A Question of Power*, and added with disarming honesty that without that book he 'would not have noticed me'. Bessie watched him go through a silent conflict:

He was a man who was proud of being honoured and trusted by his wife and the rest of the world. I certainly loved him but I kept absolutely silent. I am afraid had he approached me and so on I would not have been the honourable woman I am. All I did was remain silent and allow the man to work out his own conflict. He decided on his own that he would never approach me and I never saw him again. I have only those kinds of lessons from life. I value them because life often demands that people must not only think of themselves but make sacrifices for others'.[79]

Even this piece, with its elevated air, could be more an expression of what Bessie desired rather than what actually happened. Like some of the strong women in her village tales, she appeared to choose celibacy rather than an unsatisfactory love relationship with a man. For almost all her life, however, she subscribed to the idea that a heterosexual relationship was the desirable one. Though she was often extremely critical of men generally, she also often maintained that this did not mean that she did not like them. 'I don't have obsessive feelings. I don't exclude men and children from my life. They are always there so I don't miss them even though I own or possess nothing.'[80]

She was thus consigned to another of life's alternatives, loneliness. 'I know how endless loneliness is difficult to cope with,'[81] she once wrote. And two years later: 'It does not dismay me that I am lonely, etc. and never found love as people know it; that's never shaken me.'[82] She continued: 'What has often shaken me is the ferocity of suffering life can bring one, so that one often wonders how one survives.' Once she also said: 'I knew I could not run for cover anywhere during my dark times. The storm of it would have shattered anyone else into a thousand fragments. I haven't yet quite sorted out what happened to me: I might have had to have this backlog of darkness to clear off and I could only do it alone.'[83]

There is often an underlying feeling that her hold on life is very insecure. 'I wouldn't mind having a fairly long life but I've never felt that I had a very strong hold on life. In fact I'm always amazed when I wake up each morning. I never expect to,'[84] she wrote in 1974. In 1976 she was talking about 'not living very long anyway' and wanting to be buried in Botalaote cemetery as she 'took a fancy' to it when she visited chief Botalaote while working on the *Serowe book*.[85] That this was not a completely negative attitude is very beautifully expressed in something she wrote to the Cullinans after they had visited her: 'What we have in common is an almost inward, quiet, retreating world, a readiness to give way before life, as though one's hold on it is very precarious at most times.'[86]

History & Tale Telling
1976

At the end of 1976 Botswana could celebrate its tenth anniversary of independence and the country was flourishing in a way no one could have foreseen. In 1971 the mining of diamonds at Orapa was begun. Two years later the copper and nickel mines were opened at Selebi-Pikwe. While copper and nickel prices on the world market have since collapsed and the mine is kept open only through government and private subsidy, diamond mining has been responsible for virtually transforming the economy. From 1971 onwards minerals replaced cattle as the chief export.

In 1975 Seretse Khama's Botswana Democratic Party was returned to office for a fourth three-year term. The next year the economy was so stable that it was decided to replace the rand, which was the South African currency, with the pula (meaning 'rain'), sub-divided into 100 units called thebes. The value was fixed as the same as the rand, which was worth $1.15 in October; this was taken out of circulation on 1 December. The combination of economic and political stability within the country meant that it was better equipped to meet the regional hazards which surrounded it.

First of all there were the problems connected with UDI in Rhodesia. Though the United Nations sanctions were not seriously enforced, the country began to feel their effects from 1972 onwards. About the same time the first organised resistance to the Rhodesian regime made itself felt within the country. Black supporters of ZANU, the Zimbabwe African National Union, under Robert Mugabe, began attacks on whites on outlying farms. Later Mugabe and Joshua Nkomo combined to form the Patriotic Front, while Bishop Muzorewa led the more moderate African National Council. The Chimurenga, or liberation war, became more effective year by year, until all whites carried guns and knew how to use them and the government was calling up men in their forties and relying heavily on mercenary soldiers to defend the minority regime. Botswana provided an asylum for Rhodesian refugees and as the conflict dragged on, Botswana was one of the countries bringing pressure on Smith's government to relinquish its authority. Being so closely linked to Rhodesia through their common rail network made Botswana vulnerable. In early 1976 the guerrilla forces began blowing up sections of the line in Rhodesia. Bessie had the following comment to make on the situation:

A lot of bombs have gone off on the Rhodesia/Botswana railway line, the last being on Friday 29th October. For one bomb that goes off, so the news says, the Rhodesian forces manage to kill off a lot of freedom fighters – nineteen on Friday. If this is true, I don't like it at all because the toll in young lives is too high . . . Do so many people die for liberation?[1]

She felt that it was because Botswana was 'tied to Rhodesia through the railway line' that Seretse Khama was engaged in long talks with the presidents of Zambia and Mozambique:

For years Seretse made non-political speeches. They were so boring and empty of content that one stopped reading them. They kept the situation peaceful. The Boers and the other horrors could do nothing with those speeches. Everyone likes the way the country is run because we keep on with everyday affairs when everything is falling to pieces very hard around us. We don't know what happens at those meetings in Zambia but central to them is the survival of the country. When Rhodesia falls Botswana can come to a standstill. If the rail is not kept open we can't survive.[2]

In 1974, after years of destructive civil war, Portugal withdrew from its two colonies, Angola and Mozambique, leaving chaos behind. In Angola the new 'non-nation' consisted of three warring independence groups, with Russian, Cuban, American and later South African support. When the Portuguese flag was lowered for the last time, the last High Commissioner, Admiral Cardosa, took it off to Portugal with him: there was no one to whom he could hand it over, he maintained.[3] Independent Mozambique's new President, Samora Machel, had close links with China, then the USSR. Shortly after he assumed office he closed his border with Rhodesia, an act which had serious consequences for the Rhodesians but also for Mozambique, whose main source of food supply had been Rhodesia. Both Mozambique and Angola provided new training bases for the Zimbabwe People's Army guerrillas.

In 1972 Botswana took a large American loan to build a road to the Zambezi River and Zambia. The Kazungula ferry, linking Zambia and Botswana, provided a lifeline for both nations as sanctions against Rhodesia made themselves felt. Airlinks were also established with Lusaka.

After the Soweto uprisings and the consequent student unrest, Botswana found itself inundated with young South African refugees. The government had frequently stated that it had an 'open door' policy to refugees and it now took these young people in, to the annoyance of the South African government. But in December 1976 it announced that it could no longer harbour nationalist guerrillas though it was under pressure from the other front-line states to do so. With its economy so closely linked to South Africa's, it could not afford to; nor would it allow ANC bases or training camps in the country. Both the Rhodesian government and South Africa began to punish Botswana's independent stance with attacks over the border. In December 1976, for example, Rhodesians attacked the police barracks near Francistown in an exchange of fire that lasted twenty minutes and injured one person. The next June, Bessie reported that bombs in a bar in Francistown had killed two people and injured 80.[4] No one knew who was responsible though it was believed to be Rhodesians. From 1979 onwards there were many border incidents involving South Africans.

Inside South Africa the political climate became increasingly tense throughout 1977. A year after the Soweto risings, the young students, generally referred to as The Children, had taken charge in the township. They commemorated the grim anniversary by enforcing a two-day strike. Black sports and entertainment events were cancelled; even the 400 shebeens were closed at their insistence. Church services were held to celebrate their 'Black Christmas'. The radical student groups were asserting an authority and leadership the older generation had not been able to achieve. Thanks to The Children, one black activist teacher said 'the good African mask is now coming off'.[5] No longer would maids and office workers smile all day at work and come home vowing to poison the whole family or slit the employer's throat. This was Black Consciousness in action.

Bessie commented on the situation thus:

So you see how simply it began? 'Where will we get our servants?' Very much like the nobility in Russia, who ceased to work and had all their work done for them by bonded serfs. These riots and uprisings are a part of South African history . . . This time, with Angola and Mozambique free right on their borders, the Boer for the first time resinded [sic] his decision to impose his stinking language on children in the schools. May he swallow his bastard language. This has been the only victory out of 200 people dead.[6]

The banishment of Winnie Mandela to the remote township of Brandfort, 370 kilometres from Soweto, in late May 1977 did not ease the simmering discontent. Nor did the news of the death of Steve Biko in September, especially when it became clear that he had not starved himself to death as first stated, but had incurred such serious head injuries in detention that velvet draping was needed to cover part of his skull when his body was displayed in the coffin.

At the end of 1977 Botswana acquired a new 'neighbour'. The second tribal homeland to gain 'independence', Bophuthatswana, came into existence. The name means 'that which binds the Tswana' and the homeland was certainly in need of a cohesive force. It consisted of seven patches of territory spread across the western Transvaal and into the Orange Free State, with a thin slice bordering directly on Botswana. At independence it had a population of two and a half million people from 76 different ethnic groups, mostly sub-tribes of the Tswana nation. The only two countries to recognise the new 'state' were South Africa and the Transkei, the other tribal homeland. By creating Sun City, a resort given to gambling and pleasure, Bophuthatswana was soon to draw thousands of South Africans over its borders in search of forms of entertainment their own puritanical regime would not countenance.

Botswana refused to recognise Bophuthatswana, just as it would not comply with the other three demands South Africa was constantly making: to stop issuing anti-apartheid statements, expel South African refugees and sign a non-aggression pact.[7]

There was also constant unrest in South West Africa, Botswana's neighbour to the west. It came as a surprise to many people when South Africa's Prime

Minister, Vorster, agreed to negotiate for the country's independence, which was originally set for December 1978. Bessie was both excited and sceptical. 'The news this week has been so exciting as regards Namibia (South West),' she wrote in April 1978. 'The Afrikaner Boer can never do anything decent and when I first heard the news I thought it was a hoax.' She went on to say that she did not believe in a happy ending.

Nothing will make me believe that evil is ever overcome until the end of the world itself . . . The only thing that will break South Africa is the supernatural and unknown . . . the unexpected sort of judgement day . . . No one can fight evil in the ordinary way with ordinary weapons. So I hold out for the miracle.[8]

Her friend Mona Pehle, to whom she had written this, took her up on that last remark. She sent her a quote from her Quaker magazine saying that we don't always recognise miracles when they are happening. This led Bessie to respond, 'I do believe in a greater miracle. It has become accepted in a psychological way that the white man is no longer a political force or a governing power in Africa and the South African whites are really irrelevant in every way already.'[9]

The University of Botswana was being established during these years. During the Writers' Workshop Bessie had attended there in April 1976 the campus was still very much under construction. Students were actively engaged in fundraising for what they called the Botswana University Campus Appeal. In September 1976 some of the students from Swaneng School in Serowe decided to support these efforts. This was to be the innocent cause of what Bessie calls 'the terrible storm that shook us'. In her long and vivid account of this incident to one of her correspondents, she casts light on the way she saw her relationship with the village at that stage of her life. She also gives us the first draft of a village tale that was never written. She tells it thus:

In early February this year our co-operative movement in Serowe, which is very large and owns several businesses in the village, purchased a small mini-bus. It was to operate within the five-mile radius outside Serowe. A young man aged 27 and named Fantisi was employed to drive the bus. The young man lived next door to my yard with his married brother, so he always ran the bus down for parking in his brother's yard. I was in a fortunate position as the bus could stop right at my door and on every occasion when the weather was bad for cycling into Serowe, I took the mini-bus in.

I am afraid I did not focus on the young man until a row brewed over the conditions under which he was to run the bus. A certain Pat van Rensburg, who co-ordinates the co-operative movement and other projects in the village, gave him a mad order. Only people who had paid a R2.00 membership fee could ride in the bus. We had all paid R2.00 membership fees to start co-operative businesses in Serowe and no one wanted to pay a further R2.00 for such a perishable commodity as a bus. There were huge savings from our businesses and we felt that the bus could run on those savings. So no one paid to get into the bus and for a week the driver coasted up and down with no passengers. Then, to our great delight, the bus driver quietly took the bus over. He had been given a bus route and a time table which he never followed. He drove the bus wherever people wanted him to go and very soon he had a roaring business going. His takings for the day were very high and since he had become such a millionaire bus driver, he took quite a lot of people in for no charge. Children took absolute advantage of him and rode the bus up and down for free; and that includes my own son, Howard.

I am inclined, in an absent-minded way, to take note of everything about people especially when they express lovely qualities. It did not take me long to note every detail about the young man, Fantisi. He was a very serene young man. It never took much to evoke a smile out of him. He had a very nice face and the ease of manner of one who dispenses kindness towards people in an indiscriminate way. His only protection was a kind of delicate withdrawal and reserve. Otherwise he was completely at the mercy of people and in his element. People and children never let up on him. I once saw him eating a meal in a yard with a whole lot of children clambering over him and he sat in the clamour smiling and smiling. When we drove in the bus through the village children stood outside their yards and saluted the bus. My own behaviour was as clamorous as the children. I began to insist on my right to sit next to the driver.

'Fantisi,' I'd say anxiously, 'please reserve my seat next to you.' More often than not, I would simply stare at his face in wonder. Really perfect people arouse worship like that. I noted absent-mindedly that the young man was quite aware that I adored him because he'd smile to himself now and then. One can get so well-known in the village that people will, of their own accord, grant one one's preferences. My preference to sit next to the young man became so well known that no one would take my seat. Once a man got in the bus ahead of me next to the driver and I got into the back. The man turned around and said uncertainly: 'Wouldn't you like to come and sit in the front?' I remember feeling very surprised and replying: 'No, it's all right here at the back.'

This absent-minded worship of the young man was to hit me very hard the day he died. I was entirely unaware of it.

Events of the night of the 12th September were to combine to give us one of the most horrific tragedies we have ever seen . . . It was the night on which the students of Swaneng Hill Secondary School were to hold a function in the community hall in the central part of the village as their contribution to the university appeal fund. At about 6.20 Fantisi and his mini-bus passed my home, on its way up to the secondary school to relay the students to the function. At 7.00 p.m. my son, who is a student at the secondary school, came home and anxiously asked for his supper so that he could attend the function. When he arrived at the school he found the queue of students lined up for the mini-bus service too long for his liking so he and two other students began the five mile walk into Serowe. When they were half way in to the village the mini-bus passed filled with 16 students. He waved it down but Fantisi, without slowing, signalled that he was full and would pick him up on the next round. A second later my son heard a tremendous crash.

A huge long-distance bus doing the 36-mile run from Serowe to a neighbouring village, Palapye, had left the central part of Serowe full of ready made catastrophe. The driver of the huge bus had tanked himself up on beer. When he started out, his main headlights failed to work, so he drove the bus on parking lights. The bus was full of people. The parking lights were so dim that they failed to throw up the red reflectors of a slowly moving tractor ahead of him. The big bus was just about to crash into the tractor so the driver of the bus lurched violently to the right and straight into the little mini-bus. It caught it head-on, pushed it some yards into a gulley and sat on it. The driver, Fantisi, and four young girl students were instantly killed. All the other students were badly injured or crippled.

The storm we went through! The mothers of the girls who were killed had to be admitted to hospital with recurring fainting fits. The principal of the secondary school collapsed and was taken unconscious to hospital. She is a lady, Mrs Matome. A large number of people dropped to the ground apparently stone dead with a cessation of pulse beat and were also admitted to hospital. The driver of the big bus went insane on the spot. He flew through the front window on impact and sat for a moment on the ground. Someone asked him how he was and he sprang to his feet and ran wildly into the night. After a while he too fell to the ground stone unconscious.

One half of the village was absolutely hysterical. The other half remained sane and functioning. A whole section of the sane part of the village moved into the yard next door to my home. They brought goats for slaughter, huge stacks of firewood, huge drums of water. They prayed quietly and ceaselessly. They stepped forward one after the other with a little speech of praise for the driver of the little mini-bus service. What had been an absent-minded concept, sharply came to the fore – never had such a perfect young man lived on this earth before! The sane section of the village quietly subdued the hysterical section.

I found myself living through a strange comical side drama. People would corner me in a quiet, determined way, look off in the distance and ask, detached: 'Well now, Mrs Head; how do you get home?' And I would reply: 'I am afraid the child Fantisi took our hearts though we did not know it . . . ' Then the person would turn and stare at me directly and say sternly: 'Don't say that!' But I noted that my questioners were vigorously nodding their heads in agreement with me.

An old man stopped by my fence. For some months he had been helping the young man Fantisi build a small house opposite my own yard. On the day of his death the old man and the young man had spent the whole Sunday clearing the thorn trees and weeds out of the yard. The old man said to me: 'I know how much you liked Fantisi so I want to tell you something. He knew his end had come. He knew he was going to die. That morning he said to me: "Hey, uncle, I had a strange dream last night. I dreamt that my dead mother was sweeping my yard with a Tswana broom. I went up to her and said: 'Mother, I am going to build a rondavel house for you on the eastern side of my flat so that you may come and stay with me.' What can that dream mean, uncle?" So I said: "It means that your dead mother has come to bless your yard." So he said: "No, uncle. The dream disturbs me very much. Something bad is going to happen to me today . . ."'

The young man's mother died in 1974 of cardiac failure. For twenty two years she had reared him on her own. He was illegitimate. His father, who lived in the village, never acknowledged his existence. His mother had given him a very humorous name at his birth. Fantisi means 'Jumble Sale', you know, where things come cheap. She could never have known then that you get very good bargains for your money at jumble sales.[10]

Bessie gave additional details of Fantisi Gaothogogwe's death to Betty Fradkin, who was anxious to send a contribution to the Campus Appeal in memory of the young people. Here she emphasised the secluded nature of their village life:

We have never seen anything like this in Serowe before, Betty. Since I have been here a little boy was killed on the main road then a few dogs and one goat. Some adults tippled off the slippery gravel of the main road but they seemed to be strangers speeding some-where. Then a car had a blow-out and killed a brigade student. There were very few cars when I came. There are a lot more cars on the road now.[11]

Most shocked was Howard, who watched the mangled bodies being pulled out of the wrecked bus. He told his mother the news, veering 'from terror to manly calm'. Some days later he said that he dreaded facing all those coffins, four at the school and one next door. Bessie told him to go out and find some of the other students: 'You are not alone in this. It involves all the other boys at the school.' The boys got together and sat in silent groups. 'But the tragedy took its toll. One of the students, a boy, committed suicide a week later. He hung himself.'

In the same letter Bessie dwells in more detail on Fantisi's exceptional quali-ties. He was able to give everyone his 'instant love . . . He turned and smiled at you, and "you" meant everyone', in a simple and uncomplicated way. 'He smiled once with his whole mouth and then twice, with the corners of his mouth, so you were sure it was for you and that was the proper way to greet people.' Someone summed it up thus to Bessie: 'Here you set a limit on everything you do with people because you know people can injure you. With Fantisi you set no limit. There was nothing inside him that could injure people . . . '

Bessie sensed an affinity between them:

That young man's method of operating among people, reaching out across barriers was so identical to mine that I actually stood still with quiet wonder and looked back carefully on all that had happened. I cried with shock at the violence of the accident but it was like a more beautiful and more perfect extension of myself had died and I did not really know what to do about it. It was just gone . . . I have never felt this way about death before. I can tell you people liked that instant love very much and he was the only one who had it. No one can do an imitation of it.[12]

Bessie had introduced the story of Fantisi by saying that she had had an affair going with the village for a long time, 'a kind of marriage that turned out to be quite stable although I did not think so at first'. She concluded the account with the hope that it would give some indication of how her 'Victorian marriage of convenience'[13] was progressing. At times she seemed to suggest that she had become completely integrated into village life; perhaps she dreamt that this would happen one day. But she still recorded, with a degree of resignation, remarks made to her in the village: 'Mrs Heady, everyone knows your name but you are not really known',[14] someone had said to her about eighteen months before the Fantisi incident. And six years later, shortly before her 'Serowe book' finally appeared, she was told with a frankness that must have hurt: 'You are like someone who is looking in on a birthday party to which you will never be invited.'[15]

After her break with her agent and publisher, Bessie had returned to her historical research. But her chronic financial worries made it difficult for her to 'settle to the sustained high-pitched concentration needed for novel writing'. She admitted that 'part of last year' (1976) she 'hid in research'. She needed to earn money and she could do this with shorter work: 'Once I have money to live on without the hell of all this worry, I'll be able to take on that terribly long haul. I found that it is possible to maintain very high standards with short stories and still keep a worried eye on how the household pot is boiling,' she explained to Betty Fradkin. And concluded with the exclamation: 'Let me get rich, Betty!'[16]

The short stories Bessie was now working on she called her 'historical tales'. She had been planning them for some years. In fact shortly after sending off the stories that were to comprise *The Collector of Treasures* anthology, she asked Giles Gordon whether she should send him some of her historical tales. He was not keen. He felt that they should not flood the market with any more of her writing. He suggested that she collect about six and then send them to him.[17] About a year later she had a couple of these stories ready; and in May and June 1977 she was working on two more. In August 1980 she wrote that she had 'typed out six historical short stories and felt so depressed about the work that I switched over to concentrating entirely on the novel'.[18] These six stories were in all probability those entitled 'Property', 'A Period of Darkness', 'The Lovers', 'A Power Struggle', 'A Colonial Experience' and 'Son of the Soil', and were produced in that order. They were organically related to her historical research, often bordering on the documentary.

'Property' was actually of a much earlier date. Bessie, with her usual housewifely thrift, had kept it in a drawer since before 1969 when her agent had considered combining it and two other short stories with the rather short novella *Maru*.[19] Rather surprisingly, 'Property' had been and continued to be overlooked. It is written with much of her early verve and restrained humour, derived largely from a situation in which a young girl who is paid for with twelve head of cattle and thus accepts the fact that she has become her husband's property, is totally unnerved by his gentle and considerate behaviour: 'No slave owner asked a purchased slave if the slave was tired . . . if something was your property you expected it to keep the place spick and span and occasionally you roughed it up with a good beating to keep it in place.'[20] Only when the young man beats his wife is she relieved to find that she has a normal marriage at last; and tribal greed and individual snobbishness are also treated as norms from which both the young man and, a generation later, his son dissociate themselves. 'Property' is thus one of Bessie Head's portrayals of the type of sensitive, imaginative, apparently unmanly man who, because of these qualities, lives a 'magic life' his family and friends 'would never know'.

In 'A Period of Darkness' and 'A Power Struggle', apparently both straightforward accounts of tribal unrest, it is the psychological insight we get into the personalities of her characters and the constant light cast on the mechanism of power that make them interesting. Underlying both stories is the idea that 'a ruler only existed because there were people to rule' (p. 78); 'that people always held a position of ascendancy in matters of government (p. 83); that people 'under duress' were forced to 'make elaborate choices between good and evil' (p. 77). She again examines the paradox of the good man making a weak ruler. People understand the qualities of 'happiness and laughter ... They are the natural gifts of a good man. But these very gifts can be a calamity in a ruler. A ruler has to examine the dark side of human life and understand that men belong to that darkness' (p. 75). Though the good weak man is sometimes forced out of the tribe, Bessie explains that 'the people would take over ... They would abandon evil. What I did in the story was to romanticise the power of the people as a whole to abandon evil. It cost them a lot.' She adds that she loves this theme 'as to give way and find a new world seems to have been all I may have ever lived or died for in my whole backlog of soul history'.[21]

Trying out the same theme in 'The General', almost certainly a much earlier story, Bessie says: 'People may be unreasonable in the way they change their mind about their chosen Gods but they are not fools' (p. 103). She describes a fictional African dictator, who as President and Saviour of the people calls himself 'the composite type of all the dictators in the world'. Despite, or because of, an unusual intellectual brilliance, he soon starts sending his bright young advisers into exile and surrounding himself with 'men of dull wit or mediocre intellect' until the people depose him, preferring instead the upright General Askan. Though he takes on the dangerous job of President, enlisting the help of his friend Professor Okala to 'strike a blow in the name of truth and justice', it does seem as if two innocents are now pitting themselves against 'the thousands of crooks awaiting their turn to live off the people's blood like leeches' (p. 114). With the years Bessie had developed a somewhat irreverent attitude to African politics and 'The General', which was only published posthumously, might have originated about the time she made the following comment to a friend in 1972:

I laughed like hell this morning. General Somebody of Uganda made a coup last year against Obote. Then last month he invited Dr Busia to the celebrations to celebrate the coup, only to have Dr Busia couped in Ghana. Then he invites the couper to his coup celebrations, just the same. CAN YOU BEAT IT? This news came over the B.B.C. world service, reported in the ordinary, prosaic voice of those fellows.[22]

The story on which she lavished the most care and detail is undoubtedly 'The Lovers'. It is her re-working of one of the great love-legends of Botswana; the story of the haunted hill, Letswe La Baratani, the Hill of the Lovers. It tells of a young couple who defied the social and sexual taboos of their tribe by choosing each other instead of allowing their marriages to be arranged by the family. This causes 'raging storms and wild irrational deliberations' in each family and in the tribe as a whole. The lovers are banished for a while and are seen to be going up onto the nearby hill on which they had originally met. But they do not return when they are due to and when one of the women goes to investigate, the whole drama of their disappearance is 'recreated before her eyes'. She hears groans of anguish and has a vision of the rocks on the hill parting and closing over the lovers again. After that, everyone who goes to the hill hears groaning sounds and the tribe has to pack up and move away. Later strangers settling there 'saw the same phenomenon, heard the loud groans of anguish' (p. 100).

Bessie retains a careful balance between the simple narrative thread of the original legend and her own more probing psychological interest in the complexities of human behaviour. In fact the two threads represent the predicament a closely knit community faces when individuals refuse to comply with its customs: 'If you question life you will upset it. Life is always in order,' says Mma-Monosi, Tselane's father's second wife and her great friend. The advantages and complications of communal life are depicted just as carefully as the attractive, dangerous road of the individual. We realise in fact that Mma-Monosi's 'precarious inner balance', which is so easily upset if there is any disruption or disorder, hints at her own inability to accept her own maxim.

Tselane's painful process from emotional adolescence to adulthood, moving away at the same time from a collective consciousness into individual awareness, is finely portrayed. In her case the process is so concentrated that it makes her ill: 'I know now what was making me feel so ill. I was fighting my training. My training has told me that people are not important in themselves, but you suddenly became important to me, as a person' (p. 96).

Above the framework of tradition and superstition, the rational logic of a more sophisticated observer emerges: the fact that Keaja has carefully planned an escape route which would enable the lovers to 'disappear' forever; the fact that the originator of the story of the haunted mountain is none other than Mma-Moroni, the woman who has a delicate nervous balance and is perhaps overexcitable. But with the perception of the true storyteller, Bessie leaves unresolved ambiguities at the conclusion of her tale.

When Bessie sent 'The Lovers' off to the American journal, *Atlantic Monthly*, she wrote that when she heard the love story, it 'so haunted' her that she 'could find no peace' until she had written her own version of it. 'Sanely, a hill could never open and swallow people, so my story dwells on what happened before the lovers disappeared so mysteriously.'[23] She wrote to Betty Fradkin about the same time, praising her short story: '"The Lovers" is a beautiful story. I post it with a high heart. I usually know when I have a good thing going.'[24] To her disappointment it was returned from America; and also from the South African magazine *Drum*. She had hoped they would like it and publish it, considering all the love stories she had written for *Home Post* so long ago.

'A Colonial Experience' has never been published. Bessie wanted it that way. She withdrew it from her New York agent because she wished to rewrite it. 'It does not have a proper focus on people,'[25] she said, but never had the opportunity to rewrite it. 'Son of the Soil' was probably written in late 1979, after Bessie had read Sol Plaatje's *Native Life in South Africa* for the first time. She is obviously interested in depicting the earliest waves of black protest in South Africa and contrasting them with the mass protests of the 1950s and early 1960s. She takes in the main sweep of events and does not focus on individual personalities. 'Son of the Soil', also only published posthumously, relates both to 'Coming of the Christ Child' and to her later 'Foreword to *Native Life in South Africa*' and this is quite significant: it balances between fiction and non-fiction. Read alone, it might seem dry and uninteresting. Read in relation to other pieces of her writing, its purpose emerges.

Giles Gordon once made this point with reference to Bessie's village tales: they improved if they were grouped together.[26] The same can be said of her historical tales. In simple direct language she conveys the flavour of her period and the mental climate of her characters, allowing one tale to colour another; the mood of one to flow into the next. As it turned out, however, this was not a style that appealed to many editors. 'A Power Struggle' was the first to be rejected because its style was 'unattractive'. Bessie told a friend that this 'absolutely deflated my ego as a budding historical fictionist'.[27] For the next few years she was to be struggling more and more with the concept of 'historical fiction'.

Towards the end of 1976 Bessie Head was contacted by a South African lecturer from the University of Witwatersrand, Jean Marquard, asking whether she could come to Serowe and interview her. This she did in December 1976. She taped an interview which she later used in connection with a feature article which was published in *London Magazine* a year afterwards.[28] Later the BBC African Service also broadcast the interview. The weekend Jean Marquard spent in Serowe was very congenial for Bessie; Jean invited her to several meals at the hotel; and paid for her drinks. Jean Marquard thus pioneered an area that was soon to become very popular: interviewing Bessie. And Bessie was soon to be given a singular opportunity to perfect the art of giving interviews.

View of Serowe

Outside Africa
A Broader View, 1977–1986

Bessie after her trip to Nigeria, c. 1982–3 (courtesy Khama Memorial Museum)

13

Ohio
1977

At the end of July 1977 the quiet rhythm of Bessie Head's life was shattered by a letter from the American Embassy in Gaborone. Every year the United States State Department sponsors a large international Writing Programme at the University of Iowa. The American Chargé-d'Affaires, Frank Alberti, had nominated Bessie Head to represent Botswana. The Office of the President had approved the nomination. The University of Iowa had accepted her application. The State Department would cover all her travel expenses and there was $1000 available for Howard's maintenance while she was away.

Only when everything was cut and dried, only then was Bessie informed. She was overwhelmed. 'A week ago I was peacefully planning my summer garden and muttering curses about the horrific Botswana sun. This week there is absolute chaos in my household . . . I fear this is the pot-luck of a writer's life – one day there is absolutely nothing and the next day there is a big rainbow,'[1] she wrote to Betty Fradkin at the end of July. In a pencil note at the top of the letter, she added, 'You angel. I think the worst is over. I would not have survived without your help.' In the letter she had also written and underlined: 'I pray God this is the beginning of a way to steadily earn my income.'

She was to leave at the end of August for Iowa City, Iowa. Howard would be writing his Junior Certificate examination while she was away, and it was very important that he pass. His school results having been bad for the preceding three years, this could by no means be taken for granted. Obviously arranging for his care was the most important task facing Bessie, but this proved easy. His form teacher, Wendy Willett, and her husband Tony offered to look after him, which they did very successfully, keeping Bessie informed of his progress throughout her time in the United States.

The staff at Swaneng, Bessie's neighbours and friends in the village, all took an active part in the preparations for her departure. Someone gave her an evening dress which had to be shortened considerably. Others advised her about the warm clothing she would need for an American winter. Ruth and Per Forchhammer, a Danish couple recently arrived at Swaneng School, where Per Forchhammer was teaching biology, organised a collection amongst staff members and friends and presented Bessie with a cheque at a farewell party at their home just before she left. There was much excited chatter, Bessie reacting with exaggerated panic to Per Forchhammer's teasing warnings about tornadoes in America.

Generally she kept her anxious feelings hidden, though she was naturally apprehensive about facing so many 'firsts': her first air flight; her first departure from the African continent; her first international confrontation with other creative writers.

The Embassy had arranged the necessary travel documents because Bessie had no passport. Originally the plan was to book her on a Pan American flight from Johannesburg via Rio de Janeiro and New York to Cedar Rapids, the nearest airport to Iowa City. As she could not enter South Africa with the travel documents she had, she had to be re-routed via Lusaka, Nairobi, London and New York. It was a much longer and very tiring trip; Bessie suffered badly from swollen legs.

However, it gave her one advantage. She stopped over in Lusaka for a couple of days and visited her sister-in-law Caroline Hlaba (née Head) and her family. They had moved from Kitwe to Lusaka about eighteen months before and Caroline Hlaba now had three young children. The two women used the time together to re-establish their friendship and strengthen the family bonds that Caroline Hlaba needed almost as much Bessie did, having lived in isolation from her family for many years.

Professor Paul Engle and his Chinese wife, Hauling Nieh Engle, had conceived the idea of gathering writers from all over the world through the Iowa International Writing Programme and giving them respite and inspiration for their task. Respite in the form of pleasant living conditions and plenty of time for their writing; inspiration through the exchange of ideas amongst themselves and contact with American academic circles and admirers. The living allowance was extremely generous. There were 6 women and 20 men on the exchange that year. They were accommodated in a comfortable apartment block, the Mayflower.

Bessie and a writer from the Philippines, Ninontchka Rosca, were paired off. It was no easy matter for the organisers to allocate accommodation to suit the temperaments of 26 sensitive individualists. Shortly after arriving, Bessie reported that some people refused to share apartments and 'so for two days people were shuttled to and fro'. Others had wasted no time in forming close friendships and already had 'their lives, beer and food all mixed up'. She felt that her own shared apartment could well have been one of the few that was 'not a madhouse'.[2]

The first few weeks were taken up with settling in; relating the information they had been sent to the lives they would be leading. Rather nervously she studied the university campus that was to be the frame for all their activities. Then she headed for the library. She was amazed to see how large it was. 'Africa? Fifth floor,' she was told when she launched into a long explanation of her research project at the information desk. When she had taken her courage in both hands and a lift to the fifth floor, there was no librarian ready to find all her books for her the way they did in Gaborone. Gradually, however, she warmed to life on the fifth floor. She was almost alone up there in a 'desolation of solitude, silence, and books'.[3] And such books! Many on African history long out of print but essential to her research she found in the library. The fifth floor became her paradise.

There were introductory meetings where the participants sized each other up. Bessie felt strange and confused. None of them knew her writing but, to be honest, neither did she know theirs. There was a weekly seminar designed to allow each one to present his or her writing and country to the group. Bessie met the lecturer from the Department of African Studies who was her contact person with the University and he too had never read her work, though he admitted having heard of her. 'I'll have to see how all this nonsense works out. Phew!'[4] wrote Bessie to Betty Fradkin, shortly after arriving in Iowa City.

There were also a couple of cocktail parties held to welcome the group to the University. She put on the evening dress she had brought along, grateful to have it, and sallied forth to do her part, but found the atmosphere strangely stilted. The University staff 'huddled in a corner',[5] after rather hurried and embarrassed greetings, and the 26 foreign writers stood around talking to each other.

Bessie had to adjust herself to the American gadget world. She was fascinated by the slot machine in the entrance to her block, which provided any number of commodities from snacks to milk. The code to open the combination lock of her post box gave her some trouble: 'Two turns to the left, three turns to the right, turn to 13. Lo! most times the box won't open.'[6] Even using the washing machine was an experience. The first time she did so, she sat beside it and timed the various processes. And afterwards, she spent a day sewing all the hems of her dresses in again, as these had been spoilt in the spin-drying phase. Television was the other important innovation but she never really took to it. She seemed to find it disturbing.

What pleased her most was the bus service, though this too she found somewhat complicated. She enjoyed the friendly courtesy of the bus drivers: 'You get on and they say: "Hi" or "Nice weather today". You get off and you say "Thank you" and they say: "You're welcome." This is a fixed routine. Everyone says "Thank you" to the bus drivers.' She added a rather telling little comment: 'The atmosphere of the city is very friendly and I feel happier in it and doing shopping and finding my way around than at the parties I have been to.'[7]

Bessie enjoyed shopping for Howard and herself and sent parcels home regularly. 'Never have I had so much money and so many dresses. I only wore one dress a year in Serowe! Talk about becoming a millionaire overnight!'[8] There was an anecdote she told again and again. Shortly after her arrival in Iowa she needed some typing paper and a few items of stationery. She walked into a store and asked for a rubber. 'We only sell them in packs of three,' said the shop assistant. 'But I only want one,' said Bessie. 'I told you, we only sell them in threes,' said the man again, clearly annoyed. 'Well, let me take three then,' said Bessie. Whereupon he went to the back of the shop and came back with a pack of three 'male prophylactics' as she called them. She looked somewhat horrified and said, 'I'm looking for the thing you rub out mistakes with.' To which the assistant replied: 'Oh, you mean an eraser.'[9] Bessie commented to Betty Fradkin: 'Ah me, life here ain't what I am used to … I am going to be in a mess.' When shopping she also soon encountered a familiar phrase: 'Sorry, we're out of stock right now.' When she heard this she thought: 'Well, I'm home. This is Serowe again.'[10]

In fact, she had not been long in her new surroundings before she recognised the rural nature of the place. Iowa City was only slightly larger than Serowe. 'It delights me, rural villager that I am, to say that nothing happens here too. One day is just like the next. There's only a lot more cars than I have ever seen and lots of houses, all done up with pretty front lawns.'[11] While Serowe was sun-scorched and rocky, Iowa City was surrounded by lush farmlands and there was everywhere 'this massive earth coverage of green grass and a big, broad slowly moving river'[12] very near Bessie's apartment. The trees were very tall but she had seen 'Botswana-type weeds in the gulleys and nooks around here'. The news-papers were usually concerned with local stuff, 'so that chicken manure and other farming matters made the daily headlines until Baader was killed in prison and Sadat went to Israel.'[13] Bessie was thoroughly startled at the change in headlines when world events intruded. It was undoubtedly the recognition of underlying universal patterns and points of similarity that did much to make her time in the United States as happy as it was. She saw that though people lived in an insulat-ed and conservative environment, they were anxious to know about other ways of living and were kind and generous to strangers. That was how it was in Serowe too.

Unfortunately Bessie's relationship with her flatmate deteriorated. The two women were very different. Ninotchka Rosca was a revolutionary who had been in jail for opposing the regime in her country; she was slim and very beautiful and dependent on male company. Their different eating habits might have been one of the original causes of the irritation they felt for each other. Ninotchka Rosca was constantly watching her diet, eating melons and drinking coffee, while Bessie liked plenty of butter on her bread and sugar in her tea. Apparently Ninotchka had passed derogatory remarks about Bessie's eating habits to the others.[14] And Bessie had retaliated by stating that she was not chosen to go to Iowa because of her 'vital statistics' and she did not think of her figure but of her work.

The real cause of the clash between Bessie and her flatmate had its origins in their totally opposed behaviour patterns. Bessie was by nature a recluse; she had lived a very secluded life for years; she had very strict sexual norms. She described Ninotchka as being 'very emancipated' and having many dates and admirers. Bessie did not approve and the atmosphere became so strained that Ninotchka would not even return her greetings. After that, Bessie did not talk to her at all, sometimes communicating with written notes. Ninotchka was now hurt and spread the word around that Bessie refused to speak to her. As each woman worked out her own routine, the sources of friction were reduced and they coex-isted in a state of cease-fire.

Bessie was of course completely out of touch with all the eating fads of the Western world. She was only interested in enjoying some of the luxuries she sel-dom could afford at home and making herself meals that did not demand much time. The wife of one of the lecturers, who was designated to help her with her shopping in the beginning, was shocked to hear that she planned to eat eggs for breakfast every day. 'Only eat one egg a week,' she was told. 'Our eggs have a high cholesterol content and it will affect your heart.' When she mentioned this to someone else, this woman replied that women do not die from eating eggs, only men. 'I wondered WHERE they got all this strange information from.'[15]

Bessie struck up a short friendship with the lecturer in African Studies and adviser to the foreign writers, Peter Nazareth, who had not read any of her writing. She told him details of her nervous breakdown and listened to his records until the day she felt that he was behaving in a condescending way to her: 'I have been astonished at how deeply prejudiced Asian and such like people are towards Africans.'[16] When he tried to sort out the misunderstanding, Bessie locked him out of her apartment. Then he retaliated by not speaking to her again. She refused to sit on a panel with him and missed out on a lecture engagement on that account. While he started using her novels in his courses and with the years acquired expert status as an exponent of her writing,[17] Bessie obliterated him from her life, as was her habit.[18] 'Life is mostly quiet for me here. My friends are outside the programme,'[19] she wrote to Betty Sleath in early December.

Two such friends were the Carvlins. Though she had forgotten to bring their address with her, she managed to trace them. They visited her from Chicago for a day and took her out for a drive and a meal. Considering the forceful nature of her writing, Tom Carvlin found Bessie less of an extrovert than he had expected. Her friendliness and warmth charmed them both. They discussed current events rather than existential issues and exchanged family news. Towards the end of the day, when they were taking leave of her outside her apartment, three wild turkeys appeared out of the woods nearby. This was a rare experience even for the Americans and reminded them all of Bessie's interest in fauna, especially that of Botswana, illustrated by the many stamps depicting birds which she had collected and sent the Carvlins.[20]

By the end of her first month in Iowa, Bessie was settling down to long stretches of writing. As well as the research for her Khama novel, she hoped to work on further historical short stories. All the writers met for discussions twice a week, but this left much time for her own work. 'Days and days would go by filled only with one's own work. One could take risks with time, turning day into night and working at all sorts of odd hours.'[21] She alternated her periods of intense writing with walks in the surrounding countryside, very aware of the fiery show of autumn colours on the trees followed by a papery carpet of fallen leaves, biting winds and bleak days. Rural villager though she was, she could not relate to such climatic displays and she awaited her first snowfall with a mixture of anticipation and anxiety.

Bessie was not allowed to bury herself in her writing for too long at a time. Shortly after arriving in America, she was contacted by Cecil Abrahams, a relation of the South African writer Peter Abrahams. Cecil had been active in the ANC in South Africa before going into exile and settling in Canada, where he lectured at Bishop's University in Quebec. Bessie was invited to visit there for three days in early November. She talked at student gatherings, took part in informal discussions and attended a dinner party.

Before she went to Quebec she had another lecture engagement lined up. In October the writer Margaret Walker had visited them in Iowa. When she sent word that she was coming, she sent a special message to Bessie to tell her that she had all her books and that it would be a dream come true to meet her. She hoped Bessie would visit Jackson State University, Mississippi, where she was head of the Department of Black Studies. She was twenty years older than Bessie but her novel of a black girl's view of slavery and the civil war, *Jubilee*, written in 1966, had become a classic and inspired many of the younger black American writers. The special regard she had for Bessie had been strengthened after Nikki Giovanni had met her in Botswana. In 1974 Nikki Giovanni had written a book about Margaret Walker, *A Poetic Equation: Conversations Between Nikki Giovanni and Margaret Walker.*[22]

Margaret Walker's message gave Bessie some much needed encouragement and prestige. The trouble was, she had never read any of her books. In all haste she started on *Jubilee* and found it a remarkable and moving novel. It was the introduction to Margaret Walker, and the South that Bessie needed. It was agreed that she visit Jackson, Mississippi, in December.

She suddenly found herself with a run of engagements. On 7 December she took part in a lecture tour to the University of Northern Iowa at Cedar Falls. By this time winter had set in and she was accustomed to falling snow and the caps, coats, gloves and boots that became part of her daily clothing routine. The day they went to Cedar Rapids the weather was particularly cold and fierce. The next day she and one of her colleagues, Jack Lahui, from Papua New Guinea, were due to fly to Jackson. If anything, the weather became worse. The plane departed from Cedar Rapids with only a short delay, but when they arrived at Chicago, where they had to change for Jackson, the temperatures had sunk further and huge drifts of snow swirled across the runways. Their plane was grounded. They were delayed an hour and had to have hot oil sprayed onto the wings of the plane to defrost them before take-off.

In Jackson winter had hardly made itself felt. The grass was green, the trees had all their leaves, there was a warm sun shining. Bessie was rushed from the airport directly to the auditorium where the students and lecturers were already waiting for her. The lecture and discussion lasted two hours. She had prepared a paper which she used on each occasion, describing how Africans lost their land to the whites in South Africa. It was based on the most recent aspect of her research for her Khama novel. 'Everyone loved me,' she reported, 'and audiences sat in deep silence . . . Almost everyone asked for a copy of the paper.'[23]

If Jackson University liked Bessie, she also liked being there. She was amazed to find that she had moved into an all-black world, the University consisting of a 90 per cent black student population, and the city being 70 per cent black. During her three days there, she addressed a class about her writing; gave a television interview; went to a Christmas concert; and took part in other social functions.

It was a rare period of success for Bessie. Her personal life was ordered and her economy considerably more stable than it had ever been. Her research was continually opening up new areas of thought for her. She was not only getting the complicated history of Southern Africa straight for the first time, she was also being confronted with her own microscopic role in that pattern of events. When she had written her *Serowe* book, she had begun to sense how she could come to terms with the problem of her background. Now here, in a land distant from her own, she understood it more clearly.

For once she was not constantly creating her own crises and drawing disasters down upon herself. But an event from the outside world did intrude to cause her distress. In the middle of October she received an official letter from the Ministry of Home Affairs in Gaborone. It was headed 'Application for Citizenship' and read: 'I regret to inform you that after careful consideration, your application for citizenship was not successful.' She was naturally very unhappy, partly because of Howard's future: 'There are no openings for non-Botswana citizens and life will be hard for him.' Furthermore, as she wrote to Betty Sleath, she had been refused citizenship at a time when she was actually representing the country abroad, presenting the sum of all she had done in Botswana, which 'was not bad but favourable to the country'.[24]

When she went to Quebec this problem was foremost in her mind. Cecil Abrahams tried to help her. Her main concern was that she would not be allowed to re-enter Botswana and he was doing what he could to find her work in Canada. He was friendly with Bessie's husband and pointed out to her that as she was in fact still legally married to Harold Head, a Canadian immigrant, he would be able to sign papers to gain her admission to the country. Bessie considered the idea. However, an anxious letter she had sent to Frank Alberti brought the reassuring reply that the refusal of citizenship had in no way affected the validity of her travel documents. She had been refused citizenship, but her status as a refugee would permit her to enter the country freely and allow her to reside there as she had done earlier. It was frustrating for her to have had such a refusal, said Frank, but it would not affect her present way of life.

The other event from the outside world that made itself felt during those months was the publication of *The Collector of Treasures and Other Botswana Village Tales*. Heinemann African Writers Series brought out a paperback edition in London while David Philip published a small hardcover edition in Cape Town at the same time. Naomi Mitchison wrote to congratulate her on her 'charming stories'.[25] Betty Sleath felt a midwife's pride in her friend's achievement and Mona Pehle, too, praised the collection. It had been a long time on the way. Bessie must have registered, during her many hours of introspection, the much more subdued nature of its publication as compared with the appearance of *A Question of Power*. She must have thought back on the friends who had helped her then – Giles, Paddy, Dulan for example – with whom she no longer corresponded. She was almost reaching the stage of admitting that the unnatural degree of her personal involvement in that novel at the time of its publication had affected her judgement. It was humiliating to have to do so.

She was much less vulnerable to the reactions of critics this time. There were fewer reviews than she had been used to but her fine little collection was runner-up for the Jock Campbell *New Statesman* Award for 'new or unregarded talent' among authors born in Africa or the Caribbean. She was described as putting 'a woman's as well as a black's case' in her short stories, which both reached back 'into tribal legend and cut deep into modern Africa'.[26] A review in the *Listener* distinguished between the 'less convincing' historical tales and those dealing with Botswana just before or after independence, which were 'wonderfully alive'.[27] The

South African reviews were generally positive too, except for a short hostile one in an Eastern Cape newspaper. But even this could not upset or unsettle Bessie the way any mention of insanity had done when *A Question of Power* appeared.

With the approach of the Christmas festivities, the four months that had seemed to stretch ahead with the promise of endless possibilities were suddenly reaching their conclusion. The group of writers had gradually learned to accept, perhaps even respect, each other. The bi-weekly seminars had often been stormy but they had also been stimulating. Bessie quoted the Hungarian writer as saying: 'We all come from different countries and people say interesting things about their countries. We like to hear.'[28] In their special circle, the writers had done much to make their ideas and culture available to American students.

Bessie remained in her apartment until the end of December writing and packing. For the first time in her life her baggage was becoming unmanageable and she was grateful for yet another service provided by the Writing Programme: an excess baggage allowance of 25 lb.

Bessie was to stay with Betty Fradkin for her last ten days in America and during this time the two women took a trip to New York. Here Bessie met Alice Walker. Bessie now felt that Alice Walker must be mocking her secretly because of her appearance and excess weight, because Alice had written various critical remarks about obesity in her stories. She definitely disapproved of Alice's love affairs and in her cloud of moral indignation forgot all the pleasure they had once had from discussing their writing. When she returned to Botswana she wrote that she hoped she had put over the proper picture of herself: that she was 'a cow that moves slowly'. She said that she was 'still stunned' that she had managed to get around the world like that.[29] Alice Walker had got the message by now and did not reply. All the same, Bessie remained one of her favourite writers.

Bessie also contacted a Frenchman named René Philombé, whose special area of interest was the Cameroons. Through an interpreter he conducted a long and stimulating interview with her comparing social and political structures in Africa. This was later sent to her.

The partly healed sore of Bessie's old disillusionment with Botswana had started to fester again. For this reason she and Betty Fradkin also attended to one important business matter in New York. They went to the United Nations High Commission for Refugees. The lady whom Bessie consulted there proved very sympathetic, having read her books. Bessie told her about her earlier attempts at finding resettlement, showed her the letter of refusal of Botswana citizenship and asked for her file to be re-opened. This was done immediately. Bessie was told that it would probably be easy to find a country that would be willing to re-settle her. 'They reeled off a list of names. None of the names were of countries in Africa.'[30] Bessie also spoke to the High Commissioner for Refugees himself. Wherever she went, she put forward the special difficulties with which refugees with children in Southern Africa had to contend and they admitted that this group had not been given sufficient consideration. She was given names of people to whom she could refer in New York as well as contacts in Gaborone. These she consulted as soon as she returned to Botswana and they were as helpful and sympathetic as their counterparts in New York. Bessie felt that she had made a genuine breakthrough.

The rest of the time was spent sightseeing on a grand scale and Bessie added photographs, souvenirs and tourist brochures to her bulging suitcases. Suddenly it was time for her to leave America. Betty Fradkin had been a tremendous help to her throughout her stay there, combining practical and moral support in a calm and selfless way. She knew almost more about Bessie's financial affairs than Bessie did herself and had had detailed accounts of her bank balance during the last four months, just as she had been given reports of its less fortunate state during the previous year. 'You told me when you left America that you had enough to live on for about a year,' Betty later wrote to her, once more sending out feelers as to the real state of affairs. The monthly maintenance sum which Betty had been giving her prior to her departure for America, and which she regarded as a gift and Bessie as a loan, was not repaid. Bessie still hoped to repay it 'when I win the Nobel Prize for Literature'. She added that 'no one would have done for me what you have done . . . You're terrific you know. You watch all the quiet pockets of despair in life and take care of them.'[31]

Despite Bessie's fears that she might not be allowed to return to Botswana, the United States State Department was willing to give her a seven-day visa to allow her to visit her friends in London. Bessie was not interested: she was anxious to get home. This meant that she had twelve hours at her disposal in London and a very full programme. About a year earlier she had begun to correspond with an Englishwoman, Jane Grant, who was working on a doctoral thesis and wanted additional information about her writing. They exchanged some lively letters. Jane Grant had written to her in Iowa, suggesting that she visit them for a few days in Essex, where she lived with her husband and three children. Though this could not be arranged, Jane met her at the airport, helped her to get her bulky luggage disposed of for the day and then accompanied her to a luncheon arranged by James Currey.

The afternoon was booked up with a visit to the publisher Rex Collings. He had become interested in *Serowe: Village of the Rain Wind* through David Philip in Cape Town and Bessie was hoping very hard that they would decide to publish it together. However, the meeting proved a disappointment. Bessie again heard the criticism that had been voiced by others: the book was of an uneven quality. Its very structure was responsible for this. Editors liked the parts she had written herself: the lyrical touches in the Introduction, the stirring historical survey. But the interviews were verbatim records of what the villagers and volunteers had told her. Bessie thought it was important that they remain a documentary tribute to the people themselves, but those far removed from the life and traditions of an African village found them less interesting. Rex Collings said that he was interested in publishing only the first section relating to Khama III. Bessie could not 'dismantle' the book like this and they failed to reach any form of agreement.

The typescript of *Serowe: Village of the Rain Wind* was sent to Anna Cooper at John Johnson's, Bessie's new literary agent. She had been managing without an agent in both London and New York since her spectacular clash with Giles

Gordon and later Davis-Poynter. It was through Randolph Vigne that she had approached John Johnson Ltd. She did not meet Anna Cooper but spoke to her on the telephone and thought that she was 'nice-sounding'; and in fact it was the start of a thoroughly harmonious partnership. While she and Betty Fradkin were in New York, Bessie had arranged for Anne Elmo, who had her own agency, to represent her in America and, this too, worked out very well. Simply to get these practical matters straightened out was a great relief, not least for Betty Fradkin who had been trying tirelessly, and unsuccessfully, to get Bessie's short stories placed with American publications.

After the Rex Collings meeting, Randolph Vigne had arranged for Bessie to meet some old friends from her time in Cape Town. He had gathered them together at a hotel near Victoria. Suddenly Bessie was face to face with Ken Mackenzie and his wife Myra Blumberg; and with Randolph himself. Also in the party were Betty Sleath, whom Bessie had never met, and James Currey. Randolph could see that Bessie had become stouter and older but her breathy, high-pitched voice and precise enunciation had not changed. There was not a great deal of time at their disposal and too many years separated their last actual meeting. Neither really felt that they managed to bridge the gap. When she wrote a short note to thank him, she added: 'You haven't aged much except that your hair is on the thin side',[32] the nearest she could get to the old bantering tone she had so often used with him earlier.

The flight from London was delayed almost a whole day on account of engine trouble. While her friends pictured her heading south towards Africa, she was spending a very disturbed night in a hotel in Brighton. Exhausted and travel-worn as she was, Serowe was a welcome sight when she finally arrived there.

Two shocks awaited her when she got to 'Rain Clouds'. The first was the wild and luxuriant growth in her garden. The second was the state of her little home.

She had been hearing a great deal about the weather while she was away. First of all, her friends had complained of an unbearable heat. She could write back with descriptions of autumn leaves, gusty winds, bursts of rain and the joys of central heating. In late October it had looked as if the drought might end. Rain clouds gathered along the delicately etched mountain range to the south but it was only as they swelled and darkened in colour that people began to regard them hopefully. By late afternoon they seemed genuine. Then they became black and threatening and suddenly the village was being battered by a violent hail storm. The hail stones were the size of a human fist and they drove down relentlessly. People fled for cover, but two were killed. Many animals suffered the same fate. The villagers feared that this must be Judgement Day, as they cowered together watching the destruction raging around them. Then suddenly the storm abated; the clouds rolled on, relieved of their burden; jagged clumps of ice covered the red sandy earth, making it look like some lunar landscape.

At least this seemed to herald the rainy season, people thought, as they repaired the damage. But no. The temperatures soared again and the sun baked down. Any vegetation that had not been destroyed by the hail, now succumbed to the heat. People said that the heat was so excruciating that it was an agony to be alive, especially for the frail and elderly.[33] On Christmas Day the rains came.

This time it was a deluge. For forty days and nights, the locals maintained, it rained and rained. Bessie arrived towards the end of it.

Very shortly after the rain started, the most hardy trees and shrubs began to sprout and weeds sprang up in profusion. Huts made of mud suffered badly as the rain washed the dry walls away. Bessie's little brick house also had problems. The damp penetrated its thin walls. Howard was not at home and a green mould spread rapidly inside, covering walls and furniture. When Bessie opened the door, she was hit by a dank and mouldy smell. She was horrified.

The first week she spent cleaning up the house. Then she tackled the garden. Betty Fradkin expected her to get busy straight away with her seedlings, now that the rains had come. But Bessie was not interested. She tidied up everything and then she said that she was going to let it lie fallow. 'This year I am going to be a lady with lily-white hands. The only work these hands will do is some hard pounding at the key-boards.'[34] There were others who had gardens and she was planning to put a basket over her arm and go off and buy someone else's hard labour. 'The sun shall not smite me by day nor the moon by night,' as she put it to Betty in March.

Bessie found Howard quiet and depressed when she got home. He had written his first public examinations while she was away and as the date for the publication of the results approached, he was becoming very uneasy. It was Bessie who went over to the school and studied the lists on the noticeboard the day they were released. To their great relief, he had achieved a very satisfactory pass. His only weak subject proved to be Setswana and many of his classmates had received similarly disappointing results. The problem was that the local dialect they all spoke made it difficult to write standard Setswana.

Howard now had two years of schooling ahead of him before he would write his Senior Certificate examination and thus complete his secondary education. His teachers advised him to take the commerce and business line of study. Bessie was pleased when it was decided to get Howard studying 'business matters and things of this world'. She added that the 'less vague artistic types we have around this house, waiting to win the Nobel Prize for literature, the better'.[35]

The question of Howard's future could thus be shelved for two years if they were to remain in Botswana. But would they? The feeling of resignation, fatalism and genuine love for the country that had made her reverse her decision to go to Norway in 1974 had now left her. Despite her decision then to die and be buried in Botswana, she was once again thoroughly dissatisfied and restless. The inspiration she had gained from contact with Americans made it very difficult to return to her intellectual isolation in the village. But cutting much deeper was the Botswana government's refusal of citizenship. In America she had perforce represented the country, not only on a formal level because it was the country of her residence, but also on a cultural level. She had explained her views of village life, the cooperative movement and most of all the country's historical background. In return she had been told that she was of no use to Botswana. She was a refugee, without any political rights, and she would remain one. She made the firm decision never to apply for citizenship again.[36]

Mary Benson in particular was very concerned about this area of Bessie's life.

Throughout the early months of 1978 they corresponded on the subject and in March Bessie wrote:

The refugee situation is such a mess here because it is only black people who are refugees. I know the whole road, of lack of resources, of a basic struggle to survive on the bare minimum and below that. We can run so far and no further due to lacking resources. You have never heard of a white refugee stuck here, have you? It's an unheard of thing.

She went on to say that her life had earned her 'a quiet honour and respect' all the same. She knew the people who would offer her that. 'I am not likely to appeal to the wrong sources because from them one can only get degradation, obscenity, filth, horror, muck, dirt, stink, rot, hell and more and more filth. I know what it is like to swim in such an endless sea of filth and horror.'[37] It would probably have infuriated Bessie to hear it, but her vivid descriptions of evil outdid many a Bible-punching evangelistic preacher; perhaps even Miss Farmer's constant admonitions to avoid the fires of hell. The tone of hysteria in the letter suggests that a period of depression was threatening again. There was another reason for this, apart from the refusal of citizenship.

About a month after returning home, in February 1978, she heard on the radio one morning that Robert Sobukwe had died of cancer. The news was much more of a personal shock than it would have been if she had only remembered him as the great political hero of her South African days. For in 1972 she had conducted a short but lively correspondence with him after having met someone on a visit to Serowe who lived next door to him in Galeshewe Village in Kimberley, South Africa. They discussed the dramatic events of 1960 and Bessie sent Sobukwe copies of her novel and a letter so frank and spiced with gossip about members of the PAC that it might not have made it past the South African censors. He had never replied. With the news of his death she cried for days: 'He was the only man I loved and trusted,' she wrote, rather thoughtlessly all things considered, to Randolph Vigne.[38] She found some typed pages of his political ideas that she had kept for all those years. As she read them, and mourned him and thought back on those weeks of historic significance which had ended so dramatically for her, a short story began to form in her mind. Because Sobukwe had been educated at the large Methodist mission school, Healdtown, near Fort Beaufort and later at Fort Hare College, Alice, she thought that he was a Xhosa. In fact, although his mother was Xhosa,[39] and he was born in Graaff-Reinet in the Cape, his father was of Sotho origins. She recalled how it was a Xhosa custom for a Christian congregation to gather together on Christmas Eve and sit in silence, awaiting the coming of the Christ Child. Almost before she began, she had her title.

She decided to write a story about a political hero, the perfect leader. Though she kept her protagonist nameless, she wrote as realistic an account as she could remember of the political events leading up to the pass campaign and the Sharpeville massacre. It was unmistakably Sobukwe she was writing about. She described the growing tension within the ANC as the 'Africanist' group expressed its discontent with the leaders more and more clearly. She gave her version of the final break, more dramatic than in real life. She quoted excerpts from Sobukwe's paper to show the wide, generous sweep of his ideas. She described the indefinable quality he had, a mixture of dignity, humility and courage, that made him soar above other politicians, and ascribed it to his rich rural background. In taut, direct prose and with an immediacy she did not always achieve with her short stories at that time, she created her own cohesion from events she had been part of but not deeply involved in. Years later, far away, with no one to ask or old newspapers to consult, she showed how a man of unusual stature had stood there at one of the critical moments in history. And no one could use him.

Calling her story 'The Coming of the Christ Child', she sent it off to Anna Cooper. Great was her surprise to hear the reaction of the first editor who returned it: it was far too obviously a portrait of Robert Sobukwe. She had not expected English editors to be that wide awake. Then she began to worry about her facts. On the one hand, she had quoted directly from his papers. On the other, she had only a very limited knowledge of Sobukwe personally and she did not want her piece to be taken for a documentary account. The fact that she made her unknown hero a Professor of Bantu Languages at the University of the Witwatersrand illustrates this. This was a position far indeed from Sobukwe's humble one of language assistant, but his friends and admirers called him 'Prof'[40] in recognition of his achievement of getting any sort of appointment at such a prestigious institution. She wrote asking whether some acknowledgement of the quotations would be necessary, but nothing was decided and the short story continued to be returned from magazines and journals. Towards the end of the year she allowed it to be published without a fee in a magazine called *Callaloo* from Atlanta University, Georgia. The editor, David Dorsey, had written asking for a contribution to a special edition dealing with African writing. Here she asked for an acknowledgement to be included. In 1980 it was published in *Marang*, the journal of the English Department of the University of Botswana.

Bessie had not corresponded with Tom Holzinger for some time. In fact she had not contacted him while she was in America. When he heard she had been there, he wrote saying how disappointed he was not to have seen her. In July he returned to Serowe, bringing a friend, Ruth Cooper, with him. They had come into Botswana from Zambia, crossing over on the Kazangula ferry and intending to visit all Tom's favourite haunts, including Selebi-Pikwe. His own rondavel in Newtown ward happened to be empty when they arrived. They moved in, Tom Holzinger soon re-establishing contact with his friends in the village. Ruth Cooper and Tom Holzinger saw Bessie frequently. She was quieter, more introspective than she had been five years earlier; and seemed to have fewer friends. But after some time, she and Tom Holzinger re-established the old repartee and he was given a detailed account of her trip to America, about which she was now very critical. She referred to its flashiness and lack of depth and said that she was glad to have gone to see how bad it was.[41] Tom Holzinger's visit brought back to her his earlier years in Botswana: the everyday events that had made up her life about the time she joined Boiteko. Until now she had never seen anything good in those years, because she associated them with her nervous breakdowns.

The truth was that Bessie had been suffering from intense loneliness since she returned from America. She wrote to Betty Fradkin in June telling her that *When Rain Clouds Gather* had been translated into Dutch. 'Life is so lonely here', she added, 'that I never talk to anyone about my work, triumphs or successes.'[42]

In August she had an unnerving experience which highlighted her own sense of isolation. There was a very pleasant Norwegian doctor, Unnlaug Lingåf, at the Sekgoma II Hospital in Serowe. Bessie had actually met her right at the beginning of her time in the village in 1974. Howard had been having a lot of trouble with his tonsils and her doctor thought they should be removed. There was no surgeon in Serowe to perform the operation, however, so they had to wait until this doctor arrived and as her first operation she removed Howard's tonsils. Bessie had insisted that he remain in hospital for four days. The doctor was mildly disapproving of this exaggerated motherly concern. 'In Europe,' she said, 'tonsillectomies go home the same day.' In August 1978 Howard fell down a flight of steps and broke his wrist. When they arrived at the hospital, this same doctor was in attendance. At first she did not recognise Howard, but as Bessie bustled in she looked again and in amazement at the tall young lad. Her calm glance in Bessie's direction seemed to say: 'So you're still hovering anxiously over that boy.'[43] With expert precision she set his wrist in a plaster cast. That same evening, with equally expert precision and with an extra syringe as stand-by should the first fail, she took her own life with a massive overdose of some sedative. No one knew why she had done so. She had no friends to whom to reveal it. 'It was the starkness and sheer solitude of her death that upset people so much.'[44]

What upset Bessie even more was the fact that she 'saw her at her beginning and her ending and this really made me feel ill for the rest of the week'. Mona Pehle, to whom she was writing, would understand the reference. About six weeks earlier she had herself referred to T S Eliot's concern with time past and time present and his use of Mary Queen of Scots's motto: 'In my end is my beginning.' Bessie, who had long felt a special affinity for Mary Queen of Scots, responded immediately and just a fortnight before the tragic incident she had written to Mona: 'nothing is more poignant than that last statement.'[45] Later Mona was to send her Eliot's *Four Quartets*. Bessie particularly liked 'East Coker', where Eliot uses both this phrase and 'in my beginning is my end' as a promise of regeneration. The fact that he also chose the two phrases for his tombstone was a further indication of how significant he found them. For some months they were to discuss this concept of one's end being in one's beginning and one's beginning being in one's end. But in August this death in the village unsettled Bessie seriously.

It seems to have occasioned what she later referred to as 'another of my nervous breakdowns'. Her insomnia returned and she could not digest her food. She began to take brandy and water to settle her stomach. And beer, apparently. Later that year she told Betty Fradkin that she looked fat because she had 'a passion for beer' which she made 'no effort to control'. She added: 'Otherwise I can live on very little food.'[46] Naturally Betty was concerned. Anxious as she was not to 'preach', she begged Bessie to keep away from the dangerous combination of poor nutrition and alcohol. They could only make matters worse and immobilise her just when she needed to 'ACT'.[47]

In July Bessie met a young Englishwoman whose husband was attached to the University of Botswana. Her name was Jane Clegg. She visited Bessie in Serowe and they found that they had a great deal to discuss. 'It was certainly love at first sight between you and I,'[48] Bessie wrote after she left.

Jane Clegg planned to write an article on *A Question of Power* and they continued to correspond regularly for the next eighteen months, with Jane doing much of the asking and Bessie the answering. So Bessie's thoughts were often centred on that novel during the last months of 1978 and she gave Jane Clegg some of her most lucid expositions of it.

The first point she made was that *A Question of Power* was what she called 'a lived book'. It was not planned in her mind. It was not 'the work of a creative artist laboriously laying out a novel', though she knew that process too. She said that there were two sides to her: 'a functional, realistic and utilitarian person combined with a mystic dreamer ... *A Question of Power* is my perfect expression – the utilitarian realist and the mystic dreamer going at it at the same time'.[49] To these two sides of her personality she related the writers who had influenced her so much: Lawrence, Pasternak and Brecht.

Out of this arose another point that she made in several different forms about this time. She had begun to think that 'the book should not read the way it does', that she had 'made mistakes'. Not that this means that she was admitting that she ought to have paid more attention to the advice offered by Giles, Paddy and Dulan. Her dissatisfaction seems rather to have been directed towards the fact that she did not record events as she should have: 'I tried to be as accurate as possible ... but ... I am no longer certain of the whole of Part Two.'[50] Six months later she told someone else that she knew that *A Question of Power* was 'badly scrambled'.[51] And much later that the 'key of the book is high pitched and hysterical'.[52]

These references to her inadequate understanding (and thus recording) of the evil she was depicting relate directly to her assertion that *A Question of Power* was a 'lived book'. If she was doubtful about the success of her recording of the experience, she was not at all doubtful about what she had experienced: 'The only thing I am certain of is that I never encountered goodness but an evil, the ferocity of which, the brutality of which really defies description.'[53]

This led once more into a discussion of that evil. She gave the clearest explanation ever of what she meant by someone forgetting the point at which he becomes evil. She maintained for example that when a whole race subscribes to racialism 'that race loses the initial thread. They forget the point at which they become evil. Here I was able to catch that initial thread. I saw racial evil here right at its roots and beginnings. It is a blind and stupid emotion and it is tied up to royalty and class.'[54]

Jane Clegg had annoyed her by taking it for granted that the evil she portrayed was a form of white South African racist evil. Bessie indignantly returned one of her letters to show how she had tried to link Robert Sobukwe to 'the hissing obscenities of the demons in *A Question of Power*'. She pointed out most emphatically that it was not written in South Africa but in Botswana. It was a record of what happened to her there. 'No reviewer could review the book nor accept it as it was written. Every single reviewer re-set the book back in South Africa.' Not that she tried for a moment to defend white South Africans: 'I lived in South Africa for 27 years. I noticed then that all whites, all of them would stare silently at a brown or dark brown skin, with hate. They never talked to black people ... they never knew what they hated.' 'But', she continued, 'no white South African had the power to invade my mind, nor to arrange a wide range of hisses and obscenities for me, day after day, day after day, for fourteen years.'

In *A Question of Power*, she says, her vision of evil was 'vividly clear and coherent'. It could not be broken up into little bits, as reviewers chose to do to prove that she was insane. 'I recorded everything as I heard it because I believed this was evil making itself coherent at last. The book not only relates to evils practised in South Africa but the Belsens and Dachaus of Hitler's time, more to Hitler than anything else.'[55]

Towards the end of the year, Bessie began to tire of the discussion:

I am sick to death of all that has been written about *A Question of Power* by white reviewers. I am sick to death of it. In the mind of any white, whether racialist or liberal, a black man is not a whole man, with whole, horrific, satanic passions. A black man is a wee, sleek-it, timorous, cowering beastie they mowed down with maxim guns a hundred years ago. A black man could not possibly be the characters in my books, so hugely vile, so hugely demonish.

Having made such a controversial statement, she asked if Jane expected 'sweet simpering' ones from her. 'Did I look like a wilting empty-headed female who has learned nothing from life?' And she concludes the letter by saying that she wants no more questions about that novel. 'No more this-couldn't-possibly-be-our-darling-little-pet-black-men-whom-we've-exploited-and-aren't-they-sweet, kind of thing. No more. If you don't like the view I have you are free to write the rubbish all the white reviewers have written.'[56] There is only one comment to sentences like the last ones: 'Phew!'

The novel has shown an apparent coming to terms with the racist and sexist implications of Elizabeth's state as a victimised half-caste female outsider. In real life, however, Bessie, who 'is' Elizabeth, has apparently been unable to reach the new level of awareness of the strength to be found in these despised roles which would have given therapeutic value to the writing process. In the novel this process occurs: Elizabeth is reminded that in the individuality of the outsider and victim lies her god-like quality; she rises above references to her colour by remaining uncowed: 'Too many people the world over were becoming mixed breeds and shading themselves down to browns and yellows and creams' (p. 63). Bessie on the other hand confirms in these discussions with Jane Clegg what her life had already shown: the healing process implied in the final sentence of the novel – Elizabeth's placing of a hand on her land in 'a gesture of belonging' – was at best only temporary, a mere literary expedient. In Bessie's terminology, the evil had not been exorcised after all.

She refers to using her writing as a safeguard – 'I hoped my books would save me, next time round' – in other correspondence from this period, for she had not been forgotten by the outside world. Christopher Heywood, a South African lecturer living in England, sent her one of his articles, 'Traditional Values in the Novels of Bessie Head'.[57] Their exchange of letters included discussions on D H Lawrence (Heywood saw himself as a 'guide' to the Lawrence 'ruins'), the San people and Breyten Breytenbach. After having lived in exile for years, this South African poet, of Afrikaner origins but bitterly opposed to apartheid, made an amateurish attempt to break through forced powerlessness into action by starting an underground newspaper and establishing resistance groups. He was arrested and the eight-year sentence he received after his much-publicised trial shocked the intellectual world. 'I am filled with dismay,' wrote Bessie. 'Breytenbach's crimes were small – entering the country under an assumed name (surely only eight months imprisonment), wanting to start an underground newspaper (surely only touching idealism).' She saw him as a man who

wanted to involve himself in a hideous situation though he did not appear hideous himself. People do not choose their place of birth but they become tainted with it . . . And yet, when a situation causes so much anguish, it draws forth gestures like that of Breytenbach. I only loved one man in South Africa, Robert Sobukwe, and I place Breytenbach beside him.

This idea of being tainted by one's place of birth led to a reference to her own situation: 'Generally, as a writer, it was fairly easy for me to make records of black people's lives as I am part of that. But as an individual I needed more. I needed a message of anti-greed and anti-self-seeking.' It was the foreign volunteers in Serowe, in her opinion, who had 'that message completely worked out', but she had not, despite the comments of some reviewers, associated only with white people. She had taken hold of 'what is a universal trend' and made haste

to record it, for an inner need. Personally I am absolutely terrified that I will be born in southern Africa again, in some other life. I cannot stand such small, life-throttling worlds. I hoped my books would save me, next time round, just remind me that there are a thousand things to do other than living off people like a parasite. I did not want to be tainted like that.[58]

14

Berlin & Denmark
1979–1980

❉

It was about this time that Bessie admitted to a friend that she had too many Germans in her life. Not that it was a derogatory remark. In July she had been approached by the German Ambassador in Gaborone, asking if he could nominate her for the Humboldt Scholarship. This was an award the German government made to writers whereby they could study at a university of their choice. Bessie was asked to say where and what she would like to study. She was not keen on African literature. 'The writing world does not interest me much. It's a bit phoney.'[1] Her main interest was in development studies and she chose an American university, Michigan State, and the department of Third World Studies at the Institute for International Studies. After waiting hopefully for some time, Bessie heard that her nomination had not been successful.

Before this happened, she had been contacted by a German cultural group called the Künstlerhaus Bethanien. They were arranging a 'Berlin Festival of World Cultures' and Bessie was invited to take part in the section relating to African and Caribbean writers for a week at the end of June 1979. Bessie refused: 'How do I reply to your invitation . . . when I am at the point of a complete nervous breakdown.' She continued by listing the woes that had befallen her and attacking in an incoherent way the 'grinning apes performing in public' who made up the government, and their 'arse-creeping' ways. She ended by saying that she was 'broken', by asking whether 'near-broken corpses are ever attended to'. Should they not be left to die? She said that she did not want to die in an independent African state: 'I want to die where corpses are registered as being dead from an identifiable disease . . . I am almost out of my mind with terror. So? Who cares?'[2]

What exactly lay behind these macabre statements is not clear. What is clear is that a new emotional storm was brewing. The thought of having a concrete invitation and no passport to travel had released an outburst of the old resentment, though in her more balanced moments she knew that she could be issued with travel papers. While the recipients were trembling with philanthropic indignation in Berlin, however, Bessie was penning an extremely well-formulated letter totally devoid of hysterical undertones on Calvinism and religion in general to her friend Mona Pehle. Such were the vacillations in her mental and emotional states. But shortly after Christmas, she sent Frank Alberti at the American

Embassy in Gaborone a telegram: 'Desperately need to leave Botswana', followed by several letters, all indications that this was a period of great mental strain for her.

The organisers of the Berlin Festival would not accept Bessie's refusal. They asked her to reconsider her decision and promised to send someone to discuss her problems with her.

Unexpected good fortune came Bessie's way in January 1979. It concerned *Serowe: Village of the Rain Wind.* Some months after having left the typescript with Anna Cooper, Bessie had been told that Heinemann Educational Books had asked to see it. Since then there had been some correspondence between Bessie and Penelope Butler from Heinemann in which Bessie was asked to explain certain difficulties in the text and express her view on any pruning of the material that might be necessary. If Heinemann accepted the book for publication, it would be without any of the illustrations that had been planned earlier. In fact it would include only three photographs: of Khama III, Tshekedi and Patrick van Rensburg. In January the publishers made their decision and sent a telegram saying that they were accepting *Serowe: Village of the Rain Wind.* Great was Bessie's delight. She said that 'Heinemann was the last publisher that could afford to hold a non-commercial writer like me'. Her 'Serowe book' had had a rough passage and she had never felt such sheer relief at having a book accepted: 'I am ashamed to admit (atheist that I am) that the pleas and entreaties from my side silently took the form of: "Please God, make Heinemann make an offer for my Serowe book."'3

She could hardly have expected any other news that year which could top this. Less than a month later, a letter arrived which did. It was from the Botswana government, dated 12 February: 'Dear Madam, You are herewith informed that after careful consideration your application for Botswana Citizenship has been approved.'4 This was news that had to be digested. Standing on the steps of the post office, very close to the spot where she had once put up the notorious notice, she could only give little gasps of puzzled amazement as she read and re-read the short communication. 'Your application . . .' Which application? She had never re-applied after her previous one had been refused. Her common sense warned her that this was not the moment to quibble. She relaxed enough to register that a huge burden was falling from her shoulders. It swept away her favourite apple of discord, the 'Botswana and me' crises.

Bessie had no one to whom she could rush to share the news. Nor would that have been her way. She went home, told Howard about it when he returned from school and agreed with his point of view: it made the future look much brighter. To friends she remarked matter-of-factly that she was accepting citizenship because it solved many practical problems.

It was never revealed why the authorities had changed their minds. Had it been Bessie's own energetic efforts in New York, her contacts with and sympathetic response from the people in the highest positions in the High Commission for Refugees? Had it been the loyal and persistent pressure from her friends in the American Embassy, backed by those in the German Embassy? Had it simply been that the authorities had realised that the tubby little lady with the extraordinary obsessions was proving quite a valuable ambassador for the country?

There was an element of timing in the granting of citizenship which must have shaken Bessie. A fortnight before the historic letter from the Botswana authorities, she had told Jane Clegg that she was suffering badly from some sort of nervous breakdown, 'a kind of stop and pause to look back and look ahead'.[5] She was once more thinking about her confrontation with evil. A few days before, she had met, greeted and been greeted by the shopkeeper who so many years before had refused to sell her some cheese shortly after she returned to Serowe. Memories from those months came flooding back. Suddenly she was telling Jane Clegg details which she had never told Randolph Vigne or Paddy Kitchen and which probably only her closest friends in Serowe knew.[6]

Another aspect of the looking-back process was to realise that she was 'finding out the real truth about God'. Once more she stated that the 'title of God must go to mankind. They must feel a tenderness and reverence for each other. Then the killing will stop.' It was in her vision of Buddha that Bessie believed herself to have found the 'real image of God. He looked into himself. He looked at nothing but himself.' She described how she always took 'a kind of double look' at the people who began to 'traffic through' her life in Serowe. 'They'd quietly inform me that they were Buddha too. That life was a blue-print for perfection. Once you live the details and set up the blue-print, mankind takes it and lives it for themselves.'[7] The reference to 'taking a double look at people' throws interesting light on Bessie's frequent references to people, especially people she had not met, her friends' husbands for instance, having 'holy' faces: 'I saw the face of the man against whom the murder charge had been rigged. That face was holy to me even though I do not know the truth,'[8] she had written a few months earlier. What Bessie never elaborated on was why so many of the 'holy' people she met turned out to be devils later on.

Bessie summed up this review of her philosophical beliefs by repeating that the whole process of assessing everything had unsettled her. She could now see clearly the evil that had been done to her:

That rejection of my application for citizenship was one of the gestures of evil that was done to me. Whereas I have only offered constructive work and help, to these people ... They still think they can treat me as the coloured dog. I am coloured indeed but the life of the soul is deeper than one's appearance.[9]

Ten days later she was granted citizenship. Gods or not, Bessie, like most of the rest of fallible humanity, had drawn up a Balance Sheet of Life in which the space allocated to 'credits' was restricted and entries here were often neglected. The 'debits', on the other hand, were entered in great detail, tabs kept on each section and sub-section. Though she soon began to enjoy the practical benefits of her changed status, it is difficult to assess whether she ever made the corresponding mental adjustments to her Balance Sheet.

Bessie realised immediately that a trip to Berlin would now be considerably easier to arrange. Three days after receiving the letter from the Citizenship Office of the Ministry of Home Affairs she had completed a letter to Dagmar Heusler, the organiser in Berlin, thanking her for her concern, which she would 'always appreciate' and 'never forget',[10] accepting the invitation, and including biographical material required. Each writer was expected to give a 25-minute public reading from his or her work. They also had to present a paper on one of several available topics at the Writers' Workshop, which was open only to students. For the reading, Bessie chose the excerpt from *A Question of Power* describing the opening of the rural development project shop, where each group describes its production process. As the subject for her paper she chose 'The Writer in Africa: Political and Social Commitment'.

Bessie also gave an excellent account of the influences there had been on her writing. She named D H Lawrence and Boris Pasternak, of course, and more surprisingly, Bertolt Brecht.

Lawrence and Pasternack [sic] absorbed the mystic dreamer in me but Brecht gave the functional realist the courage to write novels like *Rain Clouds* and *A Question of Power*, where facts, figures, and real hard concentration on questions of poverty and suggestions about their solutions are absorbed into the novel form.[11]

It seems to have been the recollection that 'Berlin was the city of Bertolt Brecht' that brought him to the fore again. She said that she had not really 'lived with' his writings, the way she had with D H Lawrence's and Boris Pasternak's, but she had read his biography twenty years earlier and never forgotten it. She had learnt from him that 'the artist must no longer write poems to trees and flowers. His consciousness must be geared to the real world'. She explained how reviewers had noticed the didactic element in her work but had 'poured scorn on it' because she refused to make a commitment to Marxism and had said several times that she hated politics. She continued: 'I do not refuse a commitment to solving questions of poverty and human misery but I do not want to rule the world; others are more capable of that job than I. I only took Brecht's dictum: We must help.'[12]

She concluded by saying that her first and third novels were entirely didactic. 'I would never have had the courage to write like that had Brecht not done all that before me.' She referred to the extract she had chosen, 'the facts, figures and actual day to day living experience' as they were depicted there. For her purpose, she could hardly have found a better one. It did not entirely meet the approval of the committee, however, who asked for a short story instead, not aware of what a little pearl of a 'short story' she had chosen. So she settled for 'Life', from *The Collector of Treasures*.

Within three days Bessie had made all the necessary plans and sent a closely typed four-page letter off to Germany. 'I can set up the loudest wail in the world about any situation with all the gory details',[13] Bessie had long before said of herself. While it certainly could not be said that her miseries were fictitious, she seemed to survive them and achieve a great deal besides, perhaps because of the loud wail. In the present situation she again demonstrated the amazing ability she had of rising, phoenix-like, from a period of depression and producing in a flash a piece of work so well coordinated and planned that it would require weeks of careful preparation from most people.

The organisers of the Berlin International Literature Days, as that section of the Festival to which Bessie was invited was called, were planning to gather together the cream of black writers: Chinua Achebe, Ayi Kwei Armah, Mongo Beti, Camara Laye and Wole Soyinka were among them. Ama Ata Aidoo and Bessie Head were the only women. Bessie's old friend from Cape Town days, Dennis Brutus, was also invited. As it happened, Bessie had never read any of Ama Ata Aidoo's work. This gave her a problem as she imagined the two of them thrown together a good deal. She did not have much of a chance of getting any of her books locally.

An American friend came to the rescue. Charlotte Bruner was a lecturer in Foreign Languages and Literature at Iowa State University in Ames, Iowa, who had hoped to meet Bessie while she was in Iowa City. Though her visit to Ames had fallen through, the two women had corresponded and Charlotte Bruner published three articles on Bessie Head's writing and included one of her short stories in an anthology she edited. A few months before Bessie was due to leave for Berlin, Charlotte Bruner sent her a copy of one of these articles which compared the writings of Bessie Head and Ama Ata Aidoo.[14] Bessie wrote back thanking Charlotte and saying that she could hardly think of a 'better way of saying how-do-you-do' than handing Ama Ata Aidoo her paper.[15]

The formalities for her passport as well as for her trip were completed and she left for Berlin on 19 June via what she called the Lusaka route: a small local flight from Gaborone to Lusaka and then an international flight. This time she did not see Caroline and Max Hlaba in Lusaka.

The writers were given extremely comfortable accommodation at the Hotel am Zoo, in the Charlottenburg area of the city. It was midsummer in Berlin and the flowers and trees were at their best. 'Never have I seen a city of such fantastic beauty,' Bessie wrote. She was particularly taken by the roses. 'They blazed away in deep red and pale pink hues on every available patch of earth.'

The writers lived in an expensive part of the city but worked each evening at the Künstlerhaus Bethanien, in the slums of Krozberg. Bessie noted the contrast between Charlottenburg, which was an 'endless stream of women with slender figures and not a child in sight', and Krozberg, 'crowded with Turkish immigrants and thousands of little children playing in the streets'. A German writer, Erika Runge, took her walking through 'the stark horror of Krozberg where blocks of old buildings were massed together and where no air or sunlight penetrated'.[16] She was nevertheless amazed to see that the slum area of the city was as spotlessly clean as the expensive area.

One of the first things Bessie was told on arriving in Berlin was that Ama Ata Aidoo had broken her leg and was in hospital. That meant that she was the only woman. This certainly did not dismay her. She kept on amiable terms with the other writers and said afterwards that she was pleased to find that 'the top writers were dignified, courteous, ordinary and wonderful'.[17] There were two familiar faces: James Currey and Lewis Nkosi, the latter now an established academic and critic, whom she had known when he worked for Drum in Johannesburg.

Here Bessie once more met up with her old friend from the Cape Town and

Port Elizabeth days, Dennis Brutus. She later expressed regret that they were no longer on the same wave-length,[18] and he observed her various outbursts with unease. She and Dennis Brutus shared the same platform for their 25-minute readings. In Bessie's opinion, this had been successful. Her paper to the students attending the Writers' Workshop, now entitled 'Social and Political Pressures that Shape Writing in Southern Africa',[19] also went off well. She had a naturalness, when she made a public appearance, that endeared her to people. And she was good at getting her version of the Socratic dialogue going. The students liked her and she responded by inviting them to visit her in Serowe should they ever wish to. One of them found her writing and her personality so appealing that she made the decision to embark on some field work in Botswana when she had finished her studies, a decision she kept.

Bessie's paper had been carefully prepared. As always, it related to her life and her writing. Through her historical research she could also show how her work had covered 'the whole spectrum of Southern African preoccupations – refugeeism, racialism, patterns of evil, and the ancient Southern African historical dialogue':[20]

In my eyes Botswana is the most unique and distinguished country in the whole of Africa. It has a past history that is unequalled anywhere in Africa. It is a land that was never conquered or dominated by foreign powers and so a bit of ancient Africa, in all its quiet and unassertive grandeur, has remained intact there.

At the same time, she contrasted this state with her own background, where a sense of history was totally lacking and where 'we, as black people, could make no appraisal of our own worth; we did not know who or what we were, apart from objects of abuse and exploitation'.[21]

Despite small successes, Bessie did not fit in very well in Berlin. She was not interested in small talk, which meant that unless she could find someone with whom she could engage in an intense discussion at the various social gatherings such a conference required, she was often very helpless and very bored at them. The discovery of an element of ruralism in Iowa had made her visit to America enjoyable for her. Nowhere could anything similar be found in Berlin. The extreme materialism of Europe horrified her: 'I was repelled by what I summed up as greed and harshness. There is little help for the young. There are millions of unemployed. They run the world with the computer there and have dispensed with human labour and brains.'[22] She found the media men aggressive and 'vicious' and felt harassed by people always asking her for her opinion on something or other. 'There were days in Berlin when I was terrified for my survival.' A friend later commented that 'she was the odd-woman-out among the well-heeled successful writers . . . we had a vivid picture of this very natural human being among sophisticated people and surroundings so unlike any she had known'.[23]

There was also an undercurrent of unrest at the Berlin Literature Days. This apparently had its origins in the organisers' inability to work together and in fact resulted in Dagmar Heusler's being fired before the conclusion of the conference. Several writers felt that she had spoken to them in derogatory tones and Bessie heard her referring to one of the others as 'that coloured'. As a 'coloured' herself this appalled her. When she realised that there was general discontent she knew, as she put it, that 'Ms Heusler had her head on the block and I lifted my verbal axe and chopped it off'.[24]

A journalist who wrote to her afterwards regretted that there was so much bad feeling at the festival because it had thus not provided its guests with one of the most important things a festival should have, in an African sense at least: joy. There was a sad lack of feeling for one of the greatest cultures in the world, the African culture. 'Sometimes', he added 'it was not bad will but just inability and awkwardness or even shame that hindered true communication or fostered wrong impressions.'[25]

Bessie in her reply said: 'I do agree with you that love lay just beneath the surface in Berlin. Actually I loved many people . . . If I said: "I will never come back to Berlin again", it was only a part of the loud shouting I did to ensure that Ms Heusler never came near me again after I had that showdown with her.'[26] According to Bessie, the incident caused people to thaw towards her. 'People had seemed cold and removed,' she said, but afterwards 'I don't know how many people embraced me and kissed me really hard on both cheeks.'[27]

After acquiring citizenship, Bessie had wasted no time in trying to find some form of occupation and there were many people anxious to help her. Before she went to Berlin she had two visits from people involved in the United Nations World Food Programme in Botswana. Because the per capita income had risen in the country, there was talk of stopping the food distribution programme. But it was also recognised that there were many very poor people in the rural areas, especially as there had been a year of drought again. What the programme required was a way of distributing the food to the really needy, instead of indiscriminately, as was being done at the moment. They had approached one of the big women's organisations to ask if they would take it on, but they were not interested. Now they wanted to know whether Bessie would consider taking on the job. They paid her many compliments and said that the only way to understand Botswana was through her books. She was interested but doubtful too. She knew only about life in Serowe, she pointed out.

Later another delegation arrived. The World Food Programme had decided to continue its help to Botswana but to combine it with some project work. In India they had had remarkable success with a silkworm project among rural women. One of the visitors was wearing a blouse woven from silk produced there. They had hoped to start up something similar in Botswana but the women they had approached would have nothing to do with it. They were asking Bessie for advice.

She showed them extracts from *Serowe: Village of the Rain Wind*, not in print yet, describing Marit Kromberg's efforts to educate the women in nutrition at the clinics she established and talked generally about getting into contact with village women. They copied her material and asked her if she could discuss the matter further in Rome on her way back from Berlin. So she stopped over in Rome after the Berlin conference and was whisked from the airport in a flashy red sports car.

She did not hesitate to express her scepticism about the silkworm project and the meeting did not lead to the direct offer of a job although the people she met paid much attention to all she had to say.

As the end of the year approached, Bessie began to fear that there was no job for her with the United Nations after all. She and the organisers did not really agree on the basics of poverty. More and more her thoughts were returning to her research for her Khama novel, pitifully neglected in all the preceding months. Howard was now approaching the final months of his schooling and examinations loomed on the horizon. When he finished school at the end of November, they would be free to leave Serowe for a while. Originally she hoped she could get some form of government employment in Gaborone. This did not prove easy. 'It would seem as though it is a dead loss to try and get a job through government . . . It appears as if they do not employ people who are over the age of 35.'[28] She began to consider getting a much more humble kind of job as a copy typist to enable her to do some research and Howard to find some employment there as well.

Early in December Bessie and Howard left Serowe. They stayed with the Cleggs for a week, not a very successful visit, then with some other friends for a few days before acquiring a government flat. The British Council helped with the rent for the first month, then Bessie was given a grant from the Canadian University Services Overseas which covered the next six months. With her royalties, a few short typist jobs and Howard paying a share of the household expenses for the first time, because he had found a job at the Botswana Book Centre, they managed. When the grant ran out, she moved into the flat of some friends and stayed there while they were in England. In this way they spent almost a year in Gaborone.

It was a year that broke with old routines and introduced some new ones. Bessie spent much of her time at the University library. Here she became very friendly with two librarians, Pat Spann and Thandiwe Kgosidintsi. They helped and encouraged her with her research and became close friends as well.

She seemed to be on an even keel again, mentally. Her present concern for facts and figures apparently helped to keep her anchored in reality: 'B. Head, history has had a very good effect on your sanity. How harmonious has your life been since you uncovered the history of the land,'[29] she would write with her usual ironic touch a few years later. However, the mystic dreamer in her had to be nurtured and Mona Pehle and Tony Hall saw to this. In their correspondence they discussed a wide variety of subjects relating to religion.

Bessie and Mona Pehle, for example, started up a dialogue that went on for over a year about Calvin and his teachings. Bessie had read a book by René de Villiers on the Afrikaners and Calvinism and though she knew very little about Calvin she soon decided that he was 'stark raving mad' because he wanted to found 'the rule of God . . . Who was this fixed, rigid God who divided the world into the happy and unhappy?' She assumed that Mona Pehle, with 'the usual pious attitude to anything associated with religion',[30] did not find anything alarming in this. Mona Pehle was quite unperturbed by the comment. She simply fed Bessie with information which she had looked up in the library about Calvin and found another book, W A de Klerk's *The Puritans in Africa: A Story of Afrikanerdom*, which made Bessie change her mind about some things. She said in her next letter that Mona Pehle did not 'seem at all terrified by the wild and heretical views I expressed in my last letter to you and of course, this delights me'.[31]

Bessie always made it clear that she had no time for Christianity. She was relieved that Marxism had dislodged Christianity from its dominant position: 'What's the point of praying to some unseen being in the sky?' The only person in the New Testament that she seemed to have any regard for was the apostle Paul. Mona Pehle had said something about his formalising Christianity. 'You are wrong about Paul . . . It was his organising powers that gave Christianity its base. But there was nothing rigid in his thinking.' She said she loved Paul, first of all because he was a good letter-writer! (This may have indicated that she had not totally abandoned the belief she had held ten years earlier that in one of her earlier incarnations she had been the apostle Paul.) She also admired him because he had 'a wildly unpredictable mind' and produced his great masterpiece to love 'under pressure'. She thought that his idea that without love one simply becomes 'a tinkling symbol' (as she spelt it) 'and a sounding brass' was 'very sound . . . it is better to love than to hate'.[32]

Not only was Mona Pehle not to be ruffled; she had a way of surprising Bessie with her own unconventional views and background. As a Quaker she was not regarded as a 'Christian', she told Bessie, in the sense that Quakers have only observer status at the Council of Churches and she was not allowed to join the Christian Librarian Society. She regarded herself as a Seeker after the true Light, and as someone dependent on silence and meditation. When Bessie referred to her own interest in Hinduism and added rather condescendingly: 'Much of what I write about Hinduism will not sound unfamiliar to you as you have the writings of Jim Kirkup who explored this world',[33] Mona Pehle replied that she had known a great deal about Oriental beliefs since she was eighteen and had later worked in a library in Switzerland, Quo Vadis, which specialised in Eastern religions.[34]

This led to a discussion on Ramakrishna and Vivekananda, both of whom Mona Pehle knew about. Bessie gave a fascinating insight into the reason for her admiration for Ramakrishna. He was an illiterate man, she said, 'but with an astonishing grasp of things spiritual'. He taught spiritual truths using 'vivid everyday detail of life in India to illustrate his thoughts. As you read . . . a whole village unfolds with its everyday work and you know India in intimate detail.'[35] In this way Ramakrishna and Jesus were very alike. They were also both paranoiac, she added. Jesus was crucified for his paranoia. Ramakrishna's paranoiac delighted his Hindu audiences. In a previous letter Bessie had said: 'The huge body of work that makes up Indian philosophical thought seems to [be] rather a science, exact and precise, rather than vague yearnings and feelings.'[36] Mona Pehle questioned this. What did she mean by 'Indian', she asked, 'Jains, Sikhs, Hindus or Buddhists?'[37] Bessie also considered herself quite an authority on Tolstoy; Mona Pehle mentioned in passing how she had known Tolstoy before she was ten, as her parents read his books and she remembered looking into them as a child.

Mona was not afraid to contradict Bessie. These examples are from one letter:

'Both he AND YOU jump to conclusions which are not correct'; 'False!'; 'You are also wrong about homosexuality having its root in Empire days!! Don't get cross with me!!!'; 'You can't think things out starting with inaccurate facts.'[38]

Much less direct criticism had toppled earlier friendships, but theirs survived. Both Mona Pehle and Tony Hall tried to relate Bessie's concept of mankind as God to Christianity. 'Surely that is the doctrine of the Incarnation?' said Mona Pehle without getting a response from Bessie. Tony Hall was extremely interested in theological questions. He wrote papers for Bessie's perusal. When she received a letter from him with such enclosures, she could spend a weekend reading his work and then writing her comments. Also relating to Bessie's desire to give the title of God to mankind, he said that 'If you truly follow Christ you will only be content when all are Christ.' But Bessie shied away from the demand of Christianity to 'place implicit faith in a single dominating personality: No one comes to the Father except from me. Take salvation from me alone.' However, she admitted that she could not solve the mystery of Jesus Christ.

As always Bessie tended to the broad view: 'When you take in world literature and man's spiritual experience as a whole you find that there is mutual agreement and not hostility but oh the anguish this had caused me – the big rich view. I've had a sense of people wanting to kill me all the time for the big rich view.'

She said that *A Question of Power* was her 'great bow to the ordinary man as opposed to the powerful, single dominating God'. And she reiterated a statement she was fond of: 'Perhaps I imagine a world where people see they are God and the greeting changes and people say to each other: "Good morning God". You couldn't possibly kill God if it was you, could you? You couldn't possibly exploit and do any evil to God and God and God.' She admitted to Tony Hall that this is 'more or less' his 'triumph of love'. But still: 'I do not like the hysteria of Christianity but the broad and natural.'[39]

She gave a very good exposition of the Hindu concepts of Shiva and the Kali Yoga. Shiva, she said, is one of the few untranslatable terms. 'It was the great symbol of God as man and there are a thousand Shivas, all lost in the clouds of meditation. So many living men were Shiva.' She explained how the religious disciplines were mapped out according to people's different temperaments. There was the Bakhti Yoga, the discipline of love for those who are 'all love', the Jana Yoga for those who wish to follow the path of knowledge and the Raja Yoga for the warriors. 'Lord it's a strange beautiful free-flowing world full of unusual insights that many people outside would find unacceptable.'

The Kali Yoga in Hindu beliefs corresponds in some ways to the Second Coming of Christ, the Golden Age to which Tony Hall had referred. It is the last of four historical cycles in the destiny of man, each lasting about two thousand years. But the Kali Yoga has never been completed. It is that cycle dominated by the female principle and it has always brought with it destruction. Should it be completed, though, it will lead into the Golden Age. Mother Kali is the name of the goddess who dominates this cycle and a fearful personality she is, combining motherly tenderness and the terror of destruction. She 'deals out death as she creates and preserves'. She strikes 'dismay into the wicked yet pour[s] out affection for Her devotees'.[40] Perhaps this explains Bessie's belief that she was called to 'fix the bastards' she encountered on her way.

Bessie and Tony Hall had kept up a long discussion concerning this habit of hers. In 1976 she had written a particularly abusive letter to the wife of one of the Swaneng Brigade managers. This woman had complained that Bessie would not greet her. This came to Bessie's ears so she launched into a long written list of reasons why she would not. The woman's hypocritical religious views seemed to be part of the trouble.

Since Nouannah Hall had also suffered under this person's miserly ways, Bessie sent a copy to Tony Hall. He showed that he could really stand up to this budding Mother Kali. He admitted that it was better to point out someone's faults to her directly rather than to spread slander about her. But it was simply 'stupid, childish and wrong', he continued, to tell people that you never wanted to have anything to do with them again 'no matter who or what they are or what they have done'. He continued: 'You exaggerate the faults of people you dislike and you exaggerate the virtues of people you like. You kid yourself that you are full of generous feelings, but you are only generous to people it is easy for you to be generous to and how generous is that?' Bessie accepted the criticism, perhaps because Tony ended by saying that she was his 'kind of girl'.[41] He loved everybody but some people were easier to love than others and his heart warmed to anyone who was 'capable of shocking those who were stuffy enough to be shockable'.

A couple of years later he made another reference to her spiteful treatment of this woman. This time it was Bessie who sailed into the attack: 'Not at all. I am a hard-headed saint with no slop and sop in me.' She regarded her action as holding up a 'clear detailed analysis' of the evils the woman had in her for her perusal. In effect she said: 'Now look what you are like. Is this what a human being should be? See yourself.' She added that she had written several letters like that to 'demons' that came her way 'giving them a clear picture of their evils'. She concluded: 'You tend towards sloppy sentiment, Tony, and you don't use your brains. You depend on Jesus too much.' She said she did not have Jesus' talent to touch people and say 'Sin no more'. Her talent was to write letters, clearly bringing demons face to face with themselves. 'No one takes them on except me and that is what really shocks you – that I have the guts to do the impossible.'[42]

Bessie seemed less and less reticent about talking about her past life. If people asked, she told them. For example, a lecturer from Zambia, Charles Sarvan, distressed at being able to get so little information in their own library because of the University's straitened economy, wrote asking her about her writing and background and she sent full and interesting replies.[43] Mona Pehle, on the other hand, only heard the story of Bessie's mother quite late in their friendship because only then did she ask about it. Bessie's accounts became more and more standardised. She said that the mechanical relating of these facts had made her childhood seem totally unreal to her.

The President, Sir Seretse Khama, had been plagued by poor health for many years, because he suffered from diabetes. He had taken several trips to England to consult specialists, but in June 1980 people were stunned by an announcement made in London that the President was suffering from cancer and incurably ill. He returned to Botswana almost immediately and died a fortnight later, on 13 July. The country was plunged into the deepest mourning. A huge memorial service, attended by an estimated 20 000 people, including six African heads of state and the Duke of Kent representing Queen Elizabeth II of England, was held on 24 July in Gaborone. The day afterwards, at a funeral service in Serowe, the Bamangwato could pay their last respects to the man who had been their traditional chief for so long without actually ruling them. He was buried beside his famous forebears in the royal burial ground above the *kgotla.*

Just the previous year Sir Seretse and Lady Khama had been present at a huge ceremony in Serowe to witness the installation of their eldest son, generally called Ian, but officially known as Seretse Khama Ian Khama, as Paramount Chief of the Bamangwato. Seretse Khama had originally agreed to relinquish his and his heirs' right to the title when he returned from banishment, but after the death of Rasebolai Kgamane, whom the British had appointed as Chief of Native Administration during the conflict, the Bamangwato regretted this state of affairs, still feeling the need for a hereditary chief, even though the position had become largely ceremonial since independence.

With Seretse Khama's death, the Vice-President, Quett Masire, was elected President on 18 July, and Seretse Khama's cousin and childhood friend, Lenyeletse Seretse, was appointed Vice-President.

Some months before he died, Sir Seretse Khama played a leading role in the establishment of SADCC, the Southern African Development Coordinating Congress, the economic extension to the front-line state-alliance. At about the same time, a collection of his speeches, *From the Frontline*, was published. Its content reflected Botswana's thirteen years of independence and the way the President had shaped national development. As he said in the Preface: 'They were the years during which we learnt to survive as a democratic and non-racial nation in the midst of countries that respected neither democracy nor non-racialism.'[44] In the Foreword to the same book, the President of Tanzania, Julius Nyerere, said of Seretse Khama: 'He is a man whom it is impossible to watch without respect and admiration. Completely honest, he will only undertake what he is able to; but having agreed to do something he will carry it out regardless of difficulties which are encountered.' He concluded by saying that he was honoured to pay tribute to President Seretse Khama, 'an African leader who brings honour to our continent'.[45] Though they had not been intended as such, his words proved to be a fitting obituary.

Though Bessie often related local events with ardour in her letters, she refers only briefly to this one, saying that things were peaceful: considering the number of times Quett Masire had acted as President on account of Seretse Khama's ill health, it could hardly be said that Botswana had acquired a new President.[46]

South Africa too was undergoing change. After a record victory for the National Party in the general election in 1977 – an expression of the country's approval of the handling of the Soweto uprisings – Prime Minister John Vorster became involved in a propaganda scandal. Secret government funds were found to have been supporting the establishment of a pro-government national daily newspaper, the *Citizen.* John Vorster was implicated and had to resign. He was succeeded by P W Botha, a dedicated leading member of the National Party for many decades. All the more surprising therefore that in 1979 Botha began making statements that amazed the outside world and shocked his fellow South Africans: 'There are higher things in life than to stare at the colour of a man's skin,' he said and added that though white South Africans allowed black people into their kitchens to prepare their food, they would not stand beside a black man in a post office queue. After that P W Botha began to repeat his warning, 'Adapt or Die'. Apartheid would have to be dismantled.

It soon became apparent that P W Botha's reforms were pragmatic; he had no intention of sacrificing white supremacy in South Africa. Nonetheless, his move was enough to split the National Party. In the next few years, South Africans were to be confronted by P W Botha's constitutional reforms, a limited attempt at power-sharing with the minority coloured and Indian population groups, leading to the new constitution in 1983. That the blacks were in no way represented was to be explained by the fact they had voting rights in their own black homeland areas. Despite massive black protests, the white population would endorse the new constitution in November 1983.

These events, the historic processes that were to be steps on the way to the dismantling of apartheid from within, lay some years ahead. During the first part of 1980, as Bessie sought to impose some order on her own small area of history, her research was not going well. At the beginning of the year, she told her agent (now Christine Green, as Anna Cooper had left the agency the previous July) that she was 'trying to complete work on an historical novel'. She said that she had many notes and a thorough grasp of the historical situation she was dealing with. 'But now added to this is a happy feeling of certainty that the novel is falling into shape the way I want it to.'[47] In October she reported that she had originally mapped out twelve chapters and had planned to have it completed by August or September. She had been enjoying the work, but finding it much slower and more painstaking 'assembling research data into novel form' than she had expected. She had only six chapters completed: 'Much of my time was taken up re-reading research data and then painfully deciding how to arrange it in novel form. I worry that I have made some of the wrong decisions about the novel because parts of it are very dry and didactic.'[48]

While she was thus slowly working on, yet another invitation arrived to cause some excitement in the little home. This time the Danish Library Association wanted her to go to Denmark and take part in the celebrations connected with their seventy-fifth anniversary. To mark the occasion they had published an anthology of African writing translated into Danish. Her short story, 'The Prisoner Who Wore Glasses', had been chosen as the title piece. She and Ngugi wa Thiong'o were to be the guests of honour and it was hoped that they would take part in the launching of the anthology and be available for talks and interviews.

Bessie knew many Danish volunteers from Serowe, and during her stay in Gaborone she had become very friendly with Eva Haahr and others at the Danish Volunteer Services office in Mengwe Close. So there was general excitement when they heard her news and she felt happy about accepting without further ado. In her reply, she did ask for a special favour: that Howard be allowed to go along as well. This the organisers agreed to.

To coincide with their annual conference to be attended by 200 delegates, the Danish Library Association had arranged a series of festivities to mark their special anniversary. Bessie, Howard and Ngugi wa Thiong'o were established at the same luxury hotel in Copenhagen as the delegates and took part in the official luncheons and dinners. On the afternoon of the launching of the anthology, Bessie Head and Ngugi wa Thiong'o each delivered a short address.

Once the Library congress was over, Bessie, Howard and Ngugi wa Thiong'o moved to a smaller, more informal hotel in the heart of the city. Their own visit was to last another fortnight and it was a time of great official activity. Bessie made eight public appearances during her time in Denmark. She talked to students at the Departments of English and Anthropology at the University of Copenhagen; and to students at Emdruporg Teachers' Training College. She was interviewed on television and she addressed a women's group on the role of women in Africa. The students she found very sympathetic and well prepared. They all had copies of *The Collector of Treasures*, which they had read and considered carefully. The subject matter naturally led on to a discussion of the role of women in Africa and many stimulating views were expressed.

The women's group she was asked to address was more feminist in tone than any other she had encountered and she was constantly being called upon to express her own views on that subject. Her refusal to take a radical stand made some of her listeners annoyed, especially as many saw her as one of the foremost African feminists.

Bessie was in a strange position. It was clear to everyone that she had a far greater personal knowledge of the difficulties lone mothers face and the discrimination women suffer than most of the educated and privileged Western women in her audience. In one of her discussions with Alice Walker on the same subject, she had made an illuminating remark five years earlier: 'When you are truly alone and unpampered', she had said, 'the question of women's lib does not even arise. You just do everything for yourself and every now and then a male buddy knocks in a nail you can't reach.'[49] Her habit of disregarding theory and attitude and focusing on the essential issue could have an infuriating effect on her discussion partners, mainly because of the authority of sheer experience which her words carried.

All the same, her most recent writings, especially *A Collector of Treasures*, expressed many feminist attitudes. She later said that she regarded the collection of short stories as a 'practical' record: 'I didn't think up a sex war. It was the truth. The men are just like that and the women suffer'.[50] In a letter to Tony Hall in 1978 she had said that 'everything' looked so much more hopeful because royalty and class were disappearing. 'I think things go up in flames when power is concentrated in the hands of a few people.' These people, she said, were served by life. They did no work.

I feel the new age belongs to those who serve life. Women's lib for me tends to fall into this broad category. The independence of women is certainly a needed thing; it overcomes problems of prostitution and if a woman is independent financially it gives her time to find out if she really loves a man and is not merely dependent on him for support.[51]

Yet she would not adopt the slogans and clichés of the women's movement. 'I am not a feminist,' she kept repeating as the question was asked again and again, 'in the sense that I do not view women in isolation from men.'[52] For all that it was worth, Bessie still maintained that she belonged in the category where a man was of central importance to her existence.

It was in Copenhagen that she saw how lesbianism and a very aggressive attitude to men were becoming part of the women's movement. She met many women in love with each other and in her opinion they confused these emotions with the idea of women's liberation. She thought it most unnatural but concluded that it must be a phase in the movement.

She made her final statement on the subject five years later and a year before she died: 'I view my own activity as a writer as a kind of participation in the thought of the whole world . . . Writing is not a male/female occupation . . . I do not have to be a feminist. The world of the intellect is impersonal, sexless.'[53]

At one of these official functions, Bessie was placed beside the Minister of Cultural Affairs, Lise Østergård, who asked penetrating questions about her research and next writing project. She offered to investigate the possibilities of getting a grant for Bessie to complete her research for her historical novel in Denmark. Bessie pointed out that most of her research was complete. She now needed time to write the book. The idea of spending some time in Europe appealed to her, however, because she was now suffering badly from insomnia and a change of climate sometimes helped. So she hoped that some plan could be made, but in fact nothing came of the idea.

Once again Bessie took it upon herself to have a showdown with a journalist who had been closely involved with the arrangements for the visit. Because of this person's knowledge of African literature, she had been responsible for introducing the two guests on more than one occasion. Intentionally or unintentionally she had behaved in a way that Bessie found slighting. Such was Bessie's emotional vulnerability that she reacted violently to any hint of patronisation.

On the other hand, when a university lecturer teased her mildly about her beer-drinking, referring to Jean Marquard's interview and the notorious photo of her surrounded by three beer cans, in *London Magazine*, she responded heartily. 'I'm sorry to admit it', she said, 'but I'm an alcoholic. These two chins and that second stomach are all beer.'[54] With a twinkle in his eye, the lecturer produced a pint of beer instead of a glass of water to place beside the lectern during her address to his students, and she thought it a huge joke and referred afterwards to the broad-minded attitudes which Danes have.

People responded very differently to her. Attitudes ranged from devoted admiration of her writing ability to sympathetic acceptance of her idiosyncrasies, including her enormous appetite for Danish pastries.

The Danish writer Karen Blixen, famous for *Out of Africa*, was not amongst Ngugi wa Thiong'o's favourite authors. To most Danes she was a revered national symbol. While they saw her involvement in life in Africa as deep personal concern for the blacks, Ngugi wa Thiong'o detected the more ambiguous notes: her strange possessive attitude to 'her' people and a 'concern' that could turn to manipulation. Bessie had never read any of Karen Blixen's writing, but Ngugi wa

Thiong'o had inspired her. During a television interview she got herself into trouble.

She made the point that while African nations as such enjoy international respect on an equal footing with all other nations, individual Africans were still treated condescendingly in the Western European culture. She had observed this discrimination functioning in subtle ways; and this, of course, she was entitled to state. But she then chose Karen Blixen to illustrate her point. Karen Blixen, she said, referred to blacks as 'savages' and 'savage animals'. Her interviewer handled her gently. She did not ask her to substantiate her remarks, much to the annoyance of at least one critic the next day, who pointed out that in Karen Blixen's artisti c universe 'savage' and related terms were highly complimentary.[55] But Bessie did not present a very convincing front when she had to admit she had not read *Out of Africa*. Nonetheless she enjoyed being part of this controversy, and told her friends in London that her criticism of Karen Blixen had been 'dead accurate'.[56]

Before leaving Denmark, Bessie had two days in Århus, on the mainland of Jutland. Her purpose was to visit her old friends Amin and Maria Mohammed. After moving from Francistown to Maun in northern Botswana, where Amin Mohammed tried to eke out an existence as a fisherman in the Okavango Delta, they had been accepted as refugees by the Danish government and had arrived in Denmark earlier in 1980. Amin Mohammed was sent into hospital for four months almost immediately. The many years of extreme poverty had taken their toll: he had advanced tuberculosis. One of the children was severely handicapped and after years of struggling with this problem, the Mohammeds were gathered up into the hospitalisation and rehabilitation programmes suddenly available to them. The meeting with Bessie at the end of this important year was a great reunion for both families. 'She was our very good friend,' said Amin Mohammed many years afterwards.[57] He was later, with his old resourcefulness, to start a small eating place in Århus, which became a popular venue for university students.

It was approaching midwinter while Bessie was in Denmark. She found the short days and long dark nights hard to adjust to and later referred to the 'three weeks of darkness' she had experienced there.[58] She was given a glimpse of Christmas preparations, Danish style: the tastefully decorated shop windows, the ritual preparations of endless Christmas culinary specialities and always, everywhere, the obsessive concern for light, preferably candles in cosy massed clusters, to drive back the darkness.

From Copenhagen, Bessie and Howard flew to London. Randolph Vigne, detailed off by James Currey, met them at Heathrow on 13 December and drove them to Heinemann's. With James Currey, they had tea at Randolph Vigne's flat before going on to stay with Jane Grant for the few days they were in London.

Three weeks of high-powered living had not daunted Bessie's urge to communicate. She could talk 'as none other',[59] as Jane Grant put it, and no sooner were she and Howard comfortably settled in the Grant home, than she launched into descriptions of both her travels and her travails. Jane Grant soon became aware of Bessie's precarious nervous balance and the complex mother–son relationship during those busy days and evenings. But Bessie's vivid and original ideas were also very evident. Four days of providing for Bessie's and Howard's needs, especially transport, as well as keeping up her end of the discussion, left Jane Grant exhausted. However, when Bessie finally departed from London, she was still talking.

In Holyport Road, Fulham, London, there was sudden excitement. A friend of Paddy Kitchen's had phoned her to say that she had noticed that the writer Bessie Head was giving a talk at the Africa Book Centre two days later. Paddy Kitchen immediately made plans to go. Later that evening Bessie phoned her.

The two friends did not meet at the Africa Book Centre, but Paddy listened to Bessie's address as a member of the audience. Bessie was in good practice and it went off well. The thought of the discussion afterwards did not even distress her, though in Denmark she had begun to dread the questions people could think up. She almost laughed when she heard the old faithful: 'Would you say that with your last two books, *A Question of Power* and *The Collector of Treasures,* you have established yourself as a feminist writer?' She had her reply ready: 'I am not a feminist,' she said, 'in the sense that I do not view women in isolation from men.'

The next day, 17 December, Bessie met Paddy Kitchen and Dulan Barber at the pre-publishing party Heinemann gave to mark the appearance, soon, of *Serowe: Village of the Rain Wind,* dedicated, along with Jackie Alberti and the people of Serowe, to Paddy Kitchen. Giles Gordon, originally also one of the chosen, had been struck off the list when the tax affair raged. At the top of the stairs leading into the room where the party was to be held, Bessie and Paddy Kitchen suddenly stood face to face. Bessie took in the warmth of Paddy Kitchen's brown hair, rosy cheeks, observant and tolerant brown eyes, and generous smile. She plummeted towards her. Paddy felt herself enveloped in a pair of short, firm arms and pushed into the comfortable friendliness of a generously padded female frame. Bessie's close-cut curly hair, dusted with grey hairs, tickled Paddy's cheek. It was a bear hug of huge dimensions and it provided the complete bridge from the good years across the sad years to the present moment.

Suddenly Bessie saw it. The woven bag. Paddy had her gift from Bessie with her, made in Serowe nine years earlier and looking as good as new. It had survived breakdowns, misunderstandings and the complete collapse of the Boiteko movement. In every way the meeting re-established the old, strong bonds. Bessie, used to her old pictures of Dulan Barber with long black hair, was surprised to see him short-haired and beginning to go grey. 'Dulan asks me to say that he is still the Wild Man despite the hair cut!' said Paddy in her first letter after Bessie's return to Serowe.[60]

Paddy was pleased to meet Howard. There were so many links from the old days, not to mention the fact that she knew about boys and the problems of growing up. Her son Dan and Howard had the same interest in music and one of the results of the meeting was a tape Dan made and sent to Howard, including some numbers he and his partner Barb Jungr had recorded as the duo, The Stroke. Howard was greatly honoured. 'They've already got themselves some fans out here,' he wrote.[61]

In some ways the time in London was the highlight of the trip for Howard. He was eighteen, had just finished school and was fond of lively company. It had not always been easy for him to follow in the tail of his comet-like mother in Denmark. He was not particularly well versed in her writings nor particularly interested. None of her admirers could find much to say to him. They had done some sightseeing in Denmark – seen the statue of the Little Mermaid sitting on its rock in the harbour, walked along Langelinie quay, watched the changing of the Amalienborg palace guard, seen the royal palace of Rosenborg. This he enjoyed. But he enjoyed London more and hoped to return one day.

Bessie made a new friend while she was in London. She met Brian Willan, who had just completed a doctoral thesis on Sol Plaatje. Plaatje had been one of the outstanding South Africans of his generation: a famous political leader, journalist and writer. He belonged to the Barolong people and Setswana was his native tongue. Among his many other achievements, he produced, in 1930, the first novel in English to be written by a black South African, *Mhudi.* This Bessie had read in 1976, when she attended the Writers' Workshop in Gaborone and had been very interested in him ever since. Brian Willan was preparing to edit a new edition of Plaatje's political treatise, *Native Life in South Africa.* Concentrating on the South African Natives Land Act of 1913, it was first published in London in 1916 while Plaatje was there as part of the South African National Native Congress delegation to protest about the passing of this Act. Brian Willan now revived Bessie's enthusiasm for Plaatje and she started to read *Native Life in South Africa.* She found it moving:

Having access to the writings of Sol Plaatje has been one of the richest experiences of my life. Never was there a man richer in spirit than he. *Native Life* is an astonishing book, crowded with information about all aspects of a black man's life, though it purports to be about the Natives Land Act of 1913. It astonished me that a people so rich in spirit, and Plaatje represents black people totally, could be so overwhelmingly overcome by evil. One feels him describing this with a sense of complete disbelief and despair and being unable to halt the process.[62]

15

Nigeria, 1982

A Bewitched Crossroad

By Christmas time the travellers were home. And home now meant Serowe. The trip to Denmark had brought their time in Gaborone to a natural conclusion. The research was complete. Now it was up to Bessie to get her book written. But what about Howard? It was much harder to get anything in Serowe than in Gaborone and they had some serious planning to do.

Friends come and friends go, as Bessie had said. She returned to Serowe with the glowing knowledge that she had found two old friends again. She enjoyed the thought of telling Mona about her meeting with Paddy Kitchen and Dulan Barber, for Mona was planning yet another trip to Gaborone. Bessie had written to her from Denmark telling her about that part of her journey and making plans to see her in Botswana. On returning home, however, Bessie found a sad letter from Hope Lovell, Mona Pehle's sister. Mona was dead. A few days before she was due to leave for Gaborone she had collapsed, and died shortly afterwards of what was apparently heart failure. With the years, Bessie's correspondence with Mona had become a stimulating exchange of ideas, unlike the more usual pattern where she tended to start off a friendship with a flourish and then end it with an explosion. Bessie must have been shocked to hear this news and deeply grieved by her death. Yet this was another indication that the habit she had once had of 'setting up the loudest wail in the world' when disaster struck, no longer seemed to encompass every form of disaster. She was from now on singularly silent about the saddest events of her life.

Two other old friends also disappeared from Bessie's life about the same time. Though she had met Randolph Vigne in London, they had not been able to gather up the old threads and Randolph did not attend the Heinemann party. He was going through a period of great strain in his business life and felt that he was no longer 'part of' Bessie's 'private life'.[1] Equally sad, Betty Fradkin had also ceased to write. In late 1978 Betty Fradkin began on a new, radically different phase of her life. She joined a Sufi abode and was initiated into the Sufi order. She became an active participant in anti-nuclear-power demonstrations. Her carefully worded warning to Bessie at the end of 1978 about letting alcohol immobilise her when she needed to act, may well have brought down one of Bessie's notorious letters on her head. The correspondence tailed off. In a letter in June 1979, Betty Fradkin added a remark: 'I hope you'll feel like writing', which suggests that something like this had happened.[2] In 1981 Jane Grant asked Bessie something about the early interview 'Conversations with Bessie', which Betty Fradkin had recorded. Bessie replied: 'Betty Fradkin . . . was rather a strange woman. She wrote for a time and then stopped writing.'[3] During the course of her life, Bessie made many damning remarks about people, but none showed her up as badly as that one.

Bessie had wasted no time in writing to Paddy Kitchen and Dulan Barber on her return: 'One feels a sorrow at the way friends become innocently involved in the tragedies of one's life and there is a period of my life that I cannot undo or re-live in a different way but I've longed not to have lived it. That was the cause of my long silence.'[4] Paddy replied that they both understood 'the effects of such a stormy passage', having been touched by 'something similar' through a close friend. Such experiences could not be 'comfortably contained and explained' but if one was able to come out on the right side in a 'calm and positive spirit', then something good could be said to have come of it. 'And, oh, the welcome one wants to give when friends come through,'[5] she added.

There was another letter from London in the post the day Bessie received this one from Paddy Kitchen. It began: 'Dear Bessie, Remember me? as the ghost of Hamlet's father said, not to mention the last words of the first (or was it second?) thief hanging on the cross beside Jesus.' It was from Giles Gordon. He was bitterly disappointed not to have seen her in London, especially when he realised that she had been giving a reading of her work only a hundred yards or less away from the Gollancz (and the Davis-Poynter) offices: 'I'm miserable, my lovely lady, that I wasn't allowed in on the act.'[6] He wondered whether he would hear from her, or whether 'thunderbolts' would be 'hurled' in his direction again. But Bessie was in an expansive mood. And pleased, very pleased, to hear from him. She began her reply:

I remember you well, Giles Gordon. I failed to inform you of my visit to London as I was under the impression that you were roasting away in hell fire. I am not exactly the Devil but I've tended to pass people on to him. I've been standing outside the gates of hell for some time, very vigorously pitching my foes into the fire. Lo and behold, I failed to check if there were fire escapes and exits from that permanently burning dungeon. I note from your picture that you got out of one of the exits without your hair being singed and quite unroasted too! Not even Jesus Christ thought about the exits! I remember him saying that the goats shall be caste [sic] into hell fire and gnash their teeth forever in anguish. An amendment is needed to that line, isn't it?[7]

She told him about the talks and interviews she had given in London and ended up by saying how pleased she was that he had written. She had not forgotten that she still owed him £100 plus the cost of a year's subscription to the *New Statesman*! This she would pay back when her ship came in. But Giles Gordon cancelled the debt forthwith.

He said in his reply that he was delighted to hear that he was to receive a copy of *Serowe: Village of the Rain Wind* when it was published: 'the original type-script is in many places engraved on my mind. Engraved is the word too, as your descriptions of people were so incised, so definitive.' He told her as he had often done before that he thought her best writing, 'the sheer prose and perceptions', was in her letters: 'Oh, if you were to put together – deliberately or after the event – a book of extracts from your letters, your occasional writings, what a lovely book it would be, a kind of commonplace book.'[8]

Shortly after returning to Serowe, Bessie's librarian friend, Pat Spann, brought Hilda Bernstein, very active in the South African anti-apartheid struggle and an exile from that country, to visit her. It was a cold day with a sharp wind catching up the dusty soil outside, but in Bessie's little room the three women talked in a lively surge of warmth and understanding. Bessie had read Hilda's book *Women in South Africa* and knew of her and her husband Lionel Bernstein's part in the struggle in South Africa. Hilda impressed her in a very special way. In the first place she admired her writing, her ability to depict 'the secret silent tragedy' of the lives of women evicted from their homes and resettled in areas where they could hardly survive. There was one picture in Hilda's book that was 'so stark, bleak and bare ... one gets the feeling that the people are eating earth and dying there'.[9] But it was Hilda's personality that made the greater impression.

Bessie was still not making much progress with her historical novel, despite the fact that she had apparently been half-way through it when she returned to Serowe at the end of 1980. However, other articles were being written. She had been in touch with *Drum* magazine in Johannesburg a few years earlier, when they had asked her if she had anything they could publish. When they turned down her story 'The Lovers', they asked her to write something about her own background instead. She then wrote a long and very frank account of her birth, childhood and adult life in both South Africa and Botswana, relating all this to her writing experience. She called it 'Biographical Notes: A Search for Historical Continuity and Roots', sent it off but heard nothing further from *Drum*.

About the end of 1981 she was approached by three lecturers, Margaret Daymond, Johan Jacobs and Margaret Lenta from the University of Natal. They were compiling a collection of contemporary South African writing and asked her for a contribution. She replied promptly, sending the article she thought that *Drum* had rejected. At the same time she wrote to the editor there and asked what had happened about the material she had sent. His reply disconcerted her. They were publishing it in February 1982 as 'Notes from a Quiet Backwater'. She had to recall her contribution to the University of Natal publication hastily and promise the editors something else.

When she received the *Drum* article, however, she could see that they had chopped off her original piece at the end of her description of her life in South Africa. She realised that the remaining pages had a unity of their own and without altering a word she sent them off to the Natal editors. In 1984 the piece appeared in *Momentum: On Recent Southern African Writing* as 'A Search for Historical Continuity and Roots'.

The tone of this second section is less harsh than that dealing with her life in South Africa. She talks here about how she was already committed to 'an involvement in questions of poverty and exploitation' but she 'needed an eternal and continuous world against which to work out these preoccupations'. She talks about her need as an African to find 'a sense of historical continuity, a sense of roots'. The old image of the borrowed clothes, somewhat clumsily used in the earlier pieces, is perfectly incorporated here: 'I remember how tentative and sketchy were my first efforts, not finding roots as such but rather putting on layer after layer of patchy clothing.' She balances philosophical considerations with passages of lyrical description, and, presenting a visual image of the dichotomy, she then explains: 'Such peaceful rural scenes would be hastily snatched to form the backdrop to tortuous novels. Perceptive fans sensed the disparity, the disparity between the peaceful simplicity of village life and a personality more complex than village life could ever be.'[10]

In about March 1981 Brian Willan wrote to Bessie asking her whether she would write a foreword to the new edition of *Native Life in South Africa* that he was editing. She agreed but did nothing serious about it. In October he wrote again, asking for the foreword fairly quickly. Ten days later she sent it off, explaining that she had all her notes from the previous close reading, so it was easy to write. 'Foreword to Sol Plaatje's *Native Life in South Africa*', written crisply and incisively, is informative but not dull. Bessie calls Plaatje's work 'the history of a mute and subdued black nation who had learned to call the white man "baas".' *Native Life*, she says, is 'astonishingly crowded with data of the day-to-day life of a busy man who assumed great sorrows and great responsibilities, who felt himself fully representative of a silent, oppressed people and by sheer grandeur of personality, honoured that obligation.'[11]

In March 1981 Bessie received her next invitation to travel abroad. She was becoming quite used to the procedure. This time the invitation came from Holland. The Netherlands Organisation for International Development Cooperation, Novib, which had been responsible for publishing *When Rain Clouds Gather* in Dutch, wrote inviting her to take part in a television programme to mark their twenty-fifth anniversary. It would be a programme that covered some of Novib's work in the past and its future role in Third World cooperation. Bessie wrote back accepting but she laid down one or two conditions. She had had an unpleasant experience with two Dutch television reporters in Berlin and she said that she would not take part if they were in any way involved in the programme. Secondly, she wanted a fee for her appearance. Novib was naturally sponsoring the whole trip. Mrs Joke Junger wrote back assuring her that the television men in question had nothing to do with the production and offering her a fee of $125 for an article that would be published in Novib's monthly magazine, *Onze Wêreld*. She also mentioned that Bessie had $800 due to her in royalties from the sale of her novel. Thus satisfied, Bessie left Botswana on 20 May.

The whole arrangement went off smoothly. The television show was an ambitious affair, with fifteen people appearing on a panel. Bessie was one of a group of five guests and co-workers from the Third World. The others came from Zambia, Jamaica, Brazil and the Philippines. Amongst other things, they were asked to give their views on the overall picture of development cooperation and what the main task for the next twenty-five years should be. Bessie contributed successfully to the discussion.

For a person whose life had formed itself as a series of confrontations and crises, Bessie found herself in a remarkably quiet period at this time. There were no missionary teachers to victimise her, no racist whites to humiliate her, nor was there a profligate husband to wound her. The devils that had plagued her earlier years in Botswana seemed to have been laid. The Botswana government, with its unexpected gesture, had removed her chronic sense of insecurity; her agents and publisher gave her all the support they could. Her 'problem book' was on the point of being published and she had only herself to blame if her historical novel was taking so long to be produced. The three or four problems threatening her peace of mind at this stage of her life seemed manageable in comparison.

The first concerned her mail, which was being tampered with, and this worried her. At one stage she received a letter from her agent in an envelope addressed by Paddy Kitchen.[12] A letter from Bessie to Paddy went astray, too, and interrupted their correspondence for a while.

There was also an incident that could have had serious consequences, and resulted in a clash with Heinemann during the process of publishing *Serowe: Village of the Rain Wind*. It concerned gift copies of the book for her interviewees. She had made it quite clear from the start that she could not pay the people she interviewed for their contributions, but she had promised each one a copy of the finished product. She had 94 contributors on her list. When Giles Gordon, Patrick Cullinan and Reg Davis-Poynter had held their famous meeting in London in 1975, this question had been under discussion. Patrick Cullinan, thinking that he had taken over the primary publishing rights, promised to provide Bessie with these copies free of charge as an extra service. All those plans fell through and when finally Heinemann agreed to publish *Serowe: Village of the Rain Wind*, Bessie again stated the need for these copies. Heinemann agreed but they were not mentioned in the contract. Bessie thought that this meant that the publisher would provide them free of charge, while Heinemann thought that she intended to buy the books at a reduced rate, paying for them out of her royalties. When Bessie discovered that she was expected to pay, she wrote to James Currey saying that she had assumed throughout that this would be 'a kindly informal arrangement' on Heinemann's part and that she felt 'very bitter indeed'[13] about their treatment of her. However, there was no dramatic confrontation. She got her way and Heinemann provided the presentation copies.

Bessie's transaction with them was actually complicated by the fact that she also wished to order 500 copies which she could sell to friends in the village. Though she usually complained about her poverty, she was now indignant with James Currey for being unwilling to send her so many: 'you treat me as though I am living in the poorhouse . . . My standing with the bank . . . here is of a high order and the bank manager would only be too delighted to treat this matter as a special project.'[14] They later agreed on Heinemann's sending 100 copies first of all, with the possibility of more copies if required.

Serowe: Village of the Rain Wind appeared officially on 29 June 1981. In his foreword, Ronald Blythe praised the book for the way it 'made sense at last of much of what has occurred' in Africa during the last century. 'Rarely has the cadence and the intelligence of the four generations which lived through these years been caught so accurately or so movingly.'[15]

The fact that it appeared only in England, in a paperback edition, meant that it attracted much less critical attention than *A Question of Power* had done. However, it was given full-page reviews in the *Listener* and *South* where Paddy Kitchen and Jane Grant, respectively, gave readers a good insight into the contents and quality of the book. Paddy Kitchen emphasised the way Bessie had ordered her material so that it told a story 'which readers will find themselves using as a text to meditate on many aspects of society'.[16] Jane Grant spoke about Bessie's language: 'Whether recording the words of the villagers or giving us her own prose, as she describes her feelings for her adopted home, the words take on the cadence of song. It is a story told from the inside, with love.'[17] In *New Society*, Elspeth Huxley, in another extensive review, predicted that *Serowe: Village of the Rain Wind* would become a classic in the literature of post-independent Africa, in the same way that Ronald Blythe's *Akenfield* had in English social history: 'Here is the warp of tradition and the woof of change . . . As for the book, every word rings true.'[18]

It might not have caused a sensation in London, but in the village there was a stir. The 100 copies Bessie was intending to sell arrived long before the presentation copies, and though this later caused trouble, she used them to give away. She put up a notice outside one of the shops to say that she would be distributing the free copies to the contributors at a certain time. In this way she disposed of some. But there were many who did not live in the village any longer, and quite a number of the older people who were dead. It took time but she traced everyone to whom she had promised a copy. Grandchildren or daughters of the older generation often wrote her appreciative notes. Kethamile Kgasa, for example, told her that her grandfather, Gaboutwelwe Kgasa, had 'a shortage of time' but he thought of Bessie often. He had been the organiser of Serowe Tannery Brigade when the book was written and Kethamile said that the book made sense to her too because she had 'heard about his dealings'.[19] Bessie said in a letter that only 14 of her contributors were in fact literate, the rest were 'ordinary illiterate villagers',[20] but this can hardly include the volunteers and traders she had interviewed.

The second parcel of books was sadly delayed. This meant that many of the people she had been hoping would buy a copy had already bought one in Gaborone by the time the parcel arrived. As it turned out, Bessie had quite a lot of trouble getting rid of these copies. Nevertheless, the complicated process of getting *Serowe: Village of the Rain Wind* published and distributed went off well when it was finally effected.

Two other subjects caused Bessie considerable distress about this time. The first concerned the payment of royalties. Her trip to Holland opened her eyes to something that brought all her reserves of indignation surging to the surface. She realised that she had not been receiving any royalties from the Dutch translation of *When Rain Clouds Gather*. The Dutch publishers, Wêreldvenster, had been paying this money to the agent originally responsible for the contract for the novel, A P Watt, but Bessie had not received any. Bessie felt herself badly cheated and engaged Hilda Bernstein's sympathy and energy: 'Your poverty and need is always on my mind,' Hilda Bernstein wrote in 1982.[21] She actually employed a lawyer from the Defence and Aid Fund to look into the matter, without achieving any results. Partly because Wêreldvenster, in the midst of a large-scale accountancy reorganisation, had not kept the proofs of payment of royalties over the years in question and partly because A P Watt maintained that they had paid the money, though Bessie had never received it, no legal action was ever taken. At a very early stage of the discussion, Wêreldvenster simply reimbursed Bessie and eventually counted the money lost. One of Bessie's hysterical accusations, 'If you do not return enclosures I will know that you regard me no higher than a dog to exploit',[22] provoked a serious reply from the head of the publishing firm. He said that they had a very high reputation for treating their authors correctly, as the fact that they had long since reimbursed her money also showed. They had borne the loss and she had received the money due and he hoped that she would no longer think of them as a publishing firm who treated their non-white authors as dogs.[23]

The royalties affair was something Bessie continued to bring up periodically as the latest example of the way she was mistreated. In actual fact her real problem lay much nearer home and only a few of her friends were given an insight into it. It was Howard. His teenage years had been difficult for both of them. She had sometimes confided some of her problems to Mona Pehle. At about four-month intervals, Howard would get into some mess or other, Bessie would pull out all stops to rescue him, and he would settle down for a while. In moments of need, Howard knew he could count on his mother. A description she gave of herself trying to help one of his friends is amusing and also revealing: 'A real parent would weep, lament, beseech, pray – the whole works. Of course, as I said, I have a huge repertoire of drama that I turn on for Howard and there was enough left over for the other boy.'[24]

Howard had had no traditional upbringing. Bessie once told Mona Pehle: 'I am afraid things are wildly unbalanced like that in my household. Whole crises build up and we live through them and the solutions are never conventional ones.'[25] She was explaining how she had never given Howard any religious instruction but he had had a period of being very religious, being baptised in the Anglican Church and serving as an altar boy. Bessie herself had gone to church a few times just to show there was no hard feeling but one day he came home and asked her directly: 'Why didn't you tell me there was a God?' She replied that she did not like the idea: 'They want to give it to someone special in the sky. I want the title of God to belong to all the people in the world. I want all people to be God.' Howard thought about this and then said: 'I like that. I like your idea.'[26] After that, he lost interest in church. Howard could infuriate Bessie with his lazy habits; he could be unreasonable, rude and very demanding. But he had an open nature that meant he would suddenly discuss a problem in an adult way, then disarmingly admit his own faults. Bessie was very proud of him and generally took the vicissitudes of life with Howard with the resignation most parents are forced to adopt.

The real problem facing them was his career. After the year in Gaborone, he was having to face some harsh realities about further education. In most fields the number of applicants far exceeded the intake. They had tried to get him into the agricultural college but there were 3 000 applicants hoping for the 150 vacancies. They had tried for something in journalism, community development and at the new diamond-mining town of Orapa, but all to no avail. Howard's examination results were far from good and he was not able to find an opening in such a competitive market.

Suddenly an unexpected solution was found. After 17 years of silence, Howard's father, Harold Head, contacted them at the start of the new year. He was wondering what plans Howard had for the future and whether he could help: he offered to pay for an airticket for Howard and to support him while he acquired some form of training in Canada. Here were indeed new prospects. Both Howard and Bessie thought that Canada would be an ideal place to complete the last stage of his education. He accepted the invitation eagerly and made the necessary arrangements without delay. He left Botswana on 26 May 1982.

If Bessie's progress on her novel seemed so slow, one of the reasons was without doubt the growing number of other activities in which she was asked to participate. She had been used to addressing local groups occasionally. In 1975, for example, the Danish Voluntary Service had asked her to address a meeting at Moeding College on the subject 'Why I Write My Books'. This could well have provided the basis for her later article 'Why Do I Write'.[27] Later that same year she addressed the students of both the Francistown Teachers' Training College and the Tutume Community College. At Tutume she was guest speaker at the annual Prizegiving Day.

Her television and personal appearances in Germany, Denmark and Holland had made her known abroad to socially and politically committed young people, many of whom were considering involving themselves in African community development schemes as volunteers. Her writing provided the best practical insight into the role of the young volunteer in Botswana that could be found.

That is why volunteers from most countries were encouraged to read *When Rain Clouds Gather* as soon as they arrived in the country. From 1981 onwards she was often in demand to address these groups. She began to have a standing arrangement to address the new group of American Peace Corps trainees every six months. She was fetched and taken to St Paul's mission at Molepolole, where the training took place, and was greatly appreciated as a speaker. She was paid P40, later P70 for her time. The only trouble was that she insisted on taking her dog Pa with her. She assured the organisers that he was 'very clean with no ticks and fleas'.[28] But he was not as phlegmatic as she had thought. The first time she took him she expected him to lie peacefully at her feet while she delivered her lecture. Instead he went into one of the dormitories and returned proudly showing off some soiled socks he had found, much to the amusement of the audience. Then he caught sight of a kitten and 'went beserk. People began screaming: "Get the dog out! Get the cat out!" and chaos reigned.'[29] After that, he was banned from the lecture hall.

From 1981 invitations to workshops and conferences also began to stream in. Bessie handled these in three ways. Those over which she would incur any personal expenses she dismissed immediately. For this reason she turned down invitations to the African Literature Association Conference in California in 1981, the Zambia National Association of Writers' Annual Workshop in Lusaka in 1982, the European Association of Commonwealth Literature and Language Studies in Barcelona in 1984, and the 27th Annual Meeting of the African Studies Association in Los Angeles in 1984. Then there were those which would not have cost her anything but which she turned down for personal reasons. For example, she refused to attend an Arts Festival in Gaborone in 1982 and turned down an invitation to the Writers' Workshop at the University of Botswana in 1985 because she did not want to have anything to do with some of the other guest speakers. In 1982 she would not attend a Women in Southern Africa Conference in Zimbabwe because of a 'personal crisis'[30] and in 1986 she was invited to the Second African Writers' Conference arranged by the Scandinavian Institute of African Studies to be held in Stockholm but she refused because she had plans that kept her in Serowe.

The remaining invitations she accepted. She was in Gaborone for a symposium on 'Creative Writing in Botswana' in October 1981. In July 1982 she was back to give an address at a symposium entitled 'South African Culture' arranged by a small cultural group called Maru a Pula, and in October of the same year she took part in a Writers' Workshop arranged by Macmillan publishers, also in Gaborone.

Early in 1982 Bessie received an invitation to go to Nigeria. The University of Calabar was holding its Second Annual International Conference on African Literature and the English Language from 15 to 19 June. Bessie Head and Ngugi wa Thiong'o were invited as the keynote speakers. To be sharing the platform with Ngugi wa Thiong'o, whom Bessie knew and respected, promised well for the whole arrangement. Nuruddin Farah from Somalia was also invited, as well as six Nigerian writers and language experts.

Bessie accepted the invitation and began the necessary preparations with equanimity. She had been very busy getting Howard off to Canada, so she had not had much time to spend on her own affairs. She packed a couple of her homemade dresses, sewn as loose-hanging shifts from a simple standard pattern, a few other personal essentials and her books and papers, and set off to walk or get a lift to the village and thence go by the slow bus service, which had certainly not improved with the years, to Gaborone. The Danish teacher, Ruth Forchhammer, who by this time had rented one of the empty houses in the area beyond Swaneng School, a part that had once hummed with life when the Brigade movement was at its height, often gave Bessie lifts in her little blue truck. She saw her striding along the road that day and stopped.

'Hello, Bessie, are you going to the village?'

'No, I'm going to Nigeria,' Bessie replied.[31]

In Nigeria the conference guests were taken good care of. Bessie was shown hospitality by a lecturer at the University of Calabar, Chikwenye Okonjo Ogunyemi, who was very familiar with her writing. They had actually met in Gaborone some months before the conference when Ogunyemi was there in connection with her research. Through her, Bessie gained a good insight into the Nigerian way of life. Later Bessie and 'Mrs Chi' enjoyed a lively exchange of letters, which seemed to reflect the general success of the visit.

Apart from lectures and workshops, a concert and a banquet with a toast to the writers had been arranged. And Bessie was asked to take a class at the university. The students were highly excited, she said, having studied *A Question of Power* closely – 'which is a mistake because it is a wild, mad, book'.[32] Bessie reported that she was 'too strange and different' to be liked. She was 'not African'. She discovered that *When Rain Clouds Gather* was not popular because Makhaya dissociates himself from politics. *Maru* and *A Question of Power* were disliked because they are so 'strange'. The character Dikeledi provoked most discussion. The students felt she was not credible: 'a girl like that does not belong in a village . . . she is a mis-cast . . . She is not African.' This reaction surprised Bessie, considering that the students seemed to accept 'the vivid, highly original Maru, the other strange characters, Margaret and Moleka'.

Bessie took the criticism very calmly: 'Me, I did not care. I am supreme and I know it. I was asked by a Nigerian politician to liberate the people of South Africa and I replied that South Africa had had Steve Biko and they did not need me. There'd be another Steve Biko soon.'[33]

Another thing that amused her was the general reaction to her person. Because *A Question of Power* is 'full of swear words I invented myself', everyone expected a 'towering, violent, loud-spoken woman'. As it happened, the audience had trouble hearing what she was saying; they kept complaining that she was whispering. Someone said to her: 'I am stunned to find that the author of *A Question of Power* is such a softly-spoken woman.'[34]

Bessie thought the Nigerian countryside beautiful; 'like England and Europe, crowded with vegetation and pretty wild flowers'.[35] What is more, she found clothes there after her own heart. She returned to Serowe with a love for the colourful Nigerian kaftans and several in her suitcase which she used for the rest of her life, giving her wardrobe a stylish lift.

The visit, however, left her rather shocked by the extreme forms of good and evil she saw in Nigeria. The traffic was violent and dangerous and accidents abounded. An angry crowd could gather round a driver who had caused a serious accident and lynch him on the spot. She was appalled by the modern airport, beautifully appointed but with telephone booths without phones inside them. It seemed to be symptomatic of the way Nigerian life functioned. 'Everything associated with modern government and modern service has no meaning for the people.' At the same time she was conscious of a tradition of the 'deepest love and respect for human life'. This she experienced in Calabar. As they did in Serowe, everyone greeted everyone else. To her amazement they used English. 'Good morning,' they said. English as the lingua franca of the country had a 'unifying influence', which with an 'estimated number of 499 different local languages cannot be over-emphasised'.[36]

On her way back, Bessie spent two days in Harare. This too she found a beautiful city. She stayed with people attached to the University, and the English department naturally made hasty arrangements to have her talk to a class. Her books were not on the syllabus but 'Ngugi, Armah and the eternal Achebe' were. However, two of the students had studied *A Question of Power* and questioned her aggressively:

'When we read Achebe and Ngugi and Armah, we find things there we can identify with, but with you we are disorientated and flung into Western literature.' I replied that I was a story teller before I was an African, with a special writing technique, that of the broad horizon view of the born story teller. I know myself quite well. I can never live down in an environment and even if I had been born midnight black, green or blue I'd still dominate and be above an environment.

Bessie was never more convincing than when in the magnanimous role of the cosmic organiser. Though she unsettled the students, the lecturer, at least, was intrigued. He asked her if she would accept an invitation to visit them at some future date. 'We will have to warm the students up to you,'[37] he said.

It had been a good and challenging trip, a fact worth remembering in the light of later events, but as always after a time away from Serowe, she was, she told her sister-in-law Caroline Hlaba, 'relieved to be home.'[38]

In July the Grant family visited Serowe. They stayed at the Tswaragano hotel and spent some happy days with Bessie. They invited her to meals at the hotel and, while Jane Grant's teenage son looked on in open-mouthed amazement, Bessie consumed large quantities of beer and piled the empty bottles around her on the table. 'I wish I could win the Nobel prize for literature so that I could build some extra rooms for my friends to stay in when they visit,' Bessie said afterwards. Jane Grant enjoyed absorbing the atmosphere of the village she felt she knew so well. It worried the family that Bessie lived such a lonely life but, as Bessie said, she 'could do nothing to change it'.[39]

It was on this visit that Jane told Bessie that one of her students, named Jane Bryce, was anxious to correspond with her. She wrote soon afterwards, one of an increasing number of graduate students who contacted Bessie. She had already resorted to having copies made of a typed sheet with her biographical details which she could enclose with her replies. She answered every letter. Nor did it upset her that some students wrote to her for what seemed like quick essay-fodder: 'Which are the most important themes in the book? What is the meaning of Sello in her dreams? Meaning of the cesspit? . . . Why did you write this book? Autobiographical?'[40]

As the years went on, she took on their questions and essays in a more and more indiscriminate fashion. The interpretations of *A Question of Power* were as varied as the papers written; she liked them all. Even when students used the word 'insanity' and said that she was describing her South African experience, she took it calmly. To one student she wrote that she loved his thesis with her 'whole heart' and that she had to 'fall to the ground and read it in a prone posture'.[41]

Earlier on, she had said to a researcher:

I hardly recognized my novel in your symbolic interpretation of it, but you are excused. *A Question of Power* is a novel readers take fierce possession of. The canvas on which the tale is drawn is BIG, the tale drawn on the canvas, small, sketchy and uncertain . . . This very attitude of uncertainty is an open invitation to the reader to move in and re-write and reinterpret the novel in his/her own way. So *A Question of Power* is a book that is all things to all men and women.

To a psychiatrist it is a description of a wretched form of schizophrenia which is very distressing, but it throws light on the world of insanity about which not much is known.

To a woman's liberationist the book is pure woman's lib. illuminating some dark and hidden intent on the part of the male of the species to eliminate the female of the species.

To an idealist who would remove poverty and suffering from the world, the book is the ultimate in wonder, the great answer to human suffering.

To the idealist who dreams about the riddle of life and puzzles over it, the wide open spaces of the book are an endless delight, a temptation to re-write, re-dream and reinterpret the story.[42]

Such tolerance and breadth of interpretation seems hardly credible in the light of her earlier frenzied explanations. Perhaps the fact that Bessie's novel had been written in blood, toil, sweat and tears made her inclined to forget the D H Lawrence admonition: 'Never trust the artist. Trust the tale.'[43]

She took a special liking to Jane Bryce. She was preparing a post-graduate dissertation at the University of Essex and wrote to Bessie with a number of questions. She had also been in touch with Paddy Kitchen. She said that Paddy had told her that Bessie related intellectually better to men than to women. This Bessie denied vehemently, and it turned out to be a misunderstanding. Through Jane Bryce the postal confusions were cleared up and Bessie and Paddy took up their regular correspondence.

Botswana was in the grip of one of its periods of drought. The previous year had brought very little rain and the summer of 1982/83 was worse. The sun beat down cruelly and the rain clouds did not even gather. Bessie told Paddy Kitchen that about midsummer the birds fled, so she no longer woke up to her special joy, the 'first hesitant peep-peep, followed by a chorus of bird song'. Insects had gone back into hibernation; 'an eerie silence and desolation'[44] prevailed in the village.

In early 1983 the Vice-President of Botswana, Lenyeletse Seretse, died. To the people of Serowe, this was a personal loss. Like the former President, Lenyeletse was one of their own and would be laid to rest in the Khama royal burial ground in Serowe with almost the same ceremony and respect that had been accorded Seretse Khama two years earlier. The country was plunged into mourning. Solemn music was broadcast over the radio twenty-four hours a day.[45] Bessie had known Lenyeletse Seretse well; but the ambiguous feelings she had had for him in life meant that she kept to herself her reaction to his death.

In actual fact, the 'huge chunks of solitude'[46] that Bessie said made up her life had been invaded by a group of South African visitors at this time. Susan Gardner, a lecturer from the Department of Comparative and African Literature at the University of the Witwatersrand, brought a group of four Honours students, Michelle Adler, Tobeka Mda, Richard Salmon and Patricia Sandler, to interview her. They had discovered Bessie Head's short stories through reading Alice Walker, who regularly referred to her own indebtedness to Bessie. It surprised them to find 'the best woman novelist Africa has produced'[47] living in complete anonymity. Only after some hours of enquiries were they finally directed to Bessie's little rectangular house by a Danish volunteer worker.

They were given a warm welcome. Bessie's ability to establish an immediate intimacy with people has often been recorded. An hour after entering her house, she and Susan were walking hand in hand in the excruciating summer heat, discussing Bessie's nervous breakdown. The visitors invited her to dinner at the hotel and sat for hours in lively conversation. The subject matter ranged extensively. Bessie could at one moment be giving them intimate details about the way her 'persecutors', at the time of her breakdown, had linked her racial deficiencies to her sexual inadequacies (with phrases like 'impotent vagina', in her clearly enunciated breathy voice, filling the hotel dining-room) and at the next turn treating them to a discussion of the music of Dollar Brand[48]

The students ended up with an interview filling three sound cassettes. Bessie was generous and uninhibited. None of the South Africans had realised the extent of her international acclaim. She produced five files of book reviews and revealed something of the extent of her correspondence while they eagerly noted dates and sources and registered the fact that she had copies of so many of her own letters.

On returning to Johannesburg, Susan Gardner wasted no time in contacting the National English Literary Museum in Grahamstown, and a discussion about making her material available to South African scholars was begun. Bessie agreed to lend the library her five files of reviews for copying, but refused to donate her manuscripts or any of her private correspondence: 'Life is just never going to be simple and without pain and the private correspondence reflects this.'[49] The director replied that she might feel differently about donating her correspondence at some future date 'when the years have dulled the sharp edge of experience'.[50]

Meanwhile the students had written their theses and sent her copies. She was clearly uneasy about seeing some of her more outspoken comments in print, especially as she had agreed that a journalist from a Johannesburg newspaper, the *Sunday Times*, might use the transcript of the interview to write an article about her. Patricia Sandler had collected the various statements Bessie had made about refugeeism. 'I know I said all that over the years,' she admitted to Susan, but they 'can sound pretty bad in a newspaper.'[51] Apart from this, however, she was very pleased to have the students' work. She made constructive comments and told both Patricia Sandler and Tobeka Mda that their theses would become a treasured part of her household.

During this time Susan Gardner was perhaps making too good use of her wealth of new information about an important neglected writer on their very doorstep, and this may well have been what began to upset Bessie. With the well-trained academic's highly developed sense of propriety, she asked Bessie's permission before every move she made. For example, when they met in Serowe, Gardner had asked her, very correctly, how she wished to be addressed. Bessie apparently hesitated and looked disorientated. Gardner was later to interpret this as a sign that it was 'not a matter of courtesy inflecting and hedging her voice; it was the terrible fact that she did not know who she was, though she had pieced together a legend about herself which almost everyone still believes'.[52] A more likely explanation was that Bessie was simply not used to being treated with such

propriety and it was this painstaking correctness, combined with a startling efficiency, that later was to unnerve her.

The plans for the copying of her book reviews were under way; Susan Gardner
was writing to ask for permission to send the transcript of the interview to more
and more people; there was some talk of trying to get Bessie to the University of
the Witwatersrand as a writer in residence.[53] Though there is no record of this
in Bessie's correspondence or any indication of her reaction, it may well have
caused her to panic.

Now Bessie began to notice certain things. The students were getting fine
results, Susan was getting access to her large collection of reviews and articles, the
Museum was getting a bibliography. But what was she getting? She apparently felt
that the scale had tipped. No longer were the friendliness and generosity shown
by her visitors enough. She felt cheated.

Suddenly, on 18 June, Bessie wrote Susan Gardner an explosive letter. With
that icy coolness which she commanded just as well as her more usual exuberant style, she began with some short paragraphs thanking her for services ren-
dered:

Thank you for all the feedback material. Many people have taken from me and given nothing in return . . . Thank you for your great courtesy in handing my re-typed page 2 of the
interview to Prof. Mphahlele which stated that I did not work with him at *Drum* publications because he had just left the office when I arrived. I am no social pusher and name
dropper.

These were merely the fuse. Then came the explosion:

The mistake in receiving you and the students was entirely mine. I work in a world where
there are no rules. For what I offer there is sometimes a bottle of wine, more often there
is nothing. My relationship with the University world has been most unpleasant. Very seldom do I take trips abroad. The University people despise me, the self-made writer.

She went on to say that some things choked her. The students had thanked
their department 'for generously allocating money . . . to subsidise the trip to
Botswana'; Susan herself had recently written that 'Wits' would pay for her (and
anyone Bessie wanted to see) to drive up to Serowe again. There was money for
all this but it 'was anticipated that I would work a whole day with you and the students for nothing. Never, never again will I do this. Never, never again will I receive
students and lecturers from South Africa . . . Why should I be so anxious to see
the well-heeled. I am desperately poor.' She added that any further correspondence would be returned unopened. 'Should you make a mistake of trying in any
way to contact me or approach me I will write a letter of complaint to the
University administration.'[54] This she did a year later, in connection with another lecturer,[55] but there are no records of the letters Susan Gardner maintains
Bessie wrote to 'the Vice-Chancellors of nearly every South African university'.[56]
Shortly afterwards, Gardner began to do research into Bessie's genealogy, and she
it was who established that Bessie's mother had spent several periods in a mental home and was much older than earlier believed when she gave birth to

Bessie.[57] This information she published only after Bessie's death.

It would be easy to dismiss the whole affair as yet another example of Bessie's mental instability. However, to suggest, as Gardner does, that she was suffering from 'a "progressive" brain disease'[58] seems too convenient an explanation. Bessie's reaction was unreasonable in many ways. It could be said that she was out of touch with academic practices and that she should have required a fee from the start; but her comments on the affair suggest that she was distressed and indignant, not deranged. Subjected to a barrage of academic efficiency, she felt flattered at first, then increasingly out of her depth. She felt discriminated against economically and no doubt all the old feelings of racial discrimination also welled up. Commenting on the incident to a friend in July 1983, Bessie said that there was 'something wrong . . . with a University like Wits that will accept a service from a writer and not pay for it. My poverty just made me rebel against this kind of exploitation.' In the same letter she made another interesting remark: 'A writer's only material is mankind and a writer has a razor sharp observation of mankind . . . She [Susan Gardner] kept on saying "take care" – I was a mentally ill writer who wrote mentally ill books. In the end I could stand it no more.'[59] In September 1983 she said that she had got the feeling that she had 'suddenly and hilariously been promoted to "Bushman Curio Department of the University of the Witwatersrand." Oh, I was so popular with the students and batches and batches of them were coming up.'[60]

The consequence of this clash was that Bessie thereafter refused all requests for personal interviews, never missing the opportunity of giving as the reason for her refusal the treatment she had received from a South African lecturer. Soon afterwards she turned down a request from a Canadian lecturer for an interview, though offered $100, considerably more than she usually received as a fee. But this amount she described as showing the 'usual University contempt for my person, the self-made writer'.[61] It is in fact in her later obsessive preoccupation with the affair that the clearest traits of mental instability are evident, in this way replacing such earlier obsessions as refugee status and dishonest agents.

By adopting this attitude, Bessie was cutting off one of her last forms of direct intellectual contact. She had always been generous with her time and there is no doubt that visits from students or lecturers had been a pleasurable event for her. 'I was so touched when young people from South Africa visited me. The life of an author is a wide open world. Everyone calls. The whole world visits me on the excuse that they have bought my books,'[62] she had written in 1979. She was commenting on the visit of Susan Harvey and Mokononyana Moleta from the English Department of the University of the Witwatersrand, the first students from this university to approach her.

An incident from the same period illustrates her inherent warmth. The South African visitors had brought with them for Bessie a letter and book from Tim Couzens, of the African Studies Institute of the University of the Witwatersrand. It was the anthology of black poetry, *The Return of the Amasi Bird*, which Tim Couzens and Essop Patel had recently edited. Bessie plunged into reading it and in no time the whole anthology was 'wildly dog-eared' as she read and re-read poems that 'aroused a wonderful sense of wonder' in her.[63] She wrote to Tim

Couzens, thanking him for the way he had introduced people 'to worlds full of wonder and magic' and for all 'those careful sensitive historical introductions' he had written. 'Did no one ever thank you for all you have done, Tim Couzens? I do thank you and have said so quite openly about the re-discovery of Sol Plaatje.'[64] Couzens was so touched by the sincerity of her comments that he said in his reply that her letter had 'all the warm generosity of a true intellectual (not a cold or dry one, but someone who is full of human curiosity and interested in people and ideas) and that is how I've always thought of you'.[65]

Early in February 1983 Bessie received a letter which was going to prove of utmost importance in her life. It was from Michael Chapman, consultant editor at the Johannesburg publishing firm Ad Donker. Originally from Holland, Adriaan Donker had already published four of Bessie's short stories, 'The Prisoner Who Wore Glasses' in 1974,[66] 'Witchcraft' in 1976,[67] 'The Deep River' in 1978,[68] and 'The Lovers' in 1982.[69] Michael Chapman now asked her if she had anything that could be used in a special series of books by women in Southern Africa that they were planning.

She wrote back admitting that she had a manuscript that ought to have been finished long ago. Instead of working on it, she had accepted lecture engagements and 'generally fled the horror of the solitude of my life which the novel seemed to accentuate'.[70] By working very hard, she said that she could have it ready in two months. 'My writing life could do with a vigorous shaking up,' she admitted, implying that Heinemann was slow about getting her books reprinted. Though she also added that she was not a good investment for a publisher, Michael Chapman expressed great interest and she agreed to submit her manuscript when complete, with the end of the year set as a deadline. This was the sort of motivation Bessie desperately needed if she were ever to see her novel about her beloved 'Khama, the Great' in print.

There were plenty of distractions to keep her from her typewriter. In the hyperactive aftermath of the Gardner affair, she began to revise her assets, as she now saw her correspondence and manuscripts. With a typically dramatic gesture, she sent off copies of three sets of correspondence, including one to the librarian of the School of Oriental and African Studies, University of London. These concerned what she called the 'big rip-offs': her clashes with two of her publishers and with Gardner. She stated that the material was open to inspection and publishing but three days later she recalled it all.

She also decided that she needed someone to take care of her papers should she die. Howard had been away for over a year now and though accounts of his life in Canada were far from encouraging, she had to face the fact that he could well remain there permanently. Even if he did return, she knew that he would never be able to cope with 'the sorts of people' who were 'stealing' from her'.[71] She had recently received a copy of yet another thesis. This was by Jane Bryce, the student introduced by Jane Grant with whom she had corresponded the year before. The more she read it, the more impressed she was. Here was someone who approached Arthur Ravenscroft, Bessie's ultimate yardstick for a perceptive critic, in her assessment of Bessie's writing; in fact she surpassed him 'in love both for me and my work', as she put it. She made a sudden decision. She wrote to Jane Bryce, explaining how she needed to be able to place her papers 'in the hands of a professional person', and asked her if she would consider taking on the job of literary executor. Paddy Kitchen had told her many times that her letters were valuable. 'Something so bad has happened to me that I finally agree with her. On my death the University people will rip into my house and seize every scrap of paper in sight.'[72] Jane Bryce, somewhat hesitantly, agreed to consider the appointment, and Bessie was very pleased. However, she never drew up the legal papers as she had planned to and the agreement remained informal. After February 1984 their correspondence lapsed as Jane Bryce travelled to a teaching post in Africa.

At a time when Bessie could hardly have felt more isolated, she received a letter that brought the unreality of her childhood into unexpected focus.

'Dear Miss Head,' it began, 'Looking through one of the school magazines, I came across a photograph of you which resembled a long-lost Aunt of mine.' The writer added that her aunt's name was also 'Bessie', so she had written straight to the editor and asked for her address. 'But', she continued, 'I have some explaining to do. My name is Veronica Samuel [née Billings] . . . My mother's name was Rhoda . . . Her mother was Nellie Heathcote, who reared me.'[73] Bessie's childhood companion and admirer had traced her. The magazine article was that which had appeared in *Drum* in 1982, 'Notes from a Quiet Backwater'.

Bessie and Veronica Samuel exchanged letters regularly after this. It transpired that they had children of almost the same age. Veronica's eldest children, twins, were born the same year as Howard. Veronica wanted to see her aunt as soon as possible. Bessie explained that she could never return to South Africa until 'the Boers' were out of power 'for that is their law'. Veronica and her husband Lionel Samuel then began to make plans to travel to Serowe.

This contact with Veronica Samuel revived memories of her childhood that Bessie believed she had discarded forever. She had studied the stamp on Veronica Samuel's letter and noted that 'the city hall looks the same'. She recalled the Afrikaans name of the local river, 'Die Dorp Spruit', and mused over the fact that East Street and Boom Street and the Voortrekker Museum were all still there. 'I have travelled a long distance away from Pietermaritzburg, where I was born,' she continued, obviously not referring only to geography.

I am always forced to give biographical information, so everything on me begins rather pathetically: "Bessie Head was born the 6th July, 1937, in Pietermaritzburg, South Africa." It had become an almost meaningless statement as I had left that small town, oh, so long ago. But I was forced to write it so. One had to begin somewhere, even though one travelled far away from home. Your letters begin to make that small town not so meaningless now.[74]

In 1982 Bessie was supposed to attend a conference in Zimbabwe entitled 'Women in Southern Africa: Strategies for Change'. She had been given the invitation rather casually, at the last moment, because the chairman of the local committee did not know how to get in touch with her. Though she was surprised about this she accepted, only to send a telegram cancelling her participation at the last moment when she was again treated in an off-hand way by the same woman in connection with the final travel arrangements. 'I saw a vista of ill-treatment ahead of me,'[75] she later confided in a friend. Afterwards she regretted having done so and consequently apologised. This was when she explained she had had a 'personal crisis going'.[76]

Despite this refusal, a new invitation to Zimbabwe arrived in early 1983. This time the Zimbabwe Publishing House in Harare was planning the first Zimbabwe Book Fair in August. In connection with this, a workshop for African writers had been arranged. Bessie Head and Mongane Wally Serote were invited from Botswana; Nadine Gordimer, Alex La Guma, Ingoapele Madingoane and Lewis Nkosi from South Africa. Bessie was apparently in the midst of a new crisis. She again made a sudden decision not to attend. This time the telegram stated that she was dying of lung cancer. 'Please keep this confidential,' she added. The news naturally leaked out. James Currey, attending the Book Fair on the Heinemann stall, was completely shocked, as were Bessie's volunteer friends now working in Zimbabwe. Their shock turned to puzzled anger as they gradually learnt the real state of affairs. Once more Bessie regretted her action, though no more than to refer to the telegram as 'light-hearted' and 'jocular' two years later.[77]

Another important international invitation now arrived. She was asked to attend the Writers' Week at the next Adelaide Festival in Australia. The arrangement was scheduled from 28 February to 10 March 1984, but Bessie was offered additional speaking engagements at universities in Melbourne, Sydney and Hobart, Tasmania, extending her visit an extra week. She accepted without hesitation. The only other guest speaker from the African continent was André Brink from South Africa. Bessie had perforce to depart from Africa via Harare airport.

Before she could give any attention to preparing her material for this trip, however, she had an important obligation to fulfil. It was the completion of 'the damned difficult historical novel'. As she put it to Paddy Kitchen: 'The damn thing isn't finished yet. Damn and blast.'[78]

As yet another summer of drought hit the country, Bessie stuck more and more doggedly to her typewriter. The year before, she had been given a special gift. Her friend Pat Spann had long been concerned about the trouble she was having with her old typewriter. While Bessie was in Gaborone, they went out together and bought her a new one, an event they celebrated grandly. Bessie told Paddy Kitchen how hard she had found it to adjust to it: 'For years I typed out 5 books on a light, tinny Remington. You know how long a book journey is so one's fingers get entirely adapted to the little tin thing one works on. I suffered agonies with the new typewriter. It was heavy and almost immovable . . . For weeks my wrist and fingers ached until they built up muscle for the new typewriter.'[79]

In the same way as when she was writing *When Rain Clouds Gather*, the heat beat down on her as she worked and the world outside shimmered in eerie stillness. 'It is even deathly silent as I type now,' she had written to Paddy Kitchen in October. 'In good years we walk through a perfumed village because the Makoba tree blooms at this time but this year the Makoba stands black and stark against the horizon. A sort of dead weight of despair settles on one's mind.'[80] By December the situation was even worse. Bessie flung off her clothes and, clad only in bra and panties with 'a fearful eye on the window in case someone should call',[81] she typed from dawn to dusk. As she described the drought and rinder-pest epidemic of 1895–6 in dismal sentences such as 'The whole earth died that year', she looked out through her window and saw that it was so.

Christmas came, increasing her isolation. Usually there were breaks for shopping or fetching the post from the village but even these were now excluded. Early in the new year *A Bewitched Crossroad* was finally finished. With indescribable relief she sent off three copies of the manuscript, one to each of her agents and one directly to Ad Donker.

A Bewitched Crossroad had taken ten years to materialise. At times driven by great energy and determination, at times working in fits and starts, Bessie struggled to shape it into a satisfactory form.

Typing away at the final chapters in the heat of a Serowe Christmas, she must often have thought back ruefully on the simple, enthusiastic plan she had had in 1973 to write a novel on Khama III. Yet it was her unwavering admiration of him that had kept the plan alive. Later she called it her major obsession.

In early 1974, when she was planning to emigrate to Norway, one of her regrets was that she would have to abandon the idea of writing any more about him. 'I had found the key to Southern Africa in Khama, The Great,' she wrote to Wendy and Patrick Cullinan, 'and I kept on thinking that I'd have to do much more on him – perhaps that great novel on Southern Africa because my generation never accepted that we were the dogs of anyone.'[82]

Though the completion of *Serowe: Village of the Rain Wind* shortly afterwards rounded off her first written account of Khama, the fact that she decided to stay in Botswana after all left the possibility of something better – 'the great novel on Southern Africa' – very open. In July 1974 she was already working on this idea: 'Here is my grand proposition and opening lines: "It has always been black man's country . . .",'[83] she wrote to Betty Sleath then. She added the story about how she had been standing in a queue in the post office and chatting to one of the local cattle farmers, who had said, 'Well of course Botswana has always been black man's country.' 'There,' thought Bessie, 'there I have my opening lines.' As it happened, she changed her mind; but she did not waste those lines.

It was not until her trip to Iowa that she was again able to give the project her full attention. In those months in America she was borne on a wave of productivity. On the other hand, only now did she begin to realise how intimidating the task was. Yet she returned to Serowe feeling that she was well into her stride: 'Most of it is of such personal benefit to me that I have never enjoyed writing as much as I do now,' she wrote in July. In the same letter she began to indicate what exactly her work was encompassing: 'I am mainly working on . . . the manner in which the people lost the land.'[84] Two months later she told Mary Benson that the book was 'not so much Khama – I may have him in mind all the while – but a struggle to pull together the whole southern African experience at that time. I am mainly concentrating on the land question so he focuses only in that direction.'[85]

During this period Bessie had called her novel *Mother Winter*. It was a title of respect given to Khama III by the Bamangwato in a praise poem, expressive of his austere, dry and ascetic personality. Friends did not think it at all good but she stuck to it grimly: 'I do not care if the European mind appreciates it or not.' Bessie gradually became critical of her own rather sentimental adoration of Khama: 'I adore Khama, but I love his achievements more. I have always kept a great balance and sanity in my work and I don't want to discredit myself by showing blind worship for an idol. So I skid around Khama very carefully,'[86] she wrote. With a closer study of the original sources, Bessie had begun to realise that the garbled versions some history books give of Khama III can partly be blamed on the fact that he was 'very tricky material indeed. Some of him was good and some of him was very tricky.'[87] She admitted that several of her comments about him in *Serowe: Village of the Rain Wind* had been 'gushy' and she altered some of them before publication. 'But', she wrote to a Heinemann editor in January 1979, 'I'd love the other gush-gush to remain. Khama earned some of it.'[88]

The next bout of genuine concentration came in 1980, when Bessie and Howard moved to Gaborone. She was certain this would be her final tussle with Khama. Although she reported that she had the happy feeling that the novel was falling into shape, she returned to Serowe with the manuscript only half complete.

In August 1980 she discussed the question of obsessions with Patrick Cullinan:

I loved Robert Sobukwe obsessively. I have a number of such obsessive loves and sometimes obsessions do not allow for accuracy. Khama III is one of those obsessive loves and I struggle to wash that man right out of my hair and get it down on paper. It has been my major obsession, the Khama novel.

But she was enjoying her work:

My days though are often lit up with the sheer humour of Bamangwato history. [It] has been dominated by Khama men from 1875 when Khama III became Chief of the Bamangwato, to Tshekedi Khama and right through to Seretse Khama, who died on 13th July 1980 ... What makes me sit back and laugh and laugh is the strange and unique personalities of the three men. They were shocking, original and like jack-in-the-box surprises people could hardly cope with.[89]

With the novel at this half-finished stage, a new interruption occurred: the trip to Denmark. Others followed. It needed Michael Chapman's direct enquiries at the beginning of 1983 to push this protracted work into its final phase.

Throughout the years Bessie had continually referred to it as a 'historical novel'. The limitations she had felt imposed by the documentary nature of *Serowe Village of the Rain Wind* were not to hamper her this time, for she regarded herself first and foremost as a novelist: 'I have been the sort of novelist who took great liberties with the novel form, throwing almost anything into it,'[90] she once remarked; and earlier she had said: 'No one cuts the ground under the feet of a novelist. That's wide, free, joyous territory. Nothing dry and dull there but a world of magic.'[91]

Yet she could not disguise the fact that part of the delay in completing her book was to be found in her choice of genre: as her correspondence in the early eighties had often revealed, Bessie was trying to solve the old problem of giving historical facts immediate relevance and making history significant for modern readers.

Finally she did so by giving up her idea of a 'Khama novel'. With her lifelong interest in factual accuracy, she could in no way set aside the historical information she had been so long in gleaning in order to make Khama a suitably semi-fictitious main character, whose thoughts and ideas she could appear to interpret. 'I could only record more or less accurately what he had said or done,'[92] she said in 1985 . Instead she chose the life of an insignificant chieftain, by name Sebina, as her focal point. His lifespan almost corresponded with the whole nineteenth century and he was inadvertently a part of the epoch-making events of Southern Africa during that time. In this way the lives and destinies of Sebina and his clan 'were to mirror the anguish and wonder of a new era,.' as Bessie wrote on the first page of A Bewitched Crossroad.

Khama, as she had already hinted in 1980, is relegated to a less central role. He is portrayed instead as one of the towering personalities of that time, confronting on more than one occasion that other dominant figure, Cecil John Rhodes. By bringing Sebina's clan under the protection of Khama III, Bessie achieves much of her double aim. She can expand the scope of her canvas to include the whole of Southern Africa while keeping her focal centre. We are still in Khama's country, as we have been in all her preceding works.

The migratory existence of Sebina's clan during the second and third decades of the nineteenth century is referred to, but the real disaster striking the clan occurs when they are caught up in the final stages of the Wars of Calamity, or Mfecane, which from about 1816 onwards had been disrupting the lives of the indigenous inhabitants of Southern Africa.

The rise of Shaka and his transformation of his small following of Zulus to warriors of tremendous bravery and stamina started the Mfecane. Tribe after tribe fled from his attacks, spreading havoc before them. When one of his most brilliant men, Mzilikazi, deserted and established himself at the head of a tribe (to be called the Ndebele) as powerful as and even more brutal than the Zulus, there was little hope for the peaceful inhabitants trapped in between. Always with an eye for generous actions, Bessie includes a story of how Moshoeshoe, powerful king of the Sotho nation, spared the life of a cannibal who had eaten his grandfather with the words: 'I do not want to disturb the grave of my ancestors.' Her comment here was that these were 'the first words of compassion spoken in a land wracked by disaster' (p. 27). The fierce wars died out, and into one of the depopulated vacuums on the highveld caused by these tremendous migrations moved a third group of people: the Trekboers, escaping the British authorities at the Cape. Everyone needed land.

The trekkers were at first received with courteous interest. By combining force and diplomacy, they acquired enough land to establish themselves in two republics, the Orange Free State and the Transvaal Republic. They were determined to run their own affairs and retain their right to have black slaves, now called 'apprentices'. At first neither republic flourished.

With the expansion of the white settlers followed the spread of the missionaries. It became accepted, indeed desirable, for the various chiefs to have missionaries living among their people. It was, as Bessie puts it, a 'simple form of diplomacy that was to be of vital importance to many leaders in southern Africa' (p. 27). It was the resident missionary who wrote letters to the Governor of the Cape and other foreign powers, asking for protection for their land; it was he who helped the ruler to bring order into his financial affairs; he who often performed a valuable service by writing down the history of the tribe; and he who could sometimes alert the king to the duplicity of a proposed agreement with white settlers.

The question of converting to Christianity was not one that troubled most chiefs. They were very satisfied with their own religion, with its ancestor worship and the many rites marking the passing of the seasons. The greatest drawback of Christianity was its demand for monogamy. 'What', said a chief with twelve wives, 'would become of the other eleven. It would be a crime to cast them off like that' (p. 50). For most dedicated missionaries the toil was great and the harvest very small.

There was one exception. In the arid region to the west of the Transvaal Republic, a leader of the Bamangwato emerged in 1875, after fifteen years of internal struggle. He shone as a Christian convert, a man of upright character and a zealous reformer. His name was Khama III. Soon John Mackenzie, the missionary from the London Missionary Society established at Khama's capital, Shoshong, was extolling his praise in letters and published journals. Khama's image, as recorded by Mackenzie, 'permanently froze into one of a perfectionist, . . . an enlightened leader . . . a man of integrity and a great Christian.' It created a pause in the activities of the Europeans, this image of the perfect black man found at last. For by now Europeans were eyeing the African landscape, noting its natural resources and knowing it could be theirs. 'The indigenous people did not really exist, they had no power, they were heathens.' Except for Khama. 'Khama', as Bessie concludes in her fourth chapter, 'was to provide a resistance of image and prestige' (p. 57).

After suffering the buffetings and indignities of the Ndebele for years, Sebina and his people settled at Shoshong under Khama's protection. The Sebina clan thus became part of the radical change Khama was introducing. Since his conversion to Christianity, Khama had realised that certain of the ritual practices which had always been part of the Bamangwato's way of life were cruel or discriminatory. First he brought his people to see that the rain-making and circumcision rites which required secret human sacrifices had to be abolished. He approached the other central issue more cautiously, that of the *bogadi*, or brideprice, which had kept women as mere chattels in the eyes of the law. After a period when there were two forms of marriage contract, the traditional one requiring *bogadi*, and the Christian one, he called a huge meeting to discuss the moral issues connected with *bogadi*. After heated discussions, it was abolished. 'The missionaries have taught us that our wives are our equals . . . What utter rubbish,' said one of those in opposition to the reform (p. 171). But the women said that a great light had been given them that day.

Khama had a still larger role to play in the history of the country. In *A Bewitched Crossroad* the tribal migrations, local disruptions and social reform of which Sebina and Khama III were part are set against a much more ambitious backdrop, the white man's unrestrained scramble for land in the last years of the century. The discovery of diamonds and gold made the early land annexations of the trekkers look almost innocuous.

Despite the philanthropic and humanitarian sentiments of the British, there was often very little to distinguish their behaviour from that of the Boers who were overtly interested in securing land. The declaring of Bechuanaland a British Protectorate illustrates this.

The southern Tswana chiefs, constantly exposed to Boer attack, had sent petition after petition to the British government asking for protection, without eliciting any response. In 1876 Khama had said: 'The Boers are coming into [my country], and I do not like them. Their actions are cruel among us black people. We are like money, they sell us and our children. I ask Her Majesty to pity me and hear me' (p. 114).

It was only when the British realised how determined the Boer republics were to expand westwards that they acted. On the south west coast of Africa, the Germans were declaring the coastal regions and interior a protectorate. Unless Britain established a buffer state between the Boers and the Germans, her corridor into the interior, the so-called missionary road, would be lost. This she could only do by offering the Tswana tribes 'protection'.

In 1885 the many petitions were suddenly remembered. Without any preliminary discussions with the chiefs, who were now taken aback and uncooperative, it was decided to establish a Protectorate in the area occupied by the Tswana tribes. Its northern boundary was to be latitude 22 degrees, a direct extension of the northern border of the Transvaal Republic. This caused some amusement when Sir Charles Warren, with 4000 British soldiers, marched up through Bechuanaland proclaiming the Protectorate and finally reached the Bamangwato. Khama's territory stretched far north of this line. 'How can protection be offered so? Can a man be cut in two? Can a man or a house be protected and only half of it attended to? Why is my country cut in two, and, if divided, why just at this line?' (p. 115). It was an embarrassing question which Warren did not attempt to answer. The boundary of the Protectorate was later extended.

Just ten years later, the British were ready to hand over the 'protection' of these people to the most blatant land-grabber of them all: Cecil John Rhodes. Rhodes, with his dream of establishing a Cape to Cairo railway through Africa, with the British flag flying throughout the continent, had tricked the king of the once-powerful Ndebele, Lobengula, into signing his land away. He had gained control of the huge area north of the Transvaal, where he established the British South Africa Company, soon to become the new colony of Rhodesia. He then cast his gaze on the large stretches of Bamangwato territory to the west. He made secret plans with the British authorities to annex this and the rest of the Protectorate into his company.

Now it was that the chiefs Khama of the Bamangwato, Sebele of the Bakwena and Bathoen of the Bangwakwetse got wind of these plans. They asked how the

British government could desert them: 'Is [it] weary of us? We refuse thus to be cast away. We wish to remain under the protection of the Queen of England' (p. 189).

To the annoyance of Rhodes, they travelled to England to protest in person to the Colonial Secretary, Joseph Chamberlain. He was a friend of Rhodes and received the delegation coolly, assuring the chiefs that they would still be under the protection of the Queen. The Company was under the Queen and it would rule them on her behalf. The three chiefs were not duped. They knew far too much about the cruelties connected with rule by the British South Africa Company. What Chamberlain had not expected was the attention the three stately gentlemen attracted in England. In a number of humanitarian organisations, headed by the London Missionary Society, Khama III was already a well-known personality, the upright black Christian the missionaries Mackenzie and later Hepburn had written about. They took the chiefs to their hearts and their complaints to the highest offices of the state. The pressure brought to bear on the British government resulted in a very different kind of settlement from that which Rhodes had hoped for. Only a narrow strip on the eastern side of the Protectorate was made available to the Company for a railway line to link Rhodesia with Cape Town; and there were a few other minor concessions.

For the time being, Bechuanaland was secure. But a dramatic event ensured its future safety. Rhodes was completely discredited when his plan to send Dr Jameson into the South African Republic and oust Paul Kruger miscarried. With the failure of this Jameson Raid, he lost his powerful position and his important contacts. The British feared further scandals and cancelled all plans to transfer land.

It has surely become clear that *A Bewitched Crossroad* can hardly be called a historical novel in the sense that historical novels often have a romantic, adventurous element, for it sticks too doggedly to historically verified events, though its angle is new. Nevertheless, the book is formed as a novel: it has no list of contents, no maps, no index, though all three would have been most useful. However, each chapter is a clearly defined entity, depicting a particular series of events. Forgoing the traditional list of contents, Bessie Head introduces each chapter with a highly relevant quotation from the text itself so as to create an organising device.

Bessie once again shows her appreciation of rural African life and the African landscape. The harmonious existence of the Sebina clan in its early period contains the soaring descriptive prose that had characterised her earlier works: 'Life was peaceful. The land which surrounded the people lay in majestic sleep and stillness and the stars swung down low in the sky at night and glowed with pure blue lights between the dark, black bushes' (p. 11).

This is one of the first instances of South African history related from the point of view of the country's black inhabitants while using the records and tools of white scholarship and research. However, it is a sad story Bessie tells – of deception, greed and violence. Many minor tribes were wiped out. Many more lost their land. 'Once people lost the land, they lost everything,'[93] Bessie had once remarked; and she quotes Cecil John Rhodes as saying: 'I have taken everything from them but the air' (p. 193) – not one of his most quoted statements in earlier versions of Southern African history. It is a story of winners and losers, as so many stories are, but in this one winning is for whites only.

The exception seems to have been Khama the Great. For Bechuanaland, including the Bamangwato and the Sebina clan, miraculously escaped destruction. The storm passed on to other lands. The concluding lines of Bessie Head's saga remind us that Bechuanaland 'remained black man's country. It was a bewitched crossroad. Each day the sun rose on hallowed land' (p. 196).

Bessie gathers up her two lines of development – history as fact and history as fiction – in this unifying image of the 'centre of the storm'. Both the historical figure Khama III and her fictional protagonist Sebina are found there, where ordinary decencies persist and ordinary life goes on. In actual fact *A Bewitched Crossroad* becomes Bessie Head's final tribute to Ordinary Man; her final condemnation of the power people.

16

Australia
1984

The village of Serowe had always been conscious of its traditions. So it was not surprising when Leapeetswe Khama, Tshekedi's son, in 1976 broached the idea of a local museum. By the early eighties the idea was gaining support. A working committee was formed to raise funds and find a suitable site. After Seretse Khama Ian Khama had been proclaimed Paramount Chief in 1979, he agreed to become the patron of the project. In 1984 Leapeetswe gave the scheme added impetus by donating a family residence, the so-called ·Red House, and surrounding premises as a museum site, as well as personal belongings and furniture of historical interest. This colonial-style house, built about 1910 with a red-painted corrugated-iron roof (hence the name), had been used by Tshekedi Khama as a guest house. It had gradually fallen into disrepair and had not been used by the Khama family for some years.

It now became clear that restoring the Red House would be more expensive than local fund-raising efforts could manage. Foreign agencies were approached. A cash donation came in from the British High Commission in Harare and the Danish Volunteer Service agreed to provide a curator. The ground was cleared and fenced, and an outbuilding, a former garage, was repainted and made ready to house the museum temporarily.

The Norwegian Development Agency, Norad, agreed to finance the restoration of the Red House. DVS donated a project car, built a house for the curator, renovated the old servants' quarters thus providing three extra offices, and later provided an education officer and architect for the project. So with a combination of local initiative and foreign support the Serowe Museum was opened in October 1984. The idea was that it should encourage the local people to take a pride in their traditional arts and crafts, to rectify, in the words of their beloved Seretse Khama, the fact that they had been 'made to believe that we had no past to speak of, no history to boast of.'[1] Shortly afterwards, the name of the museum was changed to the Khama III Memorial Museum as an indication that the museum should serve the whole of the Central District of Botswana.

The museum soon acquired another valuable gift. Leapeetswe Khama donated the Khama Family Papers, dating from 1876 to 1959. A fire-proof safe had been built for them in the temporary museum while work gradually began on the restoring of the Red House. This cultural vigour in Serowe naturally also affected Bessie. The Danish curator, Maria Rytter, was keen to include her in some of the activities, well aware that here the local community had another important person to honour.

In December 1983, as she was working hard on her manuscript of *A Bewitched Crossroad*, she was approached by Ilse Meentz, a volunteer in the village, who asked her for an interview. Bessie agreed and the result provides an excellent record of her attitude to important issues at that stage of her life. For example she explained that she had written so much about women because it came naturally to do so: 'They accept a much larger share than men of the responsibility for the species, they draw attention to their situation,' she said. It was obvious that her thoughts were very taken up with the material she was working with daily. She moved on to discuss the special burden of being a black South African. Once again she quoted Cecil John Rhodes's statement that he had taken 'everything but the air' when he conquered Mashonaland and Matabeleland. As a black person looking over the land in South Africa, you get the same shocked feeling as that statement gives you, she said. 'There is absolutely nothing you can possess or identify with.' In Botswana on the other hand 'you get an environment where African history is a continuous theme. Touch on certain aspects of society and you feel you're going back in time.' As usual, though, Bessie did not resort to sentimental phrases or political clichés when discussing the plight of the black South African. She had demonstrated on several occasions that she had no time for South African refugees abroad who capitalised on their subjugated fellow South Africans at home: 'The biggest thing you can sell and shit on is the suffering of black people in South Africa – that's why early on I would have NOTHING to do with it. I saw it and how cheap the people were and are and I would have NOTHING to do with it.' That is why, she had said at that point, *When Rain Clouds Gather* is as apolitical as it is.[2]

Bessie spoke about her writing to Ilse Meentz. She saw herself as a writer with a self-dialogue. Her books had welled up from inside her.

You do not have to travel too far away from yourself to produce a book. You as a writer are aware that something has awoken in you – a dialogue whereby you are going to make a contribution to mankind's thoughts . . . It's always been a question of people surviving with people . . . Questions of love and human survival are very central to my work. I know exactly where I am travelling and that I have started unfolding my message but it's not complete yet.

Then she went on very calmly to quote Boris Pasternak, from memory of course: 'I think the Russian writer Boris Pasternak gives the most profound definition of what I mean by mankind's survival where he says a human being is like a kind of catch-all hold-all world where you help people survive in the sense that people live in you.' She quoted the final stanza of 'Daybreak':[3]

In me are people without names
Children, stay-at-homes, trees.
I am conquered by them all
And that is my only victory.

By identifying herself again with 'people without names', she was once more showing how important this her 'only victory' was for her. She added: 'I would like that kind of world to be expressed in a more solid way, in a more positive way if eventually you impress on people that the only way in which we can survive is if we as individuals are holy to each other.'[4]

Other volunteers coming to the village also became her friends. Katrin Sell, for example, a mathematics teacher from the German Volunteer Service, made a point of contacting her and they soon became friends. Katrin would often visit Bessie over the weekend, taking along six beers which they would consume. For a long time Katrin worked on translating *The Collector of Treasures* into German, because she wanted her sister to be able to enjoy it. She was very knowledgeable on European history, and Bessie and she discussed historical events and their interpretation avidly.

Hugh and Mmatsela Pearce were now back in Serowe. After moving to Lesotho in 1974, Hugh had returned to a job as District Officer. They began to see more and more of Bessie. She would arrive at their house to tell them about some disaster that had struck her and they would try to help her sort things out. Or she would call in on one of her rounds, selling gooseberry jam. Kerstin Kvist, a Swede who had come to Serowe to work with Patrick van Rensburg on the re-establishment of the Brigades and who lived near Swaneng School, also saw Bessie regularly during her time in Serowe. They soon developed the habit of doing their shopping together on a Saturday morning. Kerstin Kvist would buy some beers for Bessie and then give her a lift home.

Bosele had always remained a part of Bessie's life. Bessie passed the Boiteko gardens on her way to town and would often call in and see her. Or Bosele would trudge up the hill to Bessie's cottage if she had not heard anything of her for a few days. In 1982 Bosele was seriously ill and spent some weeks in the hospital in Francistown. Bessie phoned the hospital every day to hear how she was; when she returned home to convalesce, Bessie visited her frequently. In this way they kept up their friendship. Bosele still dreamt of the day when Bessie would start up her garden again and they could work together the way they had done ten years before. When Bessie finally finished her book, Bosele began to hope that it would happen. But when, for the fourth year running, the country was stricken by drought, Bessie could not afford to pay for water to water her plants.

Then finally there was Ruth Forchhammer, who began to get to know Bessie better about the time she finished *A Bewitched Crossroad*. 'It is as if Bessie had friends for every purpose,' said Ruth once. 'A friend to listen to all her troubles, another one to help her solve her practical difficulties, another to lend her money, another to give her lifts to town, another to enjoy a drink with.'[5] It may seem strange, in the circumstances, that Bessie nevertheless felt herself 'an absolutely solitary person'.[6] Perhaps this sense of isolation had something to with the fact that she was in the village, but not of it: apart from Bosele Sianana, she had no real friends among the local people. She was actually better at conducting relationships on paper – more caring and considerate, able sometimes to look at herself more objectively, given sometimes to dry humour. Yet her friends accepted her as she was, enjoying her outbursts of vivacity, her loquacity and spontaneity. Her isolation was a state of the soul.

Bessie had decided to dedicate *A Bewitched Crossroad* to three friends who had played a special part in helping it to materialise. These were her 'two favourite librarians', Pat Spann and Thandiwe Kgosidintsi, and her 'brother', Cassim Kikia. He was her chief economic adviser. Since he had fled from South Africa about the same time as Bessie, he had established both a happy family and a profitable business. In vain, though, did he try to bring some order and system into Bessie's finances.

Just one month after Bessie had sent off her manuscript, Ad Donker cabled an offer to publish *A Bewitched Crossroad*. In the good old days, Bessie had been used to prompt and positive reactions to her writing. But never this prompt. Heinemann was Bessie's primary publisher, so some sort of agreement would have to be arrived at with them, but as Bessie was due to leave for Australia very shortly, it was agreed that Donker and his wife, also part of the publishing firm, would visit her on her return to discuss matters. After her experiences with *A Question of Power* and *Serowe: Village of the Rain Wind*, the present offer was an unexpected run of luck and she was determined to accept it.

Feeling exceptionally optimistic, Bessie left for Australia. In transit through Harare airport, however, she 'learned something about Zimbabwe security. It is pretty tight and alert.'[7] On both her outward and return journey she felt that she was treated somewhat brusquely by the immigration authorities. On her return, though she had a Botswana passport, they detained her briefly and issued her with a refugee visa. All this she ascribed to her own false telegram (about lung cancer) of the previous July. She had hastened to send a letter of apology to the publishing house but never heard from them. It seems likely that her interpretation of these incidents was the result of her own paranoia – and a somewhat guilty conscience. She needed a visa to pass through Zimbabwe and it may have been an irregularity there that caused the trouble.

This slight upset seemed to be the only one in an exceptionally happy trip. Bessie had rubbed shoulders with the elite of African writing in Berlin. This time her name featured beside such internationally acclaimed writers as Angela Carter, Bruce Chatwin, Russell Hoban, Salman Rushdie and D M Thomas. All in all 33 writers, about half of them from Australia and New Zealand, attended the Writers' Week arranged in connection with the Adelaide Festival, one of Australia's important cultural events.

The delegates had been asked to prepare a paper entitled 'Living on the Edge'. At an early date, Bessie asked if she could talk on 'Living on the Horizon' instead. 'Living on the Edge' was a title that made her feel a bit squeamish, she said. In fact 'Living on the Horizon' suited her philosophy of the broad generous view perfectly. It took her thoughts back to her old guru, Swami Vivekananda, who had also used this expression.

When she arrived in Adelaide she realised that this was 'a big, big do'.[8] A large marquee had been erected, with pleasant lawns and shady trees across the road from it, and here the writers gathered. They were housed in a gracious mansion outside Adelaide. Its former owner had transformed part of the bare and sun-beaten Adelaide Hills into an imitation English stately home, set in a park with fountains, cypresses and deer. Three of the guests had no intention of braving the Australian outback, however. The thought of having to share bathrooms sent them straight back to the centre of Adelaide.

In Bessie's opinion, some of the writers never really unbent. Though they sold millions of copies of their books, they could not, as she put it, 'afford to talk to people'. Others were friendly and accessible. When people approached Bessie to ask where she came from, their faces fell and they looked bewildered when she replied 'Botswana'. 'And what have you written?' they asked. She told them. The bewilderment spread. 'They knew not me nor Botswana.'9

Three days after the start of Writers' Week, Bessie made her first public appearance, reading her short story 'The Special One'. Here she spent some time explaining where Botswana was and about her own village life. As she left the platform, people flocked about her. Some told her that they were relieved to hear something light-hearted and unpolitical from Southern Africa. She could see the audience suddenly responding to her own village mentality.

'That white-dominated world is closed and narrow,' she told Paddy Kitchen. 'It is as though many small villages in Europe and England transposed themselves onto the Australian soil.' She said that it reminded her of life in the United States hinterland. 'They kept that village mentality too. But with the Adelaide Festival they open up. I talked to the most receptive audience in the world.'10

Her books were on display with all the other participating writers' works. Before she gave her talk, 'Living on an Horizon' (as she now called it), *The Collector of Treasures* was sold out. *Maru* and *Rain Clouds* went next. Before the Festival closed, she saw the very last copies of *Serowe: Village of the Rain Wind* and *A Question of Power* disappear from the stand, while she signed copies till her hand ached. She noted with some surprise that many of the important names had piles of unsold books still on the stalls. The audience, she said, 'quietly fell in love' with her. 'It was the most tender and beautiful thing that has ever happened to me . . . My village created an echo that they wanted to explore.'11

On three occasions André Brink and Bessie were called on to comment on power-sharing and the sharing of wealth from the point of view of South Africa and Botswana respectively. Bessie said that they replied in their own ways: 'He with death, I with life.'12 The crises over, she could regard society in Botswana magnanimously. Brink, too, came in for his share of praise: the first good white South African she had met, Bessie told reporters.

After the Festival, Bessie's extra week in Australia was crowded with engagements. First she spent two days in Melbourne, where Heinemann had arranged for her to give a talk. Then she flew to Tasmania where she had speaking engagements in Hobart, at the University of Tasmania, and Launceston. Back in Sydney, she addressed gatherings at two further universities. She was also interviewed twice: by Suzanne Hayes of the Adelaide College of Technical Education and Andrew Peek of the Tasmanian College of Adult Education.13 Finally, on 18 March, she began the long homeward journey.

It had been a successful trip, giving her morale a welcome boost, but she was glad to return home from her 'long trip to the end of the world'. She told her niece Veronica: 'I am getting old too. Ha, Ha!'14

Shortly after her return, the Donkers visited her. Donker's editor, Jeff Probst, had already written to her with some comments on *A Bewitched Crossroad* and Donker was willing to leave them to settle the various points he had raised. He was more interested in reaching an agreement about the actual publishing of the book. The discussions were conducted in a relaxed and friendly atmosphere. Bessie had heard rumours that the Heinemann African Writers' Series was closing down. This convinced her that she should let Donker handle her new novel. He was offering her generous terms. He wished to secure Southern African rights for the book and take on the responsibility for marketing it internationally. He hoped that he would be able to sell subsidiary rights to Heinemann if they were interested.

Karen and Ad Donker enjoyed seeing the setting for the 'Serowe' book. They noted with interest the rubber hedge which Bessie had described in the first piece of prose she had published from Serowe, 'The Green Tree'. In fact they took a slip of this *tlharesetala* home with them and planted it. Still called 'Bessie's tree', it continues to thrive in the Donker garden. Bessie was calm and pleasant throughout the visit. What is more, she avoided getting herself into an excitable alcoholic state when taken out to dinner by her guests. Considering the reports from other visitors from these years, that simple fact seems more indicative than any other of how much this contract meant to her.

By the middle of June the technicalities had been worked out and Christine Green, Bessie's agent, could write to Ad Donker giving him 'the go-ahead on the contract for *A Bewitched Crossroad*.[15] Jeff Probst had suggested that the first chapters were superfluous, but this she could not accept: 'They act as a kind of quick reference and refrain to things said and done throughout the book.' And she would not consider changing the title to 'an interesting African' one. Nor did she agree that people 'have heard it all before'.[16] She felt that what she had written about the Mfecane was new.

The contract was signed and Bessie received the first, much-needed cheque from Donker. By the end of July she was correcting galleys and the last batch was sent off in the middle of September. Still she kept revising. At that late stage she managed to rectify one 'fatal, fatal omission',[17] inserting her indebtedness to the unpublished student essay which had given her the background for her characters Dalaunda and Tumediso.

The sense of achievement and relief that accompanied the publication of her 'historical novel' is perhaps reflected in a joyous description she gave of herself about the same time. Someone had told her she had appeared intimidating when they met on a previous occasion:

People have to be. I am the organiser of the universe and very bossy. From my right hand issue planets. From my left hand issue stars. I have to see that everything stays in order and the planets do not collide with the stars. When something threatens order and peace then I get mad as hell. But an organiser is not a dictator. An organiser takes care of everything.[18]

Such glimpses of her old insouciance are rare.

Just before she left for Australia, Bessie received a special South African visitor and a letter from an old friend. The visitor was Ellen Kuzwayo, who asked for an interview. Bessie was in an expansive frame of mind and agreed. She did not regret it. Ellen Kuzwayo was in the final stages of writing her autobiography, which could also be called the story of her people. She was a highly cultivated and educated woman who had moved from the relative stability of her late-nineteenth-century rural family environment to the disjointed chaos of life in Soweto. Nadine Gordimer describes her as someone who had 'Africanised the Western concept of woman'.[19] Ellen Kuzwayo, pleased by this chance to meet Bessie. asked her to write the Foreword to her book *Call Me Woman*.[20] Bessie did so.

The letter came from Jean Marquard. She had tried to visit her in 1979, three years after her first visit, accompanied by Miriam Tlali, one of the other important black women novelists of the region. Jean became ill and the trip had to be cancelled. After battling with bad health for some time, she was now well again and working on an article on Bessie. She wrote saying that she wished to come and interview her, bringing three Honours students with her. Bessie did not feel that the embargo she had placed on such interviews applied to Jean Marquard and agreed. They arrived at the very end of March, a few days after the Donkers' visit. At first the visitors could not find Bessie's house. Serowe was then a maze of small unmarked side roads and it had been about eight years since Jean Marquard was there last. Finally she had to go into the post office to ask for directions.

Though Bessie met the party with her usual initial friendliness, the weekend was not an unqualified success. After inviting her to lunch at the Tshwaragano Hotel, and providing the fifteen beers she drank, the group spent the afternoon in one of the hotel rooms 'working'. The interview was taped but Jean Marquard did not afterwards consider the long monologue of any value for her. In fact at one stage she stretched out on the bed and fell asleep.

The question of a fee was broached. Jean Marquard gave the standard reply: the University never paid for such interviews, considering that a writer would also benefit from any article published. But Bessie was taken to the Serowe Hotel for the evening meal. Though Jean Marquard thought that both the meal and Serowe as a whole were perfectly ghastly and Bessie the most expensive interviewee she had ever encountered,[21] they parted amicably and for the last time. Jean Marquard, the pioneer researcher of Bessie Head, was to die of cancer in 1984, aged forty-three.

The next day Bessie met Katrin Sell. 'Hello, Bessie,' she called in passing. 'Did your visitors find you?' She told Bessie how Jean Marquard had been asking for directions to her house in the post office. Bessie was furious. She immediately imagined that Jean must have been gathering secret information about her from the villagers. She simply did not believe the story about needing directions because she was certain Jean knew where she lived.

This was when Bessie wrote a distressed letter to the University of the Witwatersrand complaining about the way lecturers and students had taken many hours of her time over the years without offering her any kind of fee. 'Eventually I feel that too much is being taken from me and nothing given in return. I am being exploited under the guise of adoring my work.'[22]

She received a concerned reply from the Deputy Registrar stating that the problem of paying for interviews was not one they had come up against before, but that the usual international practice seemed to be not to pay for interviews. She thanked her for all the help she had given the students and the pleasure her writing had brought to her personally. She recommended that Bessie impose whatever conditions she thought fit in future before making any agreement.[23] Bessie's reply was short and to the point. She would do no further interviews. 'This door is finally closed.'[24]

This obsessively suspicious attitude towards researchers and media people was becoming a permanent state. Her accusations this time were ridiculous, though this did not stop her from relating the story afterwards, with embellishments. She nonetheless retained her own finely drawn distinctions in this matter. She still 'adored' most students; and she would nearly always agree to an interview by post even if she refused to meet people.

One student, however, experienced her rage. She was a German girl, Hanno Egner, one of those who had participated in the Workshop programme at the Berlin Festival in 1979 and had been inspired and uplifted by Bessie's warmth and originality. 'Come and see me,' Bessie had said enthusiastically to the students. 'You would always be welcome in my humble little home.' The years passed and Hanno went on a research trip to Southern Africa. She had not forgotten Bessie Head. From Johannesburg she sent her a letter asking if she could visit her. Bessie refused, telling her of the way she had been mistreated by rapacious university people. Unfortunately Hanno did not receive the letter before she left for Botswana, and the sudden opportunity of a lift to Serowe made her decide to try her luck anyway. She had been interviewing other writers and had never met anything but friendliness. After a number of enquiries she found her way to Bessie's house. As she stood hesitating at the gate, Bessie caught sight of her from inside the house. A rotund fury, she stormed down the front path, her hand raised threateningly. Hanno Egner retreated in confusion, to the accompaniment of Bessie's choice expletives. 'You got what you deserved at my gate. But you had a lucky day, madam. I could have KILLED you at my gate for being a cheater and exploiter,'[25] Bessie later wrote to her. However, it was Hanno Egner who had the last word. She wrote explaining that she had not received Bessie's letter of refusal and reminding Bessie of her invitation in Berlin. She concluded her letter: 'I never thought that "field work" could be so dangerous.'[26]

Bessie had been under pressure for months: first to complete her book; then to have her work ready for the Australian trip; then to meet the Donkers; and finally to do the interview with Jean Marquard and the students. There were two other perennial worries that had also helped to tip the scales. The news of Howard was depressing. And her financial affairs were a mess.

When Howard had arrived in Toronto to stay with his father, the plan was for him to get some form of further education or training. He was very keen on becoming a musician. He started playing the saxophone and the trumpet, showing considerable talent, and Harold Head began to make plans for him to enrol in a university to study music. He now found that his knowledge of mathematics and physical science needed to be improved to meet the entrance requirements.

His father expected to arrange for him to have tutoring, but Howard was not sufficiently motivated to overcome this hurdle. This door was thus closed. He searched unsuccessfully for some training where his interests and his qualifications could merge, while his father became increasingly impatient. Howard moved into lodgings, seeking independence. He visited Tom Holzinger, now married and living in Montreal, but returned to Toronto. He found various kinds of work and at one stage tried a printer's course. Bessie often got news of Howard from Tom Holzinger, because Howard did not write often and when he did he did 'not supply a consistent story'.[27] His father had managed to acquire immigrant status for him, which could open up for permanent settlement in the country, but this he did not particularly value. Meanwhile, his passport had expired and he did nothing about renewing it, despite many reminders from both Bessie and Tom Holzinger.

Bessie had lived close to poverty most of her life. In her best moments, this state suited her. She could seem almost childlike in her attitude to material things. She felt no urge to amass possessions. She hardly ever bought books, though they would seem to have been an essential part of her existence. Those books her friends sent her she treasured and read again and again. She often referred to the way she copied sentences from *Doctor Zhivago* or stanzas from Pasternak's poems and stuck them up on the wall or beside the kitchen sink. If she borrowed a book from the library and found something she liked, she could well type out a whole section or a complete short story to refer to after returning the book.

Her clothing requirements were equally humble. After her trip to Nigeria she did develop a passion for the more colourful and better-quality kaftan-style smocks, but her dress pattern remained constant. She sewed her dresses herself. She bought two and a half metres of material, folded it in half, cut a hole at the folded edge for her head, and sewed a seam in the middle section of both edges. This left a gap at the top for her arms and an open flap at the bottom to swing the legs. 'I live on a see-saw. I get fat. I get thin. When I am thin I am happy or in love with someone (always very secret). When I am fat I am lonely and struggling with a private problem. A dress like this just solves the problem of a wardrobe,'[28] she wrote to her niece shortly after returning from Australia, when Veronica offered her some dress material as a present. Bessie cut her hair herself with a pair of nail-scissors if she could not get to a hairdresser and struggled with a decrepit typewriter for years until Pat Spann gave her a new one. She made simple nourishing meals, partly because Howard was not keen on exotic food, but also because she could not afford expensive cuts of meat. When Paddy Kitchen sent her a cookery book about this time, she studied the recipes avidly and began to savour the possibility of a changed lifestyle: intimate dinner parties and sumptuous cooking.[29] There is something touching in the simple way she lived her life, a constant confirmation of her desire to be 'ordinary'.

Considering these humble requirements, and the fact that she had paid cash for her house, it is sometimes difficult to see why she was constantly in debt. For her writing did bring in a steady annual sum. Until her dramatic break with Giles Gordon and Davis-Poynter about nine years earlier, she had indeed been able to manage on her royalties. Her best year had been 1968/69, when she declared her income as R2,200. There were great variations after that, but her average taxable income until 1980 was about P900, never enough to have to pay income tax. This amount represents all her foreign income from book advances and royalties. As yet another facet of her many-sided personality, Bessie showed a surprisingly good business sense. After the initial clash with the Botswana authorities over the question of paying tax, her accounts show that she had an excellent grasp of her transactions with the Department of Income Tax; just as she kept a sharp eye on her own sources of income and knew exactly what was owed her.

After she began to travel abroad in 1977, she probably came home with small extra sums of money. But it was at this stage that the cost of living rose drastically, and, with a teenage son to support, she struggled more and more to make ends meet. This period culminated in her serious efforts to get herself some form of employment after she had been granted citizenship. When nothing came of these plans, she returned to Serowe and took up her old life. Howard was still not off her hands, and though she was definitely receiving more in royalties (and had to pay income tax most years now), she lived in a state of chronic debt.

Her bank account was mostly overdrawn and she relied heavily on her friends for loans between the arrival of cheques from England. Cassim Kikia knew most about this side of Bessie's life. He could see from her expression the moment she appeared in the door of his shop, if this was a day when she needed money. She would approach him shyly, often with downcast eyes. Or she would appear with her basket of homemade jam and look at him appealingly. Cassim Kikia would buy some bottles, to add to the huge supply his wife already had on their kitchen shelf. If, on the other hand, the bank had received a money transfer from her agent, she would come bursting in, money in her hand, ready to pay her debts. Or she would see him crossing the Mall and run towards him, embracing him exuberantly, much to the man's discomfort, with the news that her ship had come in and she wanted to repay him. 'Not now, Bessie,' Cassim Kikia would say time after time, 'use that money to buy food.' But she would insist on paying something and a compromise would be reached.[30] That would mean that she could also pay Ruth Forchhammer or one of the other friends something of what she owed them, because others also gave Bessie generous help. And after having left something in her bank account to pacify the bank manager, and buying the groceries they badly needed, there was not much left of that money. All too soon she would be back on Cassim Kikia's doorstep. He could become very indignant at the thought of this brilliant writer being forced to borrow money while her books were selling well. Where was the money going? he kept asking.

Though she lived so frugally herself, she had always tried to give Howard whatever he needed. With the years, his tastes grew expensive and his needs increased. She never ignored her obligations as a mother and some friends say she spoilt Howard; clearly he absorbed much of her income. He had not been at home for some years, however, and even the trip to Australia did not seem to improve things.

Bessie enjoyed only two luxuries herself. During all her poorest months in Francistown, she never gave up smoking. With the years she became a chain smoker until suddenly, amazing though it seems, she dropped it completely. 'I never touched the destroyer again,' she later wrote.[31]

She took to drinking instead. This had always been her second indulgence. From the days when she had launched out on her writing career in Cape Town, and put the admonishing tone of Miss Farmer and the concept of sin behind her forever, she had enjoyed alcohol. She always preferred beer and could drink excessively on occasions, straight from the can, tossing the beers back like a man. No one can say when dependency on liquor replaced this social drinking. But Bessie herself would probably have said that it happened when she gave up smoking. And beers were more expensive than cigarettes. There is no doubt that this drained her income.

Bessie had once had many high-flown and impossible dreams. She still had one left. She could win the Nobel Prize for Literature. She could often joke about winning this prize and thus solving all her financial problems forever. 'It's a good thing Howard is doing commercial courses,' she wrote to Mona Pehle once. 'We can't have two artist types in this house, dreaming about winning the Nobel Prize.'[32] But the most amusing story relates to the Department of Taxes in Selebi-Pikwe. In 1984 she had written submitting evidence to show that they had over-assessed her earnings and asked in a postscript: 'One day I may win the Nobel Prize for Literature – about P40 000 (actually 2–3 million pula). Would that prize money be taxable?'[33] Three months later she received a reply: 'Dear Madam, I refer to your letter of 5th April 1984. The question of taxing Nobel Prize for Literature money will be dealt with at the time it is received.'[34]

Though this prestigious prize did not seem in sight, in early May 1984 Bessie received a letter from Christine Green with the prospect of an unexpected income. Christine told her that Heinemann were interested in commissioning her to write her autobiography. Bessie responded promptly: 'I have ample material for it in notes, in papers, in letters to private friends. There is no sex and love for these 46 years of my life but rather a rich spiritual discipline which I feel now is finally coming into its own. Go ahead and sign up with Heinemann.'[35]

Bessie said that she understood a commission to be different from a contract: a commission did not have to be paid back. She asked if this was so and said that she needed a lot of money. Howard's air ticket back from Canada had to be paid and her house needed a new roof. She suggested asking for £5000. In actual fact she was under a misapprehension as regards a commission. The advance Bessie would receive on signature of the contract was to keep her going while she was producing the book, but it was against royalties, so she would have eventually 'repaid' it.

Meanwhile she began to plan her autobiography and by the end of May had submitted some suggestions. She said she wished to call it *Living on an Horizon* because this title described someone who 'lives outside all possible social contexts, free, independent, unshaped by any particular environment, but shaped by internal growth and living experience'. She explained that she would need a year to write the book because she would have to 'set up a workshop' and draw on the material she had collected over the years. In other words, it would be more in the category of a research project than a novel and would take longer than a novel to write. She added that she had three photographs only from her early youth and they would need to be copied.

Although her life had been fairly evenly divided between South Africa and Botswana, 27 years in South Africa, 20 in Botswana, she did not think she could write much about her childhood. She did not have much information about her mother and feared that she would not be able to get any more.

Other countries honour their citizens and help them find their relatives but not white South Africa. I am as anxious to avoid any knowledge of my mother's white relatives as they were anxious to destroy my mother and disown me . . . Can the early beginnings remain as spare as that?

She then went on to say that her Botswana experience would form the bulk of the book. 'It is incredibly rich in learning, both inwardly and socially. I express a surprise about this because everything happened to me unawares, grew upon me slowly and in a natural way.'[36] She said that she had not expected books to grow out of her life or that a 'special and harmonious relationship would unfold' between her and her environment.

When she made statements of this sort, Bessie could give the impression that her life was taking on a calmer structure. The sense of fragmentation and chaos that had constantly battered her was apparently being replaced with a feeling of cohesion and stability. As she herself had admitted, history had had a very good effect on her sanity. By that she meant not only the act of writing, beneficial as that mammoth task had been for her self-respect, but the long, conscious process it had involved, the shaping of a historical framework for herself, enabling her to relate to the events of her own country and slowly building up her own sense of worth and dignity. And of course, the conviction she had had, on seeing *A Bewitched Crossroad* published, that she had here demonstrated her sense of identity with the ordinary black inhabitants of the continent. This was her gift of 'the God title'. After long and painful struggles, Bessie was beginning to realise that her rather grand description of herself as a New African so many years before was in fact beginning to manifest itself. But still there was the darker side: the outbursts of rage, the unreasonable feelings of victimisation, the knowledge that she was still an outsider in her village of Ordinary People.

Heinemann were sent a copy of the outline of her autobiography, which they found acceptable. Their main interest was to reach an agreement as far as the commission fee was concerned. Christine Green also sent a copy to the publishers Hamish Hamilton. Here the reaction was less positive. The rights director, Clare Alexander, noted that Bessie did not really want to go into detail about her childhood. If she intended to write an autobiography where she focused mainly on her fiction and its roots, she said, then Hamish Hamilton would not be interested. If, on the other hand, she could be persuaded to write more about her childhood, such a book could well have the impact of Maya Angelou's *I Know Why a Caged Bird Sings* and would certainly be of interest to them. Could it be that Bessie was afraid to research her family background, Clare Alexander asked. 'I like it not that they [Hamish Hamilton] wish to force me to write about my mother's background,' Bessie wrote to Christine on receipt of this letter. 'I have never asked for her file. The South African authorities with their sick sick attitude to people may never give it to me.'[37] Obviously, though, the comments had given Bessie something to think about.

Christine Green had a query of her own. Why was the title to be 'Living on an Horizon' and not 'Living on the Horizon'? she asked. Bessie replied that she wished to show her affiliations with the Hindu holy man, Swami Vivekananda. He had said: 'For myself I always have an horizon.' She felt that she and he were 'alike in richness of personality and interests'.[38] Though she had stated that she needed a year to write the autobiography, in her most cheerful moods she regarded it as an easy task. 'Remember, I'm the main character this time,' she told Ruth Forchhammer happily.

Ad Donker was now working on a new idea. He was considering publishing a two-volume edition of her six full-length works and Bessie was naturally enthusiastic. These works would fall easily into two groups; two trilogies in fact. The first trilogy, her first three novels, Bessie saw as having 'a tight cohesion' based on 'autobiographical material' where Serowe was used as backdrop but where 'the books welled up from inside me'. Volume Two would also have an organic cohesion. The *Collector of Treasures, Serowe: Village of the Rain Wind* and *A Bewitched Crossroad* 'are all permeated by a love for the Chief, Khama III . . . his care for women, his care and planning for his people'.[39] Bessie suggested that they could use Arthur Ravenscroft's article – 'Nothing equals it' – to introduce the first volume; and that she would write an introduction to the second. But Ad Donker shelved the idea in favour of something more in line with Michael Chapman's original purpose in contacting Bessie. He suggested a collection of a dozen or more short stories to be published in their Women Writers Series. Donker had already published four of Bessie's stories at various times. The idea was to add to those stories not already in *The Collector of Treasures* some new ones written specially for the anthology.

A Bewitched Crossroad was published in Johannesburg on 31 October 1984, just over nine months after Donker had received the manuscript. It did not attract great attention but two Botswana papers gave it sympathetic reviews, the first appearing in January 1985 and commenting on Bessie Head's 'two distinct tones', the novelist's tone and the historian's tone, and the conscious way she moved from the one to the other.[40] Other reviews also noted her ability to provide a better understanding of the past, enlivened by anecdotes and conversations serving to 'humanise the factual information of the time'.[41] A Pretoria newspaper called it a failure. *A Bewitched Crossroad* purported to 'place oracular pearls of wisdom in the mouths of chiefs at a time long before the advent of the white man and the written word', it said and continued by noting that almost every white man was condemned 'in flamboyant language'; that Cecil Rhodes was portrayed as an 'arch fiend'; and that 'almost no white skin emerges un-braaid'. The review concluded: 'All that impressed me . . . was the beautiful photograph on the dust cover.'[42]

Paddy Kitchen's personal appreciation, written after she had finally received a copy of the book, was perhaps the most warming of all. She wrote that she might have known that when Bessie said that she was writing a historical novel, that was exactly what it would be – 'a whole history, a whole land's history, plotted and patchworked on to your typewriter'. She said that she had had to read it very slowly, so closely packed with detail it was. 'And the readings are counterpointed by the nightly news on the television from South Africa. So I read of the killings and raids and wars of the 19th century, and look at the screen in our sitting room and see the killings and riots and cruelties that took place that very morning.' She added that sometimes when she caught a glimpse on the screen of a woman protecting her child from a blow or shouting abuse at the police for the way they had treated her teenage son, she wished those women could be like the one Sebina had watched, 'safely pounding corn in the late afternoon sunlight. Perhaps, one day, when enough people grasp the whole history, as you have done, that will happen.'[43]

The process of editing *A Bewitched Crossroad* and preparing it for publication had been painless, even pleasurable. 'You are the best editor I have ever worked with,'[44] Bessie wrote to Jeff Probst in January 1985. But now the disadvantage of having it published in South Africa was becoming apparent. To the amazement of Ad Donker's London agent, Heinemann Educational Books turned down the British rights. Nor were any other publishers interested. It was sold to a small American publisher, Paragon House, but did not sell well. In fact it was remaindered and the rights reverted to the author. No one was interested in translation rights; and there was no paperback edition.[45] One of the reasons for the book's curiously chequered career could have been that trade sanctions against South Africa were widespread at the time of publication and there was no interest in anything the country was producing, even histories written in glowing prose by a victim of the apartheid system who condemned white land-grabbing. Bessie did not give a thought to this sort of problem. Instead she made plans to send copies to friends and began to make arrangements to distribute it locally.

Remembering the interest there had been for buying *Serowe: Village of the Rain Wind*, she decided to sell her new book in the village too. She ordered 100 copies, and two cartons were sent post-haste from Donker. Later she ordered 42 more. All these she sold to people in Serowe, who were keen to read a 'historical novel' with such local flavour. This sale of books brought Bessie some ready cash, nearly all of which she owed Ad Donker. She had not taken much more than cost price for the books. But times were hard and she decided to wait till she received her commission from Heinemann before repaying the several thousand rands owed. Donker was quite agreeable.

Howard returned to Serowe at the end of October 1984. Harold Head had left for Africa himself earlier that month, tired of waiting for his son to find a career. Howard was talking about returning to Serowe by this time, but Harold refused to pay his ticket. If Howard was going to commute between Africa and Canada, he said, he was not interested in paying for this.[46] Tom Holzinger lent Howard the money for the air ticket, helped him pack his belongings and saw him off. Howard had still not renewed his passport, so a temporary extension had to be arranged. Much chastened by some unpleasant experiences in Canada, but still keen on music, Howard finally came home. He had grown into an extremely good-looking young man. Though he had a generous smile, there was a guarded air about him and a hesitant shyness lurking in his soft brown eyes. He had reached the stage where he recognised himself as a Motswana and Serowe as his home. '[H]e is a boy with a very strong sense of belonging' was Bessie's comment to Paddy on his return.[47] He was still interested in becoming a musician especially as he knew this would please his mother. Some years later he was to say that taking up this career was 'more like trying to say thank you to my mother . . . If she had been alive I think I would have become a musician.'[48] As it was, the whole problem of finding a career was no nearer a solution.

There was no indication that Bessie plunged eagerly into her next writing project. In fact the prospect of a reasonable cash deposit in the bank turned her thoughts in an entirely new direction: to her garden. For some years she had left the land fallow as she had had more than enough to see to. But she longed to start growing things again. The days when the Boiteko garden had flourished and she had had pleasant daily contact with people came often to mind and she thought seriously about going into production once more. This time she would run it as a small business intended to give her an income. The Botswana government had a scheme whereby it supported small independent businesses. Provided the prospective owner had saved a certain sum, it would subsidise 40 per cent of the basic equipment required to start the project.

In September 1985 Bessie wrote to Eva Haahr, working in the Danish Volunteer Service in Gaborone. They had become very friendly during the planning of the trip to Denmark in 1980. She asked whether DVS would consider giving her seedling nursery financial support. By this time she had a detailed plan. A big expense would be the fertiliser she needed. She would also have to order 'shade cloth for protection of the seedlings and other experimental work' and build 'a store room 12ft by 12ft to store equipment'. She realised that a business project, without the cooperative element, would probably be outside DVS's field of support, but she explained how she needed at least to start independently so that she could get a thorough insight into the expenses incurred and get advice on how to 'make a costing of one seedling bag, balanced against labour and cost of material'.[49] She would need to 'acquire business skills' and make use of the 'advisory service for small business' that the government provided. As it turned out, DVS could not help her, but she kept working hard to realise these plans.

Heinemann now took up the idea of producing two volumes of her full-length works. She had already discussed this idea with Ad Donker, so she was quite willing for Heinemann to take it over. There was even some talk of Donker's collaborating on the project. Heinemann considered publishing these volumes in conjunction with the autobiography and they were very interested in having Bessie come to London to launch the publications. She agreed. They went into the last phase of the agreement for the autobiography, which they wanted ready by September 1986.

In Gaborone, Patrick van Rensburg had begun to edit a newspaper, *Mmegi Wa Dikgang*, intended to challenge some of the otherwise conservative views expressed in the local press. Though not nearly as energetic as she had once been about writing articles, Bessie was always in need of money. So when he asked her for a contribution, she responded with two very good pieces. Following the recent publication of *A Bewitched Crossroad*, it was natural that she write a short article giving some of the background information to her long project. This appeared as 'Collecting Oral History' in late March 1985. Here Bessie pays tribute to the people she worked with to collect the material for her three most recent books, beginning with *Serowe: Village of the Rain Wind* where '[a] hundred year history is told informally through people's life stories'. She mentions the vivid way people made her aware of their grandparents' hatred and fear of the Ndebele, a hundred years earlier. 'Without this kind of assistance I would not have been able to write a historical novel that accurately reflected people's feelings and preoccupations at that time,'[50] she writes.

Bessie had recently written a short piece for a French newspaper, *Liberation*. She and many other international writers had been asked to submit an article saying why they wrote. This she had just sent off, so *Mmegi* also received a copy. Entitled 'Why Do I Write', it was published the week after 'Collecting Oral History'.

In 'Why Do I Write' Bessie pulls out all the stops, as she liked to say. Her introductory sentence reads: 'I write because I have authority from life to do so.' The first section of the article is concerned with her so-called lack of political commitment. 'The areas in which I have this authority are clearly outlined,' she says and she does not 'trespass into terrain' unsuited to her. She explains that she was never called on to be a politician. Though she is 'well aware of the suffering of black people in southern Africa', she knows she 'could not cope with the liberatory struggle – a world of hot, bickering hate, jealousy, betrayal and murder'. She admits to having 'such a delicate nervous balance' that when 'faced with danger or secret activity' she trembles violently. But, she adds, 'I carried this around with me like a sin. To be South African born you have to be a politician, you have to be a liberator. You have to stand aloof and not comment on the horror, the horror.'

Bessie goes on to discuss the dangers of 'closed door nationalism', the idea that there should be a 'proper' and 'recognisable' African character in African novels. 'I would worry if limitations could be placed on the African personality and that only certain kinds of writers could properly represent the African personality. All my characters are black but I reserve for them the charm of being unpredictable and highly original.'

In the final section Bessie Head refers to her solitary life. 'Friends walk through my life, talk, smile and shake hands but no one is near me.' This is contrasted with the 'thousands and thousands of people' who crowd into her dream world. Her books are 'rooted in this source', she says.

Bessie had not aired her views on God for a long time. At the conclusion of this article she states them openly for the first time in article form and rounds off the many references she had made to that 'unseen Being in the sky'. These concluding paragraphs could almost be regarded as a direct extension of the idea expressed at the end of *A Question of Power*. There is only one God and His name is Man. And Elizabeth is his Prophet.'[51] She writes: 'In my world people plan for themselves and dictate their requirements to me. It is a world full of love, tenderness, happiness and laughter. From it I have developed a love and reverence for people.' She can 'foresee the day' when she will 'steal the title of God, the unseen Being in the sky, and offer it to mankind'. From then on, people will greet each other in the street by saying 'Good-morning, God'. 'War will end. Human suffering will end.'[52] To her the basic error is still the 'relegation of all things holy to some unseen being in the sky', as she had written in *A Question of Power*. She is here showing more clearly than ever how she has placed Ordinary Man at the centre of her universe and made him holy, again illustrating her contention from her great third novel that '[s]ince man was not holy to man, he could be tortured for his complexion, he could be misused, degraded and killed'.[53]

Having nevertheless brought God down to human size, Bessie concludes with a heavenly image: 'I am building a stairway to the stars. I have the authority to take the whole of mankind up there with me. That is why I write.'[54]

Invitations to attend conferences, the other distraction from her writing, continued to arrive. Bessie could give weird and garbled reasons for refusing. For instance she would not attend the Writers' Workshop in Gaborone at the beginning of 1985 because it would mean coming into contact with two 'sick sick men': one had once smiled when he heard that she had been physically assaulted by a another man, the other had once mispronounced the title of her second book. 'All the people in the world can pronounce that simple title, *Maru*, but not that sick, sick thing.'[55]

But one thing was certain. She was not going to refuse the invitation that had come to attend the Writers' Workshop entitled 'Women and Books' at the third Zimbabwe Book Fair in early August 1985. Remembering the trouble with the refugee visa the last time she had been in Harare and all too aware that she had to pass through there every time she wished to travel abroad, she was determined to make a success of the trip this time. 'I committed myself to the Zimbabwe trip,' she told Paddy Kitchen. 'I wanted to clear up a mistake.' However, she could not conceal her feeling of apprehension: she was 'anxious about the refugee visa, anxious about the exit through Harare, anxious to clear up a muddle.'[56]

Not that Bessie made it easy for the organisers. When she accepted the invitation she said that she would be bringing her dog Pa with her. She received an anxious telegram: 'Having problems about you bringing your dog please phone . . .'[57] Bessie stepped down and agreed to leave him at home. When she arrived in Gaborone, some days ahead of her departure date, her air ticket had not arrived. There was a misunderstanding about her transit expenses. Whereas she had taken it for granted that these would be met, the organisers were not expecting to pay them. In fact, the British Council in Zimbabwe sent an emphatic priority telegram to the British Council in Gaborone saying, 'do not repeat not reimburse her'.[58] As for the air ticket, she waited all Friday and Saturday for it to arrive, with telex messages flashing back and forth between Harare and Gaborone. The situation seemed hopeless when nothing had eventuated by the time everything closed for the weekend, but she hung on doggedly over the weekend, and went out to the airport on Monday morning. The ticket finally did arrive just before departure time. But it was underpaid, with instructions for her to pay the balance. This was a terrible slap in the face for her. She may not even have had enough money with her to do so. She refused. Once more she failed to appear in Harare. The long journey back to Serowe was fraught with humiliation and disappointment. Her interpretation of the incident was that 'someone in the Zimbabwe Publisher's House planned for my non-appearance . . . That was the pay-back.'59

Bessie sent a copy of the talk she had prepared, 'Themes Found in a Writer's Private Workshop', to Patrick van Rensburg, who arranged to have it published immediately in *Mmegi Wa Dikgang*.60 She also sent a copy to the *New Statesman*,61 which also published it immediately. Again Bessie had shown that startling mixture of confused emotionalism in her behaviour and intellectual clarity and pertinence in what she wrote. In the article she acknowledges the influences that have shaped her along 'that road of super-human staying power and stamina that is needed to produce the full-length novel': 'a bit of Christianity', 'a bit of Pan Africanism', 'Bertolt Brecht', 'people, a writer's material'. It has the quality of a final statement. Which of course it was.

Bessie's proposed participation in the Book Fair had been given a lot of publicity. This was because the Zimbabwe Publishing House had recently produced an edition of *Maru*, which Bessie knew nothing about. Her failure to appear caused quite a sensation. She had a German friend in Harare who had taken a lot of trouble to get into town to meet her. She was deeply disappointed and, after receiving Bessie's letter with her version of what had happened, became concerned for her safety. Some of the participants from the Writers' Workshop on African Women's Books wrote to tell her how sorry they were that she could not be with them. They said that they 'greatly missed' her 'valuable contribution', as many had 'come a long way and were looking forward particularly to being able to share ideas and experiences' with her.62 This was signed by eight participants, including Flora Nwapa and Ama Ata Aidoo. The organisers were angry about what had happened, feeling that Bessie Head had once more let them down.

The trouble did not end there. Bessie finally received the Zimbabwe Publishing House edition of *Maru*. She was shocked. 'The book is an unreadable mess,' she told her agent. The concluding twelve pages of the novel had been jumbled badly, with one completely blank page thrown in: 'The horror, the horror! *Maru*, written with precision and care, is one of my masterpieces.' Furthermore she thought that the cover design was 'ugly and dead. It has black faces with ugly grins against a background of asbestos huts. The novel is alert and alive with thought.' Bessie knew that Heinemann did not have full rights to *Maru*, they had only a sub-lease from Gollancz, so they were not entitled to enter into any new publishing arrangement without consulting her. She immediately demanded that the badly produced edition be withdrawn. When Heinemann did inform her about their contract with the Zimbabwe Publishing House and told her that ZPH would be producing their edition 'later or early next year', Bessie retorted: 'They have already produced it and I have a copy.' She found the contract unacceptable. She feared that she had been caught in 'the teeth of big business'.[63] She felt that something very strange was going on. Why had ZPH never mentioned their imprint to her in the many letters that had gone back and forth before the Book Fair? 'If a publisher has an author alive and in person there is a joyous welcome. The author alive is an asset on such an occasion.'

She feared that some underhand deal had been made because of the currency situation in Zimbabwe: 'I plead with the John Johnson agency not to accept any money for me on this contract ... My books are not going to be used to take money out of Zimbabwe illegally.'[64]

Christine Green had left John Johnson's earlier in the year. Bessie's new agent, Elizabeth Fairbairn, carried out Bessie's instructions loyally, though it could not have been a particularly pleasant job, knowing as she did that both publishing houses were anxious to rectify matters and that Bessie was losing a lot of money by her attitude. She won Bessie's gratitude, however. 'The literary agency is good'[65] was a remark that began appearing in Bessie's letters and she wrote thanking Elizabeth, always addressed as 'Ms Fairbairn', for her support in this matter and in other ways too. She even sent her and her son small gifts at Christmas time in gratitude for some copying that had been done for her. Something of the old personal style of her relationships with 'David' and especially 'Giles' was creeping back. And perhaps something of her feeling of creativity. In the midst of all her indignation she could suddenly write: 'Merciful God, make me more alert about death from the teeth of big business ... In me still grows the great novel that changes the world, but tenderly, tenderly.'[66]

Veronica Samuel had been longing to meet her aunt ever since she had 'found' her. The journey from Pietermaritzburg to Serowe was a long and expensive one but Veronica and her husband Lionel gradually overcame the practical obstacles. They were ready to fix a date on several occasions but Bessie postponed the visit. She was actually worried about the accommodation and hoped to be able to put them up in the extra room that she was planning to put up in the yard. 'Eventually it will house equipment for the gardening project, a seedling nursery, but first it will house you and Lionel.'[67] Without a doubt, too, she was waiting for the money from Heinemann because she continued to live a hand-to-mouth existence. Then Lionel was involved in a car accident. A drunken driver crashed into his car, killing one of the passengers and wrecking the car completely. With that, they had to write off their trip to Serowe. Lionel was in hospital for some time with a damaged knee and it would be a long time before they could afford another car as reliable as the one that had been ruined. Bessie did not seem to grasp the serious nature of the accident but sent a road map ('Please take great care of the road map, niece Wally, for future use')[68] and instructions on how to get from Gaborone to Serowe. She seemed relieved to have a little more time to have her plumbing repaired and an extra room built. This, she added, would only take a month to erect.

With the need to produce something for the autobiography becoming urgent, and encouraged by her contact with Veronica, Bessie's thoughts were dwelling more and more on her past. In June 1985 she wrote to the welfare society in Pietermaritzburg that had supervised her childhood, asking for 'specific and accurate' information about her birth and about her mother's background. She was particularly interested in the letter written by her mother leaving a sum of money for her education. 'That letter . . . would be of great sentimental value to me. I have done much with her stipulation.' She added that perhaps the young social worker who had visited her at Nellie Heathcote's, month after month, would be 'the only one alive to appreciate it, that those monthly visits were not in vain.'[69] The organisation made no effort to reply. They were very conscious of the codes of confidentiality that required that they protect their clients, past and present. If Bessie was to find out about her past, she would have to look elsewhere.

Bessie's memories were a farrago of bizarre impressions. She was recalling old popular songs that she wanted to quote, and curious incidents from her childhood and youth. Gradually she became obsessed with a short story by Doris Lessing. It was entitled 'An Unposted Love Letter'. Bessie wanted to quote it in its entirety. 'I cannot break it up to analyse a similar view of love that enriches the world,' she wrote to Elizabeth Fairbairn. She said that Doris Lessing writes 'that there is a man who is God but that he is duplicated in many men . . . But his woman is God too.'[70]

Bessie turned 48 on 6 July 1985. Pat Spann sent her a card. Bessie wrote a humorous letter of acknowledgement, thanking her for the 'precious' card. 'Life', she said, 'gets lonelier as one gets older and today there was no one in sight to tell that it was my birthday.'

She then recounted a story about how she had once made a mistake with her age. For months she had regarded herself as 47 until she had had to fill in some biographical information and discovered to her amazement that she was only 46. 'I spent a day feeling completely disorganised so each 6th of July I put a memo above my typewriter which has my correct age.'[71]

Bessie was continuing to put on weight. In June 1983 she had made a bet with her neighbour, Martin Morolong, that she could reduce her waist measurement to 30 inches. If she could do that, 'Mr Morolong will lose a bet and pay me P30.00. He will get poor.'[72] At that stage her waist measurement was 42 inches. The agreement was properly drawn up and signed by them both. It is highly unlikely that Bessie won that bet. Just as it is highly unlikely that Martin Morolong ever 'got rich' on the P30 she should have paid. By the time she turned 48, she weighed 89 kilograms. Perhaps her old joke – age 48 years, waist 48 inches – still held good.

About this time Bessie slipped on her newly polished floor and hurt her knee. She was laid up for some days. 'It is heaven sitting in bed in a spotlessly clean house,' she told Paddy. She had been very busy making gooseberry jam – gooseberry bushes were the only thing that could survive in her drought-stricken garden – because once more she was penniless. But that had had to be put aside and she could concentrate on reading Paddy Kitchen's latest book. It was about her village, Barnwell. Bessie's Serowe book had lain on the desk as a talisman while she wrote. It is a delightful account of a village community and Bessie was charmed: 'I have spent some happy hours in Barnwell.' She thought Paddy's descriptions of the countryside 'breathtakingly beautiful' and responded to the way people trust each other in a village. In Barnwell, Ron the grocer not only delivered the groceries. He put the frozen goods in the freezer and the perishables in the fridge if there was no one at home. 'But', Bessie concluded, 'to quote Dulan's grandmother: I feel it in my waters that the people of Barnwell love this book.'[73]

In August 1985 Harold Head arrived in Gaborone. He had come to file for a divorce. He and his future wife, Mary Munro, had been in Zambia for some months, staying with his sister Caroline. She came down with them to Botswana. Howard met up with the little party in Palapye and stayed with them for the rest of the time that his father was in Botswana. The marriage that Bessie Head had felt to be non-existent for so long was now to be formally dissolved. She hardly discussed the matter.

Bessie seemed to be becoming more reserved. She had so often been quite unrestrained in sharing her problems, yet no one was told about how she had been reunited with her niece Veronica, though she felt that a light had returned to her life with this event. Nor did she share in any way the tragic news she received about this time that her dear friend Tony Hall had committed suicide. Thus a lifetime of learning to contain pain by burying it in compartments in her heart had emphasised the silences and spaces in her life and left her with a heavy burden of loneliness.

She still received a few chosen visitors. In January 1985 two students from the University of Natal visited her. The trip was in the nature of a pilgrimage, as one of them, Craig Mackenzie, later to become a productive Bessie Head researcher, had just completed his M.A. thesis on her and wanted to meet her. In May she allowed herself to be interviewed and photographed by a gifted young Danish photographer, Lis Steincke, who had brought a letter of introduction from Bessie's good friend Eva Haahr. 'I received Ms Steincke well with good memories of my trip to Denmark,' she later wrote to Eva Haahr.[74] Maria Rytter, the Danish curator of the Khama III Memorial Museum, also taped an interview with her. Towards the end of the year, the growing number of people who were approaching Bessie for interviews were not as fortunate. She refused everyone. She was becoming more and more afraid of facing people. 'I have developed a dread of travelling. Too many people try to humiliate and degrade me . . . I find I am happy at home. I cannot take on strange people and strange audiences. I cannot fight with the lower side of human nature.'[75]

Paddy Kitchen had begun to send Bessie detective stories, including some her husband had written. Then she sent her three cookery books. Bessie's insomnia was chronic now. She spent each night's long waking hours reading crime stories or pondering over recipes:

It astonishes me how much one can learn from rather out of the way books about living – the murder mystery writers are in a class all their own with very high writing standards and they teach deeply about the dark side of human nature. Nutritionists teach about the survival of the species . . . the Jamaican [cookery] book is rich with historical items.[76]

Elizabeth Fairbairn was still negotiating for the commission for the autobiography. Bessie asked for more money than they had offered and got her way. Then she asked for the payment to be made as one lump sum instead of in three instalments. Again they agreed. Finally the contract was drawn up and signed. In December, over P13 000 was transferred to Bessie's bank account. It was almost like winning the Nobel Prize.

One of the first things Bessie did was to buy herself a refrigerator. This meant that she could buy larger quantities of food and thus have more time to give to her writing. She made plans to pay back the money she owed Ad Donker, and began settling some of her other debts. At last she had been recognised for her true worth. At last her days of borrowing and begging were over. Though she felt so wealthy, money had a bad habit of disappearing. A month after receiving the payment, she had already used P5000.[77]

Bessie's friends rejoiced with her in her good fortune. She seemed much calmer of late. Of course there had been the 'peaks and troughs', as Hugh Pearce put it, but with money to live on at long last, they hoped – with inbuilt apprehension – for good times.

One day Ruth gave Bessie a lift. She looked very pleased with herself. 'Ruth, I have a present for you. You must come up to the house and get it.' Ruth was curious. When they arrived at Bessie's home, she produced a wrapped parcel. It was a book. In fact, it was the brand new Danish translation of *Maru*, called *Gul Marguerit*. 'To Ruth, from your best friend Bessie', she had written in it. Ruth was touched and very pleased. Bessie had gone to a lot of trouble to get an extra copy to give her.[78]

Bessie began to regard the reams of material she had collected over the years in a new light. Despite the limited space at her disposal in her little home, she had kept nearly all her correspondence. And most of it was neatly arranged, chronologically and in files. Her journalist training had taught her to keep carbon copies of all the letters she typed. The writer Stephen Gray has called her papers 'a raving, alcoholic shambles'.[79] Though this is how they may have struck him when (and if) he saw them, they were not like this when she died. As she sorted and arranged, it was as if the last twenty-five years of her life lay preserved in those brown cardboard folders.

But could she open them? Could she re-read frenzied letters that were fifteen or eighteen years old? Did she have enough hindsight now to bring some inner sense of order into things, to explain herself to other people, to give her life some sort of authenticity? She believed in herself as a writer and she was very conscious of the unfolding of an overall pattern in her writing career. But she had used so much of the material from her own life in that writing; it could not be separated from her career. And it had now to be taken up for revision. Including those years in South Africa.

Maria Rytter was a good curator and very aware of the wealth of material being kept neatly filed at 'Rain Clouds'. In her enthusiasm for the new museum, she told Bessie that she was keeping Lis Steincke's taped interview with her in 'the archives' and that one day it 'would be worth a lot of money'. Bessie immediately suspected that Maria was out to make money out of her and turned against her greed 'for power and money'.[80] 'Maria Rykker', as Bessie called her, returned the tapes with a letter explaining that she was merely interested in advertising Bessie's work. Little could she know that she would soon have those tapes in her possession again and that the little country museum was so soon to acquire its second valuable collection: all Bessie Head's papers.

Just after Christmas Bessie received an exciting parcel. Joke Junger, who had arranged Bessie's trip to Holland and who worked for the Dutch publishing house Novib, contacted Bessie. She had heard that she was still having trouble with the royalty payments for the Dutch edition of *When Rain Clouds Gather*. She investigated the whole matter, found that Bessie did indeed have some royalties due to her, enclosed a cheque for this and explained all the small difficulties Bessie had had. 'Dear mrs Head, I hope I solved your problems and that everything is alright now'[81] is how she concluded. The huge parcel which accompanied this letter contained dress lengths, stationery, and packets of tea, coffee and sugar.

Alice Walker had not forgotten Bessie either. Suddenly she was notified that she had been given the Mother Jones Diploma for being an 'unsung writer'. The January 1986 edition of the American journal *Mother Jones* had asked five important writers, Russell Banks, E L Doctorow, Grace Paley, Richard Rodriguez and Alice Walker, to name their favourite uncelebrated foreign writer. Alice Walker had put Bessie at the top of her list (followed by Camara Laye and Ayi Kwei Armah).

Bessie was finding Howard more and more difficult to live with. He was hoping to make a career for himself in the music world in Gaborone, perhaps involved in the arranging of large rock and jazz concerts. He was often away in Gaborone but when he was home he was bad-tempered and lazy. They deliberately baited each other. Bessie would nag; Howard would tell her that her voice irritated him; she would demonstratively refuse to speak to him, and write him notes.

About the end of January the unhappy relationship exploded in an outburst of violence. Bessie threw Howard out of her house and he left Serowe forthwith. Shortly afterwards she was notified that her divorce had been finalised. How much this latter event affected her mood, it is impossible to say. But the break with Howard unsettled her completely.

She cried uncontrollably for days. She confided something of the situation to Paddy, who had tried before to help her through crises at a distance of six thousand miles and tried as best she could this time too.[82]

Gradually she began to pull herself together. Her life had to go on. The autobiography needed to be started. She had said she needed a year to write it. She had agreed to deliver it in September 1986 and go to London to launch it in March 1987. It was February now and she had not begun. Perhaps it was at this stage that the first genuine fears about completing it began to make themselves felt. She remembered the sheer stamina that had been needed to complete *A Bewitched Crossroad*. Did she still have that in her? And what should she do about describing her childhood? The highly dramatised versions she had recounted until now made interesting reading but she knew that such a pitch could not be maintained for chapter after chapter without becoming decidedly unconvincing. Since her reunion with Veronica, her childhood had begun to seem more anchored in reality. Important decisions would have to be made and time was running out. As if to charge herself for the task, she turned back to 'An Unposted Love Letter'. On 29 March 1986 she told Elizabeth Fairbairn that she had 'made haste' to type out the story 'in order to keep it' with her when she had to return the library book in which it was found. 'Then night after night I read it and read it until I know it off by heart. Never have I read anything so beautiful about love.'

Ruth Forchhammer once said loyally that she had never seen Bessie drunk. Bosele Sianana tended to agree. Though she, unlike Ruth, had often seen her drinking. Bessie could walk down to the Off-Sales store on the main road and buy six beers. Then she could walk up the hill to her home. By the time she arrived, she would have drunk four of them. Or she would buy six cans of beer at the Off-Sales and get a lift into town on the back of an open truck. By the time she reached the Mall, she would have only three beers left. Bosele, a teetotaller herself, would challenge this behaviour. 'You give up smoking because you say it harms your health; then you take up drinking, which is worse,'[83] she would remark dryly. Bessie turned a deaf ear, just as she totally disregarded the disapproving reactions of the villagers. Many called her mad because of her drinking habits. Both Ruth and Bosele only remembered seeing Bessie drink beer and apparently she could take large quantities of it. If one compares these accounts with the drinking patterns of some of the great American writers such as Faulkner, Hemingway and Fitzgerald,[84] it seems that Bessie could still have had a long way to go down the path to alcoholism. There may have been binges and black-outs; but there is no record of major collapses and certainly no detoxification treatments. Yet her liver was seriously affected.

For there was another compartment in Bessie's life. Perhaps reserved at first for the long sleepless nights, brandy and gin began to gain control. By March 1986 she was drinking about a bottle a day. Had Ruth, Bosele and Hugh not later seen the cache of clean bottles without labels piled up under her bed, they would not have thought it possible.[85]

In about February 1986 Kerstin Kvist returned to Sweden. Katrin Sell went home on leave to Germany in March. Bosele was away on two different occasions. And Mmatsela and Hugh were taken up with other things. Bessie's one-time 'fan' to whom she dedicated *The Collector of Treasures*, Gothe Kgamane, who had been away from Serowe for years, saw Bessie in about March and noticed that she had lost weight. She actually looked very well, she thought.

A fortnight later, however, Bosele saw her and realised that she was very ill. Her skin was yellow. She persuaded Bessie to go to the hospital. The doctor diagnosed hepatitis and wished to admit her straightaway. But Bessie refused. She had left her dog Pa alone at home. Finally it was agreed that she could be given medication and go home but she would have to remain in bed for the duration of the treatment. She was given strict instructions not to touch alcohol.

Ruth visited Bessie daily. She did not feel particularly worried. Hepatitis was fairly common in Botswana. If treated carefully, most people recovered quickly. Bessie too was optimistic. She enjoyed being taken care of by Ruth. One day as she was lying alone, she heard the door open. It was Howard. He could see straightaway that she was ill, but she assured him that she would soon be well again. He had a long time before given up understanding the mysteries of his mother's illnesses and believed her. He had come for money; she wanted him to have some. But the bitterness they both felt had not disappeared. He left shortly afterwards for Johannesburg, where one of Harold Head's sisters lived.

After Bessie had been about a week in bed, Ruth began to worry. Bessie was cheerful and keen to get up again, but she did not seem to be showing much improvement. Ruth had several times talked about her going into hospital but she would not hear of it. 'Nonsense, Ruth. We haven't got time for that. Now help me write this letter . . . ,' she would reply. All the same it was a shock for Ruth to arrive on the afternoon of 16 April and discover that Bessie was weak and listless. She would still not hear of going to hospital, but Ruth realised that she could not be left alone that night. She went out to find someone to spend the night with her.

While she was away, one of the local librarians came to tell Bessie about a meeting she was to attend. She was alarmed to find her very weak and in fact losing consciousness. She contacted the hospital and shortly afterwards a doctor and two nurses arrived in an ambulance. Bessie was lifted into the vehicle without a protest.

News spread round the village that Bessie Head was ill. Bosele had been away at a seminar but when she arrived at work at the Boiteko gardens, one of her friends told her that Bessie had been admitted to hospital. She decided to go and visit her that afternoon. After some trouble she got to the hospital but they would not let her go into Bessie's ward. She went home, disappointed, and hoped she would be able to see her the next day. Ruth called in at the hospital on the way to work and again at lunchtime. The news was not good. Bessie was in a coma. She made fruitless attempts to get hold of Howard. When she returned in the afternoon, the nurse told her that the Pearces were sitting with Bessie for a while and so she waited outside to take her turn.

Mmatsela and Hugh Pearce had only heard about Bessie's illness that morning. One of Mmatsela's friends who was a nurse called in. 'A friend of yours, Bessie Head, is in hospital,' she said. 'And her state seems serious.' Mmatsela was deeply uneasy. When Hugh came home for his midday meal, she said straightaway: 'Bessie's in hospital. We must go and see her.'[86] 'Right,' said Hugh. 'We'll go up this evening when I've finished work.' 'No, Hugh. I'm really worried about her,' she said. 'Take the afternoon off. We must go and see her now.' When they got to the hospital they were met with grave faces. Bessie's condition was extremely serious. Her liver was not functioning and she was deeply unconscious.

'We must do something immediately,' said Hugh. 'We must get her to Gaborone to a bigger hospital. 'They can do nothing for her there', replied the doctor. 'Well, Harare, then. We must have her flown to Harare.' The doctor looked at him very directly. 'Her state is most unstable. She would never stand the journey.'

'But we have to do something . . . ,' Hugh began. Mmatsela cut him short. She said with simple dignity: 'Hugh, Bessie is dying. Sit down and hold her hand.'

So they sat there quietly, the shock and sadness overwhelming them now. Each took one of Bessie's small, well-padded practical hands in theirs. Her breathing seemed to be fading away. In the late afternoon quite suddenly the pressure they had felt in her palms relaxed. Bessie Amelia Emery, firmly supported by one black hand and one white, passed from life to death. 'In my end is my beginning.'

Bessie's grave, Serowe, July 1988

Epilogue

She was buried at the Botolaote cemetery as she had requested. It is sandy and stony, straggling and weed-ridden, but it looks out over the Serowe plain with the broad, sweeping vision that was Bessie's own. There she could, in the sentiments of Bill Salter that she had once listened to so insistently, at last transcend the stress of living and stand stripped and free.

Friends rallied round to help. Hugh Pearse, Cassim Kikia, Maria Rytter and Patrick van Rensburg, travelling up from Gaborone, with invaluable back-up from Bosele Sianana, Ruth Forchhammer and Mmatsela Pearce, did what they could to arrange the funeral and inform the outside world of Bessie Head's death. Ruth Forchhammer kept on at her particular task, that of finding Howard. Finally she did manage to send a message to him and he had to phone back and hear the news. He arrived in Serowe the day before the funeral. In London Paddy Kitchen received a telegram: 'Bessie Head died 17 April to be buried 26 April. Please inform. Pearce.' Greatly distressed, she phoned Serowe and spoke to Patrick van Rensburg. He handed the phone over to Howard, newly arrived, and they exchanged a few words, though both found it difficult. Harold Head also telephoned from Canada, as did Abdullah Ibrahim, formerly known as Dollar Brand. As the funeral approached, telegrams with messages of condolence began to pour in from America, England and South Africa.

A beast was slaughtered and friends and neighbours prepared to mark Bessie Head's passing as they had marked the Norwegian doctor's, or Fantisi, the popular bus driver's, or countless others'. The night before the funeral an all-night wake was held in Bessie's yard, with hymn-singing and quiet conversation. Bosele had moved into the house to be with Howard and stayed there for the next month. The worst part, for Howard, was still to come: the day he was finally left on his own.

The funeral was conducted by a minister from the Anglican Church and a Roman Catholic priest. Howard had insisted that they should contact the Catholic priest; it was something he had promised his mother. It was a huge affair, attended by many notables, making many impressive speeches. Patrick van Rensburg tried to penetrate further than most into the mystery of Bessie Head's creative genius. He pointed out how different she was when she was writing. From the confusions of daily living she would withdraw to her desk and her typewriter and there she would almost take on a new personality. While she sat there, she seemed to have her life under control. Her fears, anxieties and physical needs were pushed to one side as she collected her ideas and concentrated her thoughts on what she was writing. It was here the disparities in her complex personality were quietened for a while. It was here the realist and the dreamer achieved a brief communion.

The many floral tributes covering the grave were soon scorched in the hot Botswana sun. As is the custom, Bosele and other friends then covered the mound of earth with the large red stones lying all around. Bessie Head's grave merged with the other unmarked ones, as they too merged with the red and stony, unkempt ground. Let there be no markings for a grave, when I've passed on, Bessie had sung with Miriam Makeba as she typed away at *Maru* with the thunder behind her ears.

'I wonder what profound statement I'd make to God the day I die. I mean that last despairing statement about waiting and waiting to simplify one's life and all the time it was a tangle of evil,' Bessie Head had once asked. But her genius defied statements. The quality of what she would call her soul-power was not to be defined. No more, at least, than she herself could do so in her greatest novel, *A Question of Power*: 'It was linked in some way to the creative function, the dreamer of new dreams; and the essential ingredient in creativity is to create and let the dream fly away with a soft hand and heart.'

References

Chapter 1

1. Head, *Drum*, 1982, p. 35
2. Peek, *New Literature Review*, 1985, p. 8
3. *Star*, 19 December 1919
4. K Birch, 1992, letter
5. WLD trial file 121/1929, State Archives, Pretoria
6. MHG 82681, 8.3.1933, State Archives
7. K Birch, 1992, letter
8. MHG 82681, Bessie Amelia Emery, 12/6/3/1465
9. GG 1253, file 33/1947, 25.5.1934
10. GG 1253, file 33/1947, 1.7.1934
11. MHG 82681, 30.7.1934
12. MHG 82681, 27.8.1934
13. MHG 4528/43, 25.11.1943
14. MHG 82681, 8.10.1936
15. Head, *Ms*, 1975, p. 72
16. MHG 4528/43, 3.3.1944
17. MHG 82681, 6.1.1940
18. MHG 82681, 17.12.1940
19. MHG 4528/43, 14.9.1943
20. MHG 4528/43, 5.10.1943
21. MHG 4528/43, 1.9.1944
22. MHG 4528/43, 3.3.1944
23. MHG 4528/43, 19.9.1944
24. MHG 4528/43, 25.10.1944
25. MHG 4528/43, 19.9.1944
26. Laband & Haswell, 1988, p. 105
27. KMM 373 BHP 27.12.1983
28. Samuel, 1990, letter
29. KMM 373 BHP 27.12.1983
30. KMM 373 BHP 27.12.1983
31. Head, 1993, pp. 7–8
32. Head, in Barber, 1975, p. 109
33. KMM 373 BHP 27.12.1983
34. Head, in Barber, p. 108
35. Head, in Barber, p. 110
36. KMM 373 BHP 27.12.1983
37. Samuel, 1991, interview
38. Head, in Barber, p. 109
39. KMM 373 BHP 27.12.1983
40. Samuel, 1991, interview; 1991, letter
41. BEF 31.1.1950

Chapter 2

1. Yates, 1960, p. 11
2. Yates, 1960, p. 17
3. Yates, 1960, p. 34
4. BEF 31.1.1950
5. BEF 9.1.1950
6. Yates, 1960, p. 118
7. Thomsett, 1991, interview
8. Former pupils of St Monica's, 1990, interview by Phipson. Subsequent comments from here.
9. Yates, 1960, p. 110
10. BEF 15.5.1951
11. Head, *Goodwill*, 1951, p. 101
12. BEF 9.9.1951
13. BEF 9.10.1951
14. BEF 19.12.1951 Ref 33/2/4/438/51
15. Head, in Barber, p. 108
16. BEF 12.1.1952
17. Head, 1973, p. 16
18. Head, *Drum*, 1982, p. 36
19. Head, *Drum*, 1982, p. 36
20. Head, in Barber, p. 110
21. Head, in Barber, p. 110
22. BEF 11.8.1953
23. Yates, 1960, p. 121
24. BEF undated 1953. Subsequent comments from here.
25. BEF 5.12.1953 & 12.12.1953
26. Head, in Barber, p. 110
27. King, 1990 & 1991, interview
28. Yates, 1960, p. 132
29. Stock, 1990, interview
30. Thomsett, 1991, interview
31. KMM 149 BHP 24.5.1972
32. KMM 149 BHP 1.6.1972
33. KMM 149 BHP 24.5.1972
34. KMM 149 BHP 24.5.1972
35. BEF undated 1954
36. BEF 16.12.1954
37. BEF undated 1955
38. BEF undated 1955
39. KMM 74 BHP 22.1.1972
40. KMM 34 BHP 7.12.1975

41. KMM 34 BHP 27.11.1978
42. Head, in Barber, p. 111
43. KMM 27 BHP 5.12.1985
44. Samuel, 1991, interview
45. BEF 26.9.1958
46. BEF 10.9.1958
47. BEF 10.9.1958

Chapter 3

1. BEF 10.9.1958
2. BEF 26.9.1958
3. BEF 26.9.1958
4. Kiley, 1990, interview
5. BEF 10.9.1958
6. South African Library, Cape Town, 1991, letter
7. BEF 10.9.1958
8. BEF 26.9.1958
9. BEF 26.9.1958
10. Head, *Home Post,* 28.6.1959, p. 7
11. Head, *Home Post,* 16.8.1959, p. 3
12. Nkosi, 1965, p. 12
13. Head, *Home Post,* 20.12.1959, p. 4
14. Pogrund, 1991, p. 38
15. Pogrund, 1991, p. 55
16. Pogrund, 1991, p. 104
17. Pogrund, 1991, p. 95
18. Pogrund, 1991, p. 106
19. Padmore, 1972, p. ix
20. Head, *Southern African Review of Books
    [SARoB],* 1990, p. 12
21. Head, *Home Post,* 20.3.1960, p. 5
22. KMM 372 BHP 6.1.1972
23. Head, 1989, p. 135
24. KMM 372 BHP 20.4.1972
25. KMM 372 BHP 6.1.72
26. Davenport, 1987, p. 396
27. Head, *Home Post,* 27.3.1960, p. 7
28. Pogrund, 1991, p. 150
29. Pogrund, 1991, p. 153
30. KMM 73 BHP 18.11.1978
31. Head, 1991, p. 51
32. Head, *Mmegi wa Dikgang,* 30.3.1985, p. 6
33. KMM 372 BHP 29.4.1972
34. Harold Head, 1994, interview
35 KMM 74 BHP 27.8.1971

Chapter 4

1. KMM 27 BHP 5.12.1985
2. KMM 27 BHP 5.12.1985
3. BEF 26.9.1958
4. Head, 1990, p. 15
5. Head, 1991, p. 2
6. Head, 1991, p. 13
7. Head, 1990, p. 14
8. C. Head, 1991, interview
9. Head, 1989, p. 29
10. Head, in UWL JMP, A 1849, C9.12
11. Marquard, *London Magazine* 1978/79, p. 51
12. Harold Head, *New African,* 1962, p. 6

13. Vigne, 1990, interview
14. Harold Head, 1994, interview
15. Head, *New African,* 1962, p. 10
16. KMM 405 BHP undated
17. Head, 1990, p. 14
18. Head, 1989, p. 17
19. Harold Head, 1994, interview
20. Head, 1993, p. 24
21. Head, 1989, pp. 17–18
22. Head, 1989, p. 29
23. Rive, *South African Outlook,* 1980
24 Head, 1989, p. 28
25. Head, 1990, pp. 9–10
26. Head, 1990, p. 8
27. Head, 1990, pp. 8–9
28. Head, 1990, pp. 10–11
29. Head, 1989, p. 30
30. *The Wanderers Club Magazine,* 1979, p. 24; Emery,
    1991, interview
31. Brutus, 1994, interview
32. Harold Head, 1994, interview
33. Mohammed, 1992, interview
34. Head, 1990, pp. 13–14
35. Head, 1990, pp. 22–23
36. Cullinan, 1991, interview

Chapter 5

1. Seretse Khama, 1970, speech
2. Head, 1981, p. 28
3. Benson, 1977, p. 126
4. Dutfield, 1990, pp. 101–106, 214
5. Head, 1989, p. 49
6. Letsididi, 1991, interview
7. Head, 1989, p. 50
8. Head, 1989, p. 48
9. Head, *SARoB,* 1990, p. 15
10. Head, *SARoB,* 1990, p. 12
11. Head, 1990, p. 30
12. Head, 1972 / 1989
13. Head, Harold, 1971, p. 524
14. Van Rensburg, 1984, p. 13
15 Head, 1981, p. 137
16. Van Rensburg, 1984, p. 16
17. Head, *SARoB,* 1990,. p. 14
18. Head, 1989, p. 59
19. Head, *SARoB,* 1990, p. 15
20. Head, *SARoB,* 1990, p. 14
21. Head, *SARoB,* 1990, p. 15
22. Head, 1991, p. 23
23. Head, 1989, p. 59
24. Head, 1991, p. 65
25. Head, 1991, p. 23
26. Head, 1993, pp. 154–155, 158–159
27. Head, 1989, pp. 53–54
28. Head, *SARoB,* 1990, p. 13
29. Head, *SARoB,* 1990, p. 13
30. Head, *SARoB,* 1990, p. 13
31. Head, 1991, p. 14
32. Head, 1991, p. 68
33. Head, 1991, p. 10

34. Head, 1991, p. 68
35. Head, 1991, p. 15
36. Head, 1991, p. 10
37. Head, 1991, p. 9
38. Head, 1991, p. 12
39. Head, 1991, p. 14
40. Head, 1991, p. 9
41. Head, 1991, p. 14
42. Head, 1991, p. 13
43. Head, 1964 / 1989
44. Head, 1993, pp. 150-159
45. Head, 1981, p. ix
46. Head, 1993, pp. 146-149
47. Head, 1990, p. 29
48. Head, 1989, p. 36
49. Newmarch, *Current Writing*, 1990, p. 170
50. Head, 1989, p. 42
51. Head, 1977, pp. 57-60
52. Head, 1991, p. 10
53. Head, 1991, p. 11
54. Harold Head, 1994, interview
55. Head, 1991, p. 20
56. Head, 1991, p. 21
57. Head, 1991, p. 25
58. Alverson, 1978, p. 70
59. Alverson, 1978, p. 190
60. Alverson, 1978, pp. 177-178
61. Ben-Tovim, 1990, interview
62. Head, 1991, p. 48
63. Head, 1991, p. 20
64. Head, 1991, p. 21

Chapter 6

1. Head, 1991, p. 29
2. Head, 1991, p. 29
3 Gibberd, 1994, interview
4. Head, 1991, p. 36
5. Head, 1991, p. 45
6. Head, 1991, p. 31
7. Head, 1991, p. 31
8. Head, 1991, p. 32
9. Head, 1991, p. 32
10. Head, 1991, pp. 31-32
11. Head, 1991, p. 24
12. Head, 1991, p. 50
13. Head, 1991, p. 33
14. Head, 1991, p. 33
15. Head, 1991, p. 34
16. Head, 1991, p. 35
17. Head, 1991, p. 37
18. Head, 1991, p. 38
19. Head, 1990, p. 12
20. Head, 1991, p. 45
21. Mohammed, 1992, interview
22. Gabatshwana, 1966, p. 64
23. Head, 1991, p. 37
24. Head, 1989, p. 37
25. Head, 1989, p. 40
26. Head, 1991, p. 57
27. KMM 9 BHP 14.7.1975

28. Head, 1991, p. 44
29. Mohammed, 1992, interview
30. Kitchen, *Times Educational Supplement*, 1970, p. 36
31. Mitchison, *New African*, 1966, p. 28
32. Head, 1990, p. 30
33. Head, 1991, p. 59
34. Head, 1991, p. 46
35. Head, 1991, p. 17
36. Head, 1991, p. 23
37. Head, 1991, p. 24
38. Head, 1991, p. 28
39. Head, 1991, pp. 36-37
40. Head, 1991, p. 62
41. Head, 1991, p. 66
42. Head, 1991, p. 63
43. KMM 60 BHP 18.6.69
44. Head, 1991, pp. 59-60
45. Finley, 1991, interview
46. Head, 1991, p. 11
47. Head, 1989, p. 17
48. Holzinger, 1994, interview; Harold Head, 1994, interview
49. Kitchen, 1970
50. Head, 1991, p. 46
51. KMM 60 BHP 5.1.1968
52. KMM 331 BHP 18.2.1969

Chapter 7

1. KMM 58 BHP 29.11.1967
2. Head, 1991, p. 58
3. Head, 1991, p. 75
4. Head, 1991, pp. 75-76
5. Head, 1991, pp. 58-59
6. Head, 1990, p. 47
7. Head, 1991, pp. 64-65
8. KMM 43 BHP 7.9.1968
9. Head, 1991, p. 32
10. Head, 1991, p. 49
11. Head, 1991, p. 67
12. Head, 1981, p. 79
13. Head, 1981, p. 79
14. KMM 96 BHP undated 1974
15. Head, 1991, pp. 66-67
16. Head, 1991, p. 64
17. KMM 96 BHP undated 1974
18 KMM 43 BHP 7.9.1968
19 Head, 1991, p. 67
20. Head, 1991, p. 71
21. KMM 60 BHP 29.12.1968
22. Head, 1991, p. 81
23. Van Rensburg, 1984, p. 17
24. Van Rensburg, 1984, p. 14
25. Gibberd, *Botswana Notes and Records*, 1975, p. 205
26. Forchhammer, 1991, interview
27. Head, 1991, p. 83
28. KMM 73 BHP 2.2.1979
29. Head, 1991, p. 88
30. Head, 1991, p. 82

31. Head, 1991, p. 83
32. KMM Head's private papers 13.3.1969
33 KMM 68 BHP 28.3.1969
34. Head, 1991, p. 85
35. Head, 1991, p. 88
36. Head, 1991, p. 88
37. Head, 1991, p. 87
38. Head, 1991, p. 89
39. Head, 1991, p. 112
40. Head, 1991, p. 86
41. 'Three Kinds of Trauma', *Times Literary Supplement*, 29.5.1969, p. 575
42. Borg, *New Statesman*, 16.5.1969, p. 696
43. Foe, *Illustrated London News*, 16.5.1969, p. 696
44. Head, 1991, p. 90
45. Kuper, *South African Outlook*, Dec. 1969, p. 195
46. Carvlin, *National Catholic Reporter*, 2.4.1969
47. Kitchen, in *Tribune*, 11.7.1969
48. KMM 183 BHP 25.7.1969
49. KMM 1 BHP 25.4.1969
50. KMM 66 BHP undated 1969
51. Head, 1991, p. 24
52. KMM 111 BHP 24.7.1969
53. Peek, *New Literature Review*, 1985, p. 6
54. KMM 24 BHP 2.2.1970
55. KMM 24 BHP 9.2.1970
56. Only in Gollancz and McCall editions
57. KMM 60 BHP 18.6.1969
58. KMM 183 BHP 24.9.1974
59. KMM 74 BHP 22.1.1972
60. KMM 183 24.9.1974
61. KMM 64 BHP 22.5.1974
62. KMM 81 BHP 13.5.78
63. Head, 1991, p. 97
64. Head, 1991, p. 104
65. Ravenscroft, *Aspects of South African Literature*, 1976, p. 179
66. Gardner, 1989, p. 116
67. KMM 149 BHP 10.5.1972
68. Kitchen, *Times Higher Educational Supplement*, 1970, p. 36
69. KMM 24 BHP 9.2.1970
70. KMM 81 BHP 3.6.1978
71. KMM 81 BHP 13.5.1978
72. Gardner & Scott, 1986, p. 7
73. KMM 24 BHP 9.2.1970
74. KMM 346 BHP 5.11.1982
75. KMM 24 BHP 9.2.1970
76. Head, 1968, p. 143
77. KMM 74 BHP 16.10.1969
78. KMM 74 BHP 23.8.1971
79. Pinto & Roberts (eds.), *The Complete Poems of D H Lawrence*, 1964, p. 1

Chapter 8

1. Head, 1989, pp. 102–115
2. KMM 68 BHP undated 1970
3. Head, 1991, p. 118
4. Head, 1991, p. 131
5. Head, 1991, p. 89

6. Head, 1991, p. 155
7. Head, 1991, p. 69
8. Head, 1991, p. 122
9. Head, 1991, p. 98
10. KMM 74 BHP November 1969
11. KMM 74 BHP 27.8.1971
12. KMM 37 BHP 1.5.1970
13. KMM 74 BHP 7.7.1970
14. KMM 74 BHP 7.7.1970
15. KMM 74 BHP 27.8.1971
16. Head, 1981, p. 171
17. KMM 74 BHP 4.12.1970
18. Lekhutile, 1991, interview
19. KMM 74 BHP 4.12.1970
20. KMM 74 BHP 15.10.1971
21. Head, 1991, p. 127
22. KMM 1 BHP 25.4.1969
23. Head, 1991, p. 90
24. KMM 15 BHP 23.8.1976
25. Head, 1991, p. 113
26. Head, 1991, p. 123
27. Van Rensburg, 1984, p. 22
28 Van Rensburg, 1984, p. 21
29. Sianana, 1991, interview
30. Head, 1991, p. 93
31. Head, 1990, p. 58
32. Head, 1991, p. 93
33. Head, 1990, p. 51
34. Head, 1990, pp. 52–53
35. For example Ruether, 1975; Goldenberg, 1979
36. KMM 58 BHP 29.11.1967
37. Head, 1991, p. 91
38. Head, 1977, p. 21
39. KMM 38 BHP 31.3.1970
40. KMM 38 BHP 1.5.1970
41. KMM 38 BHP 17.9.1969
42. KMM 38 BHP undated 1970
43. KMM 74 BHP 26.5.1970
44. KMM 43 BHP 19.6.1969
45. Nivedita, 1959
46. KMM 38 BHP undated 1970
47. KMM 38 BHP undated 1970
48. KMM 43 BHP undated 1970
49. KMM 43 BHP undated 1970
50. Head, 1991, p. 84
51. Head, 1991, pp. 130–131
52. KMM 43 BHP undated 1970
53. KMM 38 BHP undated 1970
54. KMM 74 BHP 18.6.1970
55. Head, 1991, pp. 134–135
56. Head, 1991, p. 119
57. KMM 96 BHP undated 1974
58. Head, 1991, p. 103
59. Head, 1991, pp. 106–107
60. Holzinger, 1994, interview
61. KMM 74 BHP 15.10.1970
62. Head, 1991, pp. 131–132
63. KMM 74 BHP 27.8.1971
64. KMM 74 BHP 25.9.1970
65. Head, 1991, p. 114
66. Head, 1991, p. 119

67. KMM 78 BHP 11.1.1970
68. Head, 1991, p. 115
69. KMM 38 BHP 4.7.1969

Chapter 9

1. Head, 1991, p. 161
2. Head, 1973, p. 109
3. Head, 1991, p. 136
4. Van Rensburg, 1991, interview
5. KMM 74 BHP 16.1.1971
6. Head, 1973, p. 172
7. Howard Head, 1991, interview
8. Head, 1991, p. 134
9. KMM 68 BHP 25.3.1971
10. KMM 68 BHP 25.3.1971
11. KMM 24 BHP 27.6.1971
12. KMM 43 BHP 13.7.1971
13. KMM 331 BHP undated 1971
14. KMM 74 BHP 21.7.1971
15. KMM 74 BHP 23.7.1971
16. KMM 74 BHP 12.7.1971
17. KMM 38 BHP 4.7.1969
18. KMM 74 BHP 23.8.1971
19. KMM 43 BHP 13.7.1971
20. KMM 43 BHP 27.6.1971
21. KMM 43 BHP 13.7.1971
22. KMM 68 BHP 4.7.1971
23. KMM 43 BHP 13.7.1971
24. KMM 74 BHP 21.7.1971
25. Head, 1991, p. 144
26. Head, 1991, p. 190
27. Head, 1991, p. 145
28. KMM 74 BHP 21.7.1971
29. KMM 74 BHP 27.8.1971
30. Head, 1981, p. 171
31. KMM 74 BHP 30.12.1971
32. KMM 74 BHP 27.8.1971
33. Head, 1981, p. 171
34. KMM 74 BHP 15.10.1971
35. KMM 74 BHP 27.8.1971
36. KMM 74 BHP 15.10.1971
37. KMM 74 BHP 20.10.1971
38. KMM 74 BHP 30.12.1971
39. KMM 74 BHP 30.12.1971
40. Berridge, *Daily Telegraph*, 28.1.1971
41. *Times Literary Supplement*, 5.2.1971, p. 145
42. Barber, *Tribune*, 26.2.1971
43. Levin, *New York Times Book Review*, 26.9.1971, p. 47
44. KMM 24 BHP 22.1.1972
45. KMM 74 BHP 17.3.1972
46. KMM 74 BHP 17.3.1972
47. KMM 24 BHP 1.4.1972
48. Head, 1990, p. 47
49. KMM 24 BHP 1.4.1972
50. KMM 74 BHP 23.8.1971
51. KMM 25 BHP 23.8.1974
52. KMM 48 BHP 11.11.1974
53. KMM 75 BHP 31.8.1974
54. KMM 48 BHP 12.11.1973

55. Head, 1977, p. 48
56. KMM 60 BHP 27.4.1972
57. KMM 24 BHP 9.5.1972
58. KMM 74 BHP 19.5.1972
59. KMM 74 BHP 16.5.1972
60. KMM 74 BHP 27.6.1972
61. KMM 77 BHP 13.9.1974
62. KMM 59 BHP 24.8.1972
63. KMM 59 BHP 27.9.1972
64. KMM 44 BHP 8.7.1972
65. KMM 24 BHP 19.1.1970
66 Head, 1991, p. 118
67. KMM 44 BHP 8.7.1972

Chapter 10

1. KMM 44 BHP 8.12.1972
2. KMM 44 BHP 27.12.1972
3. KMM 74 BHP 17.3.1973
4. Head, 1991, p. 174. In Benton, *Naomi Mitchison*, 1990, there is no mention of NM's friendship with Bessie Head.
5. Holzinger, 1994, interview
6. Head, 1991, p. 174
7. Head, in Barber, 1975
8. KMM 331 BHP 25.2.1973
9. KMM 47 BHP 4.7.1973
10. KMM 378 BHP 11.10.1973
11. Harold Head, 1994, interview
12. KMM 64 BHP 2.10.1973
13. Head, 1973, p. 63; Kitchen, *New Statesman*, 2.11.1973, pp. 657–658
14. KMM 74 BHP 8.11.1973
15. Rubinstein, *New Republic*, 27.4.1974, pp. 30–31; KMM 96 BHP undated 1974
16. Sianana, 1991, interview
17. Head, 1981, p. 20
18. KMM 76 BHP 28.1.1975
19. Head, 1981, p. 127
20. KMM 49 BHP 15.11.1974
21. Head, 1981, pp. 10–18
22. KMM 70 BHP 27.6.1974
23. KMM 44 BHP 5.1.1974
24. KMM 75 BHP 4.1.74
25. Head, 1989, p. 125
26. Head, 1989, p. 130
27. Head, 1989, p. 18
28. KMM 52 BHP 23.5.1974
29. KMM 52 BHP 23.10.1974
30. KMM 25 BHP 21.7.1974
31. Head, 1981, p. xv
32. KMM 18 BHP 24.9.1974
33. Head, 1981, p. x
34. KMM 96 BHP 7.2.1976
35. KMM 75 BHP 16.10.73
36. KMM 44 BHP 12.5.1974
37. Cullinan, 1991, interview
38. KMM 183 BHP 30.6.1974
39. KMM 61 BHP 11.6.1974
40. Head, *Child Education*, 1974, p. 7
41. KMM 44 BHP 26.6.1974

42. KMM 15 BHP 28.5.1977
43. KMM 20 BHP 29.1.1978
44. KMM 96 BHP 7.2.1976
45. KMM 19 BHP 17.9.1974
46. KMM 19 BHP 24.9.74
47. Kgamane, 1991, interview
48. Head, 1977, pp. 76–80
49. KMM 76 BHP 16.9.1974
50. KMM 44 BHP 6.11.1974
51. KMM 76 BHP 28.9.1974
52. Head, *Mmegi wa Dikgang,* 23.3.1985, p. 6
53. Sianana, 1991, interview
54. KMM 48 BHP 12.11.1973; see ch. 9
55. Howard Head, 1991, interview

Chapter 11

1. KMM 63 BHP 9.8.1974
2. KMM 44 BHP 28/29.12.1974
3. KMM 44 BHP 15.2.1975
4. KMM 44 BHP 25.2.1975
5. Fradkin, *World Literature Written in English,* 1978
6. Head, 1990, p. 57
7. Head, *London Magazine,* 1975
8. KMM 44 BHP 9.9.1975
9. KMM 183 BHP 12.5.1975
10. KMM 61 BHP 18.9.1975
11. KMM 44 BHP 24.9.1975
12. KMM 44 BHP 19.10.1975
13. KMM 44 BH 25.11.1975
14. Cullinan, 1991, interview; KMM 61 BHP 17.5.1976
15. KMM 61 BHP 17.5.1976
16. KMM 421 BHP 14.7.1975
17. KMM 9 BHP 19.7.1975
18. KMM 333 BHP 4.8.1975
19. Head, 1991, p. 193
20. KMM 61 BHP 31.5.1976
21. KMM 59 BHP 22.11.1976
22. KMM 75 BHP 17.1.1975
23. KMM 75 BHP 26.1.1975
24. KMM 75 BHP 1.6.1975
25. KMM 75 BHP 25.9.1975
26. KMM 183 BHP 29.10.1975
27. Head, 1991, p. 69
28. KMM 15 BHP 4.2.1976
29. KMM 76 BHP 11.11.1974
30. KMM 183 BHP 30.6.1974
31. KMM 75 BHP 14.10 1973
32. KMM 25 BHP 23.8.1974
33. KMM 15 BHP 31.5.1976
34. KMM 15 BHP 28.12.1975
35. KMM 42 BHP 5.1.1976
36. KMM 49 BHP 15.11.1974
37. Head, 1981, p 174
38. KMM 49 BHP 15.11.1974
39. KMM 15 BHP 10.6.1975
40. KMM 53 BHP 26.2.1976
41. Sianana, 1991, interview
42. Howard Head, 1991, interview
43. KMM 15 BHP 10.6.1975

44. KMM 18 BHP 3.4.1975
45. KMM 25 BHP 21.7.1974
46. Head, 1991, p. 175
47. Head, 1991, p. 201
48. Head, 1990, p. 64
49. KKM 34 BHP 15.4.1976
50. Gray, *London Magazine,* 1991, p. 138
51. Gray, *London Magazine,* 1991, p. 139
52. KMM 128 BHP undated, early 1976
53. KMM 128 BHP 2.5.1976
54. *Newsweek,* 28.6.1976
55. *Newsweek,* 16.8.1976
56. *Newsweek,* 6.9.1976
57. KMM 84 BHP 2.7.1976
58. KMM 28 BHP 27.12.1976
59. KMM 84 BHP 2.7.1976
60. KMM 20 BHP 1.9.1978
61. KMM 25 BHP 28.2.1973
62. KMM 331 BHP 25.2.1973
63. KMM 15 BHP 10.6.1975
64. KMM 25 BHP 23.8.1974
65. KMM 44 BHP 21.8.1973
66. KMM 34 BHP 7.12.1975
67. KMM 25 BHP 28.2.1973
68. KMM 47 BHP 21.1.1976
69. KMM 15 BHP 4.2.1976
70. KMM 25 BHP 21.7.1974
71. KMM 47 BHP 21.1.1976
72. KMM 15 BHP 4.2.1976
73. KMM 331 BHP 18.7.1970
74. KMM 44 BHP 28/29.12.1974
75. KMM 25 BHP 28.2.1973
76. KMM 19 BHP 28.7.1974
77. KMM 76 BHP 28.1.1975
78. KMM 15 BHP 4.2.1976
79. KMM 457 BHP undated; see also KMM 44 BHP 28/29.12.1974; KMM 55 BHP 12.11.1982
80. KMM 55 BHP 12.11.1982
81. KMM 19 BHP 28.7.1974
82. KMM 15 BHP 4.2.1976
83. KMM 76 BHP 11.11.1974
84. KMM 15 BHP 4.2.1976
85. KMM 70 BHP 27.6.1974
86. KMM 183 BHP 30.6.1974

Chapter 12

1. KMM 15 BHP 30.10.1976
2. KMM 15 BHP 30.10.1976
3. *Time,* 17.11.1975
4. KMM 34 BHP 4.6.1977
5. *Time,* 27.6.1977
6. KMM 15 BHP 26.7.1976
7. Hanlon, 1986, p. 220
8. KMM 34 BHP 30.4.1978
9. KMM 34 BHP 9.6.1978
10. KMM 99 BHP 26.9.1976
11. KMM 15 BHP 30.10.1976
12. KMM 15 BHP 30.10.1976
13. KMM 99 BHP 26.9.1976
14. KMM 183 BHP 1.12.1974

15. KMM 44 BHP 10.3.1981
16. KMM 15 BHP 3.4.1977
17. KMM 44 BHP 1.7.1975
18. KMM 71 BHP 15.8.1980
19. KMM 60 BHP 10.9.1969
20. Head, 1989, p. 66. Following pp. refer to this work.
21. KMM 15 BHP 23.6.1977
22. KMM 74 BHP 22.1.1972
23. KMM 247 BHP 1.3.1977
24. KMM 15 BHP 18.3.1977
25. KMM 26 BHP 9.8.1978
26. KMM 44 BHP 2.12.1974
27. KMM 71 BHP 15.8.1980
28. Marquard, *London Magazine*, 1978/1979, pp. 48–61

Chapter 13

1. KMM 15 BHP 27.7.1977
2. KMM 15 BHP 3.9.1977
3. Head, 1990, p. 92
4. KMM 15 BHP 3.9.1977
5. KMM 269 BHP 28.9.1977
6. KMM 298 BHP 22.9.1977
7. KMM 269 BHP 28.9.1977
8. KMM 269 BHP 28.9.1977
9. KMM 15 BHP 3.9.1977
10. KMM 15 BHP 3.9.1977
11. KMM 76 BHP 28.9.1977
12. KMM 298 BHP 22.9.1977
13. KMM 20 BHP 29.1.1978
14. KMM 297 BHP 18.9.1977
15. KMM 15 BHP 3.9.1977
16. KMM 19 BHP 4.12.1977
17. Nazareth, *World Literature Today*, 7/14, 1991
18. KMM 3 BHP 27.1.1977
19. KMM 19 BHP 4.12.1977
20. Carvlin, 1994, interview
21. KMM 20 BHP 29.1.1978
22. Giovanni, 1974
23. KMM 15 BHP 14.12.1977
24. KMM 19 BHP 4.12.1977
25. KMM 331 BHP 20.11.1977
26. Cunningham, *New Statesman*, 1978, pp. 746–747
27. Mellors, *The Listener*, 1978, p. 510
28. KMM 20 BHP 29.1.1978
29. KMM 76 BHP 28.1.1978
30. KMM 3 BHP 27.1.1978
31. KMM 15 BHP 10.1.1978
32. Head, 1991, p. 217
33. KMM 15 BHP 9.2.1978
34. KMM 15 BHP 8.3.1978
35. KMM 15 BHP 8.3.1978
36. KMM 84 BHP 27.1.1978
37. KMM 84 BHP 13.3.1978
38. Head, 1991, p. 220
39. Pogrund, 1991, p. 6
40. Pogrund, 1991, p. 65
41. Holzinger, 1994, interview
42. KMM 15 BHP 30.6.1978
43. KMM 34 BHP 27.8.1978

44. KMM 34 BHP 27.8.1978
45. KMM 34 BHP 26.7.1978
46. KMM 15 BHP 27.11.1978
47. KMM15 BHP 24.12.1978
48. KMM 73 BHP 16.7.1978
49. KMM 73 BHP 13.8.1978
50. KMM 73 BHP 16.7.1978
51. KMM 47 BHP 30.12.1978
52. KMM 152 BHP 26.6.1980
53. KMM 73 BHP 16.7.1978
54. KMM 73 BHP 2.2.1979
55. KMM 73 BHP 7.9.1978
56. KMM 73 BHP 18.11.1978
57. Heywood, 1979
58. KMM 81 BHP 3.6.1978

Chapter 14

1. KMM 20 BHP 22.1.1979
2. KMM 187 BHP 23.11.1978
3. KMM 20 BHP 22.1.1979
4. KMM 333 BHP 12.2.1979
5. KMM 73 BHP 2.2.1979
6. KMM 73 BHP 2.2.1979. Recorded in ch. 7
7. KMM 73 BHP 2.2.1979
8. KMM 187 BHP 23.11.1978
9. KMM 73 BHP 2.2.1979
10. KMM 187 BHP 16.2.1979
11. KMM 73 BHP 2.3.1979
12. KMM 187 BHP 16.2.1979
13. Head, 1991, p. 118
14. Bruner, *Ba Shiru*, 1977, pp. 23–31
15. KMM 40 BHP 19.5.1979
16. KMM 187 BHP undated 1979 ('News about Berlin')
17. KMM 15 BHP 19.7.1979
18. KMM 187 BHP undated 1979 ('News about Berlin')
19. Head, 1990, pp. 65–72
20. Head, 1990, p. 67
21. Head, 1990, p. 66
22. KMM 28 BHP 22.2.1980
23. KMM 8 BHP 17.3.1988
24. KMM 330 BHP 28.9.1979
25. KMM 330 BHP 19.8.1979
26. KMM 330 BHP 28.9.1979
27. KMM 187 BHP undated 1979 ('News about Berlin')
28. KMM 180 BHP 31.3.1980
29. KMM 185 BHP 25.3.1983
30. KMM 34 BHP 27.11.1978
31. KMM 34 BHP 15.12.1978
32. KMM 34 BHP 27.11.1978
33. KMM 34 BHP undated 1979
34. KMM 34 BHP 22.10.1979
35. KMM 34 BHP 5.11.1979
36. KMM 34 BHP undated 1979
37. KMM 34 BHP 22.10.1979
38. KMM 34 BHP 21.9.1979
39. KMM 47 BHP 30.12.1978
40. KMM 47 BHP 30.12.1978
41. KMM 47 BHP 29.12.1976
42. KMM 47 BHP 24.2.1979
43. KMM 152 BHP 25.4.1980; 26.6.1980

44. Seretse Khama, 1980, p. vii
45. Seretse Khama, p. xiv
46. KMM 34 BHP 15.8.1980
47. KMM 27 BHP 4.2.1980
48. KMM 27 BHP 1.10.1980
49. KMM 76 BHP 28.1.1975
50. KMM 72 BHP 19.9.1982
51. KMM 47 BHP 24.2.1979
52. KMM 44 BHP 26.1.1981 (see also KMM 72 BHP 19.9.1982)
53. Head, *Mmegi Wa Dikgang*, 3.8.1985, p. 7
54. KMM 40 BHP 17.1.1981
55. Hansen, 'TV i Aftes', *Information*, 19.9.82
56. Head, 1991, p. 223
57. Mohammed, 1992, interview
58. KMM 189 BHP 10.6.1985
59. Grant, 1993, interview
60. KMM 74 BHP 9.1.1981
61. KMM 74 BHP undated 1981
62. KMM 113 BHP 13.1.1981

Chapter 15

1. Head, 1991, p. 224
2. KMM 15 BHP 27.6.1979
3. KMM 71 BHP 11.12.1981
4. KMM 74 BHP 28.12.1980
5. KMM 74 BHP 9.1.1981
6. KMM 44 BHP 9.1.1981
7. KMM 44 BHP 26.1.1981
8. KMM 44 BHP 27.2.1981
9. KMM 8 BHP 20.10.1981
10. Head, 1990, p. 87
11. Head, 1990, p. 82
12. KMM 27 BHP 7.3.1981
13. KMM 59 BHP 9.1.1981
14. KMM 59 BHP 9.1.1981
15. Head, 1981, p. v
16. *The Listener*, 2.7.1981, pp. 23–24
17. Grant, *South*, August 1981, p. 55
18. *New Society*, 9.7.1981, pp. 73–74
19. KMM 231 BHP 21.8.1981
20. KMM 71 BHP 31.5.1981
21. KMM 8 BHP 28.2.1982
22. KMM 17 BHP 7.9.1982
23. KMM 179 BHP 25.10.1982
24. KMM 34 BHP 15.3.1979
25. KMM 34 BHP 15.12.1978
26. KMM 34 BHP 15.12.1978
27. Head, *Mmegi wa Dikgang*, 30.3.1985, p. 6
28. KMM 108 BHP 26.11.1982
29. KMM 108 BHP 16.6.1983
30. KMM 362 BHP 29.7.1983
31. Forchhammer, 1988, interview
32. KMM 71 BHP 3.9.1982
33. KMM 71 BHP 3.9.1982
34. KMM 74 BHP 15.6.1983
35. KMM 28 BHP 26.6.1982
36. KMM 158 BHP 27.6.1982
37. KMM 71 BHP 3.9.1982
38. KMM 28 BHP 26.6.1982

39. KMM 71 BHP 3.9.1982
40. KMM 347 BHP 23.11.1981
41. KMM 344 BHP 3.2.1986
42. KMM 342 BHP 11.7.1980
43. Lawrence, 1924,p. 8
44. KMM 74 BHP 21.3.1983
45. Gardner, 1986, p. 110
46. KMM 7 BHP 8.2.1983
47. Gardner, 1986, p. 111
48. Gardner, 1986, p. 112
49. KMM 163 BHP 25.3.1983
50. KMM 163 BHP 13.4.1983
51. KMM 185 BHP 24.3.1983
52. Gardner, 1986, p. 111
53. Gardner, 1986, p. 125
54. KMM 185 BHP 18.6.1983
55. KMM 39 BHP 4.4.1984
56. Gardner, 1986, p. 126
57. Gardner, 1986, p. 123
58. Gardner, 1986, p. 124
59. KMM 185 BHP 28.7.1983
60. KMM 293 BHP 29.9.1983
61. KMM 202 BHP 21.6.1983
62. KMM 40 BHP 28.2.1979
63. KMM 7 BHP 8.2.1983
64. KMM 7 BHP 8.2.1983
65. KMM 7 BHP 17.3 1983
66. Gray, 1974
67. Abrahams & Saunders, 1976
68. Marquard, 1978
69. Adey, 1982
70. KMM 37 BHP 26.2.1983
71. KMM 72 BHP 21.6.1983
72. KMM 72 BHP 21.6.1983
73. KMM 373 BHP undated 1983
74. KMM 373 BHP 27.12.1983
75. KMM 161 BHP 20.12.1983
76. KMM 362 BHP 29.7.1983
77. KMM 27 BHP 30.10.1985
78. KMM 74 BHP 27.7.1983
79. KMM 74 BHP 5.1.1984
80. KMM 74 BHP 9.10.1983
81. KMM 74 BHP 5.1.1984
82. KMM 183 BHP 23.2.1974
83. KMM 19 BHP 2.7.1974
84. KMM 71 BHP 26.7.1978
85. KMM 84 BHP 16.9.1978
86. KMM 84 BHP 16.9.1978
87. KMM 59 BHP 18.1.1979
88. KMM 59 BHP 18.1.1979
89. KMM 183 BHP 16.9.1980
90. KMM 27 BHP 1.10.1980
91. KMM 22 BHP 1.4.1978
92. Head, *Mmegi wa Dikgang*, 23.3.1985, p. 6
93. KMM 84 BHP 16.9.1978

Chapter 16

1. Khama, *Botswana Daily News*, 19.5.1970
2. KMM 74 BHP 21.3.1983
3. Pasternak, 1965, p. 496

4. KMM 17 BHP 16.12.1983
5. Forchhammer, 1991, interview
6. Head, *Mmegi wa Dikgang*, 30.3.1985, p. 6
7. KMM 74 BHP 3.10.1985
8. KMM 185 BHP 1.5.1984
9. KMM 185 BHP 1.5.1984
10. KMM 74 BHP 18.6.1985
11. KMM 185 BHP 1.5.1984
12. KMM 185 BHP 1.5.1984
13. Published in *New Literature Review*, vol. 14, 1985, pp. 5–13, Canberra
14. KMM 373 BHP 28.3.1984
15. KMM 37 BHP 1.7.1984
16. KMM 37 BHP 27.6.1984
17. KMM 37 BHP 11.9.1984
18. KMM 69 BHP 11.10.1984
19. Kuzwayo, *Call Me Woman*, p. xi
20. KMM 115 BHP 13.3.1984
21. UWL JMP, A 1849, C 9.12.2
22. KMM 7 BHP 4.4.1984
23. KMM 7 BHP 15.5.1984
24. KMM 7 BHP 22.5.1984
25. KMM 337 BHP 28.8.1984
26. KMM 337 BHP 1.9.1984
27. KMM 74 BHP 5.1.1984
28. KMM 373 BHP 28.3.1984
29. KMM 74 BHP 9.10.1985
30. Kikia, 1988, interview
31. KMM 189 BHP 5.9.1985
32 KMM 15 BHP 8.3.1978
33. KMM Head's private papers 5.4.1984*
34. KMM Head's private papers 12.7.1984*
35. KMM 27 BHP 16.5.1984
36. KMM 27 BHP 31.5.1984
37. KMM 27 BHP 21.9.1984
38. KMM 27 BHP 16.6.1984
39. KMM 37 BHP 1.7.1984
40. *Mmegi wa Dikgang*, 26.1.1985, p. 10
41. *Natal Witness*, 10.6.1985, p. 6
42. *Pretoria News*, 21.3.1985, p. 24
43. KMM 74 BHP 24.10.1985
44. KMM 37 BHP 29.1.1985
45. Fairbairn, 1992, interview
46. Harold Head, 1994, interview
47. KMM 74 BHP 15.11.1984
48. Howard Head, 1991, interview
49. KMM 189 BHP 5.9.1985
50. Head, *Mmegi wa Dikgang*, 23.3.1985, p. 6
51. Head, 1973, p. 206
52 Head, *Mmegi wa Dikgang*, 30.3.1985, p. 6
53. Head, 1973, p. 205
54. Head, *Mmegi wa Dikgang*, 30.3.1985, p. 6
55. KMM 182 BHP 22.2.1985
56. KMM 74 BHP 3.10.1985
57. KMM 393 BHP 10.7.1985
58. KMM 151 BHP 26.7.1985
59. KMM 74 BHP 3.10.1985
60. Head, *Mmegi wa Dikgang*, 3.8.1985, p. 7
61. *New Statesman*, vol. 110 (2839), pp. 21–23)
62. KMM Head's private papers 30.7.1985*
63. KMM 27 BHP 30.10.1985

64. KMM 27 BHP 16.11.1985
65. KMM 74 BHP 30.1.1986
66. KMM 27 BHP 30.10.1985
67. KMM 373 BHP 14.10.1985
68. KMM 373 BHP 14.10.1985
69. KMM 225 BHP 25.6.1985
70. KMM 27 BHP 16.11.1985
71. KMM 45 BHP 6.7.1985
72 KMM 104 BHP 26.6.1983
73. KMM 74 BHP 18.6.1985
74. KMM 189 BHP 10.6.1985
75. KMM 189 BHP 27.2.1986
76. KMM 74 BHP 9.10.1985
77. Barclays Bank savings passbook, 12.12.1985; 17.1.1986
78. Forchhammer, 1991, interview
79. Gray, *London Magazine*, 1991, p. 138
80. KMM 189 BHP 27.2.1986
81. KMM 178 BHP 8.1.1986
82. KMM 44 BHP 21.8.1973
83. Sianana, 1991, interview
84. Dardis, 1989
85. Pearce, 1991, interview
86. Pearce, 1991, interview

Bibliography

Works by Bessie Head

Books

1968 *When Rain Clouds Gather.* New York: Simon & Schuster; London: Gollancz, 1969.
1971 *Maru.* London: Gollancz; New York: McCall.
1973 *A Question of Power.* London: Davis-Poynter; New York: Pantheon.
1977 *The Collector of Treasures and Other Botswana Village Tales.* London: Heinemann; Cape Town: David Philip.
1981 *Serowe: Village of the Rain Wind.* Cape Town: David Philip; London: Heinemann.
1984 *A Bewitched Crossroad: An African Saga.* Johannesburg: Donker.
1989 *Tales of Tenderness and Power,* ed. Gillian Stead Eilersen. Johannesburg: Donker; Oxford: Heinemann, 1990.
1990 *A Woman Alone: Autobiographical Writings,* ed. Craig MacKenzie. Oxford: Heinemann.
1991 *A Gesture of Belonging: Letters from Bessie Head, 1965–1979,* ed. Randolph Vigne. London: SA Writers; Portsmouth, NH: Heinemann; Johannesburg: Witwatersrand UP.
1993 *The Cardinals. With Meditations and Short Stories,* ed. M. J. Daymond. Cape Town: David Philip.

Articles and chapters in books

1951 'The Stepping Stones of Truth'. In *Goodwill,* ed. M McLarty. Johannesburg: Goodwill Council
1962 'Things I Don't Like'. *New African* (1.7):10.
'Let Me Tell a Story Now'. *New African* (1.9):8–9.
1963 'An Unspeakable Crime'. *New African* (2.1):11.
'A Gentle People: The Warm, Uncommitted "Coloureds" of the Cape.' *New African* (2.8):169–170.
'Letter from South Africa: For a Friend, "D.B."' *Transition,* (3.11):40.
'Gladys Mgudlandu: The Exuberant Innocent'. *New African* (2.10):209.
1964 'The Isolation of "Boeta L.": Atteridgeville in 1964'. *New African* (3.2):28–29.
'Snowball: A Story'. *New African* (3.5):100–101.
'The Green Tree'. *Transition,* Sept./Oct. (4.16):33.
'Letter: Transition 16'. *Transition* (4.17):6.

1965 'For Serowe: A Village in Africa'. *New African* (4.10):230.
1966 'Looking for a Rain-God: A Story of Botswana'. *New African* (5.3):65.
'West–East–South'. Reviews of *The First Book of Ghana* by Norman M.
Lobsenz, *East African Sarari* by W H Stevens and *Southern Africa* by Brian
Fagin. *New African* (June):114.
'Chibuku Beer and Independence'. *New African* (5.9):200.
'The Woman from America'. *New Statesman* 26 August:287.
1967 'Sorrow Food'. *Transition* (6.30):47–48.
'Village People, Botswana'. *Classic* (2.3):19–25.
'Tao: A Short Story'. *Freedomways* (7.1):26–32.
1968 'God and the Underdog: Thoughts on the Rise of Africa'. *New African* (7.2):47–48.
1969 'African Religions'. *New African* (53):46–47.
1971 'Letter from Botswana'. *New York Times* 12 Nov.
1972 'An African Story'. *The Listener* 30 November:735–736.
'Chief Sekoto Holds Court'. Extract from *When Rain Clouds Gather*. In *Africa Is
Thunder and Wonder: Contemporary Voices from African Literature*, ed. B.
Nolen. New York: Scribner.
1973 'The Prisoner Who Wore Glasses'. *London Magazine* (13.4):7–13.
1974 'Bamangwato Children'. *Child Education* May:7, 13.
1975 'Heaven Is Not Closed'. *Black World* (25.1/2):54–60.
'Life'. *Encounter* (44.6):3–8.
'The Special One'. *Essence* (6):38, 63–65.
'Despite Broken Bondage, Botswana Women Are Still Unloved'. *The Times* 13
August: 5.
'Witchcraft'. *Ms* (4):72–7, 121.
'Oranges and Lemons'. *London Magazine* (15.2):38–46.
'Autobiographical Sketch'. *Ms* (4):72–73.
'Dear Tim, Will You Please Come to My Birthday Party'. In *One Parent Families*,
ed. D Barber. London: Davis-Poynter.
1977 'Makeba Music'. *Donga* (4):6.
'The Village Saint: A Short Story'. *New Classic* (4):12–17.
'The Collector of Treasures'. *Ms* (5.12):58–61.
'A Period of Darkness'. *Kutlwano* (16.10):20, 28, 32.
1978 'Some Notes on Novel Writing'. *New Classic* (5):30–32.
1979 'A Note on Rain Clouds'. *The Gar* (33):27.
'Social and Political Pressures That Shape Literature in South Africa'. *World
Literature Written in English* (18.1):20–26.
1980 'The Lovers'. *Wietie* (2):1–-23.
'A Power Struggle'. *Bananas: New Writing from Africa* 22 August:23–24.
1980–1 'The Coming of the Christ-Child: A Short Story'. *Marang* (3):69–79.
1981 'Tumbale and the Onslaught of the Matabele'. Extract from *A Bewitched
Crossroad. The Bloody Horse* (3):5–8.
'Sebina and the Missionary'. Extract from *A Bewitched Crossroad. The Bloody
Horse* (3):8–11.
1982 'Notes from a Quiet Backwater'. *Drum* February:35–36.
Foreword to new edn of *Native Life in South Africa* by Sol Plaatje. Johannesburg:
Ravan.
1983 'The Old Iron Cooking Pot of Europe'. *LIP from Southern African Women*, ed. S
Brown, I Hofmeyr & S Rosenberg. Johannesburg: Ravan.
1984 'A Search for Historical Continuity and Roots'. *Momentum: On Recent South*

African Writing, ed. M Daymond, J Jacobs and M Lenta. Pietermaritzburg: Natal UP.

1985 'Collecting Oral History'. *Mmegi wa Dikgang* 23 March:6.
'Why Do I Write?' *Mmegi wa Dikgang* 30 March:7.
'Themes Found in a Writer's Private Workshop'. *Mmegi wa Dikgang* 3 August:7, 9. Also published as 'Writing out of Southern Africa'. *New Statesman* 16 August:21–23.
Foreword to *Call Me Woman* by Ellen Kuzwayo. Johannesburg: Ravan.

1987 'Some Happy Memories of Iowa'. *The World Comes to Iowa: Iowa International Anthology*, ed. P Engle, R Torrevillas & H Engle. Iowa: Iowa State UP.

1990 'For "Napoleon Bonaparte", Jenny and Kate'. *Southern African Review of Books* (3.6):12–15.

Secondary material

For the most comprehensive bibliography of works by and about Bessie Head see *Bessie Head: A Bibliography*, compiled by Craig MacKenzie and Catherine Woeber, Grahamstown: NELM, 1992.

Abrahams, C (ed.) *The Tragic Life: Bessie Head and Literature in Southern Africa.* Trenton, NJ: Africa World Press, 1990

Abrahams, L & Saunders, W (eds.) *Quarry '76: New South African Writing.* Johannesburg: Donker, 1976

Adams, H & Suttner, H. *William Street, District Six.* Cape Town: Chameleon, 1988

Adey, D (ed.) *Under the Southern Cross: Short Stories from South Africa.* Johannesburg: Donker, 1982

Alverson, H. *Mind in the Heart of Darkness.* New Haven: Yale UP, 1978

American Psychiatric Association. *Diagnostic and Statistical Manual of Mental Disorders*, 3rd edn, rev. Washington, DC: American Psychiatric Ass., 1987

Barber, D. 'A Vessel of Optimism'. *Tribune*, 26.2.1971

Barnett, U A. *Vision of Order.*. London: Browne; Amherst: Massachusetts UP, 1983

Beard, S. 'Bessie Head's A Question of Power. The Journey Through Disintegration to Wholeness'. *Colby Library Quarterly* (15.4):267–274

Benson, M. 'Tshekedi Khama As I Knew Him'. *Botswana Notes and Records* (8), 1977

Benton, J. *Naomi Mitchison A Biography.* London: Pandora, 1990

Ben-Tovim, D. *Development Psychiatry: Mental Health and Primary Health Care in Botswana.* London: Tavistock, 1987

Berridge, E. 'Recent Fiction'. *Daily Telegraph*, 28.1.1971

Borg, M. 'Victims'. *New Statesman*, 16.5.1969

Bruner, C. 'Been-To or Has-Been: A Dilemma for Today's African Woman'. *Ba Shiru* (8.2), 1977

Bruner, C. 'Child Africa As Depicted by Bessie Head and Ama Ata Aidoo'. *Studies in the Humanities* (7.2):5–12

Carvlin, T. 'Biting into the Affluent Income'. *National Catholic Reporter*, 2.4 1969

Cilliers, S. *The Coloureds of South Africa: A Factual Survey.* Cape Town: Bannier, 1963

Clayton, C. ' "A World Elsewhere": Bessie Head As Historian'. *English in Africa* (15.1):55–69

Clayton, C (ed.) *Women and Writing in South Africa: A Critical Anthology.* Marshalltown: Heinemann, 1989

Cunningham, V. 'The Feeling of Onslaught'. *New Statesman*, 2.6.1978

Dardis, T. *The Thirsy Muse: Alcohol and the American Writer.* New York: Abacus, 1989

Davenport, T. *South Africa: A Modern History.* London: Macmillan, 1984

Davies, R, O'Meara, D & Dlamini, S. *The Struggle for South Africa: A Reference Guide.* London: Zed, 1984

Driver, D. 'Reconstructing the Past, Shaping the Future: Bessie Head and the Question of Feminism in a New South Africa'. In G Wisker (ed.), *Black Women's Writing.* London: Macmillan, 1993

Dutfield, M A. *Marriage of Inconvenience.* London: Unwin Hyman, 1990

Evasdaughter, E. 'Bessie Head's A Question of Power Read As a Mariner's Guide to Paranoia'. *Research in African Literatures* (20.1):72–83

Foe, D. *Illustrated London News,* 16.5.1969

Fradkin, B. 'Conversations with Bessie'. *World Literature Written in English* (17.2), 1978

Gabatshwana, S. *Seretse Khama and Botswana.* 1966

Gardner, S. 'Don't Ask for the True Story: A Memoir of Bessie Head'. *Hecate* (12.1–2), 1986

Gardner, S & Scott, P. *Bessie Head A Bibliography.* Grahamstown: NELM, 1986

Gibberd, V. 'The Re-education of Patrick van Rensburg'. *Botswana Notes and Records* (7), 1975

Giovanni, N A. *Poetic Equation: Conversations Between Nikki Giovanni and Margaret Walker.* Washington: Howard UP, 1974

Goldenberg, N. *The Changing of the Gods: Feminism and the End of Traditional Religions.* Boston: Beacon 1979

Grant, J. 'Encounters with Remarkable Men'. *South: The Third World Magazine* (10), 1981

Gray, S. 'Crying Voice'. *London Magazine* (31.5/6), 1991

Gray, S (ed.) *On the Edge of the World: Southern African Stories of the Seventies.* Johannesburg: Donker, 1974

Hamrell, S (ed.) *Refugee Problems in Africa.* Uppsala: SIAS, 1967

Hanlon, J (ed.) *Beggar Your Neighbour: Apartheid Power in Southern Africa.* London: Currey, 1986

Head, Harold. 'Exit', *The Horizon History of America.* New York; Am. Heritage, 1971

Heywood, C. 'Traditional Values in the Novels of Bessie Head'. In *Individual and Community in Commonwealth Literature,* ed. D Massa. Msida: Malta UP, 1979

Horrell, M. *The Education of the Coloured Community in South Africa 1652–1970.* Johannesburg: SAIRR, 1970

Huxley, E. 'An African "Akenfield".' *New Society,* 9.7.1981

Johnson, J. 'Structures of Meaning in the Novels of Bessie Head'. *Kunapipi* (8:1):56–69

Khama, S. *Botswana: A Developing Democracy in Southern Africa.* Uppsala: Dag Hammarskjöld Foundation, 1970

Khama, S. *Frontline Speeches of Seretse Khama.* London: Collings, 1980

Kitchen, P. 'The Way to a New World'. *Tribune,* 11.7.1969

Kitchen, P. 'Interview by Post'. *Times Educational Supplement,* 11.9.1970

Kitchen, P. 'Surviving'. *New Statesman,* 2.11.1973

Kitchen, P. 'Peace in Serowe'. *The Listener,* 2.7.1981

Kuper, H. *Indian People in Natal.* Westport: Greenwood, 1960

Kuzwayo, E. *Call Me Woman.* Johannesburg: Ravan, 1985

Laband, J & Haswell, R (eds.) *Pietermaritzburg 1838–1988: A New Portrait of an African City.* Pietermaritzburg: UNP and Shuter & Shooter, 1988

Larson, C. 'The Singular Consciousness'. In *The Novel in the Third World.* Washington: Inscape

Lawrance, D. 'Understanding the Past'. *Natal Witness,* 10.7.1985

Lawrence, D. *Studies in Classic American Literature.* London: Heinemann, 1924

Levin, M. 'Reader's Report'. *New York Times Book Review,* 26.9.1971

Lipman, B. *We Make Freedom: Women in South Africa.* London: Pandora, 1984

Lodge, T. *Black Politics in South Africa since 1945.* London: Longman, 1983

MacKenzie, C & Clayton, C. *Between the Lines.* Grahamstown: NELM, 1989

Marquard, J. 'Bessie Head: Exile and Community in Southern Africa'. *London Magazine* (18.9&10), 1978/1979

Marquard, J (ed.) *A Century of South African Short Stories.* Johannesburg: Donker, 1978

Mbiti, J. *African Religions and Philosophy.* London: Heinemann, 1969

Mellors, J. 'Exuberant Lies'. *The Listener,* 20.4.1978

Mitchison, N. 'For Serowe: A Capital City'. *New African,* March 1966

Nazareth, P. Review. *World Literature Today,* 1991

Newmarch, D. Review. *Current Writing: Text and Reception in Southern Africa* (2.1), 1990

Nivedita. *The Master As I Saw Him.* Calcutta: Udbodhan, 1910; 8th edn, 1959

Nkosi, L. *Home and Exile.* London: Longman, 1965

Nkosi, L. *Tasks and Masks: Themes and Styles of African Literature.* London: Longman, 1981

Ogunbesan, K. 'The Cape Gooseberry Also Grows in Botswana: Alienation and Commitment in the Writings of Bessie Head'. *Présence Africaine* (109):92–106

Padmore, G. *Africa and World Peace.* London: Frank Cass, 1937; 2nd edn, 1972

Pasternak, B. 'The Poems of Yuri Zhivago'. In *Doctor Zhivago.* London: Collins Harvill, 1987

Peek, A. 'Bessie Head and the African Novel'. *New Literature Review* (14), 1985

Petersen, K H & Rutherford, A (eds.) *A Double Colonization: Colonial and Post-Colonial Women's Writing.* Mundelstrup: Dangaroo, 1986

Pinto, V & Roberts, W (eds.) *The Complete Poems of D H Lawrence.* London: Heinemann, 1964

Plaatje, S. *Native Life in South Africa.* London: King, 1916; London: Longman, 2nd edn, 1987

Pogrund, B. *How Can Man Die Better: Sobukwe and Apartheid.* London, 1991

Ravenscroft, A. 'The Novels of Bessie Head'. In *Aspects of South African Literature,* ed. C Heywood. London: Heinemann, 1976

Renou, L (ed.) *Hinduism.* NewYork: Simon & Schuster, 1961

Rive, R. 'Growing Up in District Six'. *South African Outlook,* Jan. 1980

Rubinstein, R. 'Recent Notable Fiction'. *New Republic,* 27.4.1974

Ruether, R. *New Woman New Earth.* New York: Seabury Press, 1975

Staugård, F. *Traditional Medicine in Botswana: Traditional Healers.* Gaborone: Ipelegeng, 1985

Thompson, L. *The Political Mythology of Apartheid.* New Haven: Yale UP, 1985

Thompson, L & Wilson, M (eds.) *The Oxford History of South Africa.* Oxford, 1969, 1971

Thorpe, M. 'Treasures of the Heart: The Short Stories of Bessie Head'. *World Literature Today* (57.3):414–416

Tlou, T & Campbell, R. *A History of Botswana.* Gaborone: Macmillan, 1984

Trump, M. *Rendering Things Visible: Essays on South African Literary Culture.* Johannesburg: Ravan, 1990

Van Rensburg, P. *Looking Forward from Serowe.* Gaborone: FEP, 1984

Yates, R. *A Garland for Ashes.* London, 1960

Archival material

GG1253, MHG82681, MHG4528, WLD: State Archives, Pretoria

BEF: Bessie Head File, St Monica's Home, Brighton Beach, Natal

KMM BHP: Khama Memorial Museum (Bessie Head Papers), Serowe, Botswana

UWL JMP: Jean Marquard Papers, William Cullen Library, University of the Witwatersrand

Index

Index